A YEAR AT THE BOWL

Craig Burton

Published 2017 by arima publishing

www.arimapublishing.com

ISBN 978 1 84549 704 0

Printed and bound in the United Kingdom

arima publishing
ASK House, Northgate Avenue
Bury St Edmunds, Suffolk IP32 6BB
t: (+44) 01284 700321

www.arimapublishing.com

A YEAR AT THE BOWL

Here we go then, we are sat at a glorious sunny Rose Bowl, the home of Hampshire County Cricket club, on the first day of the new season and await with anticipation as the bowler runs in for the opening ball of the 2017 summer!

Sunday 10th April

Well that's how I would have liked to have started this book but I find myself and 10 or so other odd souls still on the bus to the ground, praying that the driver hurries up and hits no traffic. It all started off ok, I got the bus from Woolston to the town centre, where I changed and found my next bus stop in time for the No.8 bus to the ground. A group of people then begin turning up over the course of the next 20 minutes, some I know well, some I recognise in passing and a few new faces who look like cricket types, and there is also our driver waiting for the bus so that he can change over with the driver already on board.

10:05am, the time we are due to leave, arrives and goes, but no worries yet as this is common on a Sunday. 10:15 comes and goes and a few among us are getting agitated now. 10:20 comes and after a few comments passed onto the waiting driver he ups and goes to ask questions. At 10:30 the crowd is in uproar but low and behold our driver appears in a bus and explains it had been there all the time, the previous driver had arrived early and dropped it off in the wrong place!!

So while that first ball was being bowled by Warwickshire to the Hampshire openers we were just arriving and by the time we'd got off, laboured up the hill, passed through the turnstiles and down through the concourses to get sight of the pitch, Hampshire are 0 for 0 off of one over and Woakes is steaming in to begin the 2nd over.

Pleased that we have arrived, and not missed too much, myself, Jim, Arthur and Ian turn our attention to where to sit today, Jim opts for the Shane Wharne stand as usual but due to a hurricane like wind blowing across the ground the rest of us head off to find a sheltered spot, which we find in the lea of the newly built Hilton hotel. Within ten minutes my mate Kev also turns up and joins us as we huddle into our coats and gloves to enjoy the cricket! Brrr

By lunch Hampshire are 66 for 6 and talk turns to today's local Sports Echo and last nights' Daily Echo and their predictions for the coming season. The reporters and players are all optimistic of a good top half finish, after narrowly escaping relegation to Division two last season on the final day. Another Twenty 20 finals day and a good run in the 50 over cup competition are also predicted. It is only the beginning of the season and not one of us present at lunch on that first day is entirely confident of us having any success coming our way after this start. To confirm this view point the bookies have us as favourites to be relegated, I can't bring myself to put a bet on it though!

During the lunch break we buy Golden Gamble tickets (a 50/50 draw with half the takings going to the academy) which is more habit than anything as I have only won a 2nd prize once in the last 15 years! Have a wander around the ground and pop into the club shop to buy the new members only tie which I am going to give to my Dad as a birthday present (he is also a member but probably won't buy one I hope). Next we have a look in the Atrium to pick up some fixture cards, a copy of the roundup, a free fixtures wall chart and to have a much needed warm up before heading back out to our seats where we are joined by the ever present Adrian.

While today is for most of us the first day at the ground this season, Adrian is here for the eighth time already after seeing the pre-season friendlies and early 2nd eleven games. If there is a game on at the ground or nursery ground be it the academy, 2nd's or a friendly then you will find Adrian here in attendance, some days he even pops in for a stroll around when no cricket is even on!

Our overseas player Ryan McClaren and wicket keeper Adam Wheater are at the crease as we settle back in our seats and as always on my first day back here after the winter I marvel at how the ground has changed in the

16 years since our move from the antiquated but homely Northlands Road, County Ground, of old. The ground now looks like a proper top flight, sporting, venue with the recent additions of the Shane Wharne and Colin Ingleby McKenzie stands plus the new hotel, but I still miss the original beer tent that stood on the berm and used to be a social hub and meeting point before the new clean and clinical concourses were built and equipped with bars and fast food outlets. It's good to be back in familiar surrounding though, renewing acquaintances and relaxing in a place loved by those of us here today (although there's not many of us today due, I feel, to the bracing weather).

Wheater is out but McLaren has gone on to make a 50 supported by our new England signing Reece Topley and things are looking up! Talking of which, this promising summer is set to be very eventful for me personally, as after 30 plus years of working for Southampton City Council I am taking advantage of what they call a voluntary solution payoff and am planning on having the whole summer off, before I think about what to do with the rest of my life. I am only 51 so retiring is not an option yet but a nice part time job in the future would suite me nicely.

Topley is out before tea after a good resistant knock of 15 and due to the lowering temperature, howling wind and a few dark clouds we all decide that the 4.55pm bus is appropriate for our first day. We wander around the ground and watch a few overs after the short tea break before darting off down the hill to the bus stop where the bus is bang on time. The bus is halfway to town when it's windscreen wipers are on, and it is pouring with rain when I get onto my 2nd bus for home. When I arrive indoors Michelle (my other half of 30 years) informs me that the teams came off at 5.30pm due to bad light and play was then abandoned for the day with Hampshire on 189 for 8 (McLaren not out on 84). We later hear that Reece Topley (while scoring his best ever 1st class score of 15) has broken his hand while fending off a bouncer (and as it happens we don't see him play again for the 1st team all season due to other injuries he sustains in his recovery).

Monday 11th April

It's back to work today, I have 15 working days left before I finish for my summer of leisure, and although it was cold yesterday the pale sun and wind have given me a rosy glow on my face and I get all the usual quips asking if I've been on a sun bed, I must remember to use more sunscreen this year to combat all the extra outdoor time I am planning on having.

At the cricket, play has been washed out totally today by rain.

As it happens the lost day today probably saves Hampshire from defeat as they can only just sneak to 202 all out on Tuesday, gaining just the one batting point before Ian Bell scores 174 in Warwickshire's reply of 360. In Hampshire's 2nd innings they score 185 -5 with Liam Dawson scoring 50 not out to get us out of immediate trouble and gain the 5 points for a draw.

I have kept up to date with proceedings at the Rose Bowl over the last 2 days by tuning into Kevin James (an ex Hampshire player) who broadcasts commentary every day of every Hampshire game on local BBC Radio Solent, which is a great way to keep up to date with what is going on.

At this point I should just clarify that the reason I am referring to our home ground as the Rose Bowl in this book and not the Ageas Bowl is because that is what I and nearly everyone I know call it. It was called the Rose Bowl when we moved here in 2001 and as far as I know, if Ageas ever pull out of sponsoring it, then it will revert to the Rose Bowl again.

This is what Wikipedia has to say on the matter which is good enough for me.

The **Rose Bowl** (known for sponsorship reasons as the **Ageas Bowl**) is a cricket ground in West End, Hampshire, England, located between the M27 motorway and Telegraph Woods, on the edge of West End. It is the home of Hampshire County Cricket Club, who have played there since 2001.

October 1985 - A life at SCC

I was going to write a long piece on my 30 years working at Southampton city council but whatever I wrote was never going to be enough to sum up all the adventures that I had over the years, so that can be another book all on it's own, if I get around to it. Suffice to say, that I began my career in October 1985 on a six-week temporary contract in the street lighting stores and 30 years later ended up as a materials & logistics co-ordinator.

I enjoyed my 30 years at the council, met lots of mates who I still see now, played and run football and cricket teams, had some great nights out and even had some good times at Shirley Depot where I ended up working for the last 4 years of my time.

After many changes though I was now in a job that I didn't want to be in so when everybody was offered the chance of leaving voluntarily with a package, I put in for my figures to see what they would be. Michelle knew of my concerns if I stayed and after discussing the voluntary solution on offer we agreed that the time had come for me to leave. It wasn't a done deal though as it all depended on how many, and who put in for it, luckily for me the unions managed to get the management to agree to all who had put in for it (approx 39 people) and in January we had the good news that I was on my way at the end of April and the end of an era for me.

Sunday 17th April

Most of the people who are finishing work under the voluntary solution all left on March 31st but a few of us for various reasons have differing finishing dates, my last day is Friday April 29th and in some ways this is good as the weather hasn't been great and I get another month's pay before leaving. It does mean though that I will miss going to Hampshire's County Championship away game at Yorkshire starting today at Headingly, a ground that I have not been to before, but evokes memories of Geoff Boycott's hundredth hundred in glorious sunshine and crowds flocking onto the pitch to give him a celebratory sip of beer.

Instead of travelling to Yorkshire this weekend I have attended another council chap's retirement party at Hamble club on Friday night, the 3rd leaving/retirement party of the month and on Saturday I went to the Southampton Punk Festival at the relatively new Engine rooms venue to see the Cockney Rejects, Anti Nowhere League, Vice Squad, 999, Tenpole Tudor and a host of other acts. A great day was had.

When I wake on Sunday though, my knees and joints are aching from the jumping around last night and after a visit from the in-laws I manage to stumble outside to sit in the garden to listen to the match commentary on Radio Solent. Hampshire begin with a few wickets so all's well and good

7

so I have a few ciders and as the sun comes out I slowly nod off. When I awake Yorkshire are 270 for 5 and have gone off for bad light, it is ok here still, but I have a wet patch over my shorts which in my sleepy haze I fear for the worse! it's ok though as my glass is on the floor and it's only cider over me and the patio. Phew!

Monday 18th April

I tune in to the radio when I get home and Yorkshire have piled the runs on today finishing on 593 for 9 declared, Lythe and Plunkett making centuries and Jonny Bairstow hitting a whopping 246. Hampshire have started their reply and in an injury packed start (Dawson and Wood are both unwell) have finished on 141 for 5.

No time to linger today though as Monday night is darts night. I play for Netley Central Sports & Social Club and we're away at the West End Brewery, a pub just down the road from the Rose Bowl as it happens. We get stuffed 7-2 but it's a good night and they are a good crowd of blokes who we've known for many years.

Tuesday 19th April

Amazingly Hampshire bat all day today with centuries for James Vince and Sean Irvine and 50's for Adam Wheater and Ryan McLaren for the loss of just three wickets. We avoid the follow on and finish on 450 for 8.

Wednesday 20th April

Hampshire have done enough, they don't add many more runs but do take some wickets as Yorkshire try to build a total to defend. In the end Yorkshire cannot score quickly enough and the Hampshire bowlers keep the runs down to restrict the total to 183 for 8 before a draw is called. A good draw all told, but the worry after this game is the growing injury list after just two games. Fidel Edwards our West Indian fast bowler is the latest casualty breaking his leg in today's pre-football warm up.

Monday 25th April - Friday 29th April

There's been no game over the weekend so I went to see Saints beat Aston Villa in Birmingham on a mini bus with a group of mates on Saturday. Then on Sunday it was the Southampton Half Marathon, so we went to cheer on our mate Kev who was running in it, and in the afternoon my mate Dave Herd was hosting his 50th birthday drink at the Encore so we went over town to celebrate with him.

There's also no game for Hampshire this week but it's my last week at work and I'm getting excited now. The days go by in a daze and various people come to say their farewells as they are not in later in the week. Thursday finishes and I am taking our little team of 7 out for a farewell meal at the local Weatherspoons in Shirley High Street. We only stay a couple of hours but it's enough time to reminisce, have a natter and talk about the future, my last day tomorrow will probably go by in a flash so it's nice to have this little session tonight with them all.

The big day arrives and at 10ish I am asked to go and get something from another office. When I return there is a fair sized crowd of people gathered and a presentation ensues, the tears that have threatened all morning suddenly well up and I get all choked up. It's a standing joke in my family that I have never liked goodbyes and in my younger days I used to break out in tears after every visit to my Nan's in Hull or after being away on holiday. At funerals I am still the same now, so it's no surprise today when it happens (and I did warn my colleagues in advance it would) but I think I may have just got away with it without looking a total wuss.

I am presented with a lovely stone slate plaque thanking me for my service to the council along with a tablet and a keg of hobgoblin beer and well wishing cards. I really wasn't expecting any of this and it is a lot more than the other 20 odd who all left en masse last month got. The rest of the morning is spent chatting to colleagues who want to know what my plans are for the future. Then at midday the office closes and we all troop off to the pub, where people come and go all lunchtime, until at 2:30pm I am chauffeured home (many thanks Pete James) in a relaxed and buoyant mood for a couple of hours' rest, before my main leaving party tonight at the Spitfire pub. It's a great turn out in the pub that night with faces from past and present turning out for me and a good night is had by all. After a lift home (thanks Jo) I arrive indoors at 2am tired but happy.

with my stone slate

My leaving has coincided with the May Day Bank Holiday and there's lots planned for the weekend. Starting on Saturday I meet Steve, Bob and Butch in the Encore pub before getting the train to see Havant & Waterlooville play Weston-Super-Mare in the Conference South. Steve has family in Weston-super-Mare and his brother in law is travelling to the game so he said as it's local he'd pop in to see him (us other 3 are just hangers on, out for the day, although I haven't been to Westleigh Park before so it's a chance to tick off a new ground for me). The game finishes 1-1 and Havant are relegated on goal difference, while Weston stay just above the safety zone after looking odds on for relegation earlier in the season. We get back to Southampton and the others are meeting friends to go and see "From The Jam" at the Engine rooms. I would normally go but after last night's late one I decline as tomorrow is another big day.

Sunday 1st May

May 1st 1976, a day etched into all Southampton football fan's memories as the club's greatest day (so far!) and today before the game with Manchester City we will be celebrating it's 40th anniversary with an open top bus tour featuring all of the surviving players (R.I.P Ossie and Bobby) who beat Manchester United 1-0 at Wembley all those years ago.

Myself, Bob, Steve, Staffy and Darren get an outside table at the new cider bar in town and watch the proceedings from there. There are lots of flags, scarves and noise and as the bus drives down the high street and passes us we raise our glasses and wave and cheer. Saints win today's game 4-2 and we all go home happy, there was a further celebration later that night to celebrate the cup win 40 years ago at the Mayflower Theatre but I didn't get tickets, by all accounts it was a great night though.

It was mentioned by a lot of people that 40 years is a long time without winning another major trophy and we wonder if we will still be celebrating our only success in 10 years' time for the 50th anniversary?

Today was also the start of Hampshire's 3rd County Championship game, at home to Middlesex and looking at the score when I get in I see that Hampshire have batted first and ended up on 315 for 7 with Michael Carberry getting a hundred and Liam Dawson on 87 not out.

Bank Holiday Monday 2nd May

The day dawns wet, cloudy and cold so me and Michelle make the decision to not rush to the ground for the start of day 2 and as happens every time we do this, play begins on time at 11am prompt. Listening to the radio commentary, the commentators are not hopeful of long periods of play though, as showers are due from midday, so that makes our minds up to stay at home. Hampshire take no notice of the weather and play on to record a total of 336 all out before Middlesex take over and score 84 for 3 before play is eventually stopped for bad light, and then rain, at 2:50.

The other interesting thing to note in this game is that Adam Vogues of Middlesex was knocked unconscious yesterday when one of his players threw the ball into the wicket keeper who failed to catch it and it clonked Adam on the back of his head while he wasn't looking. Adam cannot now play due to falling unconscious, even though he is ok, so although Middlesex can replace him in the field with a sub fielder they will be one down in batting numbers as he or a sub cannot bat.

Tuesday 3rd May

Finally, I am back at the Rose Bowl and while it is lovely and sunny, a chill wind still charges across the ground, almost as though the ground has it's own microclimate as it's ok everywhere else I have been this morning. It is the first official day today of my semi retirement (everyone else is back at work after the long weekend) but even the joy of being here in the sunshine begins to pale as Hampshire take no wickets at all in the morning session.

The afternoon session is more fruitful and me and Ian have found a spot out of the wind as Ryan McLaren and James Tomlinson each take 4 wickets for 74 runs and Middlesex are all out for 361, a lead over us of 25 runs. Tino Best who has been drafted in to replace Fidel Edwards has been hit for 93 runs without a wicket today and hasn't exactly won the fans over, inevitably he is the talk of the crowd as we head away at 5:40pm for the bus, and as we wait, we hear the news that Carberry is out and Hampshire have finished the day on 76 for 1.

Wednesday 4th May

My Dad is coming along today for his first visit of the season and unfortunately his bus is late and our next bus is early so we get the next one and arrive about 11:10am, where it's nice and sunny again but the ever present breeze is still chilly as Hampshire try to either set Middlesex a target or alternatively try and hold on for a 3rd consecutive draw.

So far this year my Dad has been in the wars with a vertigo problem that he has had for a couple of years now and which seems to be getting worse, and just recently he has picked up a knee injury from which he is still recovering from. The seats at the Rose Bowl are sometimes not the most comfortable of sitting options and I can see that my dad is struggling to get settled and find a comfortable position to sit in. It's no surprise then, when after seeing out the morning session, he decides that his nagging knee can take no more shifting about and he is going to get the bus back home and listen to the rest of the days' action on the radio. It's a slow walk for Dad down the hill but I wander over when he can't see me and I check that he gets down unscathed and watch until he is out of sight, which is just near the bus stop so I know he's got there ok. It's sad to see Dad like this as when younger he was the Dad who took all of us kids out on adventures, took me to watch

my dad

him play in football and cricket teams (and let me play if they were short), was a top marathon runner in his field and we even played in the same local cricket team where he still holds the record first innings score and first wicket partnership total. At the time I hoped it wouldn't be the last time he came up the ground this season but as it turned out it was, as although the knee healed ok the vertigo has got worse before getting better (at the time of writing he has now seen a specialist and fingers crossed there are signs of improvement so hopefully he will be back up the ground next year).

For the afternoon session me, Adrian and Ian move around to the hotel end and when the wind drops it is baking hot. Ian has brought along a jar of Jack Ratt scrumpy for us to share as he knows I am partial to a drop, and this was a present he received off of someone. We spend a pleasant afternoon chatting and drinking while Hampshire save the game and declare on 290 for 5 (Jimmy Adams scoring 70).

Hands are shaken at 5pm but not until after Tino Best takes his first wicket of the game to some sarcastic applause. Hampshire have drawn all three games so far and a look at the table sees us in the second from bottom spot, it's still early though and we're unbeaten so we take heart from that.

The rest of the week is taken up with renewing my Southampton FC season ticket, having a trip to Portchester Castle which I had never visited and going to the first of this years Kennesion birthday parties on the Isle of Wight. Our friends Andy and Carol moved to the IOW some 18 years ago and now have three children so in an attempt to see all of their friends and family in one hit they lay on a party for Andy and son number 2 in May and another, later in the year, for sons number 1 and 3. They are always great affairs and most people put them on their calendars as soon as they are announced so as to not miss them. I did make the mistake one year of missing one of the parties to attend an England v South Africa game at the Oval. It just happens that I am godfather to son number one whose party it was and I have never been allowed to forget it by my oldest mate Paul Neal who is godfather to son number 2 and has not yet missed one of his godson's parties. Oh how I am looking forward to that day when it comes!!!

a Kennesion party

Sunday 8th May

I was hoping to visit Old Trafford for today's Lancashire v Hampshire game but due to the party on the Isle of Wight yesterday, plus discovering that the Old Trafford Lodge is being knocked down and no cheap train or airfares, I have sort of given up on going. Myself and Michelle had an enjoyable weekend in Manchester a few years back staying at the Old Trafford Lodge where we had a balcony room overlooking the pitch as Hampshire beat Lancashire in a one-day game and we always wanted to go back but alas the lodge is no more so that won't happen now.

Today we are sat in the garden sunbathing and drinking beer while first listening to the cricket coverage, on the radio, before changing channels to hear Saints beat Spurs 2-1 at White Hart Lane and then turning channels again for the cricket. The Saints score is great but Hampshire have had a disaster and are all out for 109 which is made even worse as I listen to Lancashire rack up the runs and finish on 157 for 1.

Monday 9th May

Day two is all Lancashire again and they score a decent 436 in the end. It looks like we will be on the end of our first defeat this summer, especially as Jimmy Adams is already out and Hampshire are 14 for 1 at the end of the day. The only bright spark for Hampshire is that Tino Best took 5 wickets so perhaps he has taken a while to find his feet and will fire up from now on in!!

Tuesday 10th May

As part of my summer off I want to at least keep my weight down or if possible even lose a bit, so today I went swimming with a view to making it a regular weekly activity. First though I need to find out if my dodgy knees and ankles will be ok so I pay on the door and start with 20 lengths to see how I get on. My football career finished years ago when I got too slow, old and unfit to play anymore and that didn't affect me but giving up playing cricket was a harder decision. I persevered until I was 47 before my ankles and knees told me that was it time to finish and my recovery periods were getting longer and longer, I still miss playing now though.

The rain has delayed Hampshire losing today, they held out until lunch with the loss of only 2 wickets but then the rain comes and puts paid to any more play today, obtusely though the sun is out in Southampton when I get back from my swim and I sunbathe all afternoon.

Wednesday 11th May

There are no negative results from the swim yesterday so I head back to the pool in town and pay my £270 for a yearly swimming membership which entitles me to lane swimming 7 days a week at either the Quays or Bitterne leisure centres so the more I use it the better value it will be.

Five wickets from Lancashire spinner Simon Kerrigan puts paid to our faint hope of holding out for a draw today after a good morning on the defensive from Vince, Smith and Wheater. Lancashire win by an innings and 94 runs before tea. A look at the new table today shows us rock bottom which is a bit depressing but this early in the season only 20 odd points separate top from bottom so it's all still to play for.

Thursday 12th May

It's a swim again this morning and then in the afternoon I go over to the Encore for a couple of pints before meeting Michelle for the 2:13pm train to Barnham where we get the special bus to Fontwell for the first horse race at 4:55pm. Those of you who know my betting patterns will know I do not bet big money and am happy with any small win I get, so it's a surprise to both me and Michelle when a couple of £2 bets come in and in the first race I win £24 and then later £18, big money to us. The evening is warm and sunny and by the time we get home at 10:20pm the winnings have been spent on beer at the course and a chinese takeaway in Woolston when we get off of the train.

Friday 13th May

Another one of the things I want to do this summer is to go to a few music festivals. Not the big corporate ones, but the small and friendly ones who have a maximum of 500 tickets, reasonably priced beer and scrumpy, line ups of music I relate to (punk/folk and scrumpy & western), and good food.

So today Bob is picking me up at 1pm and we're off to The Curses festival situated between Blandford and Salisbury and run by a great little group called Fuelled by Cider, who have been doing these festivals for a couple of years now. The tents are up and we're sat outside drinking, watching other festival goers arrive and watching BBC South Today reporters doing a feature on the festival for their programme tonight. The headliners today are a favourite band of ours, The Skimmity Hitchers but before them are an assortment of other great bands and a chap called Dorset Phil who really gets the crowd going with songs of cider and Dorset themed shenanigans. It's early May and inside my tent it's freezing so I'm glad I brought extra clothing and mats to keep me off of the cold ground.

main stage at curses

The festival is all I hoped it would be and I thoroughly enjoy it and all of the bands (Saturday headliner is Citizen Fish and Sunday the brilliant Pronghorn). They even get a bonfire going in-between stages on the Saturday and Sunday nights which takes the chill off a bit when stood near it. The only time we deviate away from the action is on the Sunday afternoon when we listen to Saints beat Crystal Palace 4-1 to go into a temporary 5th place position (we eventually drop to 6th after Man United beat Bournemouth in a re-arranged game due to a bomb alert, but that's ok as we qualify for European competition next season either way).

enjoying the festival

Monday 16th May

we are up and away by 9am and home safe and tired by 10:15. In the evening at darts I win my pairs game with Chris in a 5-4 home win over the Swan and I'm glad when I get home and sleep in a nice warm, soft bed.

Tuesday 17th May

It is Kelvin Davis' testimonial tonight and he is donating all the proceeds to charity so me and my season ticket buddy, Andy Holman, go along to watch. It's a good game which actually gets better as it goes on which is a surprise as normally these things turn a bit jokey at the end. A good night and only marred by the fact I had my hip flask full of rum confiscated at the turnstiles when they used a metal detector on me and found it hidden in a pocket (how was I to know that security would be tightened after the Manchester United bomb scare two days ago?).

Wednesday 18th May

James Vince is called up for the England squad to play Sri Lanka this Thursday so it is announced today that Sean Ervine will be captain of the one day squad in his absence and will have his first game in charge tomorrow in a Twenty 20 warm up game against Dorset at Bashley. Tomorrow!*! Tomorrow, if they'd let me know sooner I'd have gone along but I'm booked now and can't go (as you'll see by the end of the book this wont be the last time I have issue with the club giving late notice of events on their website but that's another story for later).

Thursday 19th May

The reason I cannot go to Bashley today is I am going to see the 2nd eleven play a 50 over game against the MCC youth on the nursery pitch and straight from there to Suz and Paul's for a BBQ (Suz is Michelle's sister and Paul her fiancé and they live at Chartwell Green near the ground)

I often wondered who and if anyone goes to see the 2nds and whether it is any good so today is my chance to find out. Adrian is there of course as I expected he would be and he points out a hardcore of about 6 people who turn up every game. He then points out the players' family members who have come to see their son/grandson/nephew/cousin play. There are about 20 people in all. It's a nice sunny day though and I have brought a few cans of cider along and some crisps and I sit on a bench with Adrian and have an enjoyable afternoon watching Hampshire win. As the winning runs are scored at 5ish we feel the first spots of rain and make it to the bus stop just in time as the heavens open.

Sunday 22nd May

Today is day one of Hampshire's game against Nottinghamshire and there are a couple of reason that I am sat in garden listening to it on the radio. Firstly the weather forecast is not looking good, although the sun is currently out, and secondly I'm knackered from three late nights on the trot and am not up to full steam this morning.

On Thursday after the 2nd eleven win I popped into the Two Brothers pub for a pint before the rest of them turned up for the BBQ and when they did we proceeded to eat and drink and chat well into the night before getting a taxi home at 1am.

The following night my mate Kendo (of the Kennesion party fame) came over and stayed the night and we met Bob and Dave in the Spitfire for drinks before going to see the UK Subs at the new Talking Heads venue, we had got Kendo the ticket as a Christmas present

On Saturday me and Michelle accompanied Kendo back to the Isle of Wight for an afternoon with the kids, then the adults went for a meal at the Folly Inn before heading off to a charity night involving The Wurzels, the legends of the west country, at Brickfields near Ryde. We could have stayed over but had planned to attend today's game so we opted for the 11:15pm Red Jet which was late leaving due to a punch up in the terminal with some drunks and the police were called to sort it out. The knock on effect was that when we arrived back on the mainland we missed our bus and ended up walking back over the Itchen Bridge getting in after 1am, so we are a bit sluggish today.

Hampshire lose three wickets in the morning session and then it pours with rain and play is suspended until 4.15pm when another hour is possible before it rains again.

Monday 23rd May

Back to my usual self today after yesterday's recovery day and after a morning swim at the Quays I am on the early bus from town, with Mike who is also early today. I stop off in Asda at West End village for some food and drink and have walked up to the ground by 10:30am. A nice sunny day looms and I am shortly joined by Ian and it turns out we are both leaving at teatime today, me to play darts tonight and Ian to see his wife off as she is babysitting this week at their son's house somewhere north of London. When we leave at tea, Hampshire are all out for 270 with Tom Alsop top scorer with 72 and Nott's are a couple of wickets down in their innings and eventually end the day on 99 for 5.

Before going home today I have another job to do as Michelle is collecting a £1000 worth of euros after she finishes work so I stay on the bus and meet up so that I can chaperone her home with the dosh. On Friday we are off to Corfu for two weeks, Yippee.

Tuesday 24th May

No swim today so I get the bus from Woolston to Bitterne, change and get on the bus to the ground with the usual crowd, including Arthur who is up for only his second day this season. Arthur is a real cricket buff and a lifetime member who is always moaning about the ground and our players and one-day cricket, he is real old school in his cricket outlook. He is also a non league football fan and I have seen him a few times at local grounds such as AFC Totton and Brockenhurst, a real character.

The first hour today is slow going but then Crane and Dawson take 3 quick wickets and Nott's are all out before lunch still 81 runs behind. Hampshire struggle early on but after being 24 for 3 they pick up and finish the day on 189 for 8, leading by 270.

When I get home there is some bad news, Michelle has taken our cat Rex to the vets today, and he has had a tumour removed from up his nose. We have to take him back tomorrow at 12:40, it may be serious so I am going along as well just in case.

Arthur

Michelle with Rex

Wednesday 25th May

We taxi to the vets at 12:30 and to our relief all is ok with yesterdays tests, and how he is today, so it's straight home to turn the radio on to find that at lunch Nott's are 50 for 3. I am straight out of the door and for once fortune favours me and the buses all time in and I am at the ground by 1:45pm buying a celebratory pint to toast Rex's good news. As the weather isn't too bright I go upstairs in the members pavilion for a look around for a change and to see if I can spot any of the usual crowd around the ground, I see some of them but stay upstairs to watch as another wicket falls and Nott's are now 68 for 4, victory is surely ours.

An hour later and Patel and Taylor have added a century partnership for the 5th wicket, bugger! The home fans are getting restless, especially as Tino Best is back to firing loose balls fast and wide over everyone's heads for 4 byes. Thoughts now turn to an unlikely Nott's win!!

At 3:28 Taylor is finally out for 71 after a 108 partnership with Patel and Hampshire hopes soar again and as tea is called, Nott's need 127 off of 39 overs (which is possible) and Hampshire need 5 wickets, it could go either way!

It's cold up top now so I go downstairs for a warm up in the atrium and a pint. The general opinion is that if Patel stays in then Nott's have a good chance of winning. On the bar is a sign saying that there is a 4th day special on Ringwood's Boondoggle beer at £4 a pint which is strange, as I buy one, and it costs me £3.60? The reason I'm told is that as a member I get 10% discount, I understand this but I have just bought it in the members' bar where everyone is a member anyway so why not just advertise it at £3.60?

It's unusual for me to buy a pint in the ground as I normally bring my own, why pay £4.14 (that includes my 10% off) for a pint of cider when I can bring 4 cans in for £3.69 or less. Years ago when County Championship games started on a Tuesday I used to finish work at 1:30pm on a Thursday and I would bus up for the last 4 hours of play, then I would buy beer in the ground but that was in the good old days of the beer tent.

Play begins and I watch an over through the white gauze sightscreen before going out to my normal seat at square leg. I apologise for drawing this last day out but it's 4.15 on day 4 and it's getting exciting, anything could happen and we don't see many like this, there's 34 overs left now and they need 100 to win (Patel is 53 not out), we still need 5 wickets.

4:25 arrives and a few patches of blue are poking through the cloud and Nott's are batting as though they can win it. A few Nott's fans are getting excited and they now need just 90 from 31 overs. The sun doesn't last long though and by 4:45 the floodlights are on and it could be a late finish if it goes all the way.

Wicket! Tino Best has bowled Christian for 31 and the crowd go mildly wild as 4 wickets needed now to win!

4:52 and Tino Gets another wicket which draws a bigger roar from the crowd and then things get silly with batsmen running silly runs, fielders throwing wildly and the crowd get noisier. I've had 6 pints, need the loo but I'm not going to leave my seat and miss anything now, so I hold on.

It's 5pm and Mason Crane finally gets the wicket of Patel, caught in the slips, for 65 and they still need 70 runs to win. I dash to the loo and just get back to my seat to see the next ball and it flies off of Gurney's bat, high to Carberry who takes the catch, 9 wickets down!

But that's it, Nottinghamshire's captain Reid is not fit to bat after an injury in the first innings so Hampshire have won by 69 runs and hands are shaken in the middle.

We've just missed the next bus so I have another celebratory drink in the bar before meeting the usual crowd at the bus stop, which as it happens is 25 minutes late but we don't care, Hampshire have WON!

Thursday 26th May

The feel good factor from yesterday after Rex's news, and Hampshire's win is gone this morning when I get a call to say that my friend Jim has passed away at the age of 60 of a heart attack. Jim was a lifelong Hampshire Cricket fan, Saints season ticket holder and had worked for Southampton City Council as long as I had. The usual crowd earlier this week wondered where he was and we presumed he must be on holiday or couldn't get time off of work for the game! It turns out, he had booked Monday and Tuesday off for the game, but he died on Saturday at home where he lived alone after his mother's death a year or so ago. The alarm bells didn't ring with anyone until he failed to turn up for work on Wednesday and that was when the situation was discovered.

The cricket crowd had seen him recently at the first few games and he seemed his usual self, he had even given me a bottle of rum as a leaving present when I left work last month, Jim was one of life's nice blokes and he will be missed by us all.

I first met Jim properly at a one-day game at the Rose Bowl about 15 years ago when we both recognised each other on the bus and found out we both worked at the old Town Depot. After that we bumped into each other at football and cricket over the years as well as stopping to chat at work all the way up to when I left. Jim loved his sport and it later transpires that he was a Laurel & Hardy aficionado as well.

A sad day and a thought dawned on me today with the news of Jim's passing that I never knew his surname, address or telephone number and thinking of the people who I sit with at the cricket or chat with on the bus or in the ground it's the same for all of them as well, whether that's right or wrong I don't know. I do know though that Ian will be doing the scoring tonight for a local team called Southamptonshire and that my friends Butch and Sylvia will be there, so I send them a message on Facebook and ask the news to be passed onto Ian for me, he knows a few of the others better than me so will get the news around before I get back from Corfu. Work will let me know when the funeral is.

Friday 27th May

As soon as my letter came through at work, in February, to confirm I would be leaving, Michelle was on the internet and booking us a holiday, nothing fancy just a beach holiday in the sun for two weeks flying from Bournemouth. After checking different sites and destinations we chose Corfu (we've been a few times before) and the resort of Sidari in the north (where we haven't been before) and the hotel Christina.

Bob gave us a lift to the airport for the 6:30am flight and we were in our apartment by 1pm Greek time, a lovely big room with a balcony looking over the gardens complete with small kitchen area and table and chairs. A quick unpack and we were down to the poolside restaurant (taverna) for something to eat and drink before having a lay on the sun beds and a dip.

our home for 2 weeks

We have specifically picked these two weeks to go away so as to miss the least possible amount of Hampshire home games we can, because if you are like me on holiday, it's all about eating, sleeping, drinking, reading and sunbathing with events at home the last thing on your mind. It used to be very difficult keeping up to date with news at home anyway in Greece and you had to either phone home or try and obtain a two days' late newspaper, flown over from home if you wanted the football or cricket scores, and they always cost a fortune. Today is a different matter though and here in Sidari all of the bars have Sky TV, newspapers are printed the same day and internet signal is everywhere for your phones, tablets and other devices.

On the day we arrive, Hampshire have their opening Twenty 20 game of the season away at Middlesex and that evening as we're walking back from a wander around the resort and a meal of grilled sardines and roast potatoes washed down with ice cold Retsina, I happen to notice a bar with a big screen showing an update from Uxbridge where Middlesex got 155 and Hampshire are going well on 55-1. The screen goes back to the presenters and we head back to our hotel for drinks in the bar and then more ice cold Retsina on our balcony into the early hours.

It's only the next day while sat by the pool that I learn that Hampshire collapsed last night and lost by 69 runs.

Sunday 29th May

After watching Hull City beat Sheffield Wednesday yesterday in the Championship play off game at Wembley it's back to the pool today and at home Hampshire are starting a County Championship game with Middlesex at Merchant Taylor's school. We're having a late lunch in our hotel restaurant when Michelle has a quick look at the latest score to see that Hampshire have taken 2 early wickets. So my swordfish tastes even better now.

I should have known it was too early to celebrate though and as we're sitting in the sunset bar in town later that evening, watching the sun going down into the sea, Michelle informs me that Vogues and Malan have had a stand of 279 and the end score is 342 for 3. Another whisky sour please barman.

more drinks please waiter

Wednesday 1st June

3 days later and we're up early for a coach to Corfu town and then a boat to visit the island of Paxos followed by the mainland town of Parga (where we have holidayed many times in the past and want to see if it's changed much in the last 10 years). On the boat other people are talking about the poor weather back home and I'm hoping that the impossible happens and the weather can save Hampshire, as Middlesex amassed a massive 467 before skittling us for 101 and making us follow on.

After a long day, you know how it is on these trips when you travel 6 hours to visit somewhere for 2 hours and you think why did I do that? I should have just stayed here! we arrived back at the hotel at 8.30pm and once in range of a Wi-Fi signal Michelle checks the score. In London they have had a bit of rain today after yesterday only 17 overs being played, but not enough and Hampshire have lost by an innings and 116 runs.

Thursday 2nd June

After yesterday's non stop travelling it is a relax by the pool today and tonight Hampshire play Kent in a Twenty 20 at home so we are trying to check if it is a live Sky TV game, if it is we will find a beach bar to watch it in.

As it happens all the bars are showing the England V Portugal football friendly. Our game is not on live anyway, it's Yorkshire against somebody, so we go to bed tonight not knowing the score.

Friday 3rd June

Hampshire won last night by 9 runs. Our two Twenty 20 specialists Boom Boom Afridi and Darren Sammy both took wickets and Carberry hit 54. Matches are coming thick and fast now, tonight it's Glamorgan away.

Before tonight's game, Michelle has a massage on the beach and we both dangle our feet in a tank of water for a fish spa before going back to the room for a Greek salad and Retsina on the balcony where we stay all evening as we can't be bothered to go back out.

We find out the next day that Hampshire lost tonight by 5 wickets in a pretty low scoring affair at Cardiff. That's one win out of three in the Twenty 20 competition so far, not a disaster yet but we need a few wins now to stay in touch. I will need to go and get my wallet out of the hotel safe tomorrow as it's got my fixture list in and I can't remember when or against who our next matches are, perhaps I've had too much sun or Retsina already?

fish spa

Sunday 5th June

Upon looking at my fixture card this morning we see that Hampshire are at home to Essex in a 50 over game, the 2nd home game we miss while away, so we decide to stay around the pool and keep up to date on twitter.

I log on to my tablet, that I received as a present from my colleagues when I left work, at 1pm (2 hours ahead remember, only 11am in England) and all of the usual blurb comes up for listening live and I hit the buttons with no actual hope of anything coming up. We've done this many times on holiday before, getting excited that we'd hear a football or cricket commentary and then being deflated by an error screen or 'out of your area' message. But hold on, we have another screen to download now, we've never got this far before on BBC audio player, so I click ok. Ten minutes later, and just as I'm giving up, something has downloaded and wants to know what game I want to listen to so I click on our game and nearly fall off of my sun bed when I hear Kevin James' voice coming out of the speaker and Hampshire are 7 for 1.

Unfortunately, the signal doesn't last and in between swims, naps, and ordering beer (they even have cider here, although only Magners but that's better than nothing) I have to refresh and restart all day. We head up for a shower in between innings and Hampshire pair Wheater (90) and Alsop (84) have scored a new A list second wicket partnership of 169 in a total of 310.

Tonight we have an early meal in the hotel and then wander down to the town to people watch with a few gin and tonics. Michelle keeps tabs on the Essex score and keeps reading them out to me, they seem to be keeping up with the run rate but wickets are falling so it's still in the balance. Just as I'm on my 5th G&T and late sunlight is making me feel nice and relaxed Michelle blurts out that Essex need 18 runs off of 2 overs (connection hasn't been great, hence the surprise) but that's still a tough task so I'm not too worried. The next update when it comes has me spluttering into my drink, 3 off of the last over, What? Who bowled the last over and got tonked for 15, is that right? Unfortunately it is and when Michelle's phone refreshes we have lost by 3 wickets.

Oh well we're off to Corfu Town tomorrow by boat and have to be up for the 8.30am pick up so we pack up and wander back to our room for a commiserating Retsina on the balcony before an early night.

Tuesday 7th June

After a nice trip to Corfu town yesterday, we got a coach to Kassiopi and then a boat the rest of the way, Hampshire are back in action today in a 50 over game away to Middlesex at Radlett school. Going back to Corfu town yesterday though, there is a little cricket pitch in the middle of the town square where touring teams can or used to play, it has an all weather artificial strip and it has seen better days (full of holes and patches) so whether it is still used I don't know.

Looking at the fixture card I have, today's game is 2pm - 10pm but when I log on at the hotel pool (Greek time 4pm) for the start I am surprised to hear that Middlesex have already batted and the interval is in progress. My fault, I should have realised that the venue wouldn't have floodlights, being an out ground, and would begin early. When we next log on it is to find that play is now held up due to rain!

We have some tea in the room tonight and then head down to the beach to watch the sunset which is an angry and violent red and very impressive. We see a bar showing some cricket highlights and wander over for a drink and a watch, and it's there that we learn Hampshire have won via the Duckworth Lewis method and see footage of Liam Dawson scoring a man of the match 68 not out off of 40 balls for our first 50 Over success this year.

Wednesday 8th June

We've two more full days left before going home and Hampshire are away at Kent tonight in a Twenty 20 game that is live on Sky. We sunbathe all day at the hotel and I make tentative enquiries to the owner as to whether there is anything going on tonight in the hotel bar (they have had quizzes, karaoke and other events some nights) and as she shakes her head I get in quick and ask if we could watch Sky Sports 2 tonight. We leave the pool early today and have our showers and a cool off on the balcony with a glass or two of, you've guessed it, ice cold Retsina and at 8pm we're down and sat in front of the screen in prime seats. Nobody else seems the least bit interested apart from odd comments as to what we're watching, so good job we got here early!

Anyway Kent get down to batting and batting and batting, no Hampshire bowler comes out unscathed (although Tino took the wickets of their openers) and after 20 overs have scored 193 for 3. Luckily all of the other guests have gone out and the Greek owners haven't a clue as to what's going on, so we don't have to pretend to still be enjoying it, another bottle please Christina.

Hampshire give it a go though and Ervine and Afridi hit a few sixes to keep us in touching distance but wickets are also falling regularly and we're always just that bit behind the rate and eventually miss out by just 8 runs. It is now getting on for midnight in Greece and the bar is empty and the owners sat chatting, no doubt wondering if there is an end to this, whatever we're watching, and could we go home now.

I'm going to miss this

Thursday 9th June

Our last day dawns and we make the most of it starting with breakfast at the Sea Breeze before a sunbathe on the beach and at 4pm we have a fish spa again and as the owner is English and wants a chat we dangle our feet in, being nibbled, for nearly an hour before we say we must go. Back at the hotel we have some wine at the side of the pool and a last dip before going to pack our bags ready for departure tomorrow. About 10pm we nip down to a seafront taverna for a last meal and listen to the waves rolling up the shore. This is when Michelle checks on how Hampshire are doing today in a Twenty 20 match against Surrey at the Oval and find out that Surrey have a decent score of 188 for 5, so like last night it's not hopeful. Unlike last night though we don't get anywhere near and are all out for 108 with youngster Lewis McManus top scoring with 41. We finish our 'on the house' kumquats and Grappa and reflect that qualifying for the next stage of the Twenty 20 competition is very long odds indeed now.

Friday 10th June

We've had a lovely two weeks here and I'm sad to be going home, but go we must and we have a 8:30am pick up from outside the hotel for the 12:25 flight back to Bournemouth so we should be back home well before 5pm English time no problem!! All goes to plan until we get to Bournemouth train station and find out it's closed! There are no trains running as they have had to turn off the power due to some idiot hanging off of a bridge at New Milton station and he's been there for two hours already. We are advised that it is not going to be sorted quickly and pointed to a queue, a mile long, where people are waiting for taxi's laid on by the train company. We join it and eventually at 5pm we manage to get on a coach that is going non stop to Southampton Parkway station, at least a step in the right direction. To make things even worse, at the Ageas Bowl tonight there is a gig by Rod Stewart and the roads all the way to the station are rammed and it takes us an hour and a half to do a 40 minute trip. There is no point getting a taxi as traffic is not moving, so we manage to squeeze onto an already packed train with our suitcases, to a few murmurings from the squashed throng already on it, and get off 10 minutes later at Central where we can get a taxi home. We walk indoors at 8pm just in time to watch the opening European Championship game in France which begins today.

delayed at Bournemouth

It's a bit of a lazy weekend after the holiday and we do the usual unpacking, give some presents to our neighbours who have fed Rex and Ollie while we've been away, catch up on emails and post and do the laundry. Suz and Paul pop in on the Saturday night and we do them a Greek buffet with some of the things we brought back with us and some added Sainsbury's Greek dips while we watch England draw 1-1 with Russia in their opening Euro game.

Two main things need mentioning. Firstly I have had an email from work notifying me that Jim's funeral is on Tuesday 14th June, so that's ok I can make it after originally thinking it would be while I was away on holiday.

Secondly I do not cancel the local daily paper while I'm away. When I get back I like to catch up on what's been going on, mainly in the sports section, so when reading the report of the last day of Hampshire's loss at Middlesex in the championship game I'm surprised to see that although we gained a bonus point from the game we also lost 2 points for slow over rate#*!? So we're worse off than before the game began. How this can be when the game finished well ahead of schedule and had rain interruptions I do not know.

Tuesday 14th June

Hampshire are away at Gloucester in a 50 over game today live on Sky TV. However it's also Jim's funeral at 3:15 in the Wessex Vale Crematorium which is certainly ironic as it is only around the corner from the cricket ground and also for the fact Jim would have had this Hampshire game pencilled in as a half day from work so that he could watch it.

I make my own way to the crematorium by bus as I've not had any time to see if anybody else is going, or when, and in a mark of respect I wear my dark blue Hampshire top which I hope Jim would like if he's looking down on us. There's a good turn out from work which is good as he hasn't got a lot of family left by the look of it, just an aunt and a few distant cousins and a few old family friends. "Oh when the Saints" is playing when we walk in and it's just my luck to be sat next to Billy who turns out to be as big a blubberer as I am and before we know it tears are rolling down both of our cheeks so I don't know if it's just the two of us or if more have a tear in their eye, I hope it's not just us.

A good proportion of us head back to Woolston Social Club where his aunt has laid on a buffet. This is handy for me as I only live around the corner and I get a lift there with one of the other chaps. It's quite a nice afternoon now that the funeral has taken place and people tell tales of Jim dancing on the tables in his younger days, and of his heroics in goal when he played football. We also hear of his love of everything Laurel & Hardy related. We raise a few glasses and his aunt thanks us all for turning out, she didn't know he had so many friends and we assure her of what a lovely bloke he had been to us all.

In the club they have the cricket on in the other bar and each time I've gone up for drinks or gone to the loo I've peeked to see how things are going and as it happens it's not going well at all, Gloucestershire have racked up 352 for 3 with Dent scoring 142 and Klinger 166 not out.

Eventually people begin to leave so I take the opportunity to say my farewells as well and slip back home for the 2nd innings. Hampshire do actually recover and do well with Alsop, Dawson and Ervine all making 50's before a late flourish from Gareth Andrews who gets 70 not out and leaves us just 10 runs shy, a massive effort that gives hope for future games.

Wednesday 15th June

After the sad occasion yesterday it is back to normal today, sort of, and Hampshire have their 2nd home 50 over cup game of the season against Surrey which starts at 2pm. The game should finish at 10ish and from there I am going to Bob's where Dave will also meet us for an early morning taxi to Gatwick as we are going to the South of France for 4 nights to soak up the atmosphere of the European football championships in Nice as part of Dave's 50th birthdays celebrations.

I start the day with an early morning swim and then head home to pack my bag. It's only a rucksack, as we only have hand luggage tickets to save on the cost, and in effect we're only going for the same length of time as a long weekend away. At 12:30 I head to the ground and meet up with Ian and Kev and we settle down for the start. Michelle will be finishing work at 1:30 and will be turning up a bit later with provisions of food and drink but just in case I've brought four cans of my own cider to see me through until she arrives. The game is a thriller and after losing an early wicket, Tom Alsop goes on to score his maiden first class hundred and with support from Ervine (50) and Vince (41) Hampshire go on to score 289 for 8. Michelle has turned up ok and we have our snacks before Surrey begin their run chase. What a chase it is, they lose an early wicket like we did but instead of one man scoring for them, Ansari (62) Foakes (72) and the Curren brothers (42 + 25) all chip in with successful partnerships to keep the run rate ticking over and with 2 overs left only 16 runs are required with 4 wickets in hand. I and most Hampshire fans think that, that's it, another loss, but step up Gareth Berg who with 11 needed off of the last over takes 3 wickets in 4 balls and we secure a 6 run victory, exciting stuff.

After the end of the game me and Michelle wait for the crowds to disperse and call a taxi, it drops me off at Bob's house first before going on and dropping Michelle off at home. It's only 5 days since I got back from Greece but I am on my way abroad again, it's all go this summer!

The French Trip
Thursday 16th June - Sunday 19th June

This year's European football tournament finals are in France and as it's my mate Dave's 50th birthday year we wanted to do something memorable to celebrate it. Last year we went to Las Vegas for my 50th and Dave has already been to Niagara Falls and Toronto with his sister for his main big holiday away so a short break somewhere was required.

As none of us had ever been to a major tournament like this and we'd not been to the south of France either we decided we'd visit Nice and that's why at 1am we're sat watching Family Guy on TV waiting for our early morning taxi to come. After nodding off in the chair the taxi arrives at 4am and gets us to Gatwick well in time for our 7:30am flight. All goes well and we nap and have breakfast on the plane (cheese croissant and a yogurt) before landing in the sunshine at 10:20am. We were planning on getting a bus to the hotel, but walking out of the airport it's manic, so we go for the easy option and get a taxi to the hotel Brice instead, for 35 euros. Our room won't be ready until after 2pm so we do all the paperwork required and show our passports then put our bags in storage and head off out to get our bearings and most importantly find somewhere to watch the Wales v England game which kicks off at 3pm local time. We have a few hours' spare, so wander along the prom, admire the views and take in the bracing sea air before we get settled in Queenies bar which is all set up for the football with 4 large screens facing every direction so you can see wherever you are in the bar. It's a bit pricey, 9 euros a pint, but it's good beer and a good crowd gather for the game (60% English, 20% Welsh and 20% other nationalities). It's a good atmosphere, contrary to what we've seen splashed over the front covers of the tabloid press at home.

It begins to rain after the game begins and we're just on the outskirts of the cover because we wanted to sit in the sunshine earlier. Dave is ok as the rain is missing him, Bob is in his element drinking and watching football so he doesn't care about getting wet but I am getting soaked and don't like it, it's watering down my expensive pint. Luckily there is a shop next door so I nip in and buy an umbrella which suffices and I watch the next 1/2 hour of play from underneath it and Wales score! By the time England have made changes, equalised and then caused major jubilation all over the pavement by scoring a last gasp winner, the rain has stopped and the sun is out again.

The Welsh leave quickly but take it in good humour as they shake peoples' hands and wish them a good tournament and say well done, little do they know at this stage that they will be having the last laugh!

We go back to the hotel after the game and have a look at our triple room and unpack. It's not a bad size, has a nice window looking down the street and has air conditioning which will be handy, more for covering the sounds of us snoring than keeping us cool. We patronise the hotel bar and then go out for something to eat before having a relatively early night after watching the Germany v Poland bore draw which finished at 11pm

Next day in Nice is match day and Turkey are playing Spain this evening at 9pm. After breakfast at Queenies (our chosen home pub for the trip as it's near the hotel, easy to get to and right on the seafront) we head on down to the fanzone on the beach front. A decent sized crowd are already enjoying a variety of entertainments including human table football, 5 a side football, volleyball, water polo, video games and lots of displays of football memorabilia. There's a party atmosphere all around town and judging by the flags most of the fans are supporting Turkey today. We're not too fussed though and just hope it's a good game. We did look at getting tickets ourselves but firstly they were over £250 each on the resale sites and secondly it seems a lot of hassle to go to it, as the stadium is a long way from town, you have to go by special buses and it would take out a large part of our day getting there and back.

fanzone

After the fanzone we have a proper look around Nice, go to a few bars on the way around to soak up the atmosphere, and outside the Irish pub watch all of the people in fancy dress making fools of themselves, exactly why we came here. By mid afternoon I am ready for a sit down and I leave the other two when they decide to have a look around the shops. I head to the other fanzone in the city centre where the big screens are, and after going through the airport type security checks, I get a beer and watch some of the Italy V Sweden game. When the game finishes I head back out and watch some 5-a-side football on the beach as the sun sets into the sea and then go and meet the other two as thoughts of food now enter my mind. Nice is famed for it's seafood and fish so Dave has done his homework and picked out Chez Freddies to eat at tonight. It is in the market area of town, and that's where I'm sat with a glass of red vin de plonk when they stroll along to join me. The menu is fantastic and it's hard to choose, but we end up with fish soups, grilled sardines, squid and a fish paella which could feed four people on it's own, a splendid feast to set us up for the evening. We watch Spain beat Turkey 3-0 on TV in a bar and then somehow find ourselves in a nightclub, at the back of another bar, which caters to an audience who looked like they could be on 'Strictly Come Dancing', they had all of the moves and the music was a very Samba/Latin type style. Being in France me and Bob went for double Cognacs as a sophisticated way to end the evening but Dave let us down by ordering Tequila Sunrises which came with sweets in it! We headed back to the hotel at 1am tired but happy and luckily still walking in a relatively straight line.

Bob & Dave enjoyed their meals

Unbeknownst to me as I slept, Hampshire's Twenty 20 home game with Sussex today had been abandoned after a freak hailstorm had come unannounced and soaked the wicket before the ground staff could react. Thousands of fans poured into the ground from sunny areas of the city and couldn't believe that the game was off. The ECB did an investigation afterwards and cleared Hampshire Cricket and the ground staff of any fault but it was a talking point for weeks afterwards.

It's Saturday in Nice, so me and Bob decide to walk up to the Parc du Chateau while Dave goes shopping. It's a long walk up for us, especially in our dehydrated states, but well worth it as the views over Nice are stunning and there are lots of parks, cafes and a thundering waterfall at the top. There are a lot of people up here, locals and tourists alike and there is even a wedding party having photos taken. We have some water and a beer as it's hot again and sweat is dripping off us. We make the descent back down again, just in time to receive Dave's text to say he has taken up position in a bar along the seafront overlooking the sea and will meet us there for an afternoon of football watching and drinks.

Nice sea front

When the evening comes it's off to another seafood restaurant where we find that the dishes are even bigger than last night. The fish soup comes out in a tureen and is big enough for 4, so it's a shame that Bob has ordered it for himself as a starter. I have mussels and Dave has salmon and we leave absolutely stuffed. It's back to Queenies for the last game of the day, Portugal V Austria, and the place is full of Austrians, a boisterous bunch who are singing, standing on chairs and having a great time. In the end the owners have to ask them quiet down, especially after Ronaldo misses a penalty, and they end up threatening to chuck them all out due to the commotion they are making but the game ends before it gets too out of hand and they file out into the street to celebrate their 0-0 success. No nightclubbing for us tonight and I'm off to bed as it's now midnight.

We wake up on Sunday and it's our last day, so we check out, go along the seafront and have breakfast before sitting in the sun and drinking coffee basking in the sunshine. We get a taxi to the airport for our 4:20pm flight to Heathrow and arrive back in a dark and wet Blighty. Nice was great and I'd love to return one day with Michelle for a holiday.

hopefully be back again

While we're travelling home Chris Gayle is scoring 52 runs for Somerset as they beat Hampshire by 6 wickets at Taunton. Hampshire batted first and only Liam Dawson (46) shone in the poor total of 133 all out, Somerset won with 26 balls to spare.

N.b. England drew their next football game 0-0 with Slovakia and I watched it at the Barleycorn pub in Hedge End with my mate Paul Neal and his football team mates. They then embarrassingly lost to Iceland 2-1 in the last 16 and I watched with my darts team at Netley Sports Social Club. Wales on the other hand performed heroics and lost in the semi finals to eventual winners Portugal.

Wednesday 22nd June

There's a bit of a cricket lull this week so I take the opportunity today to go to Salisbury Races, I get the train from Woolston, then change in Southampton, so I get in to Salisbury at 11:15 in time for the free bus to the course at 11.55pm. Also waiting for the bus is Michael, a regular on the bus to cricket, and after catching up on my recent trips away he very kindly gives me a free ticket for today's meeting as he is a member and gets a few freebie vouchers each year (like we do at the cricket if you are a member). It saves me the £15 entrance fee I would have paid to get in, but unfortunately as I am in shorts and trainers I cannot take full advantage of the voucher as I am not allowed in the best stands dressed as I am. It's a good day, the rain holds off and I have an 11-1 winner which gives me my stake money back. After a few drinks in Salisbury I get back home indoors just after 8pm.

Friday 24th June

It's an away Twenty 20 game tonight at Essex and me and Michelle sit in the garden and listen on the radio as Hampshire bat first and score 135 for 8 (Carberry top scoring with 34). It's another defeat though as Essex easily make the winning runs with an over to spare, the only highlight for Hampshire being Liam Dawson taking 3 wickets in the innings). We could have gone to the Hedge End beer festival tonight and seen the Mangledwurzles live, I wish we had now!

Saturday 25th June

Cricket is due to resume at the Rose Bowl today with a live on Sky TV game against Gloucestershire in the Twenty 20 tournament and we all turn out in glorious sunshine for the 1:30pm start only to find rain clouds hurtling towards us. 45 minutes later, after a deluge of rain and thunder, we sit again in brilliant sunshine as the ground staff take off the covers and mop up the outfield and Hampshire win the toss and elect to bowl first. An hour and a half after the original start time the players are now entering the field of play to quite a good crowd (it's a family day event with lots of attractions for the kids) but before a ball is bowled, dark clouds are appearing again and lightening is seen flashing behind the main pavilion. The umpire's take the players off for their safety and leave us all sat in the open seats fearful for our own safety! Within minutes the heavens open and it lashes down. Michelle makes a brave last stand by refusing to come and stand with us under the new hotel canopy and sitting in her seat under a golf umbrella, but the torrents coming down soon force her to flee and we head indoors to the atrium to get dry.

lightning on its way

Me and Michelle are going to a BBQ later at her sister's so we phone up and they are in, so we decide to head to their house early and if play does start then we'll watch it on their TV. As we're heading out the news is that a 5 over a side game may be possible if they can start by 4.28pm but as it happens that is scuppered when it begins raining again anyway.

On the way out of the ground we bump into old pal Steve (the Woking fan), he used to be a regular on the bus a few years back, but has not been seen for a few years now. We have a catch up and he explains that due to a new job he cannot make weekday games anymore and with the finish of the 40 over Sunday games he lost a bit of interest. Today was his first game back for a while so it's a shame it's ended like this.

Before last nights' game we had to win 5 out of 6 of our remaining twenty 20 games to have any chance of qualifying for the quarter finals stage so a loss and a postponement means that's it, our chances have gone. For a side that's been in a record number of finals days that is a disappointment. Oh well, C'est la vie.

Sunday 26th June

Today is the start of a four day championship game against Somerset and although we didn't get in until 2am last night after the BBQ I feel pretty good and am at the ground for 11:40am after getting up a little bit later than planned. The sky is overcast but the pitch was ready for play to begin at 11am, which is an achievement in itself after yesterdays downpour, and we see a good morning's batting from Hampshire.

Originally when the fixtures came out I was looking at perhaps booking a hotel room at the Hilton with a pitch facing balcony for 3 nights over this weekend for me and Michelle but the cost of £200 per night put us off. In hindsight with the weather I'm glad we didn't but it would be nice one day to do it.

Hampshire are looking well set with the score on 184 for 3 and Jimmy Adams on 61 but what happens next is the story of the season so far. Hampshire lose 6 wickets for 11 runs with only Ryan McLaren putting up any fight during this period, ending up 24 not out, in a total of 219 all out.

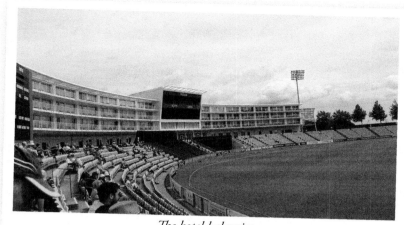

The hotel balconies

To add to Hampshire's woes today news has come from the ECB that Tino Best may be liable for disciplinary action after supposedly throwing a ball at an opponent in Friday's loss at Essex. This may result in a suspended points deduction in all competitions which is hanging over our heads from previous suspended ECB actions. The mood of the crowd is further tested when news also comes out that Hampshire coach Dale Benkenstein has come out publicly to blame Adam Wheater for under par wicket keeping and the cause of previous loses. All in all, it has not been the best day for Hampshire fans and me, Kev, Ian and Adrian leave at 4:45 when the teams come off for bad light and rain.

Monday 27th June

Hooray, the weather forecasters have got it wrong today, and in our favour. Somerset restart on 66 for 1 and it's a glorious sunny day taking most of us by surprise as red faces later in the day testify. Somerset make us toil in the field and only one wicket falls in the morning session with ex Hampshire man Johan Myburg on 110 and James Hildreth on 152 scoring well by the end of the day. I leave at tea to go and watch England's ill fated exit in the Euros to Iceland and Somerset eventually declare on 474 for 8 depriving us of full bowling points.

The lack of bonus points this season is a real worry, especially in the batting area, and is one factor in being so lowly in the table. Take the current game as an example we have a measly 3 points compared to Somerset's 8.

Tuesday 28th June

The weather forecast isn't good today and rain is expected by 2 or 3pm but it's a nice sunny morning though and we hope the Met Office is wrong like yesterday. Hampshire actually play quite well and Tom Alsop gets another 50 to add to his collection in an impressive debut season and Will Smith, Michael Carberry and Sean Irvine all chip in mid 30 scores to take Hampshire to 173 for 4 when the first drops of rain begin to fall at 3:15pm. Most people know the forecast and we all file out of the ground for an early bus.

Wednesday 29th June

The forecast is even worse for today so when after my morning swim I'm stood at the bus stop and feel the first spots of rain I change my plans and head for home, A good decision as it then proceeds to rain all day.

We are now roughly half way through the season, so let's take stock.

Hampshire are effectively out of the Twenty 20 competition with 4 games still to play (3 of them at home).

Hampshire are bottom of the County Championship division one, 30 odd points adrift of safety.

The only bright light is that we are still currently alive in the 50 over cup competition after two wins and two losses but you could, if you were being uncharitable, say that is only because nobody has been outstanding and everything is still to play for.

Not a great season then so far and it's blooming typical that Hampshire are having their off season in the one year that I have the summer off to follow them. And another thing, if the weather doesn't pick up soon in England I shall be booking another holiday abroad for some guaranteed sunshine.

Hampshire are away at Durham next in a four day championship game but me and Kev have tickets for the England Twenty 20 games at the Rose Bowl next Tuesday.

At 1:30pm England ladies play the Pakistan ladies followed at 6pm by England men playing Sri Lanka men.

Kev or his wife has a friend who can get discounted tickets, our ones' next week are £25 each so a bargain.

Sunday 3rd July

It's July now and I have a sore throat, blocked nose and a hacking cough. I managed to make it through the second Kennesion birthday party on the IOW yesterday with the help of cough syrup and a copious amount of cider and red wine but today I am wiped out and snooze most of the day on the bed with the radio next to me. It's a shame because the weather is on the up and it's a lovely sunny day out and I would normally jump at the chance of a sunbathe in the garden listening to the cricket. Especially today as Hampshire have one of their better days with everybody chipping in to score 319 for 6 and all of the top five batsmen scoring 40 runs each (Will Smith 67 and the other opener Jimmy Adams 86).

Monday 4th July

Surprisingly I slept all night after snoozing all day yesterday and I wake feeling a bit better. I do however send an email to say that I will miss darts tonight if we have enough players so that I can concentrate on being OK for tomorrows England game. Back in Durham we have achieved 4 bating points for the first time this season, normally by mid afternoon on day two when we have batted first we are in a far worse position, could our luck be changing?

Tuesday 5th July

The day is warm and the forecast good as I head to the West End Brewery to meet up with Kev for a few pints before the big games today. A couple of pints turn into 4 each before we have to put a spurt on to get to the ground in time for England women to take on the Pakistan women beginning at 2pm. There isn't a massive crowd in yet, but it's bigger than for a usual championship match here and we sit in any old seat for the time being. The game is enjoyable and we have a few more drinks in the sunshine as England win and then Kev shoots off to get some photos and selfies with the winning England players.

The ground begins to fill up in the gap between the two games so we head to our seats in the Colin Ingleby MacKenzie stand and watch the build up of excitement, and eventual fanfare as the teams come out to flag waving mascots, flame throwers and rousing renditions of patriotic songs.

filling up nicely

England bowl first and playing today are two Hampshire players, Liam Dawson and James Vince. It's Liam's day as he bowls well to take 3 wickets for 27 runs to help restrict Sri Lanka to 141 all out.

During the interval we have a wander in the sun and refill our glasses. We decide to stand on the berm to watch rather than going back to our seats for the England innings. There are no temporary seats in today to boost the attendance so there's lots of room to move around and peruse all of the stalls and food and drinks stands.

England bat well and with a 114 partnership between Josh Butler (73) and Eoin Morgan (49 not out) they cruise to an 8 wicket win. Unfortunately, James Vince only chipped in 16 runs before a bizarre stumping got him out.

The end of the game comes and this is where I am normally put off coming to internationals here, getting home afterwards! I have been to previous games and have had some bad experiences, one time even having to walk all the way home (nearly a two hour trek) after the one, single decker, bus laid on was filled in moments leaving loads of us stranded. Today however I am pleasantly surprised to find a row of buses all lined up and ready to take us to various locations, I jump onto one going into town and once full we are off and once in town I change buses and within 1 1/4 hours of the game finishing I am indoors safe and sound. A perfect day, although when I get in and count what money I have left, not a cheap one!

Back at Durham and Hampshire scored 472 for 9 before declaring. Durham then batted well to get anywhere near our score and they declared on 421 for 9 (with McLaren and Gareth Andrew taking 3 wickets apiece) trying to make a game of it on day 4.

Wednesday 6th July

Michael Carberry (59) and Jimmy Adams (49) tried to push Hampshire along today so as to try and make a game but on a flat pitch it was deemed not worth the risk and Hampshire batted out the day to end on 174 for 4 when rain came.

Friday 7th July

I have a lazy rest of the week recuperating from my cold until Friday night comes along and me and Michelle go for a meal in the West End Brewery before making our way to the ground for the Twenty 20 game against Essex. I bump into some of my old colleagues from the gas section in the pub and they are having their annual night out at the cricket today. When we get into the ground there are more of them there so I have a good catch up on what has been going on since I left, not a lot as it happens and the place hasn't collapsed without me, oh well!

It's quite an exciting game and Essex bat first and score 153 for 6 before Hampshire have a good start with Adams and Carberry climbing to 42 without loss. James Vince scores 62 on his return from England duty and just as it's looking like a home win may be likely Vince, Alsop, Ervine and Afridi are all out quickly. Hampshire need 30 off of 18 balls and McManus puts us back in with a chance with a big 6 before we need 4 off 2 balls, A lot of tonight's crowd are here because they came to the rained off game last Saturday and have swapped their tickets for tonight's instead, and they've picked a good one to come to. The Hampshire batsman, for some reason, tries a reverse sweep which would have looked good if he had connected with the ball, but he doesn't and misses it, so it's now 4 off of the last ball. Another miss, actually good bowling by Bopara, and we've all got our hands on our heads, oohing and ahhing at another defeat, we can't qualify anyway but it would have been nice to see a win, especially with the large crowd tonight.

As with the bus service laid on after the England game the other day, tonight's organisation is just as impressive and buses line up to take people away, I must remember if this keeps up to send both the club and bus operator thank you emails in the hope it continues next season. It's a nice evening so me and Michelle get off in Bitterne instead of town and walk the 25 minutes into Woolston, if it was raining we wouldn't have though.

Tomorrow Michelle is going to the 'Lets Rock' 80's music festival on the common with her mates and I am going to the Beggars Fair music festival in Romsey with my old mate Antony. All parties have a good day but I'm in first and in bed asleep when the others arrive back after midnight, not to be antisocial, but tomorrow I am off to Edgbaston for Hampshire's Championship game against Warwickshire, it's a ground I have never been to and I'm going for all four days.

Sunday 10th July

Going on the Sunday means I will not arrive in Birmingham for the start of the game and entails a lot of perusing of train timetables and fares to get something suitable. I am bearing in mind that I don't know what time train I will be getting at the end of the match come Wednesday. I could get there earlier than I do, via London, but it would entail coming back the same way and it's more expensive. In the end I opt for the 9:27 train to Bristol where I change and get the train to Birmingham and am in the ground at 2:20pm after eventually finding a taxi at New Street Station.

I have paid my £15 to get into the ground and using my Hampshire members' card I go into the members' bar and area on the 2nd floor, get a pint and sit down inside to see what's going on. Hampshire are batting and were 63 for 2 at one stage before Dawson and Alsop began an impressive partnership which is when I arrive to see Alsop and then Dawson get their respective 50's. Dawson goes on to get his century (116) and Wheater is undefeated on 89 when play is closed for the day and Hampshire finish on 304 for 4, a good days play.

At tea I had a wander around the ground and not a lot is actually open, just the club shop and members' area by the look of it. On the ticket and club website it says no alcohol to be brought into the ground so I didn't, but there are no public bars open and when I query this with a steward she says oh, don't take any notice of that, it's just Internationals and Twenty 20 games where you can't bring anything in, so same as the Rose Bowl then!

At the end of play it's time to find my hotel and check in. On the map it's just down the road, left turn followed by a right turn and it should be just in front of me and in effect that is correct, however after a long day travelling (and I had to stand on the train between Bristol and Brum), getting to know the new ground, and now walking in sweltering heat it seems a lot further than it is. Add to this the fact that my shorts are now wet and rubbing my inner thigh raw and I am so glad when I eventually walk into the front door of the Ibis budget hotel and I check in ok. The room is new and tidy with tea and coffee and a TV etc but it's a bit small if you had two sleeping in it, it's ok for me though on my own and I unpack for the next 3 nights.

Tonight is the European Championship final between France and Portugal and my plan is to go out and get something to eat and watch it somewhere. On trip advisor there are lots of posts regarding my hotel being on the main duel carriageway into Birmingham and it is on the wrong side of all of the pubs and entertainment that can only be accessed through a subway in which tramps, beggars and all forms of nightmares await. I approach the subway tentatively and am happily surprised when I find it well lit, clean and habited by nothing more than a bit of graffiti so I head in and safely come out of the other side without mishap. Only 400 yards on and I come into a nice area full of Chinese restaurants, noodle bars and pubs so I settle in a Weatherspoons with a pint of scrumpy (they've got a cider festival on at the moment which is handy) and watch the football. The game goes into extra time and I want to visit the shop down the road before it closes for supplies for tomorrow so I head off, go in the shop, and watch the extra time in my hotel room. Portugal win 1-0.

Monday 11th July

The toilet flush isn't working in the room and it's one of those boxed in affairs which I can't tamper with so I am downstairs to use the loo in the lobby and to report it on my way out. On my way to the ground my rubbed thigh is giving me more grief so I nip into a chemist and buy some plasters which I will apply once in a loo inside the ground. It seems today will be a toilet tour! I am at the ground for 10am and all patched up. I have a bacon sandwich and a cup of tea as I have not paid the extra for breakfasts in the hotel not knowing if I would have time for them or not.

There are a few other Hampshire fans in the members' area and we say hello even though I do not know them. They have replica jumpers on or club ties and they identify me from my Hampshire jacket and baseball cap which I have had to bring today as there is a slight drizzle and come the 11am start time the covers are still on. We do get going shortly afterwards though and it is another good batting day for Hampshire as Adam Wheater hits a double century, scoring his 5000th first class run in the process before Sean Ervine hits 75 and his 10,000th first class run.

Although it is nice in the members' bar and seating balcony there is no sun. After lunch I move around to the main stand for some warmth and it is a great place to view the Hampshire onslaught as the boundary is right over this side, as near as it can be to the boundary. For a top class ground though I find the Edgbaston seats a little flimsy as they twist and bend under my weight and I have to position myself just right so as not to tip backwards or sideways out of them.

Once Ervine is out Hampshire lose 4 quick wickets and are all out for 531 with Wheater unbeaten on 204, only the 4th time a Hampshire batsman has hit a double ton at this ground.

After the restart Hampshire take three fairly quick wickets and I can't help cheering, which people take note of and a few come over to chat about the game and ask what I'm doing here. One chap is even going my way and asks if I want a pint in the Fox after the game which I accept. It turns out he is called Durham Pete (Peter Hemming) who lives in Durham and travels to all of Warwickshire's games, costing him over £5000 a year in travel and hotels. He is staying in a hotel near mine and we get the bus back towards the town centre. As it happens the Fox is near enough next door to the Weatherspoons I was in last night, so I know where I am. We stay for a few pints and talk of cricket and our lives and generally talk rubbish like blokes do when having a few pints. I wander back to the hotel at 9.45pm and get some cheese and biscuits and a bottle of red to have in the room.

The toilet flush is fixed when I get back to the room so all well and good, unlike my sore inner thigh which has rubbed again and getting the old plasters off causes no end of pain as the leg hairs come off with the plasters, ouch!

Tuesday 12th July

Today is overcast with a few spots of rain as I wander to the ground and I manage to arrive before the real rain begins in earnest. It's quite cosy in the members bar with people drinking tea, reading papers and chatting while watching the rain come down. I sit with some Hampshire fans who have been here since Sunday but this is their first time in here as they've been sat over the other side of the ground. Lunch comes and goes and I go for a walk around to stretch my legs, get a bit of fresh air and eat my sandwiches in peace. A Warwickshire chap who has just arrived has seen my jacket and comes over to chat, very sociable these Birmingham types! We have a brief moment of hope when the grounds men take the covers off mid afternoon and begin drying the wicket off for a pitch inspection at 3.30pm but it clouds over again and is raining by 4pm.

Durham Pete, my drinking buddy from last night, decides to show me the executive balcony two floors above our members' level. There is a great view of the city and ground and if it clears up tomorrow I will sneak up here and take some photos. As we're heading back down Pete's phone goes off and one of his mates tells him that play has been written off for the day. We hang around the bar chatting for a bit but at 5pm I head down to the ticket office and claim my £15 entrance back and get the bus back into town.

On the bus is a South African chap whose son is Hampshire's twelfth man for this game, and who was at the Rose Bowl for last Fridays Twenty 20 game. He is here in Birmingham for this four day game before going home next week after the next Twenty 20 game in Southampton. Neither of us know where we're getting off the bus but I get off a stop or two before I should do and he stays on to who knows where?

I never did find out who his son was or why he was twelfth man just for his game?

I pop in Weatherspoons for another cider and as I get settled and 7 O'clock ticks round, I order some food before staggering off to find the hotel and hope for some sunshine and play tomorrow.

Durham Pete

Wednesday 13th July

I'm a bit late leaving the hotel this morning, I was up early enough but then got caught up reading my book and before I knew it 10 o'clock was here so I check out and have a hurried breakfast in Weatherspoons, before getting the bus to the ground in time to see the 3rd ball of the day. The sun is out for half an hour before it clouds over and the players go off for rain! Hampshire need 17 wickets today, a tall order, and this isn't going to help the cause one iota.

I get a pint in the members' bar and it dawns on me as I say hello to people that I've met these last few days, that they are sat in the same spots every day, funny people cricket fans. Play eventually resumes at 12:30 with the loss of 8 overs and it is a slow day with not many wickets falling. At lunch I have a walk on the pitch and Durham Pete gives me a tour of some of the other members' areas around the ground which I didn't know existed. He also introduces me to some of his friends in them (so that's where he has been when not over the other side! mystery solved).

I uhmm and ahh whether to stay after tea or go and catch an early train but I'm glad I stay as Hampshire take the two wickets they need for an extra bowling point and Warwickshire go all out to get up to 400 runs before the 110th over is bowled. It leads to a Twenty 20 like last five overs and they need 12 off of the last 2 balls. They hit a six and next ball we think they've gone and done it when a big hit flies off of the bat again, but the ball drops just inside the boundary rope for a 4 instead, a great finish and the sides shake hands and it's a draw, 11 points each, and an exciting end to the trip. I have even gone upstairs and got some action shots of the play and Pete has taken a few of me up there as well, which have come out well, and will be on facebook soon.

top floor at Edgbaston

Me and Pete get the bus back to town and he pops in to collect his bag from his hotel. We walk to New Street station where we say our goodbyes and part company, him to the far north and me to the far south. I manage to get the 18:04 train cross country straight back to Southampton (hence the reason my train ticket was more expensive in the end for this convenience) and after changing trains get indoors at 9pm after a great trip away.

Nb, me and Durham Pete have become friends on facebook and chatted throughout the summer about cricket and hopefully we'll meet again at another game in the seasons to come.

Thursday 14th July

It's my first day back after Birmingham and it's straight into the action with a home Twenty 20 game against Glamorgan tonight which just happens to be Michelle's sister Suz's birthday, so we are having tea with them first, a cod mournay ate outside in the open air, before it's off to get the bus to the ground. As previously mentioned they only live in Chartwell Green, so not far, but they have both forgotten their money in the rush to finish tea and get to the bus stop. Michelle gets off with them near the shops in West End and gets some money out for them to borrow while I stay on the bus and go to the ticket office to exchange 2 vouchers for tickets to get them in.

Paul has been to cricket here before but Suz hasn't, so as it's her birthday, we go the full hog tonight and get yellow fluffy hats and send our selfies in to be featured on the big screen as well as having the 4 and 6 cards to wave about like loons. It's another good crowd seeing as we're out of the competition, so it just proves that the lure of 20 over cricket works. Liam Dawson is in inspired form since his England heroics a week or so back and once again he is the star as he scores 76 out of Hampshire's total of 168 runs along with good partnerships with boom boom Afridi and newcomer Joe Weatherly.

The evening is slightly marred by the news that comes out this evening that Michael Carberry has cancer. That is why he has been ill lately, and this after his previous problems a few years back when he had a blood clot on his lung. Shocking news to all Hampshire fans and his friends and family.

Glamorgan come out to bat and put on a quick 51 for the first wicket before Dawson steps up again and takes 4 for 23, he can do no wrong at the moment. Two new faces in Brad Wheal and Gareth Griffith continue the good work and by the time the Glammies have an over left they need a whopping 35 from it to win, it's all but over.

It's been a good evening for Suz's birthday but I'm not sure how much enjoyment she got out of the cricket. That's what twenty 20 is all about though, cricket for people who don't usually go but want a night out and say they were there.

The birthday party

Friday 15th July

Me and Michelle live in a top floor flat, in a house that has been converted into two flats, and we share the garden with our downstairs neighbours Pete and Sandie. The garden sharing works out fine as me and Michelle are out all day sunbathing while they prefer the shade and cool of the evenings but it does mean that you can't be spontaneous sometimes and have a BBQ or light the fire pit as and when you want to. This weekend though they are away for the weekend, in Weymouth. We are feeding their cat (and they feed ours when we are away which is handy) and as the weather forecast is good we have arranged to have a BBQ in the evening. We will be listening to Hampshire's away twenty game against Sussex at Hove, a game I'd have like to have gone to but it's not often we get a chance of the garden to ourselves! We have the BBQ early and then get the fire pit lit and the booze out, and tune into the radio commentary for ball by ball coverage. The game is actually on Sky TV but I'm not missing being out in the garden when the opportunity arises like this in the middle of summer. At the interval Hampshire have posted a pitiful target of 135 and Michelle has gone in to watch TV (not the match though) thinking that we've already lost, a shame as I was thinking of outside romance later on, but it's not to be now, ha ha.

Sussex begin well but good bowling keeps the runs down and Sussex are only just keeping in front of the run chase leading to Kevin James on the radio getting excited for an unexpected close finish. With just four overs left, Sussex need 25 runs to win and the game is theirs to lose now. Wickets and runs come at a frenzied rate and with one over left Brad Wheal in only his 2nd game has to stop experienced batsman Taylor, who is on 46, from scoring just 5 runs to win it for the home team.

Sussex only score 3 (three) and the radio commentators are delirious, I'm jumping around the garden and when I see film of it later on TV the Hampshire players are also celebrating as though they've won the cup itself. It's a local derby and it's a great win. I just hope no neighbours were looking out of their windows though when I was leaping about, punching the air!

Sunday 17th July

After a lazy Saturday in the garden, Sunday see's us on the UNISON coach to the annual Tolpuddle Martyrs festival. We are with our friends from the Isle of Wight the Kennesions (only two of the kids though, as Son number 1, our godson is old enough to stay at home on his own so does). It's a scorching hot day and it looks like summer has finally begun, so after arriving I go off and see local musician Doozer McDoze play inside a sweltering hot tent, before me and Andy carry the Southampton UNISON banner in the annual march through the village. After a load of speakers who I don't pay any attention to, it's time for the main reason I've come this year and a performance on stage of a band from Mansfield called Ferocious Dog. I've seen them a few times before and this time is no different, a great set which has the hairs on the back of your neck standing up with their power and lyrics.

carrying the banner

56

To be here today means that I've missed the opening day of Hampshire's home championship game against Surrey. When I get in at 8pm I am dismayed to see that Surrey have made hay in the sunshine scoring 208 runs for the first wicket and Hampshire only getting a few wickets late on in the day and restricting Surrey to 320 odd for 4.

Monday 18th July

It's another scorcher today and after the setback this morning when we found out that Michelle had washed my shorts from yesterday with my wallet in them (including my weekly bus ticket, that still had three days left on it) I arrive to a lovely sunny Rose Bowl which is just how it should be when watching cricket. I had to pay another £18 for another weekly bus ticket but my money has dried out !! Thank goodness

It's a bit of a toil for the Hampshire players and fans as Surrey captain Gareth Batty bats on and on to post 637 for 7 before declaring after tea. I leave early today as I've got darts tonight but find out later that Hampshire lost 2 wickets when they eventually got a chance to bat and they end on 73 for 2.

Darts tonight is unfortunately away at the West End Brewery so it's all the way home for tea and a freshen up before getting the bus nearly all the way back to the ground again, where we narrowly lose 5-4 to the top team in the league. There are no scheduled buses after 8:30pm for me to get home, so it's a taxi with some of the others tonight for a change. After a roundabout route dropping people off I get indoors at near midnight. I hate to think how much the taxi costs but as it's a one off our treasurer Ray is paying out of our subs thankfully.

Tuesday 19th July

The forecast for day 3 is that it will be the hottest day of the year so far, up in the 30's at least. I decide that after last night's late homecoming I will have a relax in the garden first thing and keep up with proceedings at the match on the radio. McLaren is bowled first ball of the day and then in the 3rd over Tom Alsop falls as well, not a good start. By the time I arrive at the ground after lunch a bit of stability has returned and our new wicket keeper McManus scores his maiden first class century under intense pressure from the Surrey bowling. Adam Wheater gets another 50 and both Berg and Andrew chip in with decent knocks supporting McManus, however when Brad Wheal comes to the crease for the last wicket we are all wondering how long it will be until the follow on begins. I think it takes everyone in the ground by surprise though when the last two put on a 71 run stand and are still holding out by the end of play on 398 for 9.

scorching day

Wednesday 20th July

This is what county cricket is all about, Hampshire need to bat all day to gain a draw and Surrey need 11 wickets to win. I have sat many times watching similar scenarios but unfortunately with not much success for my teams. I remember numerous times when Hampshire's Nick Pothas put in heroic feats of resilience, nearly getting us out of trouble only for others to lose their wickets around him, great days. What you need in these instances is a Boycott or a Tavere', someone who can block their end up all day.

It's another scorcher and I'm sat with Ian and Adrian. Not caring about my appearance today, I strip off to the waist and don my Wurzels neckerchief to keep the sun off of the back of my neck. It's a great day as Hampshire have us going through every emotion possible throughout the day from unexpected safety to abject defeat.

Hampshire begin by adding 25 runs to the overnight score before Brad Wheal is run out by an exceptional throw which means we begin our follow on 214 runs behind. We plough on slowly throughout the day making steady progress but just before tea, two wickets fall, and it's now 107 for 4 at the break. After the break, McManus and Berg stabilise things and with the score creeping ever nearer to safety the Hampshire fans are thinking now of the draw, especially if we can get ahead and then declare which could take out 3 overs for the changeover. Surrey and in particular Gareth Batty are getting frustrated, and upset now, at the thought of not winning and they are cheesing the home crowd off with a series of petty appeals and unsporting shenanigans. Just when we think it's nearly done, Gareth Batty has the last laugh by getting first inning's hero McManus out LBW and that turns out to be crucial. Unfortunately, the resistance is broken and the likes of Crane and Wheal cannot survive and Batty ends up the victor taking 6 wickets himself, we were close but not close enough as only 39 balls remained in the day when it's all over. The next bus is in 10 minutes so the bus club, who have all stayed on for the finish, trundle down the hill bemoaning our fate that relegation is nigh.

Thursday 21st July

A rare day off for me today and it's a bit overcast so I end up sorting my finances, catching up on emails and booking some future trips. Michelle is on mornings this week so in the afternoon we take the opportunity to go for a walk along Riverside Park and watch a bit of evening league cricket as I know that local team Southamptonshire are playing here tonight. Our good friend Sylvia does the scoring for the team and Ian (from the Rose Bowl bus club) either does the oppositions' scorebook or does the scoreboard if required. Sylv's husband Butch, who we also know, plays in the team. There's bit of rain in the air at times and as it's a bit of a walk home we wander back to the train station just before Southamptonshire score their winning runs and we get a chinese takeaway on the way home.

Friday 22nd July

Me and Michelle are off to the Netley Marsh steam and craft show today, a regular event on our calendar at which I have often camped for the whole weekend before. After multiple buses getting there we arrive at 10:30am and a have a great day. We watch falconry displays, dog agility, and drink cider, wandering around the stalls. At lunch we have a walnut and cheese bread accompanied with a slab of local stilton and washed down with more cider.

We can't linger too long this afternoon though and after getting the bus back to town, having a meal in the spitfire pub and making our way to the Rose Bowl, we meet our mate Kendo and our godson Tom for tonight's Twenty 20 game against Middlesex. Everybody attending has the chance to win a luxury holiday to Barbados so spirits are high!

As it happens the game is a bit of a flop for us and Middlesex win quite comfortably with only Brad Wheal doing anything over and above by taking 3 wickets as Hampshire lose by 43 runs. We didn't win the holiday and we didn't win the Golden Gamble and to make matters worse another old Hampshire boy, George Bailey, hit 76 in Middlesex's innings.

me & Kendo

Godson Tom

Saturday 23rd July

The big news today is that Dale Benkenstein has left Hampshire as head coach for family reasons with immediate effect. It turns out he was going to leave anyway at the end of the season but perhaps Hampshire's dismal season and rumours of changing room unrest also played a factor in the timing of his departure?

This weekend me and Michelle are camping out in the New Forest with Suz and Paul. After a few hours crabbing at Mudiford and stocking up on food and drink we arrive at the camp site and set up for a relaxing weekend of eating and drinking with possibly an odd woodland walk. Very nice.

Tuesday 26th July

Our one hope of glory left this season is in the 50 over cup and today we play Kent at home. It is a 2 o'clock start so should be a good day, especially as I meet Kev in the West End Brewery first, and I have 3 pints of Old Rosie and Kev has jack Daniels. We arrive early enough to see the 30 piece Southsea Skiffle Orchestra playing live outside the Atrium, which is something different, normally we only get a band after the end of a Twenty 20 match.

It's a lovely sunny day again and Hampshire bat first unfortunately and it's a bit of a disaster scoring a measly 230 all out with still 5 overs of the 50 left to bowl. Adam Wheater is our top scorer with 65, which is a good effort in the scheme of things. During the game I bump into the Cluette brothers (Kev and Dave) who work for the council and are here for their first game of the season. We have a good chat and a catch up which is nice, they're both nice fella's.

Kent make light work of chasing the Hampshire score and openers Joe Denley and Bell-Drummond almost win the game by themselves with a 203 first wicket partnership. A little blip causes a moments panic, when the score goes from 203 for none to 204 for 3 but Kent were nearly there, and settle down for a 5 wicket victory to go ahead of us in the table. Brad Wheal actually finishes with figures of 4 for 38 his best performance yet, but is still on the wrong end of the result. It's a shame as it's been a good day, a nice social drink and due to the early finish, the bus club are able to get on a normal bus and not have to wait for the specials later on.

Wednesday 27th July

Hampshire are away at Hove today in another 50 over cup match and I am determined to go as Hove is another ground that I have not been to, although I have seen Sussex v Hampshire games at Arundel a few times. I bought the match ticket ages ago but there is strike action and disruption on Southern trains and the game will finish at 10pm if it goes all of the way. I keep my eye on the train situation and come the day of the game I am advised to travel from Southampton to Clapham Junction and then change there for a train back south to Hove. I get the 10am train so that I can use my railcard and it costs me £20.80 instead of £31.50 and all goes to schedule, and I arrive in Hove at 12.20pm.

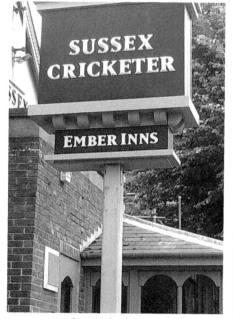

pub outside the ground

I find the ground easily enough after a ten minute walk and go into the Sussex Cricketer pub, which is right outside the entrance and pretty packed with people eating, so I only stay for one before going into the ground. Once inside I have a wander and then use my Hampshire membership to access the members' area and bar. This takes up the whole of one side of the ground, square on, and is very quaint, old fashioned and nice. There are seats outside but if you go up the steps there is a much larger seating area with a view looking over the pitch and ground. It's here that I sit and watch the first innings with a couple of other away fans who I chat to after they see me drinking out of a customised Sussex cup. You pay a £1 for the cup and each time you want another drink you take it back meaning less rubbish and more recycling. At the end of the game you either keep the cup as a souvenir or hand it back and get a £1 back - I kept mine and brought it home.

Sussex win the toss and put us in to bat and the innings is very stop/start with some good and equally bad batting. Jimmy Adams scores a great 92 but is out trying to hit a ball that flies over his head and it looks like he is trying to play a tennis shot as it snicks his bat and we're all sat gob smacked. Wheater again chips in with 42 before a late surge by McClaren, who is fast becoming my player of the season, sees him score 46 not out to set Sussex a total of 269 to win.

During the interval I'm refreshing my Sussex cup with the local Harvey's ale, which is 10p cheaper in the ground than in the pub outside. I bump into Grant, another ex colleague at the council and he has driven down with three mates and all they can talk about is Adams getting out and how bizarre a shot it was so near to his 100.

It has been overcast all day and the floodlights have been on but as Sussex begin their run chase a few rays of sun shine through to brighten things up. Unfortunately it also seems to be the signal for loads of gulls and pigeons to take to the air and it's like a scene from the Hitchcock film ' The Birds' for a while. They eventually thin out a bit but there are some swooping and diving all through the innings, my mum would definitely not like it.

The other Hampshire fans think that 268 is enough to win, but I think it will be close. After yesterday's defeat we are at last chance saloon in this competition, and perhaps in our whole season. Sussex don't start well and the required run rate steadily increases, even with Sussex hero Luke Wright scoring a quick 40 to take them to 109 for 4 before he is caught out. Things improve for the home side when Ben Brown and Chris Nash put on a 100 partnership and need 63 off of 36 balls. Nash gets his 50 and at 231 for 4 Sussex are eating into the lead and need 38 off of 24 balls, it's getting tense for both sets of fans now and being under floodlights seems to add to the excitement.

The game is swinging back and forth now and Hampshire seem to get the luck when Brown is magnificently caught behind by McManus off of McLaren and then Jordan swings the bat and is caught while hitting out. Sussex need 17 to win off the final over and Brad Wheal again takes it all in his stride so that 12 is needed off of 2 balls. It's too much for Sussex and in the end a 9 run victory for Hampshire doesn't tell the whole story. After the last ditch Twenty 20 win here a couple of weeks ago, added to tonight's win, Sussex must hate the sight of us.

I am downstairs in position at 9.20pm when the final ball is bowled and after a quick fist pump in the air to celebrate it's a quick walk to the station for the 9.50pm train to Clapham which is good, as if I miss this one it's an even more complicated journey home via Brighton and then Clapham. Once again the journeys go to plan and after a taxi home from central I am indoors just before 1am. For my first trip to Hove it's been a great day. I liked Hove, it's one of those quirky old grounds where if you want you can grab a deckchair and sit on the grass and during the interval you can go onto the pitch and have a game of bat and ball on the outfield.

Thursday 28th July

It is all go this summer and today I am off to the New Forest Show, I think I once went when I was little with my Aunt Audrey and Uncle Jim but I can't be sure. As it always falls midweek and I have always been at work I have never got to go and never had the inclination to take holiday to attend before. It's only a short journey by train to Brockenhurst and then a half hours walk to the show ground, so I'm there at 11:30 finding my bearings by looking at the map in the programme, and then just wandering anywhere anyway, looking in craft tents, food tents, trade tents and pet rabbit, weasel, hens and hamster tents. I eventually come to the place I've been looking for and sit down with a pint of New Forest cider and watch local 'Wurzel' tribute band the New Forest Yokels play their set. The day forms a pattern after that, and I go for a regular half hour wander in a different direction each time, before returning to see another band and have another drink, so by the end of the day, I think, I have seen all there is to see, but the last hour or so was a bit hazy, hic! I do cheat on the way back and jump on a special bus going back to the station and am indoors by 7:30 after a good day.

Friday 29th July

It is Hampshire's last Twenty 20 game tonight at home to Somerset with the winner avoiding the wooden spoon, and the loser coming rock bottom of the group and having the glory of being the worst T20 team this summer. I'm sat in the garden at 4pm and it's clouding over and a few spots of rain begin falling and I have one of those lethargic moments and inform Michelle that we're not now going, we'll have an early night in readiness for our trip to Swansea tomorrow instead.

I nip down to the shop at 5pm instead to get some supplies for tonight as we're now staying in, and it's pouring down, so imagine my surprise an hour and a half later when the sun comes out and the game starts bang on time. Oh well, I can take the stick I'll get from Kev, Ian and Adrian when I see them next. It's actually so nice now that I take my cider outside to the garden and listen to the game on the radio and a good evening it is as well.

Sean Irvine is out injured, he has injured himself in the warm up. Adam Wheater is out ill, and both teams actually have the look of second elevens. Hampshire's youngsters do have a lot of experience between them though and the game reflects this. Hampshire pile on the runs and when debutant Jake Goodwin is out for 32 we are 83 for 1. Tom Alsop goes on to hit his first Twenty 20 half century and boom boom Afridi hits 21 off of 12 balls in his final Hampshire game this season. Alsop is finally caught on the boundary for 85 with the score at 159 - 3 after 18 overs and Hampshire end up scoring 181.

Radio Solent are keen to stress that Somerset have a crucial 50 over game tomorrow and have a below strength team out tonight. They are proved correct, as Somerset are all out for 98 and Liam Dawson has new best figures of 5 for 15. Somerset's innings has only lasted 15 overs and my feelings are mixed, have I missed a classic or have I saved myself a late night bearing in mind our trip to Wales tomorrow. Oh well whichever it is, it's two wins on the trot and we head to Swansea in optimistic mood.

Saturday 30th July - Monday 1st August
Swansea

Hampshire are playing Glamorgan at the St Helens ground on Sunday and as Michelle has never seen the Mumbles I have convinced her that she needs to see them and that this exact weekend would be a good time to do so. The hotel, match tickets and trains have been booked for a while now and it's a rare chance to see Hampshire play Glamorgan at an out ground instead of at Cardiff. Michelle has just changed her working hours to include having Mondays off, so being a Sunday match is ideal for a couple of nights away.

We are on the 08:24 train to Southampton where we change onto the next train to Newport and then change there for Swansea. We should arrive at approx 1pm in time for the 2pm check in at the Premier Inn.

The train turns out to be full of Portsmouth fans going to Bristol for a pre season friendly. For many it's standing room only, although we do get two seats as we're first on by some fluke. This overcrowding results in the train taking longer at each station to ensure people can get on and off. The knock on effect is that we miss our connection at Newport and are told to stay on now, until Cardiff, and change there instead. In the end we are only about 15 minutes late arriving in Swansea so not too bad.

Our hotel isn't far from the station but does turn out to be in the middle of 'party district central' and we are surrounded by pubs, clubs, restaurants and bars. There is already a party feel to the place as hen and stag parties are roaming the streets in various states of inebriation, and it's not even 2pm yet. Once we've checked in, and I won't need to say what the room is like as all Premier Inn's are the same throughout the land, we go for a walk around the marina. A regatta is on so we have a quick watch and the ladies are out rowing the men in a charity boat race quite easily, before we head down to the beach and the glorious miles upon miles of the Mumbles. Unfortunately, just as we're taking in the view it begins to rain so we have to take refuge in a pub to wait for it to stop.

In the evening the main street outside the hotel is closed to traffic and everywhere is heaving with people dressed to the nines, out for a good time. We sit in a bar and people watch for a while and I will say one thing for the Welsh women out that night, they looked like proper women with lots of curves and flesh on show. Not one anorexic supermodel in sight, even Michelle commented on this, even though some of the sights bordered on the too much flesh and curves variety! Michelle had set her heart on crispy duck to eat tonight and after failing to get into one fully packed Chinese restaurant we wandered a little away from the party area and found a lovely one, half full. The service was great and we spent a few hours there before walking back through the, now worse for wear, hordes to our peaceful room.

Match day dawned bright and sunny and after breakfast we had a nice walk along the beach path to the ground at St Helens. This is a venue that normally hosts rugby but today was providing a yearly treat for Swansea's cricket following population. After the beer mess up at Edgbaston where it said no beer to be brought into the ground, and then they let you in with it for non international and T20 games, I presumed that Glamorgan would be the same when it said on the tickets no alcohol. Oh no, this time it was real, so after having our bags checked at the gate and alcohol found we were asked to go and get rid of it ourselves or it would be confiscated and not returned! Michelle was not happy with my misdemeanour, especially when she was told that no cans of any description were allowed in, so she couldn't even bring her cans of diet coke in! oops. I tried to say that it wasn't my fault, it was just the Welsh trying to fleece more money out of us, as if you can take cans into Lords why should a piddly out ground in Wales be different, but it was still my fault apparently. There was only one thing to do in this situation, especially as we were early anyway, so we retired over the beachfront, sat on a bench, and I knocked back two cans of cider (I would have had all four if I was on my own but Michelle was taking a dim view as it was only 10:30am).

drinking on the seafront

The rest of the cans we ditched and in we went to the unusual looking ground, to see some people even stood on terracing, watching the teams warm up. We grabbed chairs and sat around the boundary rope and it was a good view.

Hampshire won the toss and decided to bat first with everybody chipping in runs heading towards a reasonable score. Michelle even thought that we'd get over 300, to which I replied that ' I'd eat my hat if we did!' This was the cue for Will Smith to score 84, some fireworks as Ryan McLaren hit a quick 33 and a fantastic 100 not out from Liam Dawson, who scored a six off of the last ball to get his century and set a target of 316 for Glamorgan to chase. When the six dropped over the rope just in front of us I couldn't help but jump up and cheer, which got me some funny glances from the Welsh fans around me, but there were enough Hampshire fans dotted around the ground (including Grant who was at Hove the other day and who I bumped into earlier at the bar) to make me feel safe. During the interval Michelle took a photo of me pretending to eat my baseball cap and posting it on facebook for all of her friends to see.

Swansea

The sun continued sending down it's glorious rays as Glamorgan started their innings. I was on my way round to the beer stall as the first ball was bowled by McLaren, and Wicket!, first ball of the innings. Glamorgan never recovered from that early setback and before our unbelieving eyes collapsed from 22 for 2, 22 for 3, 23 for 4, 25 for 5, 29 for 6, 59 for 7, 59 for 8 before their, brief, last two wicket stands take the score to 130 all out. Me and Michelle make our way over to the main stand and applaud our heroes off as they walk up the steps inches away from us, especially McLaren and Berg who have taken 4 wickets each from their 10 overs and Gareth Andrew who took 2 from his 5 overs.

The crowd have dispersed quite quickly and the game has finished over an hour earlier than it should have, so we walk back along the beach and have a relaxing hour back at the hotel before venturing out again. A few people are about but compared to yesterday the place seems dead and deserted, so we have the pick of eating places to choose from tonight.

heroes coming off the pitch

The journey back on Monday goes to plan and we get the 10:30 train, change in Cardiff and are back indoors by 2:30pm where our two cats Ollie and Rex are waiting to greet us home, or waiting for food at any rate! It was raining when we left Swansea this morning and it rains all the way back and all afternoon and night when we get back, it just shows how lucky we were yesterday, although Glamorgan may wish that the game had been rained off.

The Sussex and Glamorgan wins have lifted Hampshire to 3rd in our 50 over cup table and the top four qualify for the quarter finals, we have

Somerset, who are top and have already qualified, at home next in our last match, so if we win that tomorrow it will be a great achievement. A note of caution though as the table is also so tight that a loss and other results going against us may mean we cannot qualify and it's season over for any silverware or a cup final day out at Lords!

Tuesday 2nd August

It is raining when I awake but the forecast is ok for later so I head off to meet Kev in the West End Brewery for some pre match drinks and also, as it happens, to be regaled with some tales from Jim Steele, a Saints 1976 FA cup winner, who sits down with us for a chat. By the time we head off to the ground for the 1.30pm start it is drying up nicely and the game begins on time.

Somerset win the toss and elect to bat first and the opening pair of Jayawardena (55) and Jim Allenby (69) put on 108 for the first wicket so it looks like a good call from the opposition. The Hampshire bowlers do hit back though and two wickets each from Dawson, McLaren and Wheal limit Somerset to 250 for 9 after their 50 overs. Hampshire start their innings ok with Adams scoring a 50 and Will Smith 59 but the first 4 batsmen all fall to LBW decisions and we're on the back foot, especially when a couple of showers come down and Hampshire are behind on the Duckworth Lewis comparison score. Play continues though and with Lewis McManus scoring 35 and some big hitting from Gareth Andrew, Hampshire remain in the game right until the end where they fall short by just a measly 5 runs. It is a great end to the game but it sadly means Hampshire have just missed out on a quarter final spot as results elsewhere have not gone in our favour and we end up 5th just a point behind Surrey.

Due to the earlier start today I am not sure what the bus situation is so I take a chance and just head down to the bus stop, thinking a long walk might be in store for me tonight, however not 2 but 3 buses come around the corner so I jump straight on. Even better news arrives when the driver informs us that Bitterne Road is closed for road works tonight so all of the buses are being diverted over the Itchen Bridge, exactly where I want to be, so I jump off of the bus in Woolston and am home indoors within 35 minutes of the game finishing, superb.

Thursday 4th August

After the routine all season of County Championship matches starting on a Sunday it is all change now until the end of the season, with all different starting dates. Today's game starts on a Thursday and there will be no Ian to sit with me for this game, for the first time I think this season. He is away but will be back for the last two days of play, so I say hello to Mike, Adrian and a few others and head off to find my own spot for the day. For Hampshire it is an enjoyable morning as no wickets fall and Adams and Smith take us to lunch on 69 for 0. Both openers go on to bring up their 50's after lunch and actually go on to equal the second highest partnership against Lancashire of 191 before Adams gives his wicket away again with a loose shot and is caught out. It's a slow but enjoyable day for me and if you realise that Sir Geoffrey Boycott was a big influence on me in my playing days, it will tell you what sort of day it was, but Tom Alsop ends up on 50 not out and Will Smith on 99 not out as Hampshire finish the day on 257 for 1. Inevitably some people on the bus are complaining about slow scoring and run rates etc but I loved it today especially sat on my own in the sun for a change.

Friday 5th August

Day two at the Rose Bowl and I am not going to be there today as I am off to the Rebellion punk festival in Blackpool for the day. This is a 4 day festival and previously I have been to all 4 days. Last year Michelle got me a ticket for my 50th birthday present, and I wouldn't normally have gone this year but it's a special one. It's 40 years since punk music is officially accredited to have begun and it's also the 20th anniversary of this particular festival. I am compromising this year by just going for the one day because A) it's expensive, a day ticket is £60 compared to the £135 weekend one, B) I don't need the cost of a hotel - which was £160 last year, C) I will save a lot on beer and merchandise. It all sounds great on paper but when I am sat outside a closed Blackpool North train station on Saturday morning at 3:15am with no sign of life, apart from a few rowdy drunks in the distance, waiting for the hopefully on time 3:40am train to Manchester, I envy all of those tucked up in their hotel rooms and vow not to do this again at my age!

But that's later on, back to Friday morning and I'm all excited to be on my way there and it's a military operation as I am meeting my mate Gary Watts at 11am in a pub along Blackpool seafront. The alarm goes off at 4:45 and it's dark out as I have a wash, get dressed and check for the umpteenth time that I have all tickets and paperwork for the day. I make the 5:13am bus to Southampton Central station for the 5:40 train to Southampton airport just as it's getting light. I am well in time for the plane to Manchester, thanks to Michelle printing my boarding card out yesterday at her work. For some reason the train fares at this time of day to get you north for a decent time are astronomical, even by booking well in advance, so I have taken this route a few times now going up north. Once at Manchester airport it's straight on a train, change at Piccadilly and I'm in Blackpool and walking along the sunny seafront taking photos of the tower and beach at 10:45am.

I am in the pub before Gary and if you are not a music or punk music fan then feel free to skip ahead to the next chapter. Back in the early 1980's and 1990's I spent my time, amongst over things, going to punk gigs and along with a small group of like minded people putting on our own gigs, producing our own fanzines, playing in bands and selling our own records and tapes. Gary was a part of this group and still produces with his friend Tony the 'Suspect Device' fanzine which has now been running for over 30 years. Even though Gary has now moved to Norwich to live, we all still keep in touch and see each other when we can. Gary is here for the 4 days and it's great to see him again and catch up before we both head off, me to exchange my ticket for a wristband and him to say hello to other people he knows. We will be meeting up again throughout the day so it's not goodbye just yet.

The Rebellion festival, if you haven't heard of it, is the Glastonbury of the punk music world and every year it's a fantastic line up of all things punk, Oi, skinhead, alternative, experimental, weird and loud. It has had various venues over the years but the Blackpool Winter Gardens is it's spiritual home and that's where it is again this year.

Once I am in, my first aim is to get into the outdoor concert stage, which is new for this one year only, where I see Hasting sisters ' Maid of Ace' followed by London's 'Wonk Unit' and the great 'Ferocious Dog'. It's now time for a wander indoors and between looking at all the stalls selling

me and Gary in Blackpool

clothing and music, having a drink and bumping into people I know, I see The Crows on the acoustic stage. I then see an interview with Animal from the anti nowhere League in the Tower Street Theatre before heading back outside to see Vice Squad, Argy Bargy and Discharge. There I bump into another old Southampton punk 'Spud' and Southampton taxi driver Steve who it's great to see. The festival never stops once it starts each day (as many of us know from being sat at 1am in previous years slumped in a chair, or in the corner on the floor) so there's no time to rest today and it's back inside to see The Ejected, The Men They Couldn't Hang, the Exploited, Anti Nowhere League, The Cravats, Naked Aggression and last but not least The Lee Harveys to name a few of them. Gary has sloped off at 1am after The Cravats but Taxi Steve stays with me until they chuck us out of the venue at 2am prompt.

Welcome back if you left me for the last part of this story. I was hoping to while away a bit longer in the venue before they threw us out, but the security are well organised and we're out on the street in mere moments of the last band finishing. I have a ticket pre booked for the 05:25 out of Manchester which I can only use on that train. So after a bit of aimless wandering I arrive at the station with an hour to spare before the scheduled 03:40 from Blackpool, which should get me to Manchester in time. My hopes of sitting in the station concourse, while waiting, disappear when it's pitch black inside and not a sole about, so I sit on a rock in a rock garden and wait, and wait and wait, getting more worried as the time ticks on. Eventually at about 03:25 a couple turn up and ask when the station opens? Then 3 chaps get out of a taxi and ask the same question which fills me with a little bit of hope as they obviously think that there is a train due, the same as me. Just as I'm thinking that there is no train and we're all mistaken and that I'm going to miss my train from Manchester, a small side gate opens and a guard beckons us in, points in the direction of the train and within what seems like seconds we've left. I've only paid £20 for the return trip home but it involves changing at Watford Junction and then Clapham Junction so I set my phone alarm to wake me up before reaching Watford and it does the trick. I wake up thinking who's playing games on their phone that loud? before I realise it's me making the racket and turn it off and apologising to all and sundry around me.

Everything times in well, and after a bus home from the station, I arrive indoors at 10:45am to find Michelle and the cats all out sunbathing in the garden. I am tired, have sore feet and am shattered but I'm glad I went. I wont be going for just the day again though, so if I even mention it please talk me out of it.

Saturday 6th August

After a bath and breakfast it's nearly midday so going to day 3 of the game is out for me today, and it's a day in the garden listening on the radio instead, but first to catch up on what I missed! Firstly, Will Smith completed his hundred and went on to score 210, which, with the help of an 81 unbeaten knock from Ryan McLaren took Hampshire's score to an impressive 548 for 6 before declaring and then restricting Lancashire to 68 for 1 by end of the day's play.

Back to Saturday and I doze off periodically throughout the day on my sun bed and as well as being tired, this can be partly put down to the slow goings on at the game, so at least I'm not missing anything major, luckily. Only three wickets fall all day and Lancs. finish the day 238 runs behind with a draw looking very likely now.

Sunday 7th August

I am quite refreshed today, so me and Michelle head to the ground in the hope that we are in for a classic day, with Hampshire needing just 16(!) wickets to win, ha ha. Still, no Ian today and it turns out he never appeared yesterday either according to Adrian, so I presume he has either extended his holiday or doesn't fancy a day here after the slowness of the previous days. It turns out that Ian has injured his back and couldn't physically make it to the ground, but I don't know that until later in the week when I see him. It's a very sparse crowd today possibly the lowest I've seen here so far this season. A lot of people have given the game up as a draw already, but Mike is on the bus and is optimistic of some swing this morning and he is proved correct as wickets fall early, even if it is the spinners who take the wickets! Lancashire miss out on avoiding the follow on by 10 runs so Will Smith our captain today puts them back in leading to a surge of hope for a win. This doesn't last very long though as the play goes back to being even slower than it was before and the Lancs. openers are on 18 runs after 19 overs. Tea is at 3:40pm and there is a bus at 4:05pm (hourly on Sundays) so Michelle decides that, that is it for us today, and we set off home, but not before checking our Golden Gamble tickets. We were undecided as

golden gamble winner

to whether bothering getting any tickets today due to the low crowd but when the ticket seller came round she convinced us that the less sold meant more chances of winning, so I bought two to make her trip around the ground worthwhile. WE WON, only 2nd prize though so not a fortune, a whopping £15 in fact, but it's been over 15 years since I last won anything so that hasn't dampened my mood. I'm over the moon and make Michelle take a photo of me and my winning envelope full of money (3 x £5 notes).

When we get in and are sat out in the garden I am surprised to find, when turning the radio on, that play is still in progress? It turns out that after tea Liam Dawson has taken three quick wickets to rekindle some small hope and this has extended the game a bit longer. Not for much longer though as one of the Lancs. openers is still in and looking solid and hands are shaken on the draw.

Monday 8th August
Southern Vipers v Yorkshire Diamonds

Something a bit different today as me, Michelle and Kev are going to see a ladies Twenty 20 game. This is a new competition based on the principles of the Indian premier league (IPL) where top players are split or auctioned between various franchise teams and play each other. The Southern Vipers are our local team and are playing their three home games at the Rose Bowl. The first game was last weekend against Surrey Stars when me and Michelle were in Swansea, but a good crowd of over 2000 turned out to what was a good opening win. The Vipers 2nd game against Lancashire was coincidently at Blackpool on the same day I was there at the Rebellion festival and they recorded their 2nd victory.

Today we meet up in the West End Brewery for a meal and a drink before heading to the ground for the 2pm start. Being a Monday we are expecting a much smaller crowd but we reckon it is still over 500, and it turns out later it was officially over a 1000 with quite a few fans sporting the bright orange colours of the vipers.

The Vipers bat first and things don't begin well with four quick wickets falling for not many runs and jokes of we'll be home by three start circulating in the crowd. Then a brilliant stand of 99 from Suzie Bates and

Arran Brindle takes the total up to 118 for 4 and gives the Vipers a fighting chance. Yorkshire are currently bottom of the table and unfortunately, they get nowhere near to improving that statistic today as they are bowled out for 64 with 4 overs still remaining.

It's been a pleasant afternoon and we've been well entertained so hopefully this format of cricket will take off and continue next year, especially as Hampshire members got in free, so it's an added benefit for us. It turns out that today's win for the Vipers will be enough to get them to finals day even if they lose their remaining two games so well done to them.

The evening is rounded off nicely when my darts team win 8-1 at the Bitterne pub and I win my first singles game of the season 2-1, I have only played in the pairs for some reason in the last few games.

Tuesday 9th August

Our godson Thomas (Tom) who is now 15 is coming over to stay tonight from the IOW, this has been a yearly tradition during the school, summer holidays since he was small, and he is now old enough to travel over by himself. I meet him off of the Red Jet at 12:15 and we have a wander around the Saints shop and eat some sandwiches at Ocean Village before going to see 'Suicide Squad' at the pictures. We have a minor blip when the lady at the ticket kiosk asks to see some ID as the film is a 15 certificate and although she admits he may look 15, she cannot let him in without it. Luckily his mum is home when he phones her, and after a few minutes she has emailed something over with his date of birth on it. I'm not sure what it is she emails but it works, and in we go.

The main reason for picking today for his trip over is that local non-league side Sholing are playing Cowes sports from the IOW in a league game tonight, so he will be attending as an away fan. Kev who comes to cricket with me also wants to take his 5 year old son Martin to a non league game as well, so it's ideal for them to come along. After we have tea Kev picks us up and we all see an entertaining game end 2-1 in favour of the home team before me and Tom get a chinese takeaway on the way home.

Wednesday 10th august

Tom sleeps in until midday which is fine by me as I get a few jobs done early and Michelle has gone to work anyway. He must be home by 5pm though as the whole Kennesion family are going to a production of 'A midsummer's night dream' at Osborne House and he hasn't got his own key on him. We have a quick snack and after lunch head off for the 2:45 Red Jet to the Island. I am going back over with him, because it's Cowes Week, the world famous yachting regatta, and there will be lots on in Cowes including live music and good ales. Tom stays with me until 4pm and we have a look around at various stalls, have some snacks and generally soak up the yachting festival vibe. Once Tom has shot off home I have a few real ales and watch local bands the Nuberrez and Lucid on the promenade stage before having a wander and watching a Morris dance team and a folk band in the main street. At 9pm it's just beginning to get dark and cold so I head for the 9:15 Red Jet back after another good day out. I think that Tom enjoyed his trip over even though his football team lost.

Tom at Cowes week

Friday 12th August
Michelle's 'Jack up the 80's weekend

Michelle and our mate Jeanette are going over to the IOW this weekend for the 4th 'Jack up the 80's' music festival and are staying at the Kennesion's house. They are also going due to Carol booking the ferry travel for the bands and Kendo working at the festival over the weekend. The line up is made up of a few decent 80's bands who are still going today and other bands and singers who had their five minutes of fame in the 1980's. I have been a couple of times in the past but this years line up is a bit flimsy for my noisy tastes, and include Five Star, Owen Paul, Bucks Fizz, Leo Sayer, Johnny Hates Jazz, Bruce Foxton, Paul Young and Bad Manners amongst others.

Jeanette picks Michelle up at 6pm on the Friday, as although the festival doesn't start until tomorrow it's the Friday night's firework display for the end of Cowes week tonight. They are all going down to see it, and by going tonight they are on the island ready for an early start in the morning. Once they've gone I take the opportunity to visit the new micro pub that opened in Woolston just last week, which is called Olaf's Tun, named after the original Viking who set up a settlement in this area. To my surprise it's packed in there, so everyone has had the same idea as me. It is friendly and I have a pint of real ale and a chat to a bloke called Richard from Weston and then head back for an evening in the garden.

Saturday 13th August

It is the opening day of the new premiership football season today and Southampton are at home to Watford so I have arranged to meet my usual match day drinking partners Steve, Dave and Bob (plus Bob's mate Darren) for pre-match at Ocean Village. We have a drink in the Pitcher and Piano but it's packed with away fans from the off so we move onto Banana Wharf and then Marisimo's before heading to the game. We only manage a pretty disappointing 1-1 draw as Saints had all the late play and should have won really with better finishing.

Never mind though because I'm not off home after the game as I have arranged to meet some old work colleagues for a drink tonight. We were originally going to make it a trip over to the IOW, as we have in previous summers, but some of the group could not make it tonight, so we settle on a scaled down local drink instead. Present tonight are myself, Mike Long, Sean McGlead and Gordon, to begin with, and we're joined by Darren Ediss a bit later in the evening. It's a good night with us all catching up on what each other is doing now and we start in the Spitfire. We then move on to Goblets when the music gets too loud to hear yourself think, let alone have a conversation. At 10pm Sean, who lives out in the sticks of Totton has to go and get his bus, Mike is slightly piddled and I am now flagging a bit after being out drinking for 10 hours, so we call it a night and end an enjoyable day.

Sunday 14th August

Day two of Jack up the 80's on the Island but I'm up and off to meet Kev in the usual venue of the West End Brewery for drinks before the Southern Vipers last home Twenty 20 game against Loughborough, and as it's a lovely sunny day at the ground, it's cold ciders and shirts off as the Vipers bat first and score 156. It's during the opposition's innings though that I sense that all is not well with Kev! He is shouting out what he thinks is encouragement to the players and giggling at his remarks and people around are beginning to stare at us, the Vipers are fully in control though and the visitors are all out for under 100 and lose by 59 runs.

The bus leaves in 10 minutes (only every hour on Sundays remember) so I go to make my exit and somehow Kev is behind me and has become disorientated. He is holding onto the temporary seating that has been put in for the next England game, and with his arm around me, is now slowly falling backwards taking me with him and we both end up in an undignified heap on the floor! It turns out that in the pub before the game he had a pint before I got there and then had 2 double jack Daniels and 2 single jack Daniels with cokes. At the ground he's had 4 cans of strong lager and if you add to this he had no breakfast or lunch, just a few bags of crisps in the ground, and that it's been a scorcher, then it's all added up to take it's toll on poor Kev. I make sure he is ok, and he seems to be fine now, it was probably the getting up too quick at the end of the game that made his head swim. I make a dash for the bus and when I get indoors I check Facebook and he's messaged me to say he's in ok so all's well in the end.

Kev enjoying the day

Hampshire began a 4 day championship game yesterday, away at Nottingham, who are 2nd from bottom, just above us in the table. My next job is to see how they are getting on, and we have batted first and mainly due to Adam Wheater scoring 102 have made 319 all out. Nott's in their reply have been bowled out for 245 with new Hampshire signing Andy Carter taking 4 wickets, so a good start for him. By close of play today Hampshire are on 106 for 1 with Jimmy Adams on 69 not out, so going into day 3 we will be in a great position and may even get our second win of the season.

Monday 15th August

Michelle returns from the IOW today having had a great time at the festival but there's no time to rest as we are off to Weymouth for 3 nights. It has become a bit of a family tradition in recent years that when my nephew Nicholas goes away with his family for their 2 week summer caravan holiday, the rest of the Burton clan all have a short break to coincide with his birthday as well, and help them celebrate it. This year my nephew has booked up a caravan at the Haven holiday park. Me and Michelle have booked a room above a cocktail bar on the seafront and my Mum, Dad and my Brother and his wife and daughter have booked a hotel at Bowleaze Cove in-between the two of us.

A problem has arisen though this year, when 2 weeks ago we found out that my nephew and his partner Shelley have separated!

Shelley, Georgie and Reece are still going though as it's unfair on the kids to deny them their holiday, and it's already paid for. The rest of my family have cancelled, due to various reasons which I understand, but me and Michelle are still going regardless as we like Weymouth and have been looking forward to it. Roll on the seaside.

Weymouth is nice and easy to get to by train and after Michelle has freshened up and had a relax we are away and arrive at our cocktail bar room at 2:30pm, it's a great room with a sea view and in a prime position along Weymouth's seafront. It's a hive of activity getting ready for two days of carnival starting tomorrow. We have a walk around and tonight have mackerel baps, pea fritters and chips sat by the harbour before going into Dorothy's pub and seeing a singer songwriter live on stage.

At Trent Bridge today Hampshire have scored 393 for 7 (Adams 99, Alsop 93, Dawson 69 and McLaren 71) before declaring and setting Nott's a target of 468 to win. By the end of play they are on 42 for 2 leaving us on the brink of a win tomorrow, although with Hampshire nothing is certain!

Tuesday 16th August

It's glorious weather today and we have hired a sun bed and two deckchairs on the beach as Shelley and the kids are joining us this morning to say hello. It's nice to see them, and while Georgie and her mate, who has come with her, go off into town together shopping I take Reece down for a paddle. Luckily he doesn't want to go in for a swim as it's freezing! but I would have if he had wanted to - honest! We play in the sand and he buries me in it, before he goes on a bungee ride. Some of Shelley's family are coming down to stay with her today and they join us for a while on the beach, before they all head off and me and Michelle are left to our own devices again. This entails getting some beers and sandwiches from Marks and Spencer's, watching an air show and then sunbathing until we have to give the chairs up at 6pm. There is a stage on the beach at the pavilion end, with a cider bar, so we head off there next and watch the bands until the sun goes down and a firelight procession takes place along the beach. We go for a Thai meal this evening which is very nice.

Reece on Weymouth beach

This morning Mullaney had given Nott's hope by scoring 137 off of 277 balls but a devastating bowling display from Brad Wheal in the afternoon and evening sessions of 6 for 51 has given Hampshire the momentum they needed to bowl Nott's out for 291 with 24 overs still to play, a win by 176 runs. Hampshire have leapfrogged Nott's into 2nd from bottom spot but are still 16 points behind Durham, who have a game in hand, and 17 points behind Warwickshire.

Wednesday 17th August

It's carnival day today and although the morning is sunny enough and we sunbathe on the beach again, we have to come off when it clouds over a bit in the afternoon. We are in touch with Shelley as they are around again today, but either we miss them or they miss us, and given the crowds that have descended on Weymouth today it's not hard. In the end we both say we'll go our own ways and if we bump into each other all well and good. This afternoon we have the Red Arrows do a display, and then we take up a good position by our cocktail bar and watch the carnival go by. It actually starts raining half way through, which is a shame, so Michelle goes up to our room and has a grandstand view from there. It's not enough to get me and most others inside, and we brave it out until we realise that the street sweepers aren't a part of the carnival and they are actually now cleaning the rubbish away.

Back in Southampton on Thursday we have a lazy day in the garden after getting up this morning, having breakfast and coming home on the 9:30am train. One small detail to mention though regarding our train travel to Weymouth is the fact that I looked up the cost of our tickets on line before we left home, and an off peak period return for two with a railcard was £45. When we got to Woolston station though and used the new card only ticket machine the only fare it would give us was a £67 anytime return. There are two machines at our station so we went outside to use the old cash and coin one, where, when we tried again, it gave us the ticket we wanted for £45! A Southwest trains money making scam or just a technical error, I don't know, but it pays to be prepared.

Friday 19th August

We have a few days off from cricket now until next week but things are never dull this summer. Today Carol and numbers 2 and 3 sons are coming over from the IOW and we are going to do the Zany Zebra trail, before meeting her husband Kendo when he finishes work. We are all going to Nandos as they have got some money off vouchers from somewhere. The Zany Zebra trail is basically 40 odd sculptures of zebras dotted around the town centre. A map is needed to follow the trail around and see them all and all profits from the sale of maps and merchandise goes to the local wildlife park at Marwell so a good cause.

We begin the day at Southampton Football Club to see our first zebra which officially is something like number 46, but it's the furthest one out of town, so we're doing it first. We will then be doing a circular route from there, to end up at the Civic Centre later. Unfortunately, the rain which has been holding off so far now decides to pour down, and as we go via Ocean Village and the parks, on our way to Town Quay we end up soaked. So much so that when we arrive at the bottom end of town we give up for the moment and go into Fantini's for coffee, wine and cokes and wait out the downpour, we have seen about 8 zebras so far.

The rain eases off and it's onwards around the trail, a bit behind schedule now, so we have to improvise and go to see just those in the line of travel. As we get near to the time of meeting Kendo the sun comes out and he's wondering why we're all dripping wet when we eventually meet up with him.

the Zany zebra trail

Nandos it turns out is a mainly chicken restaurant and out of the 6 of us, 4 have the veggie option, so not quite the best place to eat, but eat we do and I make up for the others by having a whole chicken, lovely.

We say our farewells to the island crew and head quickly home, as Saints are on TV tonight away at Manchester United. Suz and Paul are coming over to watch it with us. It's a good job the Dorchester cider and music festival is cancelled tomorrow because after Saints have unluckily lost 2-0, Paul shows no sign of going home and we proceed to drink the 3 litre wine box and too many beers to count and Suz eventually drives him home in the early hours of the morning. He is a bad influence on me that man!

Sunday 21st August

It's another trip over to the IOW today, this time to the Garlic Festival which is held at the same venue as the Jack up the 80's festival and they use the same stage for both. There are far more stalls, entertainments and crafty type tents this week and of course a tent dedicated to everything garlic. We see a few good local bands in-between wandering around the attractions and finally the main headliners are on. This year 1960's stalwarts the Searchers, with original singer Mike Pender still belting out the hits.

Just as Tom has made it a tradition to come over and stay with us in the summer holidays, his brother Jacob has now done the same, and it is his turn to come back with us tonight and stay over. Kendo is kindly doing two trips back to East Cowes. Trip one is me, Michelle and Jacob who he drops off at the ferry terminal for us to catch the boat home, while Carol and Isaac wait in the pub (good call Carol) for him to come back for trip two.

at the garlic festival

85

Monday 22nd August

One of the things on my list to do this summer is to go on one of the open top bus tours through the New Forest so, as Jacob is with us, it seems like a good thing to do with him as well. Living on the Island he doesn't see many trains so we get one to Southampton Central, and change there to go to Brockenhurst. Here we can hop on to one of two open top bus tour routes. I have chosen a route that takes us to our first stop of Burley, a village associated with witches, and which just happens to be home to the New Forest Cider Farm where we stop for refreshments, and to pick up a flagon or two to take home. Then it's back on for a scenic view of the open forest before reaching Milford on Sea, where we get off to have our sandwiches on the beach. It's a bit blowy along the seafront so Jacob resists the urge for a swim as the waves are crashing up the beach. We instead walk along the spit out to Hurst Castle but turn off before getting there, and head to the little harbour of Keyhaven, where we pick up the bus again. We are on a schedule, as we need to get Jacob back to the ferry terminal by 5pm, where his dad will collect him when he finishes work at the Civic Centre. We have to miss getting off at Lymington and hot foot it back to the train station at Brock to get the connecting train. We make it in time, as I knew we would, and wave the two of them off. In the evening at darts it's the house knockout and I may as well not have turned up, as I play rubbish, and lose my first match 2-0. I put it down to tiredness having had Jacob all day, but my team mates point out it could also be that I'm just crap at darts. Thanks lads.

open top bus tour

Tuesday 23rd August

Today is a welcome day off for us. Michelle has had last week and this, off on holiday, and it's been all go so far. If I had, had my way though we'd be off to Taunton for the day, for day one of the championship game against Somerset. The reason that we haven't gone is purely cost. I had scoured the train sites looking for cheap tickets and for once have come up blank. We either had to pay a fortune to get an early enough train to get us there for the start at 11am (and if you're only going for a day you want to see it all) or we could pay £84 for the two of us to arrive after lunch. Coming after Weymouth last week, the Garlic Festival, New Forest bus tour and before going away again tomorrow to the Great Dorset Steam Fair for 5 nights, we thought it a bit much for the day. If you add to that £15 each getting in plus food and drink it all mounts up.

So that's why after getting all of our gear ready for tomorrow (and it's a hefty amount as we're camping) you find us taking advantage of a nice sunny day in the garden listening to the cricket on the radio.

After a poor Hampshire start, including a returned from England duty James Vince, they find themselves on 61 for 3 and then 92 for 4 before Sean Ervine and Ryan McLaren (have I mentioned he is my player of the season?) steady the ship with a 100 partnership. The radio commentary today is hilarious with Kevin James blasting the Taunton pitch. This has been, and still will be, a talking point in many of their games this season, and the Somerset duo defending it, so it's great listening. After the early pitch deviations, or as Somerset may say bad batting, Hampshire actually do quite well and finish the day on 281 for 6 (Ervine got 103 and McLaren 61) with MacManus still in on 41 not out.

Wednesday 24th August

We are off to the Great Dorset Steam Fair today with our good friends Bob and Jeanette Elderfield (brother and sister for the record) and are staying for 5 nights in their new blow up tent. Their luxury tent has 3 bedrooms a lounge area, larder and 2 entrances. This will be the 4th time that I have been here, the first was when me and Michelle ended up with a pot of money after a savings plan matured, and we celebrated by glamping for 3 nights in 2013. The second time I visited was with Bob in 2014 when we just went for the day, on the Saturday, mainly to see the Skimmity Hitchers play two sets. Last year the four of us went for 3 nights, taking individual tents and a gazebo which was subsequently ripped to shreds in the Tarrant Hinton winds.

This year we are going posh and have booked posh camping which entails security controlled showers, toilets and a pamper area. This is mainly hairdryers and mirrors for the girls. If you have never been to the steam fair, it is set in rolling hills in the countryside around Tarrant Hinton and is a celebration of everything steam powered. With the biggest country fair/village fete/funfair you've ever seen and combine all of this with the fact that there are 5 music stages around the site and too many real ale and scrumpy bars to count and you have a great show.

Jeanette collects us and all our gear at 2pm, we're covered for every weather and eventuality. We meet Bob at a service station near Ower, as he has just finished work, and has come straight from there. We get into the site easily enough, as the show is not officially open yet. Today is for people staying over only, and just as black clouds threaten a downpour we have the tent up in 10 minutes, beds all made up and our first cans of beer open. It is the first time we've seen the new pump up tent and we're impressed at the ease of putting it up and how big it is.

I have taken a radio for when we are sat relaxing around the tent but for some reason cannot get the cricket on it? Bugger. Later that evening we have had a wander around the site, as all the food and drink places and the funfair are open. Then we watch Lady Windwards Maggot perform two great sets in the beer tent before retiring to our luxury accommodations.

a blow up tent

At the Rose Bowl today England have beaten Pakistan in the first ODI of the series. Rain means that it is settled by the Duckworth Lewis method, and unfortunately although Liam Dawson is in the squad he hasn't played. Me and Kev had originally got tickets, through his source for this game, before we both knew we couldn't go. He managed to flog them to friends of his so at least he wasn't out of pocket.

At Taunton Hampshire were all out for 338 in the end and, although, we think that this is a good score, and that Mason Crane's spin can wreak havoc on this pitch, it didn't quite work out like that. Somerset have finished the day on 257 for 5. I find this out the following morning, when I come across a stand selling the local chronicle newspaper which includes a mystery gift! today's gift was a bottle of water or orange juice and a GDSF A4 poster, wow!

Thursday 25th August

Today the GDSF officially opens it's doors to hordes of day trippers and is fully up and running. I start the day by seeing a folk band playing popular songs in a way not heard before, while the others all go to see a falconry display followed by ferret racing. Once reunited we have a look around the massive craft and arts tents and the food village before settling down to watch some more bands and have a drink. One band I must mention are 'Lost the Plot' a feel-good covers band who get everyone up dancing. Their crowning glory is, one song, where all four members put cuddly toys on their heads, tip a bucket full of plastic bath time ducks into the crowd and during the next song the audience are invited to throw them, and knock the toys off their heads! I am sure some people are aiming at the band rather than the toys but some people's aims are so wild, anyway, after a day of drinking that you cannot tell for sure, but it's great fun regardless.

Michelle and Jeanette head back early today for a sit and relax around the tent. Me and Bob have set our hearts on getting a good early spot, down the front to see, a steam fair institution, Dr Busker who is on from 9:30 to Midnight today. They are a 30 plus piece band of all ages, shapes and genres and sing comedic, bawdy songs about steam fair antics and life in general. There is lots of audience participation expected in helping sing the lyrics. It's a great evening with regular intervals to recharge glasses, and after a late night curry, me and Bob just get back to the tent before it pours down and it continues to do so all night.

give one a throw

Hampshire didn't get going until 1pm today due to morning rain but when they did Somerset continued to pile the runs on and finished on 534 for 7. Just two wickets fell all day.

Friday 26th August

Today is a scorcher, after last night's rain, so while Michelle and Jeanette watch the horses in the parade rings I take an opportunity to plonk myself down in front of a threshing machine with a glass of scrump. I watch as a team turns grain stalks into corn, hay bales and thatch. Bob has shot home to check on his parents and walk their dog and also to see who Saints have got in the Europa draw which is today. He will be back later this afternoon in time for some cider before seeing The Wurzels tonight on the main outdoor music stage.

outdoor stage line up

It's 40 years since the Wurzels were number one in the charts but they are still as popular as ever, especially at the steam fair, so it's no surprise to find the place packed to the rafters tonight and it's standing room only if you want to get a glimpse of the band on stage. Bob doesn't normally drink scrumpy but has had a few today, since getting back, in honour of the legends from the west country. By the time midnight is approaching he's had enough and Jeanette takes him to get a pizza to soak up the juice, and get him back to the tent in one piece, so he misses the last few songs.

Back at Taunton, Sean Ervine has scored his second 100 of the match and Jimmy Adams gets 96 to steer Hampshire to a draw. The chronicle tomorrow when I get it says that we got out of jail and looked like losing at one point by an innings. Today's free gift with the paper, was a packet of Weight Watchers snacks and another A4 poster, the same as yesterdays one.

Saturday + Sunday 27th & 28th August

The days fall into a regular pattern now, with showers and a brush up first thing, followed by breakfast in the show ground and then, depending on the weather, either watching outdoor events in the arenas or sitting in the tents watching bands. On the Saturday Jeanette manages to meet up with some friends, who are there with a real live steam engine! They invite us all for a ride on it one day around the main arena. I also meet up with an old work colleague Steve Ganter and his wife for a beer and a catch up.

On Sunday, our friends Paul and Michelle turn up in the afternoon unannounced and manage to find us. In the evening they want to see some SKA tribute bands (Bad Manners and Madness) which is fine by us, so we have the evening with them before they head off home at about 11.30pm.

Bob, me & Jeanette

Bank Holiday Monday 29th August

Our last day and we are packing up to go. We were originally going to leave early tomorrow morning but as Bob has to go to work in the early afternoon we didn't want to risk the long queues of slow moving steam engines, on the road just in case.

We pack the car up with possessions but leave the tent up to dry off for a bit, while we go in and have breakfast and see if we can have a go on the steam engine. Michelle has her picture taken on the engine before Bob and Jeanette have a spin around the arena with all the other steam powered vehicles, but I see how covered in soot and grime they are when they get off and duck out of it, chicken!

Once the tent is packed away we head back to the outdoor concert stage for one of the highlights of the holiday, two sets by the Skimmity Hitchers to end our steam fair. The band are as good as ever and play to a reasonable crowd but it's over too soon, and we are heading home by 8pm knackered after all the late nights and outdoor living.

Michelle at the helm

Wednesday 31st August

After a lazy day yesterday I get up this morning and go for a swim before getting the bus to the Rose Bowl for day one of the 4 day game against Yorkshire. It's a surprise to everyone that I have no beer today! After the excesses of the GDSF I'm having a few days break from alcohol.

The big news today is that Adam Wheater, our top run scorer so far this season, is off on loan to Essex for the rest of the season. He came to us as a wicketkeeper /batsman and after losing the gloves to Lewis McManus earlier this year, and coming in for some harsh criticism from the management, it seems as though he has been unsettled for a while now and wanted a change.

It's a scorcher, and the earlier rainy weather in June is well forgotten. Yorkshire win the toss and decide to bat first to take advantage of the conditions, however it soon clouds over, Ha Ha, and it appears that Yorkshire have cocked up when some quick wickets fall early on. Kev is with me today as he has taken two days off from work to come along, more on that later! We see Hampshire have a good day by restricting Yorkshire to 275 for 9 (Berg has got five of them) before bad light stops play at 5:45pm. "Typical", says Ian who normally goes for the 5:40 bus, but has stayed on tonight as there are still quite a lot of overs left to be bowled. He is less than happy when the 6:10 bus then comes along late.

Thursday 1st September

Due to my dad not being well this year he hasn't been up to the ground much this season. As a Yorkshire man this game would have been a must see one, pencilled in to come and see. Today I nip up to see him early and drop off a scorecard and a roundup for him to peruse while he listens to the commentary on the radio while sat in the garden.

An early wicket finishes off the Yorkshire innings and to our surprise Hampshire start well. We have hopes of a good score when Vince and Ervine put on a 100 partnership taking the score from 38 for 3 to 199 for 5 but disaster is approaching for Hampshire and Kev!

Firstly, Hampshire collapse and are all out for 222 even with Ervine getting 80 and Vince 60. We are trailing 59 runs behind before Yorkshire add another 69 for 1 before the end of play to go in 128 ahead.

Secondly, unbeknown to me, Kev has taken the two days off from work for this game but not told his wife! So when she and his son Martin pop in to his place of work to give him a message, she is somewhat surprised to find him not there! The story unfolds when he receives a text and walks off to answer it, only to come back with his son in tow, after his missus has driven straight here and dropped him off outside the entrance turnstiles for his dad to look after him.

should Kev be here?

Friday 2nd September

Today is the day of an almost annual event, where I go for a days cricket with old chums Andy Veal and Lee Page. This began many years ago back at the old Northlands Road ground. I will never forget turning up one Thursday afternoon about 2pm and wondering where they are, only to hear them laughing and giggling, half cut, right in the front row of the members stand. It wouldn't have been so bad but they weren't even members like me, and after I turned up we were all asked to leave due to their noise, tarring me with the same brush, the shame of it!

I have known Andy since 1985 when we both started working for the council together. I have known Lee for 20 years since he came and started playing in my works cricket team, before he eventually took it over himself when I retired from playing in 2010 due to a dodgy ankle. Over the years we have had some great times playing cricket and snooker and being thrown out of pubs for having Christmas singsongs together. Even though we do not work together now, this is one day when we get together and have a catch up.

Andy lives in the New Forest so after my swim I meet him outside the Civic Centre to get the bus together to the ground. Lee lives in Hedge End so he is meeting us there, where his wife will have dropped him off.

It's a pity we have chosen today as our day though, because after 16 overs, play is halted due to rain and we have to head for cover. Bad light and more rain ruin the cricket and all in all we see 19 overs, 74 runs and 1 wicket before we give up at 3:40 and head for the bus home. It's been a good day though and we had a laugh, you can't fail to with those two and their wicked sense of humour, which is what the day is all about.

Lee & Andy

Saturday 3rd September

Yorkshire start the day on 143 for 2, a lead of 202 runs ahead. As the bus hurtles towards the ground, the bus club are speculating on what Yorkshire's tactics will be, given that rain is forecast from 3pm today. Yorkshire are in 2nd place in the league and with leaders Middlesex unlikely to win today in their game due to the weather will Yorkshire go for it or not?

As it happens Yorkshire lose some early wickets and then bat on until 11:30 before declaring and giving us 298 to chase. If the rain comes in then a draw is on the cards, but if not it's game on for both teams. If Yorkshire expected to bowl for 20 minutes, before lunch however, they are thwarted as rain begins falling in the change over period and we all dive for cover. Lunch is taken early and when the teams are back out, one look at Yorkshire's bowling attack of Brooks, Bresnan, Patterson and Sidebottom are enough to make us quake in our boots. The Hampshire players must have felt the same as us bam, bam, bam, bam and 4 wickets have fallen before we know it, and it's a case of can we hang on for the draw? If the rain doesn't appear now it's curtains - OH MY!

As it happens the umpires take the players off the field for bad light, before it begins to pour at 3:45pm, to save us, and it continues to pour all day then. Not the end of the game we were hoping for, but one we will settle happily for now. Two games still to play and relegation feels even more of a certainty now than ever.

Tuesday 6th September

After a couple of free days, I'm off to London today for the County Championship game versus Surrey at the Oval, which is our last away game of the season. Due to the cost of train fares I wont be in London for the earlier than usual 10:30am start, but I hope to be there by lunch. If I leave before 10am my railcard is not valid and it'll cost me £84 return, by leaving after 10am the cost goes down to £29 so I feel that the £55 saving is worth missing a couple of hours play out of 4 whole days. On the same train as me are three chaps in blazers and Hampshire cricket ties so I'm not the only skinflint trying to save money.

When we get to Waterloo I pop into Marks and Spencer's to get some liquid refreshments for the afternoon. My sandwiches are already packed in my bag, and once I add the cider then it's on to the tube to the Oval, and I'm inside watching Surrey batting at Midday and they are 69 for 1. Over the other side of the ground from where I'm sat is an IOW flag and I presume that this belongs to a chap who gets on the bus with us to and from home games, and who I saw at Edgbaston earlier in the year. I will pop over and see him later and say hello.

25 minutes after the lunch break the players are taken off for bad light. That's the story for the rest of the day, with the umpire's taking the players off every time it clouds over. The crowd don't like it, one little bit, and show their dissent with boo's and slow handclaps ringing around the ground, enough so that the tannoy announcer has to ask us to be patient and respect the umpires doing their jobs. At the tea interval I meet up with the chap from the IOW (whose name is Steve I notice from his members badge) and

some Surrey fans I recognise, as they were at the Rose Bowl earlier in the season, for a beer and a chat.

After tea I sit with Steve and when the players go off, yet again, for bad light at 5:30pm play is abandoned for the day with only 80 overs being bowled. Steve is staying with his mum in Fleet and getting the train in each day, so we say our goodbyes until tomorrow and I set off for my hotel for 2 nights in West Brompton which doesn't look too far to walk on the map! I picture a nice walk over the Vauxhall bridge, a scenic trip along the Chelsea embankment and then a right turn, inland, up to the hotel Lilley. Unfortunately, the sky is grey and overcast, and it's extremely muggy, and a lot further in practice than it is on the map. When I arrive one and a half hours later I'm dripping with sweat and hobbling on a sore knee, not to mention having chaffed thighs again from my shorts rubbing my thick, chunky legs. To make matters worse, Chelsea embankment is a major route for speeding cyclists and joggers so I am constantly alert and dodging them. One lady cyclist crashes into me and spins off into a tree, while dodging a jogger who is also overtaking me. She was extremely apologetic, and I made sure she was ok, before she whizzed off again into the throng. Back to the hotel and for the last half hour I've been dying for a wee, so I'm pleased when there is no queue at reception and they give me the key and room number quite quickly. I dash up the stairs to find that on floor 3 there is no sign to say which number rooms are which way. I'm in 324, so I follow the corridor down 319, 320, 321, 322, 323 and through the next door to the fire escape! what, no 324? I retrace my steps and 324 is next to 318, 317 and 316 for some unknown reason and when I get in to it, the room is like a sauna, all the windows are closed and there is no air conditioning. The room does have four beds in it, so I hope they've given me the right one and nobody else is joining me later.

First things first and I have a cold bath to cool me off, and ease my now aching limbs. After that, there's a pub next door called 'Lilly Langtries' that serves real ale, so I have a pint in there and then have a hobble around the local area, where I pop into the Goose and find out that they have just stopped serving food 5 minutes ago. After a couple more pints my legs are up to carrying me back to my hotel and I pop into a shop and buy a bottle of red wine and some cheese and biscuits to eat in the room.

Surrey by the way finished on 262 for 6 with Burns the opener scoring 101.

Wednesday 7th September

I'm up at 7:30am and breakfast in the hotel is ok, with unlimited tea and toast. Then I head to the tube for the trip to the Oval, there's no way I'm walking back after last night's hike! At the tube station, I explain my journey plans to a guard and he advises me to use my contactless debit card for all my journeys, and at the end of the day I will be charged the cheapest rate automatically for all my trips. I've never even used my contactless debit card before, and I plan at least three journeys today so I'm a bit hesitant and hope I don't get stung for a fortune when I get home, I do get to the Oval ok though.

I sit on the top tier, members roof terrace, this morning. It has great views out over London, the houses of parliament, the London Eye, St Paul's and the Shard. I notice Steve from the IOW is in the same seat as yesterday, so I must pop over and buy him a drink at some point as he got me one before play finished last night.

To the game, and Jimmy Adams drops an early chance, but a couple of overs later the same batsman is bowled for 48 and in comes the Surrey captain, Gareth Batty. We want him out quickly as he didn't conduct himself too favourably in front of the Hampshire fans a few months ago. Ian has specifically told me to give him some stick in this game. Not long after, Smith drops another catch as Surrey bring the 300 up.

At the lunch interval, I meet Steve at the real ale bar and buy him a pint. A Surrey chap called Tim, who was sat with me upstairs after he saw my Cocksparrer band tee shirt and who I got chatting to about music, joins us as well. The sun is now shining down on us and I am planning to sit out in it this afternoon when Tim asks us if we've been in the new members garden area yet? Neither me or Steve have a clue as to what this is so Tim's mission is now to take us up to see it. The garden area is at the back of the Peter May stand and consists of 4 rows of padded seats, complete with drinks holders, like at the pictures. Behind it is a standing, drinking area with Astroturf, potted plants, tables and chairs plus the piece de resistance, a real ale and wine bar. The whole area is very plush, new, and has it's own toilets within a 20 second walk, so all in all a great place to watch cricket from.

The game today becomes part of the background as some of Tim's friends join us. Some complete strangers to Tim also join us as well, and it's a party atmosphere as rounds are bought and we talk of music, football and cricket, just glancing up occasionally to keep an eye on what's going on down on the pitch.

the garden area and new mates

Surrey are all out for 329 and Hampshire finish the day on 213 for 3 with Tom Alsop scoring his first 100 in championship cricket and he is 117 not out.

After play finishes Tim is three sheets to the wind, but insists that me and Steve accompany him, and two of his mates, to a local pub for a post match chat and more beer. It's been a great afternoon, so it's nice not to dash off straight away. By 9pm the beer has flowed and Tim's mates have managed to convince him it's time to go, and he's in no state to argue. We say our farewells in a blur of handshakes, and promises to meet again, and go our separate ways.

I'm starving by now so I head for the tube and make my way to central London where I go to China Town and have a chinese buffet, before going on a tourist walk around Piccadilly Circus, Soho and Leicester square. It's late when I the tube back to the hotel and I sleep the sleep of one who has had a great day.

Thursday 8th September

I feel surprisingly fine when I wake up. This is a good thing as I'm meeting my Auntie Kay who lives in south London and she's coming to the game with me before I stay at her house tonight. We meet at the ground at 10am and as she hasn't been in the members' areas before, I take her in using Michelle's membership card. We view the long room, main pavilion and the roof terrace from where we watch the morning's play. Alsop is out 2nd ball of the day, but this is a minor blip in Hampshire's day and no more wickets fall before lunch.

Once again the roof terrace is in shade, so as the sun is blazing down, we head on round to the garden area, saying hello to Steve on the way round. Kay is really impressed with the view and seats and we crack out the pork pies and sausage rolls that she has brought along. There are a few faces from yesterday so I say hello to them and have a quick chat, but I'm being on my best behaviour today with my aunt here, so I make do with just 3 cans of cider and 2 cans of gin and tonic that I have brought along myself. I leave the real ale bar to them today.

Me and Steve are both wrong in how Hampshire will play this game now, and our predictions for a Hampshire win come and go as Ervine hits another century, taking his tally to over a 1000 runs this season. My player of the season, Ryan Mclaren also hits a ton, meaning that 3 players have scored hundreds in the same innings for Hampshire at the Oval for the first time in over 24 years. We need to bowl Surrey out again to win this match, so it's a surprise to me and Steve when Hampshire bat on and on leaving ourselves less and less time to do so. Even Sean Ervine seems to be looking at the dressing room for the call to come in, but the call isn't coming yet! Still to come is 39 from McManus, 42 from Berg, 25 from Andrew and finally a 10 from Brad Wheal before the captain, James Vince, eventually calls Ervine and Wheal in with the score on 582 for 9. A lead of 251 runs and only 9 overs to bowl at Surrey tonight.

Before going to back to my Auntie's for the night, we head back to Tooting and get takeaway curries to take to my cousin Claire's, where I am introduced to one of our families newest members, London, a baby girl named after her Dad's stage name of Sean London. We have a nice couple of hours with the London family and then tired and sunburnt, we head to

Mitcham and a cup of tea before bed. Kay now knows how tiring a day at the cricket can be, ha ha and we're both soundo by 11pm.

Friday 9th September

Kay is working today so drops me off at Tooting Broadway tube at 8am on her way to work. I get a train to Vauxhall and have a sit along the river looking down towards the London eye, while reading the Metro newspaper and having breakfast of some fruit and a cup of tea. Other games, elsewhere, this week are either over or are just about to finish and results have gone in Hampshire's favour for a change. A win would pull us out of the bottom two, with one game left to play at home to Durham. Even a draw would reduce the gap between us and the teams above us so it's all still to play for today.

On the way to the ground, I spot Steve who is already inside, and he is not optimistic of our chances. We agree to meet later in the day to catch up and have a last beer together. The crowd is a lot smaller today as Surrey fans don't have much to cheer for. It's either bat out all day for the draw or lose, for them, so I take the opportunity of lax security to have a look around the large OCS stand. I take some photos from where the posh, rich and corporate people normally sit, and very nice it is too. I don't linger too long though, and am back with the hoi polloi in time for Surrey to resume on 23 for 0, and I'm dreading a long, slow day with nothing to show for it for Hampshire. I open an early can of beer to get the day under way. After 45 minutes and 11 overs, Burns, their first innings hero, is out and it's 53 for 1 so another can is opened to celebrate, a bit too premature perhaps as it doesn't last for the hour it takes before the next wicket falls, just as hope was fading again.

At lunch I go for a wander onto the pitch and take a few selfies from the middle before going to meet Steve at the real ale bar. He is looking on the bright side now that a draw will keep us in with a chance of avoiding relegation. it will be a good result, and give us a chance of survival in the coming last weeks of the season! I wish that I could share his optimism.

I'm back in the garden area for the last afternoon session, chatting to some of the faces from previous days. I normally enjoy seeing a team batting to save a game but today I am frustrated by Hampshire's lack of cutting edge in their bowling attack. Steve has packed up his IOW flag now and comes over to sit with me for the last two hours of play. At 4pm the umpires take the players off for bad light and then the heavens open, and that's that for the day. We wander around to the members' lower bar to finish our drinks. The announcement comes over that hands have been shaken on the draw, so we say our farewells and I'm at Waterloo for the 5:05 train to Southampton. I change to the connecting 6:40 train to Woolston and am indoors again with Michelle and the cats, Rex and Ollie, just after 7pm.

me and IOW Steve

Saturday 10th - Monday 19th September

A week off for Hampshire now, but other teams are playing this week and the games could have a big effect on the situation that Hampshire will find themselves in next week. I'm glued to the internet and on the 4th day, Radio Newcastle who are commentating on the crucial Durham v Surrey game

Rain washed out our planned visit to Romsey show on Saturday, which was a shame, so we did some bets on the horses and had a bottle of wine instead.

On Monday 12th I am having some fillings at the dentist, and as I haven't been in 3 years, it's costing £314 which I could have done without just now.

Wednesday sees me on a day out to Pompey seafront with old mate Antony Young. We have a walk past my Nan's old house in Southsea, a cup of tea at the boating lake cafe, a game of pitch and putt, a pub lunch and a walk around old Portsmouth before heading home.

On Thursday I saw Saints beat Sparta Prague 3-0 in the first Europa league game in our group.

Friday saw me and Michelle go and see her favourite local country band ' The Paper Trains' at a new venue called Note's cafe in Southampton

On Saturday we went to Dorchester for the cider and music festival that has been rescheduled from a few weeks back, and a good day it is. Billy Bragg opens proceedings with a short set of songs, followed by various acts including the Jimmy Hillbillys and main act Neck, a rowdy, Irish band in the mould of the Pogues. It's all free except the cider, and I will certainly keep an eye out for it again next year, as it finished in time for the 9:22 train back and in time for the last bus as well.

On Sunday me and Dave met in the Chapel Arms before seeing Saints finally win a home league game at the 3rd time of asking by beating Swansea 1-0

Back to the cricket though and Lancashire got a valuable draw against league leaders Middlesex, to make them just about safe but not quite mathematically safe yet. Durham beat Surrey in the last session of their game, after looking at one point like losing. Hampshire cannot now overtake Durham so it's a straight race between Hampshire who are at home to Durham next week and Warwickshire and Lancashire who are playing each other.

Tuesday 20th September

Hampshire begin the day 8 points behind Warwickshire and 14 points behind Lancashire. A win with 22 points or more will be enough to stay up regardless of the result from Edgbaston, but with only two wins all season, and both of those against already relegated Nott's, we are still favourites to go down.

It is always a sad moment, when the end of the cricket season is nigh, but this year it hits me especially hard as it will mean that I have had my summer off and will soon have to start thinking about future employment and what I want to do. That's in the future though, so lets forget about that for the moment and enjoy the here and now first. After my morning swim it's into town for the 9:37 bus which is full of the bus club today as it's an earlier 10:30am start for games in September Normally when I get this bus I'm at the ground and have half hour on my own before the others turn up, but not today, even Arthur is on the bus and I haven't seen him for a while.

I'm still wearing shorts, the last time I wore long trousers was for Jim's funeral in early June. Autumn is showing now, and leaves are beginning to fall from the trees. There's a nip in the air, so even I have a jumper today, which is a rare thing for me to take to cricket. The crowd isn't massive, perhaps because it's midweek, but I bet a lot of people will be keeping their eyes on the score and will turn up if it gets interesting. Hampshire do begin well and as the sun comes out, Jimmy Adams and Will Smith put on 111 for the first wicket partnership before Adams is out for 53. James Vince continues the good work and gets 50, before Smith is eventually out for 90. Vince is eventually out for 92 after a silly run out between himself and Ervine, but the good batting continues as Dawson adds 62 and Ervine himself gets a 50 which means 4 batting points gained at the end of the day. Hampshire finish on 370 for 6. A decent first day which means we should go on to get the maximum 5 batting points tomorrow, by taking the score past 400. At the bus stop everyone is bubbling, especially as news comes in that Lancs. have bowled Warwickshire out for 219 This means they only get one batting point to our 5, and that if Lancs. win we can still stay up with a good draw.

Wednesday 21st September

Hampshire got their 5th batting point early on today and were then all out for 411. A decent first innings total, which hopefully Durham will get nowhere near to. If we bowl them out for less than 261 we can make them follow on and bat again. The first Durham wicket falls with the score on 2 and it's their danger man 'Jennings', who goes so the crowd are jubilant. The second wicket soon follows and at lunch Durham are 44 for 2, so far so good, it's all going to plan.

After lunch, a few small partnerships get Durham up to 186 for 7 and hope abounds that they will now be scuttled for a low score. Victory and safety are now in everyone's minds and a probability! Oh what a nice thought. Durham are on the rack, but this is Hampshire we are talking about, and we're not in the relegation zone for nothing. As the afternoon ticks on and no more wickets fall, the fans hopes dwindle a little more, but at the end of play with the score on 242 for 7 it's still an optimistic bus club but with a twinge of caution thrown in.

The bus is late today but I'm not going home as Saints have a league cup game at home to Crystal Palace, whose players have been in the hotel at the ground this afternoon. Some of them were on their balconies for a while watching our game, notably Jason Puncheon who once played for Saints.

Before the bus arrives, my mate Bob stops and gives me a lift, to the envy of those still stood at the bus stop. When I get to town I pop in the Frog and Parrot for a few punk Ipa's and see that Lancashire have let us down, by being bowled out themselves for 152! not a good development for us at all. Saints win 2-0 to take my mind off the cricket and after a couple of pints in the Chapel Arms I get home to find out that we've got another home tie in the next round, this time it's Sunderland.

Thursday 22nd September

The mood in the bus club this morning is quite jolly with the prospect of us getting Durham's last 3 wickets fairly quickly, before setting them a decent score to chase. Possibly even putting them back in later this afternoon. What we didn't all take into account though, is a downpour before play even begins. It has been quite nice on the bus journey so far but when we hit West End village, a few drops appear on the windows and within a couple of minutes, it's a full blown squall. Hats, coats and umbrellas are coming out of bags in preparation of the walk, from the bus stop into the ground.

The usual crowd find Adrian and we all have a sit together. Huddled at the back of the Shane Wharne stand, we chat for a while before all popping off individually to stretch our legs. I have a look at the sale which starts today in the club shop and watch some of the Middlesex V Yorkshire title decider which is live on sky TV, and perversely is being played in brilliant sunshine just 80 odd miles away. As the time ticks on with more showers and news that the players will take an early lunch, I head up to the top of the members' pavilion to have my sandwiches. I try to get the free wifi unsuccessfully and to look out at the views towards Winchester.

Play eventually begins at 12:40pm with the loss of 16 overs, and I find Ian in a usual spot, in front of the Hilton hotel, as the sun does begin to poke through the cloud. It's frustrating to think that Durham should be all out by now. Then to make matters worse the Durham tail end play blinders and make stand after stand eventually racking up 361, just 50 runs behind us. It's not just the Hampshire fans who are frustrated though, as the Durham batman Richardson has played superbly and is left stranded on 99 not out, when his number 11 batsman takes a big swing and is out. Richardson stays in the middle for a few moments not believing what he has just seen, and I wouldn't have wanted to be in the dressing room when he eventually walked in.

Warwickshire have had a second wind against Lancs. and now look like winning after their first innings debacle, which means for us, a Hampshire win is essential now.

Hampshire's second innings begins ok, with both batsmen scoring quickly, and 50 is reached for no wicket. Everything gets a bit frantic from now on though with wickets falling and runs being scored at a Twenty 20 sort of pace. This is due to time now being of the essence to set a decent score and have the time to bowl Durham out. Hampshire's quest backfires somewhat as more wickets tumble than they'd have liked. It's only a partnership by Liam Dawson and Lewis McManus that gets the score to a respectable 176 for 7 by end of the days play. The Durham spinner Pringle was our main antagonist as he took 5 wickets in just 45 balls, giving hope that our spinners can emulate him tomorrow. On the bus things are bad as even IOW Steve, who has been the biggest optimist of us all, concedes that our chances of winning are low.

Warwickshire are near certainties to win tomorrow, so Hampshire know what they have to do now with one last day left of the season. In some respects it's a miracle that we are even in with a shout of survival at this stage, when you take into account that we have been without world class bowlers Reece Topley, Fidel Edwards and Chris Wood all season. We have had Vince and Dawson away on England duty, have lost Adam Wheater due to him falling out with the management and missed the batting prowess of Michael Carberry due to his serious illness. Things certainly haven't exactly gone to plan.

Friday 23rd September

At least the sun is out and the sky blue as we settle down for today's tense finale to the season. It's Jimmy Adams birthday and Dave Allen's last day as official Hampshire archivist, so let's hope they enjoy the day. Giles White, the Hampshire manager, said in a radio interview last night that we would bat for an hour today, before declaring, and seeing where we are at then. This is what we do, but the more cynical fans on the bus this morning expressed concern that we could actually bat for another hour, myself included.

Anyway, young McManus got his 50 and Gareth Berg hit a valuable 36 off 43 balls to finish up on 245 for 9 when we declared after the hour, setting Durham 296 to win off 78 overs. News is also in from Edgbaston, that Warwickshire have won by 238 runs so it's now the Lancashire team and supporters who will be on tenterhooks seeing if Hampshire can take 10 wickets and relegate them instead of us.

Adrian, Arthur & Ian on the pitch

At lunch today we have a rare treat. The Hampshire fans are allowed onto the pitch to have a stroll about and look at the wicket close up. I know that most other supporters will be wondering what I'm on about now, as they can do this everyday at their grounds. I've been on the pitches at Warwickshire, Swansea, Hove and the Oval this year to prove it, but at the Rose Bowl this is one of the pleasures denied to us apart from this one day of the year when the hoi polloi can wander onto the hallowed turf. I have brought my camera specially and get Ian to take some snaps of me in front of the main stand. I get some good shots of Ian, Arthur and Adrian as well. Nb. not to give anything away but looking back, this moment could be a contender for the highlight of the day!

At tea Durham are 149 for 1 and our hopes are fading fast, Hampshire are not looking like making the breakthrough needed and the umpires seem to have fallen asleep as our many shouts for catches and LBW decisions are met with total apathy. IOW Steve thinks that hands will shaken on the draw at 5pm, but upon closer inspection I think that Durham have a good chance of winning this now, and they'll go for the win. They only need to plod on at 4 or 5 an over and they'll win comfortably. Ian and Adrian think it's all over for Hampshire and leave early saying their farewells until next summer. Adrian is heading to St Mary's, where Saints under 23's are taking on Spurs under 23's who are also using the hotel at the ground this afternoon as their pre-match base. I'm staying on until the dying breath, especially as it's a lovely evening and Grant (who was at Hove and Swansea) has arrived to see the final nails knocked into Hampshire's coffin. Durham continue to knock off the runs and Stoneman hits 137 and Borthwick 88 on their last appearances for Durham, before both joining Surrey next season, and then it's left to Ben Stokes to hit the winning runs at 5:20pm.

IOW Steve and Arthur have both stayed on until the bitter end, and they get on the same bus as me. When I get off as usual at Bitterne tonight we commiserate and say our farewells until next season. I'm not going home yet though as I'm meeting Dave and Bob (from Nice fame) for a beer in the Humble Plumb at 6pm which, for them, is our usual get together for a catch up and a natter, but for me it's a beer to toast the end of a great summer.

As an aside, when I check the Hampshire website the next day I see that yesterday there was an article put on in the morning, where you could vote for your player of the season. All well and good, but the closing date was 5pm that same afternoon? the game was still going on! and I can never get decent Wi-Fi at the ground anyway so that counted me out of the voting.

REPRIEVE Monday 3rd October

You wouldn't believe it, but jumping forward now to a week later, and news is coming through that Durham may be penalised quite heavily for running up massive debts in the previous seasons. This has literally left them crippled, and on the verge of going out of business. On Monday 3rd October the ECB announce that Hampshire Cricket will remain in Division One of the Specsavers County Championship in 2017 in place of Durham who have been relegated as part of a range of conditions and sanctions imposed by ECB, following a financial aid package to help Durham meet historic and future financial demands.

I'm not sure whether to celebrate or not? I'm pleased that Hampshire will be playing in the best cricket league next season, but I do feel for Durham. It's good to see that the governing body of English cricket are taking an interest and helping them out, unlike the governing football bodies who will let smaller teams die as long as the rich get richer.

That's it folks! my summer off in one neat little package, one that I will remember for a very long time with fondness and one that is full of memories. Leaving my job at the council was a big decision, but it's onwards and upwards now to new challenges and adventures and hopefully long days and happy endings, as old Nick Thorne always used to say.

It was typical that Hampshire happened to have their worst season ever in the one season that I took the summer off to follow them. There were positives though, especially the introduction of a lot of youngsters who acquitted themselves well after being thrown in at the deep end. Mason Crane looks like a future England player although he didn't get the rub of the green sometimes. Tom Alsop in his first season fitted in well and had some match winning games. Joe Weatherly did his bit when called upon with a fair amount of success and Lewis McManus will certainly be our regular keeper for years to come, after this season's introduction. Not forgetting Brad Wheal who only came into the first team later than the others, but looks like he will go on to be a great fast bowler in the future.

To be fair most of the Hampshire team had their moments and when you look at who won the playing awards at the end of the season, I think that they are probably a fair reflection.

South-African seamer Ryan McLaren claimed the accolade of Bowler Of The Year after finishing the 2016 campaign with an outstanding 32 Championship wickets to go alongside his 869 first-class runs at an average of 51.11.

Sean Ervine pipped both McLaren (second-place) and Dawson (third-place) to win the 2016 Fans' Player of the Year Award with the all-rounder also taking home the Batsman Of the Year Award, for his outstanding contributions this season.

The 26-year old Dawson, who is currently representing England on their tour of Bangladesh, won the Players' Player of the Year, voted for by his Hampshire team-mates.

2016 Clubmen of The Year were fast-bowlers Reece Topley and Ryan McLaren.

If you look on the Hampshire cricket website there is a great video of the highlights of the season which was shown at the awards night and well worth a look if you are interested.

Coming up for me next, are trips to Milan and Prague to see Saints play in the Europa cup. A weekend away at the New Forest Cider steam pressing weekend. Gigs at the 100 club in London. The sister in laws wedding. The Levellers at Pompey Guildhall. Lots of Non League football and then the Woolston Christmas Festival. There might even be enough material for another book if you're lucky so keep your eye's open in case.

See you all at the bowl in 2017

This summer wouldn't have been the same without

Michelle Doe

Suz & Paul

The Kennesions

Bob & Dave

Jeanette

Kev Tyler

Ian Saunders

Adrian

Arthur

IOW Steve

and all of the bus club

Thanks to you all

And this book is also in memory of

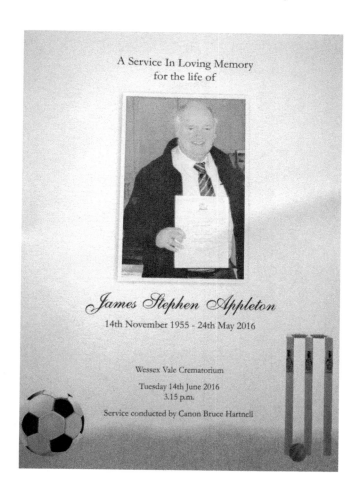

A Service In Loving Memory
for the life of

James Stephen Appleton

14th November 1955 - 24th May 2016

Wessex Vale Crematorium

Tuesday 14th June 2016
3.15 p.m.

Service conducted by Canon Bruce Hartnell

Jim

Lightning Source UK Ltd.
Milton Keynes UK
UKOW07f0452200417
299524UK00003B/5/P

ENGLAND'S SCREAMING

A fictional history of UK horror cinema

ENGLAND'S SCREAMING

SEAN HOGAN

ELECTRIC
DREAMHOUSE

Cast of Characters

CONTENTS

FOREWORD

WHY, I WONDER, WAS THE LATE-1950S BOOM IN BRITISH horror films met with such savagery and incomprehension by British film critics?

The classic examples are regularly trotted out; they came from a wide range of reviewers, but just confining ourselves to the responses of one will provide the requisite flavour. In 1957, the veteran critic CA Lejeune wrote the following in *The Observer*: "Without any hesitation I should rank *The Curse of Frankenstein* (Warner Theatre) among the half-dozen most repulsive films I have encountered in the course of some 10,000 miles of film reviewing." The following year, there was this: "I regret to hear that it [*Dracula*] is being shown in America with emphasis laid on its British origin, and feel inclined to apologise to all decent Americans for sending them a work in such sickening bad taste." And a few months after that: "*The Revenge of Frankenstein*...is, to my taste, a vulgar, stupid, nasty and intolerably tedious business; a crude sort of entertainment for a crude sort of audience; but it leaves me with a sense of nausea rather than horror. I want to gargle it off with a strong disinfectant, to scrub my memory with carbolic soap."

All three of these films—undisputed classics today—were directed by Terence Fisher and came from Hammer Film Productions, with Peter Cushing toplining all three and his regular co-star Christopher Lee appearing opposite him in the first two. The revulsion they inspired was by no means confined to old stagers like Caroline Lejeune, for in *Tribune* the young Derek Hill was just as enthusiastic in stoking what amounted to a full-fledged moral panic. Reflecting on the third film mentioned above, he wrote: "The past months have seen the most relentless corruption of public taste the cinema has ever known." This was just a warm-up, however, for his famous pronouncement in *Sight and Sound*: "Only a sick society could bear the hoardings, let alone the films." And when a controversial Anglo Amalgamated release, directed by no less a figure than Michael Powell, came along in 1960, he delivered himself of the niftiest soundbite of all: "The only really satisfactory way to dispose of *Peeping Tom* would be to shovel it up and flush it swiftly down the nearest sewer. Even then the stench would remain."

Lejeune, of course, had a word, or words, for Powell's picture too: "It's a long time since a film disgusted me as much as *Peeping Tom*." Indeed, she admitted to having left the press screening before the end. But one of the most telling responses to the film has never, to my knowledge, been reprinted before. It was from Martin Wallace of the *Belfast Telegraph*, who called it "a sad, sick British film which deserves no place on a British screen," summarising it as a symptom, like "the current rash of London's striptease clubs and pornographic literature," of "something rotten about latterday Britain."

Something rotten about latterday Britain... This, surely, was the spur behind much of the disgust expressed at the sudden, and wholly unexpected, explosion of British horror films—the mere fact that they were British, that they exposed a different side of Britishness to the cheerful image beamed out by the cosy and conformist likes of Doctor in the House and Reach for the Sky. A side of Britishness that dwelt lovingly on horror, sadism, death and, most unforgivable of all, sex. And the affront was all the greater, it seemed, when the films were set in contemporary Britain rather than, as in the first volley of Hammer horrors, the Gothic past.

It's these 'contemporary' shockers, *Peeping Tom* included, that Sean Hogan focuses on in the superb, and aptly titled, *England's Screaming*. (Count Dracula certainly gets a look in, but only really by way of those memorable moments when Hammer brought him into the 1970s.) And it's the sheer rottenness underlying the outward true-Brit façade that interests Hogan most of all; the rottenness, in fact, is key.

In these pages he draws a wealth of wildly imaginative links between the characters and events of apparently unconnected films, creating in the process a web of evil both ancient and modern. These links will impress any aficionado of British horror with their waggish audacity; such aficionados, in fact, are likely to be left somewhat breathless by the sheer scope of Hogan's insight and invention. But they'll also intrigue readers less au fait with Hogan's source material through the sheer wit and sprightliness, and often beautifully atmospheric detail, with which he lays them out.

Creating a web of evil from such disparate sources seems quite reasonable given the fact that these films are often much more connected than they at first appear. The recurrence of actors, writers, directors and technical personnel is striking, as are the Home Counties locations that crop up again and again. (Let's not even try to list all the films in which Oakley Court, adjacent to Hammer's Bray Studios, appears; even an unsung pile like Pyrford Court in Woking is common to such films as *The Mind of Mr Soames, Tales from the Crypt, The Omen* and *The Cat and the Canary*.) The intimate, borderline-incestuous connections thrown up by the British film industry are one thing, but what's still more remarkable about Hogan's elaborate web is that he spins it, here and there, not just around British films but also American, Australian and Italian ones.

Worldwide reverberations notwithstanding, something rotten in the state of Britain remains the crucial factor, and in this regard an essential signifier, it seems to me, is the Old Etonian tie—a masterstroke on the part of the film's wardrobe department—that was worn by Christopher Lee in the 1972 release *Death Line*. Here Lee played an enigmatic MI5 operative called Stratton-Villiers (the perfect name), a character fused in *England's Screaming* with a similar one, Fremont, played by Lee in 1969 in *Scream and Scream Again*. This is one of Hogan's own masterstrokes, for this shadowy character—though amounting to not much more than a cameo role in either film—says much about the Establishment corruption underpinning the whole web.

It's quite a distance, perhaps, from the "Some of our people have never had it so good" soundbite spoken by Harold Macmillan in 1957 (just a couple of months after the initial release of *The Curse of Frankenstein*) to the self-serving "Let's get Brexit done" inanities spouted by modern-day mediocrities, but Hogan shows that British horror can comfortably encompass both. To this end he focuses, not just on the 'classic' period, but also on a number of films thrown up by the new boom of the last 20 years — titles like *A Dark Song, The Borderlands, Possum* and *Under the Skin*.

After all, a political reading of British horror films is by no means far-fetched. Take an apparently innocuous example of the type, written by Milton Subotsky in 1971 and drawn from the EC horror comics of two decades before. *Tales from the Crypt* is an Amicus portmanteau picture comprising five stories, and, despite the fact that Subotsky was as American as his source material, a barbed indictment of Britain's middle and upper classes is the common theme, especially in stories three, four and five.

Ralph Jason, the self-regarding businessman played by Richard Greene in the fourth episode, is said to have sold arms to far-flung countries, presumably doing deals with dictators in the process (a detail with plenty of resonances some 50 years on). Most memorably, we're given spectacularly loathsome examples of 'Young Conservative' and 'Old Tory'—Robin Phillips as James Elliot in the third instalment and the superlative Nigel Patrick as Major Rogers in the fifth. Elliot gets a harmless dustman sacked two years before retirement age, depriving him of his pension and, ultimately, his life. Rogers, on the other hand, takes charge of a blind men's refuge only to systematically whittle down its amenities, notably such minor matters as food and heat, causing the death of one of the elderly inmates. And all the while he continues feeding choice cuts to a pet Alsatian called Shane.

Rogers, in particular, subscribes to an 'austerity' narrative that needs no elaboration in the 21st century. In revenge, Jason is reduced to a mess of undying chopped-up body parts, Elliot has his heart ripped out (with explicit reference to his essential heartlessness), and the Major's outraged charges contrive to feed him to his own dog. Lovely! — though the retribution dished out in horror-movie parables is rarely made available in real life.

Tales from the Crypt isn't touched upon in *England's Screaming*, though a couple of other Amicus anthologies—*The House that Dripped Blood* and *From Beyond the Grave*—most certainly are. (The chapter focusing on the latter film is typical of the joy to be found in Hogan's extrapolations; not only does he fuse together two Angela Pleasence characterisations, he also incorporates a couple of Ian Bannen roles and even throws in Sean Connery for good measure.) The omission of *Tales from the Crypt* isn't a problem, however. It just whets one's appetite for a possible sequel.

What might Hogan make, for example, of the tragically driven surgeon played by Peter Cushing in *Corruption*? Or the cross-dressing High Court judge (Jack May) in *Night, After Night, After Night*? Or the elderly hypnotist played by Boris Karloff in *The Sorcerers*? (Actually, this character gets a tantalising mention in Hogan's superlative Bernard Quatermass chapter.) What unholy connection might there be between the ringmaster monsters played by Anton Diffring and Joan Crawford, respectively, in *Circus of Horrors* and *Berserk*? And where might the repugnant, economy-mad Major Rogers fit into all this? Pretty snugly, I don't doubt.

These speculations may seem skittish, but *England's Screaming* is so stimulating it throws open any number of fascinating possibilities. Who knows? Maybe all those scandalised postwar critics could be worked into the fictional fabric too, wringing their hands over the exposure of England's underbelly for murky reasons that even Stratton-Villiers might approve...

Jonathan Rigby
February 2020

Jonathan Rigby is the author of several books, among them *English Gothic: Classic Horror Cinema 1897-2015*, *American Gothic: Six Decades of Classic Horror Cinema* and *Euro Gothic: Classics of Continental Horror Cinema*. He has also written *Studies in Terror: Landmarks of Horror Cinema* and *Christopher Lee: The Authorised Screen History*.

AUTHOR'S PREFACE

A FEW BRIEF WORDS OF EXPLANATION.
Firstly, I must acknowledge an obvious debt. This book would not exist without the model of David Thomson's *Suspects*, which I first discovered in a second-hand bookshop over twenty-five years ago and has been a frequent companion ever since. I could not hope to equal the erudition and graceful finesse of that novel, and while I'm sure Mr Thomson never envisaged his work inspiring someone to take a complementary look at some of the myriad oddities thrown up by UK genre cinema, it was both a pleasure and a privilege to pay homage nonetheless.

In his foreword to *Suspects*, Thomson writes: 'Is this a novel, or a non-fiction book about movies? My answer must be both.' I encountered a similar confusion in the course of writing this book. For myself, I probably leant more towards the pleasures offered by fiction—I hope the delight I took in teasing the dangling strands of these various stories into something resembling a tapestry (however cobwebbed and shabby) is evident—but undoubtedly there are elements of criticism here too. Certainly I have attempted to look at certain questions or issues raised by many of the films included here, and to address illogicalities or inconsistencies where I saw them.

As a general rule, I've tried to play fair with chronology, except for where the films themselves made it impossible. The obvious example being the fudged timeline of the *Omen* trilogy, wherein Damien ages thirty-two years in the space of a mere five, meaning that by the time of the concluding installment, his date of birth has been retconned to well before the Treaty of Rome was signed, thus making a nonsense of the Biblical prophesies alluded to in the first film. Also, if more than one iteration of a character exists, I've chosen whichever one suited the story I wanted to tell. For instance, the respective TV and Hammer Quatermass series offer somewhat different incarnations of the professor, and while I'm certain that the small screen Bernard Quatermass would undoubtedly be Nigel Kneale's preferred version, I've played the heretic and gone with the Hammer creation (meaning that mine arrives at an entirely different fate from the John Mills *Quatermass*).

Is this intended as a 'Best of British' then? Not at all. For my purposes, I have mostly restricted myself to dealing with films that were roughly contemporary in their subject matter. This obviously excludes the strain of gothic horror that is so indelibly linked with British genre cinema (and which would probably require another volume to deal with properly). Outside of that, I have made some attempt to be representative and cover the various aspects of UK genre film I thought noteworthy, but in certain cases this meant including works I don't necessarily hold in the highest esteem . . .

So — some of the movies included here are masterpieces, others are flawed-but-fascinating, a handful are no damn good whatsoever. Hopefully this book may lead some readers to interesting films they hadn't previously been aware of, but that was never my main aim. Rather, I was inspired by their stories to tell my own — in many ways, these films comprise a shadow history of this country, and I wanted to see exactly where that history led to.

The answers were not always reassuring — but since when should a horror film be reassuring?

Sean Hogan
July 2019

ENGLAND'S SCREAMING

For Lynda, whose fault it all is,
and for Evrim
(hopefully I didn't fuck it up too badly)

They're putting all your names
In the forbidden book
I know what they're doing
But I don't want to look

— "Night Rally", Elvis Costello

'I will bring the whole edifice down
on their unworthy heads.'

—The Medusa Touch (1978)

THE DUC DE RICHLEAU

Christopher Lee in The Devil Rides Out, 1968
written by Richard Matheson
based on the novel by Dennis Wheatley
directed by Terence Fisher

H E IS ALL BUT FORGOTTEN NOW, BUT THE DUC DE RICHLEAU WAS one of our most effective defenders against the dark Satanic forces that burrow beneath our world, like worms in a rotten apple. His failure to prevent their insidious rise to power should not obscure his undoubted bravery and selflessness. He acquitted himself tirelessly against numerous lesser menaces, but in the end, he fell—as would so many others in his stead—to the ultimate evil known to mankind: the Antichrist, Damien Thorn.

An aristocrat of French descent, de Richleau was a scholar and deeply moral man, albeit one whose desire to understand all that was wrong and unjust in the world had led him down some shadowy intellectual trails. An early interest in religion and philosophy had prompted his studies to take a detour into esotericism, and for a time it seemed as though these dark dabblings might irredeemably mark the young Duc's soul.

However, a subsequent encounter with the black magician Oliver Haddo proved to be a Damascene experience; the utter depravity of the man reawakened de Richleau's moral urges, and he renounced the Left Hand Path for good, content to simply study and understand the occult from a position of academic remove. Still, while foregoing the power and mastery of the Black Arts that was surely within his grasp may have saved him in the short term, his resultant lack of magical expertise would ultimately lead to his downfall.

De Richleau's first clash with the forces of darkness came in the mid-1930's, when his friend Simon Aron fell under the sway of the occultist Mocata. Although he was certainly the pre-eminent English black magician of the period, Mocata was nonetheless something of a dilettante, a moneyed libertine mostly interested in using his sorcerous abilities for his own pleasure and advancement. Had he been more focussed on mastering the occult and serving his diabolical masters, he might have been able to claim Aron's soul and destroy de Richleau with ease. As it was, the Duc was able to hold his attacks at bay and finally defeat Mocata; albeit only by resorting to his knowledge of the Sussamma Ritual, an obscure invocation that acts to disrupt the laws of time and space. For a relative novice like de Richleau, employing the ritual was incredibly dangerous, and he could count himself highly fortunate that both he and his companions survived the experience. He would not be so lucky again.

Less fortunately, Mocata's demise left a void in occult circles; one soon to be filled by the ascendancy of Julian Karswell, a far more skilled and dangerous magician than his predecessor ever was. While Karswell was not immune to the comforts and indulgences his abilities brought him, these were not his primary focus as they had been Mocata's. Rather, his singleminded ambition was simply to further the cause of evil in the world; and he ruthlessly destroyed any enemies or rivals that might thwart that aim.

It was not long before he and de Richleau crossed paths; however, each man recognised that the other might prove to be their equal, and accorded him a certain level of wary respect as a result. Thus, the two adversaries found themselves locked in a cold war; neither moving directly on the other for fear of the possible consequences. Instead, they both schemed and plotted, each using their means and influence to keep careful tabs on the other, scoring small tactical victories when and where they could.

This campaign of attrition continued for years to come, always conducted under a veil of impeccable politeness. Indeed, Karswell always made sure to invite the Duc to his annual Christmas party, and it was said that de Richleau attended on more than one occasion, albeit heavily protected by magical wards and charms whenever he did so.

Years passed, and the Duc eventually eased into a comfortable semi-retirement. He still maintained a close watch on his opponent, but for a time it seemed as though his efforts had at least succeeded in curtailing the occultist's influence. It was only after de Richleau received a visit from one of Karswell's former disciples that events escalated disastrously.

The apostate in question arrived at the Duc's country home one evening in an acute state of nervous collapse. He insisted his erstwhile master had cursed him and that he only had another twenty-four hours to live. But before he died, he wished to atone; to reveal Karswell's plans to someone in a position to stop them, and by doing so, try and save his own soul.

The man alleged that Karswell was part of a worldwide conspiracy of Satanists, all acting to usher in the Last Hour: the day upon which the Great Beast would be unleashed unto the world. When de Richleau heard this he was seized with horror; he had been successful in thwarting the relatively trivial schemes of Mocata and his ilk, but this was evil on a much grander scale.

If the man was correct, Karswell and his cohorts were conspiring to bring about the birth of the Antichrist, and beyond that, the total destruction of the world, the end of everything: Armageddon.

De Richleau begged the apostate to tell him everything he knew, but before he could learn any more, his informer became terrified of some unseen entity he claimed was watching from the darkness outside. He immediately fled the house, disappearing into the night before the Duc could stop him. The next day, his mutilated body was found in a nearby village, lying on the bed of a pond; the water of the pond had completely evaporated, and the wet mud around him was scored with large cloven hoofprints.

The Duc found himself at a deadly impasse; it was far too dangerous to confront Karswell directly, but he could hardly stand by and do nothing. He attempted to glean further information from his extensive occult contacts, but a thick forest of silence seemed to have sprung up around his enemy. It was only when Karswell came into conflict with the visiting American academic John Holden that de Richleau was offered his chance. Angered by Holden's dismissal of his magical abilities, Karswell had placed a deadly curse on the man; however, Holden was a wilier opponent than the occultist supposed, and ultimately, it was Karswell and not the academic that fell victim to the fatal spell.

When the Duc read of his opponent's death in the morning newspapers, he knew he must act quickly. He did not for a moment imagine that Karswell's passing would halt the malefic conspiracy the occultist had helped foster; the scale of the plan was too great for that. But if he moved decisively now, de Richleau might be able to gain a surreptitious advantage nonetheless.

Later that day, he travelled to Lufford Hall, Karswell's country retreat. Announcing himself as a close colleague of the deceased doctor, he managed to bamboozle Karswell's grieving mother into giving him access to his enemy's office and private papers. Desperately searching the occultist's files, de Richleau came up empty-handed until he finally stumbled across an unmarked dossier, filled with private information concerning a solitary married couple: an American diplomat named Robert Thorn and his wife Katherine.

There was nothing overtly linking the Thorns with any of Karswell's other activities; therefore de Richleau felt certain that they must somehow be a vital component in the Antichrist conspiracy, unwitting or otherwise. When he learned that Katherine Thorn was in her ninth month of pregnancy, the Duc became convinced the couple were in great danger. The file stated that the diplomat was currently stationed in Rome, so it was to Italy that de Richleau travelled the very next morning.

His enquiries took him to a large Catholic hospital in the centre of the city, where Katherine Thorn had entered labour some hours before. De

Richleau searched the corridors until he finally came across Thorn, in hushed conference with a priest. The diplomat seemed shaken, desperate; was he in the middle of striking some dark covenant?

As soon as their conversation ended, the Duc approached him. *Mr Thorn, it is imperative I speak with you.*

The man looked at him, tired and obviously distracted. *I can't. Not now. My wife…*

This concerns both you and your wife. And your son.

Thorn's eyes widened in sudden anger. The Duc had somehow touched a nerve. *How do you know about my son?*

A great many people know about your son, Mr Thorn. If indeed, he can truly be said to be *yours.*

Urgency had made de Richleau indelicate. The diplomat's face reddened. He advanced on the Duc, grabbing him by the lapels. Once upon a time, de Richleau would have been more than a physical match for the man, but those days were long past. *Mr Thorn, please!*

A nurse stepped in to separate them, jabbering furiously in Italian. Thorn gave a cursory apology, then turned back to the Duc. *Stay away from me and my family!* he barked.

De Richleau watched him stride away down the corridor. He still could not be certain how much the man knew, or to what extent he was involved, but a direct approach was clearly fruitless. He turned to look out of a nearby window, his pulse beating like a heavy cosh at the back of his neck. His gaze drifted to the branches of a nearby tree, where a lone raven kept a careful vigil, as if in anticipation of an imminent death.

The Duc paid it little mind. What could he do? He had little doubt that the Antichrist was here, now, in this hospital. A mere baby, weak and defenceless. He would never have a better opportunity to act.

He had to be sure. He took one of the hospital's ancient lifts up to the nursery. Finding the room empty of staff, he searched frantically amongst the newborns, certain he would be discovered at any moment. His heart still hammered in his chest; for a moment the Duc was sure he would be felled by cardiac arrest before he could hope to achieve his goal.

Then, at last, he found the boy—a small chart hanging at the end of the cot read simply *Thorn*.

De Richleau stared down at the child. As a Biblical scholar, he knew that if this was indeed the Beast of the prophecies, it had to bear a Mark. He reached down and began to check the baby's flesh. The child stirred and started to squall. He must hurry.

And then, he found it, a small birthmark, hidden in the thin nest of the boy's hair: *Six hundred and sixty six.* He felt uncontrollably sick, as though he might vomit all over the child. No, he told himself. It was *not* a child! He should take the creature in his hands right now, just snatch it up and beat its brains against the wall, just...

Signore!

A nurse stood in the entrance to the nursery, her face furious. He had been discovered. Mumbling abject apologies in Italian, he retreated swiftly from the room, his normally aristocratic air suddenly reduced to that of a naughty child being sent for punishment. He hurried away before she could call security and have him removed from the building.

He had failed. If there were Satanists operating in this hospital, he might never be gifted with such a chance again.

As he stumbled down the stairwell, a thought suddenly struck him. The strength ebbing from his legs, he sat heavily down on a stair. It had saved him once before, saved all of them, but *dare* he?

The Sussamma Ritual.

The risks were immense, but if he could once again reverse time, to before the Thorn child was born, then he would be better placed to act. And if he succeeded? Could he, say, murder a pregnant woman to prevent the birth? He felt numb at the thought.

But what choice did he have? It was not just the lives of he and his friends at stake now, but those of the entire world.

He hauled himself to his feet, feeling every one of his years. The words of the ritual came easily to his tongue—the incantation was almost like holding a loaded revolver in one's hands; such was its power that it conveyed an almost irresistible urge to use it.

He shouted out the words, his voice echoing emptily down the stairwell. *Uriel Seraphim! Io Potesta! Zati Zata, Galatim Galata!*

We can only speculate as to the reasons for what happened next. Perhaps the Duc had gambled one too many times with a spell he lacked the true expertise to control. Or perhaps he had simply underestimated the profane power protecting the newborn Antichrist.

Whatever the explanation, the Duc was immediately ripped from his position in time and thrust *forwards*, not backwards as he had planned.

He materialised in the hospital a full two days later. Ordinarily, this might not have proved disastrous, but what the Duc could not foresee was that the dark forces gathered around the Antichrist had swiftly moved to destroy all evidence of its birth, and had set fire to the hospital as soon as the child had been taken home by his parents.

De Richleau was thrust into the middle of a flaming inferno. He had no time to react before the blaze consumed him. His final despairing thought was that he hoped the hell his failure had consigned him to would not prove to be a dreadful premonition of what awaited the rest of the world.

Then he died, his ashes mingling with the blackened remains of the hundreds of others killed in the fire. Unbeknownst to anyone, the first battle in the war against the Antichrist had been fought, and lost.

HUGO FITCH

John McGuire in 'The Ventriloquist's Dummy', Dead of Night, 1945
written by John Baines
directed by Alberto Cavalcanti

W HEN THE NAME OF HUGO FITCH FIRST SPRANG TO NATIONAL
prominence, after the shooting of American stage performer
Sylvester Kee in the mid-1940s, it was not Hugo himself that made most of
the headlines—he was, after all, just a dummy—but that of the ventriloquist who voiced him, Maxwell Frere.

What no one understood was that it was Frere who had been the true
puppet in the partnership all along; nothing but a feeble stooge, helpless
in the face of his master's malevolent desires. One supposes that if Frere
had but one satisfaction as he was committed to the asylum cell where he
would see out the remainder of his life, it was that it was precisely this
misapprehension which denied Hugo the fame and notoriety he had
always thirsted for.

A perpetually shy and nervous man, much given to involuntary
twitching and anxious perspiration, Maxwell Frere had nonetheless always

felt the irresistible lure of the footlights. He believed that if he could just force his way onto a stage, his tics and phobias would instantly fall away, and the true Maxwell—confident, witty, handsome—would stand revealed. Despite the best efforts of his concerned friends and family to dissuade him from this path, Maxwell persisted, finally managing to secure an opening slot on the bill at the Silver Fox nightclub in Soho.

To say he bombed would be to understate the destructive power of his act that night. A literal explosion could not have cleared the room faster, nor killed Maxwell and his nascent career any more comprehensively. As the ashes of his routine trickled through his fingers, such was Maxwell's paralysed terror that some onlookers claimed he'd involuntarily wet himself, onstage, in full view of the remaining audience. Utterly humiliated, he fled the nightclub and ran, sprinting through the nighttime streets of London, until he finally collapsed sobbing somewhere on the other side of the Thames.

As he sank down onto a park bench, his gaze fell upon the public hall opposite. A large and enthusiastic crowd had gathered outside, waiting to be admitted to that night's event. Maxwell stared at their excited faces, which offered such a stark contrast to the turbulent sea of scornful patrons he had performed to just a short time before.

Intrigued by their palpable excitement, Maxwell ventured over to the hall. Upon enquiring as to the nature of the event, he received the excited reply: *Dr Karswell is speaking tonight. He's such a clever man, so wise about the way things really are. He changed my whole life!*

A life change seemed to be just what Maxwell needed, so he dutifully joined the line as it slowly filed into the building. Inside, he found himself ushered into a brand new world, one he had never even realised existed. Quickly falling under the spell of the charismatic Karswell, Maxwell soon joined the rank of his cult, eagerly seeking the self-betterment that the occultist promised his followers.

Such was Maxwell's shy malleability and unquestioning desire to please that he promptly became one of Karswell's most trusted lackeys; unsurprising given that the doctor's continuing success relied upon recruiting a steady stream of disciples who could be trusted to carry out his every instruction, no matter how immoral, illegal or blasphemous.

Still, Karswell was not an entirely selfish master. He liked to do favours for the members of his inner circle, small demonstrations of his power that helped bind them ever closer to him. So it was that upon falling into conversation with Maxwell about his aborted nightclub career one evening, Karswell promised him his performing dream was yet within reach, if he allowed his new mentor to help him.

Maxwell was incredulous, barely daring to believe such a thing were possible. He had failed utterly, he had no talent. What on earth could Karswell do?

The doctor smiled. *You just need a friend to help you along. Leave it with me, dear boy.*

A month later he proudly presented Maxwell with a ventriloquist's dummy, smartly dressed in a miniature tuxedo, its face fixed in a leering grin. The performer found himself somewhat unnerved by the frozen malevolence of the thing, contempt etched into every carved aspect of its wooden face. And was it Maxwell's imagination, or were the puppet's features a twisted caricature of his own?

Meet Hugo Fitch, Karswell told Maxwell. *He has quite a lot to say for himself, the little devil. I think you two could do great things together.*

The puppet swivelled its head towards Maxwell, fixing him with a glassy stare. *This the dummy you promised me?* it snarled.

Delighted, Maxwell moved to take him from Karswell, only for the occultist to place a cautionary hand on his arm. *Before you accept him, just remember what I always tell people, Maxwell. You get nothing for nothing.*

Maxwell nodded his head, barely listening. He fully expected that Karswell would demand a cut of any money he earned with Hugo, as was only his due. None of it mattered. Maxwell realised that Hugo was the key to unlock the life he had always dreamed of.

He reached out and took the dummy in his arms. Within a matter of weeks, he would have that life, and so much more.

Although stories of his disastrous debut had already become legendary in London's clubland, as soon as Maxwell and Hugo hit the stage, they were as swiftly forgotten. Audiences loved the mild-mannered ventriloquist and his scabrous sidekick; Maxwell's nervous affability finally proving to be an asset, perfectly positioning him to play the continual stooge to Hugo's blitzkrieg of mockery. The partnership went from booking to booking, their fame spreading like a disease. Perhaps the same disease that had begun to afflict Maxwell himself.

He did not know what Hugo truly was — had never even dared to ask — but he harboured several uneasy suspicions. At night, as he lay there in the darkness listening to the buzz and whine of the dummy's incessant chatter, like a cloud of flies enveloping his sleep, his weary mind began to free associate: *Flies. Weren't they a harbinger of the Devil? Could Hugo be housing some form of demon? If he were to dissect the puppet, eviscerate his wooden innards, what might be unleashed?*

It was during these long, sleepless nights that he first started to feel his equilibrium skittering away from him. *Nothing for nothing.* He had always thought that Karswell meant he would pay for his fame financially, but in truth, the cost seemed to be his sanity. And it was a price he could not stop paying.

On more than one occasion he attempted to lock Hugo in his box, just shut him away, out of sight and mind. But even without Hugo there, Maxwell's arm would habitually crook itself to accommodate the dummy's presence, fingers twitching to operate the ghosts of his levers. Maxwell had once met a wartime amputee who would complain of the ache he still suffered in his missing phantom limb, and now he understood exactly how the man felt. It was as though Hugo were his Siamese twin, attached to his flesh, sharing the same bloodstream — and the thought of separation was too painful to bear.

So when rival ventriloquist Sylvester Kee came to see their act at Paris's Chez Beulah, Maxwell was immediately put on his guard. He felt sure that Kee would covet Hugo for his own. Neither did he trust in his sidekick's loyalty — Hugo relished every ounce of pain he caused Maxwell, and seemed gleeful at the notion of abandoning him.

Impressed by the routine, Kee had visited them backstage, where Maxwell attempted to warn him off. *You don't know what Hugo's capable of,* he told the visiting American. Hugo swiftly demonstrated the proof of these words by biting Maxwell on the hand. Or was that all just part of the act?

Regardless, it seemed to work, for a time. Kee left the dressing room, telling anyone who would listen that Maxwell was crazy. But what did anyone care if he was? He was a hit, him and Hugo both. And weren't all stars a little bit crazy to begin with? Besides, this was a man who made his living by talking to himself. What on earth did people expect?

Alone except for Hugo, Maxwell had no safety net, no available handhold to prevent him toppling into a rift of neurosis and insanity. When Kee ran into him again a year later, in the bar of the Imperial Palace Hotel in London, he was shocked at the precipitous decline in the performer. Maxwell was now a drunken wreck, given to walking out on engagements and openly squabbling with Hugo in public. The public would only tolerate this sort of warped eccentricity for so long—indeed, Kee had to step in to save Maxwell from a beating that very night. A fracas, Maxwell insistently slurred, that was instigated by Hugo.

Kee escorted Maxwell and Hugo up to their hotel room and put the senseless ventriloquist to bed. He had to admit, the boy had talent; that little display in the bar downstairs had been weirdly impressive, what with Maxwell keeping up the dummy's patter while being falling-down drunk himself. It was just a tragedy that he had no common sense, or self-control.

Accounts differ as to what happened next. Kee returned to his own room and retired for the night, but was soon awoken by an enraged Maxwell, bellowing that his rival had stolen Hugo.

Both men later gave statements agreeing that the dummy was subsequently found in the room, but Kee insisted that Maxwell must have planted him there in a bid to justify what happened next, whereas Maxwell simply offered it as confirmation that he had been right about Kee's motives all along. (Sadly, no one thought to ask Hugo about the truth of what happened.)

The increasingly deranged Maxwell pulled a gun and shot Kee, but luckily for his intended victim, Frere's ability as an entertainer far outstripped his competency as a cold-blooded killer. Kee collapsed to the floor, but was only wounded. The police were summoned, and the gibbering Maxwell was taken into custody. There, he insisted that the real facts of the matter would not be revealed until Hugo was returned to him.

Dr van Stratten, the psychiatrist consulting on the case, persuaded the police to acquiesce to the prisoner's demand. Hugo was placed in

Maxwell's cell, only for an argument to immediately break out between the two. Hugo viciously insisted that although Maxwell was incarcerated, he still had his own career to think of, and therefore would be teaming up with Kee after all.

In response, the ventriloquist flew into a violent rage and attacked the dummy, throwing Hugo to the floor and stomping his head into fragments.

Van Stratten would later stand firm in his belief that this was merely proof of Maxwell's hopelessly split personality. (Of course, Julian Karswell might have been able to tell him differently, but alas, the legal system took a dim view of putting infamously wicked occultists on the stand as character witnesses.) At his trial, Maxwell was found to be insane and committed to an asylum. Hopelessly psychotic, he would by now only communicate in Hugo's voice.

Of course, his doctors only took this as further confirmation of van Stratten's diagnosis, but was there perhaps another, more horrifying, explanation? Had Hugo—or whatever it was that animated him—simply fled its ruined body and leapt into the closest alternate host?

Within months, Maxwell Frere would be dead by his own hand. Hugo's remains were thought to have been destroyed by the authorities, but this was far from the end of the dummy's story.

Some thirty years later, the amateur magician Charles 'Corky' Withers was holidaying in London—or so he told people. In truth, he was fleeing from his own failure, something he had already shown a decided knack for.

Having apprenticed under the legendary vaudeville magician Merlin the Great, Corky had recently made his first public performance in a local talent contest. But, despite his undoubted sleight-of-hand ability, his lack of stage charisma had resulted in complete audience indifference (in truth, with his bad haircut and cheap J.C. Penney clothes, Corky had resembled nothing less than the class nerd during Show and Tell), and—much like Maxwell Frere before him—utter humiliation.

According to Merlin, there was only one solution: *Find yourself some charm, kid.*

As it turned out, this was literally what Corky was about to do, although not in the manner either man might have expected—or desired.

Originally born in Wales, Corky's parents had moved to the United States while he was still a boy, and in an attempt to fit in, he had adopted an American accent that was as much of a failure as everything else he had turned his hand to. He had spent his teenage years hopelessly in love with a high school classmate, Peggy Ann Snow, but could never summon the nerve to tell her. Having left his hometown in search of the success he believed would grant him the necessary stature to win Peggy, he had failed at that too. So now he wandered the labyrinthine back streets of London, staring bewilderedly at his A-Z, hopelessly lost in every respect.

Stumbling down a narrow passageway, he passed a small antiques shop, Temptations Limited. Glancing up at the window display for a moment, he saw something that instantly halted him in his tracks.

There, on the other side of the glass, nestled amongst the dusty jewellery, china and other trinkets, was Hugo Fitch. The same leering grin, the same insane glare; a glare that seemed to follow Corky as he paced in amazement back and forth before the shop.

Corky was an avid student of the history of magic and ventriloquism, and knew the tragic story of Maxwell Frere by heart. He had a photograph of Maxwell and Hugo pinned above his desk, and would have sworn that this was the very same dummy. He even looked sufficiently aged, tarnished with the long decades that had passed since Hugo last enjoyed the limelight.

But he had been wrecked, destroyed! This *couldn't* be him. It had to be some kind of clever replica. His heart jittering with excitement, Corky hurried inside the shop to find out.

Finding the elderly proprietor lurking behind the counter, Corky asked about the dummy. The man looked thoughtful and chewed on his pipe for a moment. *That's a rare piece. He was a star once, that one. Hugo, his name was.*

Corky was incredulous. *I know all about Maxwell Frere. Hugo Fitch was his dummy. But he went mad and destroyed Hugo himself.*

The proprietor smiled. *Aye, there was some damage, although perhaps not as much as you've heard. But he's been lovingly restored. Take a look, if you like.*

The old man led Corky to the window and carefully removed Hugo from the display, cradling him in his thin arms as delicately he would his own child. His hand moved to Hugo's controls, and in response, the dummy slowly swivelled its head towards Corky.

We have a visitor, Mr Hugo. All the way from America.

Corky spoke, his voice hesitant. *Uh, hello, Hugo.*

Hugo spoke. *He don't sound like a Yank. That accent's a put-on.* The shrill edge of his voice had not been blunted with the years.

Impressed, Corky looked up at the proprietor. *You're a ventriloquist?*

Oh no, sir. This is Hugo talking. I do apologise for his rudeness.

Hugo snarled, insulted. *Talk to me, not the dummy!*

Corky stammered an apology. *I am sorry, Hugo. Um, in answer to your question, I was born in Wales, but grew up in the States. My mother was born there.*

Hugo cackled. *Did she have any children that lived?*

The proprietor looked pained and apologised again. Corky paid it no mind. His body was thrumming, electric in Hugo's presence. He looked eagerly at the proprietor. *Can I hold him?*

Hugo's grin seemed to widen, his voice taking on a fake American twang, in imitation of Corky's own: *I smell an oppor-fuckin'-tunity...*

The proprietor looked relieved to be free of his burden and handed the dummy over to Corky. The young man took Hugo, with the same tenderness that he had once dreamed of embracing Peggy Ann Snow. *How did you come to acquire him?* Corky wondered.

The proprietor gestured vaguely with his pipe. *Oh, items have a funny way of finding their way to this little shop, sir. Just as they have a funny way of finding the right owner.*

Corky knew he was being finessed for a sale, and he did not care. He had found the charm he was looking for.

He and Hugo returned to America the next day. Within six months, Corky had a whole new act, and a big name agent. Hugo—now rechristened Fats—had been the making of him. Corky had been liberated by the dummy's presence—and as for Hugo (for at heart, he would always be Hugo, never mind his new stage name); well, he had been set free too. No longer bound by the social constraints of a bygone era, he could be as vulgar and insulting as he wished. *The first X-rated dummy on the block!* And the more obscene he was, the more audiences loved him.

If anyone had asked Corky, he would have said Fats was just the same dummy he'd discovered in London. Sure, he'd given him a new wardrobe and a lick of fresh paint, but otherwise it was the same old showbiz trouper, built to last.

Corky did not acknowledge — or did not wish to — the fact that the contours of the puppet's face had somehow warped and shifted; features that had once resembled Maxwell Frere's now approximated Corky's own.

Hugo had grown more like his partner, and in exchange, Corky would now have to become more like Hugo.

Corky found himself playing to sold-out crowds, appearing on Carson, being courted for his own primetime TV show. This was everything he'd ever fantasised of, lying there at night in his lumpy single bed, dreaming of worldly success while trapped in a cramped studio apartment; a tiny room that seemed to grow smaller and smaller by the day. He knew he owed it all to Hugo, but what of it?

His old mentor Merlin had warned him that using another ventriloquist's dummy was bad luck, especially one as ill-starred as Hugo, but Corky chose to ignore him. It was just superstition, showbiz bullshit.

Had Julian Karswell still lived — a man who understood the truth of superstition — he might have warned Corky, just as he once did Maxwell Frere: *You get nothing for nothing.* Hugo extracted a heavy price for the fame he bestowed upon his partners, and his hunger could never be sated.

Corky got his first inkling of this when the network insisted he undergo a medical check before recording his TV pilot. All of a sudden he felt irrationally panic-stricken. He was certain he would fail the medical, be exposed as a flake and a weakling, become a laughing stock all over again. Only this time it wouldn't be just a half-empty nightclub laughing at him, but an entire nation.

Despite his agent's blithe reassurances, Corky knew he could not do it. Panicking, he fell back on his original talent, the one thing that had sustained him through all those early years of failure: he ran away. Only this time he took Hugo with him.

He fled to the Catskills, to his old hometown. He'd barely dared hope to find her there, not when everything else in his life was falling apart, but when he went calling, Peggy Ann Snow was still at home. And still beautiful, although by now her beauty was shaded with sadness. She too, had known failure, although of a more humdrum sort: the collapse of her business, the slow disintegration of her marriage. In her eyes at least, Corky was still a success.

Needing charm now more than ever, he introduced her to Hugo. The dummy goggled, saying all the things Corky had thought but could never allow himself to utter, lewdly commenting on Peggy Ann's breasts and ass.

To Corky's amazement, she loved it. Was this what women really wanted? Was this the sort of man he should have been all these years?

Peggy Ann's husband was away on business, and one night, she and Corky ended up in bed together. Suddenly he understood that this was all he'd ever desired. The fame, the success—it had only ever been a means to get back here, to win Peggy Ann. In a flush of post-coital happiness, they started making plans to elope.

But Corky had reckoned without the partnership he had already made. Hugo had not finished with him yet, and without another prospective Sylvester Kees around, the dummy was not about to let himself be abandoned or shut up in a box. As ever, he still had a career to consider. His claws were already tightly in Corky; it was time to flex them. The boy had always been weak-minded—could Hugo pick 'em or what? Now to show him who was really boss.

So when Corky's agent tracked him down to Peggy Ann's, Hugo had his partner kill him and dump his body in the lake. And when Peggy Ann's husband returned, Corky murdered him too. Hugo was almost proud of him. For such a shy boy, he was already proving far more adept at shedding blood than Maxwell. Now all he needed to do was dispose of the ageing tart, and they'd be home free.

Corky had come very close to doing it, too—lurking outside her bedroom door with a knife, crooning to her in the voice he'd borrowed from Hugo, waiting patiently for her to emerge—but at the last moment something in him had resisted, the dummy turning against its master—and he'd stabbed himself instead. These damn kids today; no profess-ionalism.

Corky had stumbled away from the house, a wounded animal seeking a private place to die. He'd lain down with Hugo, tears in his eyes, wondering which of them would be the first to expire. He was so pitiful that even Hugo barely had the spit to tell him the truth.

Besides, there was a more pressing problem. With Corky dead, what would happen to Hugo? Would he be destroyed again? Shut away in an evidence locker for good? It had been hard enough to find his way to the antique shop the last time, and now he was in a whole new country, one he barely knew.

Then he heard her outside — Peggy Ann, calling outside for Corky. She'd come to him at last.

Could he do it? Maxwell and Corky had been simple enough, but they'd been *chosen*, and besides, he'd had time to work, to carefully pick the locks of their minds.

She shouted again. *Hey Cork! Don't play hard to get with me! I can always change my mind again!*

Or perhaps — Hugo could change it for her.

He leapt.

Peggy Ann's voice suddenly rose in pitch, becoming a nasal whine, no longer her own. A voice both Maxwell Frere and Corky Withers would have immediately recognised. *You may not get this oppor-fuckin'-tunity tomorrow!*

But Hugo had always recognised a good opportunity when he saw one.

DAMIEN THORN

Harvey Stephens in The Omen, *1976*
written by David Seltzer
directed by Richard Donner

About Me By Damien Thorn (Age Six)

MY NAYME IS DAMIEN. I AM STARTING A NEW SCOOL IN America. Mrs Rooney is my New Teecher and askd me to rite about miself. I am Six Yeers Old. Six is my Favoritt Number. I live with my Uncel Richard and my Aunty Ann. They are Nice to me. I cayme to live here beecause my reel Mummy and Daddy are deads. Beefore I lived in Ingland in a Bigg House. My Daddy was Impourtant and worked for the Prezident Of The United Staytes. I had a nannie to look after me. Her nayme was Mrs Baylock. She was a bit Scary but Nice to me. She gave me a Dogg that was my Best Frend. She was my nannie beecause my old nannie jumpd out of a winndow with a rowpe around her neck at my partey. It was Funny but some of the other chilldren cryed. Mrs Baylock looked after me Good. Sometymes Mummy and Daddy mayde me do Bad Things like goe to Church. Church hurted my hed and I cryed. Mrs Baylock said

Church was Silly and I did not Have to goe. Daddy was Kross with her but they did not tayke me to Church again. Another tyme Mummy took me to the Zoo. We drove the Car in a feeld with Monkees in it. The Monkees got Very Kross and showd us there teeth. They were Scary and Mummy screemed. I did not lyke the Zoo. Mummy and Daddy took me lotts of Playces I did not Lyke. I do not now why they did this. Sumtimes I think they were not my Reel Mummy and Daddy. Sumtimes I have dreems of a Scary Mann who sed he is my Reel Daddy. I do not now his Name. So then my other Daddy went away on an Impourtant Trip and me and Mummy and Mrs Blaylock stayd at Home. It was Fun beecause Mummy would lye down a lot beecause Mrs Blaylock said she was Poorly. I think beecause she was Poorly she did not luv me any moor. But Mrs Blaylock luved me and let me play games so it was O K. One day I was ryding on my byke and Silly Mummy got in my way and she Fell down to the grownd. They had to tayke her to Hosspital. At the Hosspital Mummy Fell down again. She fell out of a Winndow and this tyme she was dead. She always tolled me to be Carefull Silly but I think Mummy was not very Carefull. Silly! Then Daddy cayme Home. He was Sadd beecause Mummy was dead and Very Kross. He Hurt poor Mrs Blaylock and lockd My Dogg in the sellar. Then he mayde me goe to Church again even tho it hurted my hed. I was Very Kross with him and sed No Daddy No! He did not lissen to me. I think Daddy did not luv me any moor just like Mummy. He had some Sharp Knifes and he wanted to Hurt Me. I do not know Why beecause I was a Good Boy. But then the Poleesemen came in the Church and they shooted Daddy with there Gunns. Then Daddy and Mummy were both deads. I was a bit sadd for a littel whyle but then I was better. I went to see Mummy and Daddy be buryed. The Prezident of the United Staytes was there. He was Nice to me. He sed I had to be a Bigg Boy and I sed I am. Then he sed my Daddy was a Good Mann. I said why did he try and Hurt me. Then the Prezident of the United Staytes was Sadd and sed Damien. Sumtimes Good Menn do Bad Things. If I do Bad Things I get a Spannking. One day when I am Old I want to do Bad Things too and I will be Too Bigg to get a Spannking. After that I cayme to live with Uncel Richard and Aunty Ann. It is nice here. They are Very Ritch. Uncel Richard works in the citee called Chicargoe. He has a bigg desk and sed

One Day I can have one too. They have a littel boy too. His nayme is Mark. That is a Good Nayme. Mark is my Frend now and I hope we can be Frends For Ever. He is six yeers old lyke me but I am a bigger Boy beecause my Mummy and Daddy are deads. I lyke it here. I miss my Dogg but when I woked up today I lookd out of the Winndow and I saw a burd. It was bigg and Black and it lookd at Me. So I think it can be my new Pet. Mrs Blaylock sed I shud all ways have a Pet to Protect Me. I am Happy now in America. The End.

I forgotted. I had a dreem of the Scary Mann agane last nite. But I was not Scard any moor beecause I am a Bigg Boy Now. He tolled me I was the Beest. I sed I am a Boy. He sed I was a Boy And a Beest. I sed a Beest lyke my Dogg? He sed lyke a Very Very Bigg Dogg, one Bigger than the hole World. Then I woked up. I lookd at my face in the miror and maide a Beest face. Grrrr I sed. It was Scary. One day I mite Eat Evryone.

CAROL LEDOUX

Catherine Deneuve in Repulsion, *1965*
written by Gerard Brach & Roman Polanski
directed by Roman Polanski

WHEN SHE WAS A LITTLE GIRL IN BELGIUM, CAROL WOULD spend hours playing with jigsaws. Always a quiet and solitary child, she was at her happiest poring over a fractured mosaic of tiny puzzle pieces. The adults who observed her noted that she seemed less interested in the overall picture than the gaps in-between; the fault lines splintering the image, the occasional missing piece. She would stare intently at an unfinished jigsaw for hours, until her mother was worried she would strain her eyes. It was as though she glimpsed something lying behind the puzzle; a larger picture, visible only in increments. *Tu es une énigme,* her mother would tell her.

Over time, Carol became increasingly withdrawn. The only person she seemed happy to spend time with was her older sister, Hélène. While they were both younger, Hélène was content enough to have her little sister trailing around after her; she would practically treat Carol as another of her dolls, playing dress up or tea parties with her. Carol was pliant, as obedient as any of Hélène's other toys; indeed, with her perfect features and blank gaze, she almost resembled a doll herself.

But as she grew older, Hélène began to find Carol something of an irritation. She preferred spending time with the local boys to dolls, and demanded her own private room, away from her sister.

Carol cried when Hélène moved out of the bedroom they had shared, and began to resist going to bed at night. Even after she had finally given in to sleep, she would frequently experience night terrors and wake screaming that strange men were standing over her bed. Her mother, groggy with tranquillisers, would groan at her husband to attend to Carol; often, he would go to his daughter and spend the rest of the night in her room. He claimed that it helped the little girl to sleep peacefully; no one seemed to notice the fearful way she began to look at him, even after it was captured in a family snapshot.

As she grew into adolescence, her withdrawal became more pro- nounced; without warning, the light would suddenly fade from her eyes as she stepped into some private, hidden world. She would flinch from loud noises or human contact, and sometimes simply walked away in the middle of a conversation. The nuns teaching her at the local Catholic school became increasingly exasperated at what they saw as wilful rudeness and punished Carol accordingly, but it only caused her to drift away even further.

Her mother wanted to take her to a doctor, but her father insisted it was merely a phase that she would eventually grow out of. Adolescent girls were highly strung, prone to outbreaks of hysteria; everyone knew that. In time her hormones would settle down and all would be well again.

Life continued like this for some time. Even after Carol blossomed into a beautiful young woman, no one seemed to question whether it was normal or appropriate for her father to spend so much time in her room at night. Her mother moved through life in a chemical fog, and Hélène often spent her nights elsewhere. Carol was left alone, in a world increasingly consumed by shadow.

Matters came to a head one night when Carol awoke screaming from yet another nightmare. Hélène returned home soon afterwards to find her mother in shocked tears and her father staunching the bleeding from a wound in his shoulder; apparently he had gone to calm Carol and she'd stabbed him with a kitchen knife concealed under her pillow. Where was Carol now? She had barricaded herself in the room by dragging a wardrobe in front of the door.

Hélène went upstairs to speak to her sister; she returned grim-faced with Carol an hour later, each of them bearing a suitcase. She was going to take Carol away; her sister would never be safe or well as long as she lived under this roof. She stared into her father's eyes, daring him to try and stop them; he merely shrugged and poured himself another brandy for the pain. *Loufoque*, was all he said.

The sisters first moved to Brussels, then England. For a time Carol seemed happier; she had her sister back, and the night terrors subsided. But when Hélène took them to Kensington, lured by the promise of Swinging London, Carol's fears began to overwhelm her once more. Hélène was out a lot of the time, drinking and dancing and pursuing a series of affairs with married men; she tried to invite her younger sister along, but Carol knew what it would be like, all those vile animals leering and pawing at her. London was a zoo; it stank of unwashed male bodies and urine, and the food here was disgusting, fit only for wild beasts. She could barely stand it, any of it.

Hélène didn't try too hard to persuade Carol otherwise; she could see how the English men looked at her sister, and she didn't need the competition. God, even her current *beau* could barely keep his hands off Carol. Michael was spending more and more time at the flat, away from the wife he promised would leave any day now. Carol could barely mask her resentment of his presence; it seemed as though she could no longer bear the company of any man, no matter how wealthy or handsome. Hélène had tried to convince her that not all men were like Papa, that they could be kind and funny and caring; she had even introduced her to a nice good-looking boy, Colin.

But Carol knew the truth; she had long since trained herself to see past the lying surface of things, and she understood what lurked behind men's eyes. They were interested in nothing but their own pleasure. She could hear the noises her sister and Michael made at night, and they were the same grunts and moans Papa used to make. They were all animals, and spoke the same bestial language. What then, was the difference?

When Michael whisked Hélène away to Italy for a holiday, Carol's reality finally began to crack irreparably, the jigsaw of her existence shattered into its thousands of constituent pieces. The animals could sense her loneliness and abandonment, could smell her fear; and one by one they came, scratching and pawing at the door, desperate to taste her sweet flesh.

At first she was terrified, but then she remembered the look of fear on Papa's face when she had produced the kitchen knife; she remembered that under their ridiculous bravado and displays of machismo, men were small and weak and stupid, and could be hurt.

First she killed Colin—she had given him every opportunity to leave her alone, but he would not listen—and then the landlord, initially greedy for money, then for her, his sweaty fingers clutching at her pale body. She thought perhaps that she would be safe then, but everywhere she looked, there were more of them: lurking behind her in the bathroom mirror, hiding in the shadows of her bedroom at night. They were even watching her from behind the walls; when they thought she was unawares, their hands would eagerly tear through the plaster to reach for her body, just as the landlord had.

She finally understood that this was a world owned solely by men; they controlled it all, could see and hear everything, and there was no escaping them. She had run from Papa, and it had only brought her here, to this stinking cage of a flat, locked in with savage, drooling beasts.

When they finally found her, she was catatonic, hidden under her sister's bed. The doctors tried to reach her, but she had nothing to say to them—they were, after all, men—and so she was committed to an institution, a hopeless case.

There, she was placed under the care of a young doctor, new to the staff, Dr Channard. Yet another man, but his manner was gentle, and looking into her eyes, he seemed to understand something implicit about her, without any need of words.

He did not try and force her to speak; instead, he began to bring jigsaw puzzles to her room—small, simple ones at first, intended only for young children. Initially, Carol did not respond, preferring to sit and stare emptily at the cracks in the walls, but gradually, as Dr Channard would do his rounds in the mornings, he would start to find pieces of the puzzles assembled on the floor of Carol's room, random fragments of an as yet-unrealised bigger picture.

As time went on and she moved past the more childish jigsaws, he gave her bigger, more elaborate sets, abstract images divided into thousands of tiny pieces, practically impossible to solve. And yet Carol would sit there for hour after hour, wordlessly assembling them, piece by piece. She was never frustrated; never thwarted by a puzzle's difficulty. This was the limit of her engagement with the world, but Dr Channard had succeeded in giving her a purpose, however small it may have been.

Finally, one evening, after he brought Carol her nightly dose of medication, he produced another kind of puzzle—a small lacquered wooden box. He placed it carefully in front of her. *This is a different kind of puzzle, Carol. One I've never been able to solve. Perhaps you might have more luck.*

After he left her alone, Carol gazed at the box for a while. By now, she was adept at seeing past the surface of things, and could recognise the puzzle for what it was: a door to another place. The box frightened her—she could not be sure what she would be opening a door *to*—but she felt compelled to pick it up, to solve the mystery of what lay beyond; the other world she knew existed and had spent all these years desperately straining to see.

In the end, the puzzle was deceptively simple to solve. As the last piece slid into place and a musical chime began to play, an impossibly bright light suddenly flared through the cracks in the walls she had studied so intently, rendering the room as a negative image of itself. At last, the world beyond was revealed.

A bell tolled somewhere in the distance, announcing the arrival of the Hell Priest.

Carol looked up into his pallid face, intersecting lines carved into its flesh almost like a jigsaw, brass pins marking the corners of each piece, his emotionless expression a puzzle no one could solve. The Cenobite studied Carol with interest.

I sense much anger in you. You wear the perfume of blood and suffering. Why have you summoned me?

Carol stared at him, saying nothing. The Hell Priest gazed into her eyes. He recognised madness, understood how to read it.

You are in a Hell, child. But I can show you another, if you wish. Perhaps you can find a voice there. A purpose.

He held out a hand to Carol. Slowly, she reached up and took it.

The Cenobite helped his new disciple to her feet and led her away, down those long endless corridors, so reminiscent of that dark hallway in Kensington. There, in the depths of Hell, she would become a child again, a pliant lump of unformed clay, ready to be sculpted anew. And although Carol hated to be touched, she found that the sensation of the knives and hooks in her skin was different; far more delicate and precise than the brutish gropings of the men she had left behind.

She welcomed it.

Afterwards, once she had been transformed, her flesh pierced, the soft meat of her throat peeled open to the air, Carol learned to talk again, to speak the language of pain and misery and sweet, sweet suffering. She found her rightful place at the side of the Hell Priest, where, for the rest of eternity, she would show the lustful men that summoned her the true meaning of pleasure.

EDITH EASTWOOD

Yvonne Mitchell in The Corpse, *1971*
written by Olaf Pooley
directed by Viktors Ritelis

"*W*HY DO YOU COMPLAIN OF YOUR FATE WHEN YOU COULD SO *easily change it?*"

Edith read these words in *Justine*, the novel by the Marquis de Sade that she had so carefully smuggled into the house. If her husband Walter were to find such a book in her possession, she had no doubt her own resultant suffering would be Sadean in its cruelty; she kept it concealed amongst her cookery books for just that reason, knowing Walter would be about as likely to peruse them as he would a copy of *Das Kapital*.

She found much about the book repugnant, abhorrent; yet it spoke to her in ways her so-called women's magazines could not. She had only ever wanted to be a virtuous, loving wife, but marriage to Walter had plunged her into a small hell of suffering and despair. Much as de Sade's Justine is only ever punished for her decent impulses, so too Edith found herself paying a fearful price for the crime of doing only that which she had been raised to do: to provide her husband with healthy children and a spotless, comfortable home, never an ornament or rug out of place.

On the surface, they had it all: a large house in an excellent neighbour-hood, plus a cosy country getaway; they moved in the right social circles; their income and investments were sound; and their children were well-educated and beginning to make their own way in the world.

But underneath his Savile Row suit and his impeccable manners, Walter was a depraved tyrant worthy of de Sade's own imagination. While his hypocrisy was such that he would undoubtedly declare *Justine* to be pornographic filth and confiscate it, Edith could easily picture what would happen next; her husband's clammy fingers flicking through the pages as he dipped into the novel at random (purely to satisfy himself that it was as appalling as he expected, you understand); his flushed cheeks and mounting excitement as he marvelled over the accounts of beatings and perversions on a level of depravity that Walter's petty humiliations could only aspire to; and finally, his soft tread in the hallway as he looked to exorcise those forbidden feelings and searched for a likely victim; either Edith or, more likely, their sixteen year-old daughter Jane.

The thought sickened Edith; while she was (almost) certain Walter had never touched their daughter sexually, one did not need to have read de Sade to recognise exactly what he was sublimating when he took it upon himself to discipline her with rod or (eager) hand. Why, just the other day, she had looked out of the window and caught her husband fondling Jane's still-warm bicycle seat after she had returned from a ride.

Edith wondered how much longer it would be before Walter's abuses did finally cross that line; of course, from his perspective it would just be one more lesson that their daughter needed to learn, purely and simply for her own good.

She would not see her daughter walk the same path as Justine de Bertole. Edith gave Jane the book and told her, *This might open a few windows.*

Jane was shocked at first; she could not imagine her mother reading of the perversions she discovered within the novel's pages. But it became a shared conspiracy between them, as though they were agents in occupied territory. They would whisper passages to each other when Walter was safely out of earshot, like an illicit, shameful code, and Edith could not deny that she and Jane were both as excited as they were horrified. Finally, they felt as though they understood what manner of monster they were facing.

The book was only the start of it. Edith still remembered Walter taking her to see that awful French film all those years before. Being foreign, he'd assumed it would be something artistic, refined; instead, they'd watched in shock as a grubby tale of adultery, betrayal and murder had unfolded onscreen. A brutal philanderer was killed by the two women he held in his sadistic thrall, their desperate attempts to dispose of his body culminating in a scene of almost unbearable horror as he returned from the grave to take his revenge.

It was all a trick of course, another twist in the tale; such things didn't really happen. Appalled, Walter had complained to the cinema manager afterwards about such immoral rubbish being screened and demanded his money back. (The man's retort that he'd managed to sit through the entire film before complaining was treated with the contempt that Walter felt it deserved.)

But Edith had often thought of the film in the time since. It was inevitable really, given how much her own life had come to resemble it. Not simply in its humdrum quotidian violence, although that was certainly present. She also recognised the same sour effluvium of contempt filling their lives, those horrendous endless dinners during which Walter would wheedle and belittle them, chipping away at the two women in tiny, painful fragments. Sometimes Edith felt as though she and Jane were statues in a public square, their once-delicate features slowly being rendered formless by the elements.

So when she turned to her daughter one morning—her poor Jane, bruised by the beating she had suffered the previous night—and said, simply, *Let's kill him*, it was as if she were only mouthing words which had been scripted for her years before.

She planned the murder fastidiously—years of marriage to Walter had taught her precision, if nothing else—and after her initial shock subsided, Jane willingly fell in with the scheme. Edith supposed that she should have acted alone and spared her daughter this final horror, but in truth, it was far too late for that. She had involved Jane from the very moment of her birth — if she'd meant to spare her anything, it would have been better to smother her in her crib. But in her selfishness, she'd kept Jane for herself, fed her weakness like mother's milk, and now they were utterly dependent on each other. They shared a single nervous system, the same heart and mind, the same instinct to survive; they were Siamese twins in victimhood.

They packed Walter off to the country cottage for a shooting weekend, then crept down after him in the dead of night. He'd been dozing in front of the fire when they arrived, but in her clumsy nervousness, Edith had shattered an ornament on the mantel and alerted him to their presence. Very well, then; she would have to look the monster in the eyes before they slew him. She only hoped her limbs would not turn to stone before she could act.

When Edith pointed the hunting rifle at Walter's chest, he'd seemed more appalled that a mere woman might touch his prized weapon than at any apparent threat to life or limb. She knew his arrogance was such that he would not envisage her having the strength to pull the trigger. She quickly disabused him of that notion by firing into the ceiling; he'd rapidly retreated back into his chair and gulped like a clogged drain at his tumbler of whisky, his dark eyes smouldering as he awaited his chance at retribution.

A chance that would never arrive; the bottle of whisky that Jane had spiked with sleeping pills saw to that. He passed out with a final indignant croak of outrage; the two women then forcefed him with more alcohol and sedatives and carried him up to his bed. Edith had no idea how large a cocktail it would actually take to kill a man — fiction was always annoyingly vague about such matters — but as she looked at her husband's scrawny, inert frame, she felt sure she'd erred on the side of overcompensation.

They left Walter to die and drove back home in silence. The whole event quickly began to seem dreamlike to Edith: had she really murdered her husband? Was it really that surreally simple? The burden of waiting for someone to discover his body quickly became far more of a torment than the murderous deed itself. She would not be able to rest until he was pronounced dead and safely interred in the ground. Of course, she was thinking of the French film again; she laughingly chided herself that corpses do not get up and walk in everyday life, only in ridiculous thrillers.

So when Walter was not found; indeed, when it began to appear that he was not even dead, Edith took refuge in the notion that this must all be some kind of dream, a jumbled nightmare version of that old film from which she would soon awake. Far better to go back to the waking horror of her everyday existence with Walter than this.

But Edith did not emerge from the dream; if anything, she plunged ever deeper into its labyrinth.

When they returned to the cottage in a forlorn bid to put their minds at rest, Walter's body had vanished from the bed. It was as if he, too, after watching the film on that night all those years ago, had foreseen the winding trail of events that had brought them all here, and was now taunting Edith by playing his own assigned role — the revenant husband — to the letter. Was his control over them so total, that he knew everything they were thinking and planning?

Events continued to unfold with the same dreamlike logic: Walter's corpse would appear, then vanish again, and all the while others would insist they'd seen him alive. Edith's life began to take on a harrowing air of deja vu; she recognised these events, had seen them play out before, and knew there was only one manner in which they could possibly end.

She waited, resigned, for the inevitable climax; the dreadful resurrection.

But when Walter finally returned for them, his bloodless features leering grotesquely as he pursued her and Jane through the house, Edith finally realised that there was no hidden plot; there would be no last-minute revelation or narrative twist. Everything was precisely as it appeared to be; they *had* killed Walter, and he *had* come back. Their lives were indeed a shared nightmare, far worse than any horror film fiction.

For what Edith now understood was that they were *truly* trapped; not simply in their life with Walter, but also in this appalling, endlessly looping chain of events. Their fate could *not* be changed.

They would continue to suffer at Walter's hands, and in turn, they would continue to murder him for it. And time and time again, he would continue to return from the grave to claim his vengeance, the only difference being that, with each reprise, his revenge would be more and more terrible, more Sadean in its exquisite viciousness. She knew now that Walter lived, and died, only to torment them further.

Finding herself seated back at the family dinner table, enduring yet another loathsome meal, Edith suddenly felt certain she had lived through this chain of events innumerable times before. As Walter's features contorted in a ghastly death's head smile, she could feel the wearied torment of those years engulfing her like a flood, reducing her skin to worn grey parchment, her eyes to fogged marbles.

A tear trailing down her ravaged cheek, she silently prayed to be granted the only escape she could now envisage—not via any futile resistance she or Jane could muster—but by simply fading away to oblivion.

JOHN EBONY

David Hemmings in Unman, Wittering and Zigo, *1971*
written by Simon Raven
based on the play by Giles Cooper
directed by John MacKenzie

T HIS WASN'T THE WAY HIS LIFE HAD BEEN MEANT TO GO.
Ebony had always hated school: the teachers, the pupils, the lumpen
sludge of the lunchtime meals, the ritual humiliation of physical education. He'd dreamt about those days ever since, little bubbles of anxiety
rising out of the stew of his unconscious. Dreams in which he'd be late for
school but unable to find the way there, or walk into the exam hall and
realise, too late, that he was half naked. All he'd ever wanted was to leave
rules and timetables behind, to cast off the shackles of state-mandated
education and dwell forever in the tobacco-fogged bohemia of bars and
clubs, talking of life and love and art.

He'd announced his intention to be a writer, but when after several years
doing battle with his muse had failed to produce so much as a completed
short story, let alone a novel, his parents had lost patience and kicked him

out. Fuck them. What did they know anyway?

He'd drifted into advertising, but soon soured on it and quit. *It's all the same bastards I was at school with,* he told his wife Sylvia. *They had their heads filled up with useless crap and now they're selling it to the rest of the world.*

But what else could he do, he wondered.

Sylvia looked at him, kittenish. *You could try teaching,* she said with a smile. *Don't teachers always know better?*

Sometimes he thought his wife viewed his life as nothing but a joke for her own private amusement. He imagined slapping her—the murkier pleasures of discipline were not entirely lost on him—and Sylvia must have glimpsed something in his eyes, for the next moment she was leading him into the bedroom. *Teaching? I'll teach you a thing or two,* he said as he pushed her down onto the mattress.

As he lay spent in bed afterwards, replenishing himself with a cigarette, Sylvia appeared with the classified section of the newspaper. *Look at this,* she said. She'd picked out a job vacancy at a small public establishment in the southwest, The Chantry School. *It's a temporary position to begin with, and private accommodation is included. You could try it out and see how you get on.* Wearily stubbing out his cigarette, he agreed to apply, privately certain that he'd never be considered for the post. But his own education had taught him that sometimes, you just had to go through the motions.

Much to his surprise, he was called in for an interview. Arriving at the gates of the Chantry, his stomach had curdled at the sight of the school buildings, huddled together against the brisk coastal air like beggars. As he stepped inside, his nausea intensified; the faint odour of urine and despair in the hallways made him glad he had not eaten breakfast that morning. He should not be here. He was an unwelcome outsider; the pupils in the corridor stared at him with feral eyes, as though he was a stray animal intruding on their territory. He was seized by a sudden urge to light a match and burn the place down.

Ebony went into the headmaster's office determined to fail the interview; of course, they immediately offered him the job. It transpired that the previous teacher, Mr Pelham, had died in an accident on the nearby cliffs, and a replacement was needed urgently. He suspected he'd had no competition for the post and told himself it was simply down to superstition; word quickly got around about such things and it was probably considered bad luck to take a dead man's job.

He didn't give a damn; his misfortune had been Sylvia spotting the job advert in the first place. He listened politely as the headmaster prattled on about the school's academic record and its allegedly distinguished alumni; amongst them, Ebony recognised only the names of the crank writer John Morlar and Miles Sercombe, the government minister. *Marvellous*, he thought to himself. *It's a school for misanthropes and moneyed idiots.*

As it turned out, that wasn't altogether far from the truth.

When he began to call the class register on the first morning, he was suddenly sure the whole thing was indeed some sort of elaborate prank. Those surnames! *Aggeridge!* he called out. *Bungabine! Cloistermouth!* He felt as though he was chanting a spell to invoke a horde of devils.

In truth, he would rather have been greeted by a legion of hellspawn than the spiteful ranks of young men—for The Chartry School insisted that they *were* men—assembled before him. They stared glassily back at him, their sallow suet faces pocked with entitled contempt. *This* was Britain's future. These places were nothing more than hives, breeding swarms of privileged insects that would burst forth and swarm across the country, poisoning it with their greed and cynicism.

For a moment, he was granted a premonition of the decades to come; the nation slowly being bled white, sinking under the weight of their parasitic infestation. He choked back a bitter laugh. What could he teach pupils such as these? Their programming was already complete, instilled deep in their genes from birth.

He would soon learn the extent of their monstrosity. As he expected, the class spent their initial time together testing him, discovering his limits. Growing weary of their insolence, he threatened the entire class with a Saturday detention. The boy—no, the *man*—called Cloistermouth responded, oh so matter-of-factly: *It's not a good idea, sir. Mr Pelham tried it once, sir. And that's why we killed him, sir.*

Obviously it was a lie, but to even say such a thing! To a teacher, a figure of authority! They were trying to cow him, to bludgeon him into submission, much as they'd done to Wittering, the class weakling. He must resist. This was no mere anxiety dream, nothing he could leave safely behind in sleep for the waking sanctuary of his wife's warm embrace. This was cold, harsh reality; tribal, territorial. He must *command* their respect, grind it out of them if necessary.

Ebony strode into the next lesson prepared for battle, but quickly found himself ambushed once more. He opened his desk drawer to find Pelham's diary waiting for him, the pages curled and bloodstained. They'd taken it from his broken body as evidence of their brutality; all at once he saw them for the depraved children they were, seeking approbation for their crude handiwork.

He fled to the headmaster for aid, feeling like a child himself. He could almost imagine himself shrinking in stature as he stood before the man's desk, his manhood withering between his legs, reduced to an impotent pubescent once more.

The headmaster dismissed him impatiently, blind to the corruption festering in his school. As Ebony retreated from his superior's office, he began to consider that perhaps the man's blindness was wilful; that it harboured some tacit approval of what these tailored monsters had done to his predecessor. Was this the true purpose of such schools then, to turn out a master race of unfeeling psychopaths?

He tried in vain to convince his only confidants—Sylvia, his fellow teacher Farthingale—of his predicament, but neither believed him. Rebuffed, he concealed his mounting paranoia, nurturing it in the dark like a fungus. Biding his time, he came to an arrangement with the class; he would do the bare minimum of teaching necessary to get them through the year, and agree to place racing bets with the local bookie on their behalf; in return, they would leave him in peace.

The compromise suited him; it would give him time to try and uncover the ringleader behind the murder. Increasingly consumed by this obsession, he was oblivious to Sylvia's mounting frustration at Ebony's neglect of their marriage. Crucially, he was also oblivious to the boys' voyeuristic interest in his wife; they would linger in the lane and make conversation as she walked home from the village, or find excuses to call at their cottage while Ebony was out.

Matters came to a head after he clumsily tried to intimidate one of the pupils into implicating Pelham's true murderer. When he was informed shortly afterwards that his employment would not be extended, that the school preferred an old Chantryian for the post, he realised that ranks had closed against him; he would not be allowed to disrupt the natural order of things.

With that, his desire for justice was extinguished. He could not change the world; it was foolish to even try. He had been momentarily dazzled by the brilliant light of idealism, but in truth it was better to withdraw to the safety of the bar stool, the comforting cocktail of alcohol and cynical chatter.

The class however, were less easily deterred from their goals. They meant to ensure Ebony's silence. To this end, they lured Sylvia into the school building one night and assaulted her; only her natural resourcefulness saved her from a gang rape at their hands. She escaped their clutches and fled back to the safety of the cottage.

Upon hearing her account, Ebony was horrified, but secretly glad his wife had been taught a deserved lesson. Hadn't she scoffed at his story? Even encouraged their prurient attentions?

When Wittering's body was found at the base of the cliffs the next morning, the affair seemed to be at an end. A suicide note was discovered, claiming sole responsibility for Pelham's murder. Ebony was summoned back to the headmaster's office and given a begrudging acknowledgement that perhaps there'd been some partial truth in his earlier accusations. Still, the matter was now solved, the culprit was dead, and as far as The Chantry School was concerned, this was to be the end of it.

Only Ebony and Sylvia knew the truth, that the pathetic Wittering was simply the scapegoat of a larger conspiracy; but that shared knowledge would not save their marriage. They left the school and returned to London, where Ebony's heavy drinking (and the resentment of Sylvia that flourished under its influence) soon drove her away.

Thus abandoned, there was nothing to prevent him sinking deeper into sodden self-loathing, tormented by the knowledge of the evil he had failed to stop. He would lie writhing in his bed at night, the hairshirt of his insomnia untouched by the drink. Their faces floated up at him out of the dark. *Aggeridge, Bungabine, Cloistermouth.* He could recite the entire register by heart. Those daemonic names, branded into the meat of his brain.

Desperate for some confirmation of his fantasies, he tracked down the alumnus John Morlar, posing as a fan of his writing. The writer agreed to see him, provided he brought a bottle of good brandy along. *I'll bring two,* said Ebony.

When the writer answered the door, his glacial eyes froze Ebony like a gorgon's. Receiving the proffered gift of brandy, the writer poured them both a glass, and cut immediately through Ebony's evasions.

You're not a fan of my work. What do you want, Mr Ebony?

Ebony shifted uncomfortably. *I wanted to talk to you about Chantry.*

Ah, that shabby little ant's nest. You don't strike me as a product of the public school system, Mr Ebony.

If only Morlar would stop looking at him, he might be able to relax. *I'm not. I taught there for a short while.*

The other man drained his glass and immediately poured himself another, not extending the same courtesy to Ebony. *You don't sound impressed. Don't you believe that our public schools put the Great in Britain?* His voice dripped with venomous contempt.

I wanted to get your impression of the place.

Morlar looked thoughtful. *There's nothing wrong with it a couple of well-placed bombs wouldn't fix.*

Ebony gazed at him eagerly. Perhaps he'd finally found the approbation he'd been seeking. *Then you know? The pupils there ... well, there's no other word for it, they're monsters. They killed a teacher, and a pupil. Probably two.* He thought of the eternally-absent Zigo.

Is that all? said Morlar. He suddenly sounded disappointed. *Didn't you ever want to murder your teacher?*

Not literally, no! The brandy burned like acid in Ebony's gut.

Morlar strode to the window, as though he were about to address a gathered audience. *Well, you'll forgive me if I do speak literally, Mr Ebony. You see, I too, killed a teacher there once. Copley, his name was. No great loss, one less sadistic little bastard in the world.*

You ... ?

Oh yes. I've killed a great many people, Mr Ebony. Almost without thinking about it. You see, that's all I have to do. Think about it. The slightest whim, and snip! The strings are cut.

The man was obviously quite mad.

Morlar turned to face him, his eyes glittering in the dusk. He continued on, relishing his moment. *I discovered my talent at a young age. So I did not require the ministrations of a public education to understand what I was capable of. But if you're asking my opinion of the rest of them, all those plump little parasites lining up to suck on the tired bones of the British Empire, well.*

He paused for effect, enjoying the theatrical flourish. *They're vermin. If I only could, I'd stamp on the heads of every last one of them. Do you understand, Mr Ebony? They should all die.*

Ebony felt that if he were to spend another moment in this flat, breathing in Morlar's insanity, he might just throw himself out of the window. But he had his answer.

Thanking the writer for his time, he hurriedly made his excuses and left. Scurrying away from the building into the encroaching darkness, Ebony finally realised something.

It was *he* who had been the pupil all along.

He bided his time until the school holidays, then commenced his task. He'd bribed Farthingale to gain access to Chantry's records and get him the information he needed. He chanted the familiar litany of surnames to himself.

If you knew a devil's name, you had power over it.

Aggeridge would be first.

He tracked the boy down to his parents' home, a cancerous old Home Counties pile, and watched from a safe distance. He did not have to wait long for his moment.

One morning, when the youth was out fishing in the nearby river, Ebony crept up behind him, pushed his face down into the water and held it there, reciting latin conjugations until Aggeridge's struggles subsided. He'd thrown the corpse into the river and left with the two plump trout the boy had already caught that morning. Enough of this country's resources had already been squandered on Aggeridge and those like him; he would not be responsible for wasting any more.

As he strode up the riverbank, he was already calling out the class register in his head.

Aggeridge! Aggeridge?

Absent, sir!

Bungabine came next.

THE SPIRIT OF DARK AND LONELY WATER

Donald Pleasence in Lonely Water, *1973*
written by Christine Hermon
directed by Jeff Grant

*S*EE THEM, THE CHILDREN PLAYING. THE BOY ON HIS BICYCLE, *the little girl pushing a wheelbarrow. A damp Sunday afternoon, a quiet country house.*

See the children's parents, cosy by the fire, their bellies full of roasted meat, their senses dulled by alcohol. They are content. They are unaware.

Sometimes my work is all too easy.

The little girl moves closer to the pond. She has always felt herself drawn to it. Even before she could walk or speak, her mother would sit with her on the bank and she would gaze out, transfixed by the glitter of the sun on the water's surface, her chubby arms straining for my embrace. She was too young to fear me then, and something of that childish bravado remains. She has been taught not play too close to the water, to tread carefully on the slippery grass. But her mind is sensitive—she knows things, sees things others cannot. Her father is the same, but he buries his talent under rationalism and doubt. His mind is firmly closed, but hers is still an open door, through which my long fingers can reach.

I speak to her through the doll she carries—'Fall in!'

She can feel me beckoning, and draws closer to the pond, finding its lure irresistible, too guileless to feel my cold hand nudging at her shoulder. I have my first taste of her, her reflection teasing across the pond's surface, an amuse bouche of the meal to come. Her coat shines back at her from the water like a warning, red as heart's blood.

Others of my kind require a blood sacrifice, but I do not—their sweet breath is enough for me, the exquisite taste of their last sigh as my icy waters rush in to fill their lungs.

Mindful of her nascent talent, I am careful to remain out of sight, lest I frighten her back into the safety of the house. Instead, I coax her ball to me; wet with rain, it slips from her grasp and bounces down the slope to the pond, shattering the mirrored surface with a splash. She is too young to know of superstition, of bad luck; I will soon teach her.

Staring down at her lost toy, she looks dismayed for an instant, then her face brightens. The ball bobs close to the water's edge; I have been careful to keep it just within her reach. She should call for her brother to help, he is taller, stronger; but she knows he will make fun of her for losing the ball, and like her mother always says, she is a big girl now.

Instead, she gingerly makes her way down the wet grass towards the water. She is careful, oh so careful, just as Daddy told her, and won't he be proud once she tells him she got her ball back all by herself? Her sudden eagerness to impress her father makes her unwary, and as she reaches out for the ball, her short arm straining to claim it, I gently ripple the pond's surface. It is the subtlest of touches—I am a careful, cunning spirit—but enough to send the ball bobbing just out of her reach. She strains further, leaning out on tiptoe—and I have her. Her unsteady foot slips in the slime of the pond's edge, sending her plummeting into the inky water.

Although she cannot yet swim, she might have scrambled back to safety had I not been waiting in readiness. I reach out for her, my fingers animating the thick weeds of the pond, wrapping them tightly around her arms and legs, pulling her down into the cold dark. The pond is only a few feet deep, but to her it feels like fathoms, the deepest ocean, the sun in the sky above winking out as she is dragged down, down, down.

And there, in the black depths, I bring her lips to mine and kiss her, and if it is to be the last kiss she will ever know, it is also surely the sweetest.

Inside, her father suddenly stops in his work. Even the blind obstinacy of his logic cannot shut out her desperate, dying thoughts. In his mind's eye, he sees her pale, angelic face slip slowly under the water's surface. As his son cries out for him, he bursts from the house and stumbles across the wet lawn, feeling dulled by their indulgent Sunday meal; heavy and slow, too slow, too slow.

He lurches into the water, hands clutching desperately for his lost daughter, diving for something more valuable than the most precious pearls. But she has already given herself to me, and all he can do now is scream.

As he breaks the surface, clutching her wet ragdoll body to his, is the veil he has so studiously held in place suddenly ripped from his eyes? Does he glimpse me, even for the most fleeting of moments?

You know, I think he does.

Because, as he rises from the water and his uncomprehending eyes fall upon me, stood quietly on the other side of the pond, his daughter's shade at my side; there, for a single instant, I see him too.

I see the winding path that brought him to this moment, and where it leads. I see him months from now, in that drowned, crumbling city; his wife at his side, both of them trying to forget, to reclaim the love they felt for each other before I took their daughter. I see this man's tragedy—that he refuses to acknowledge the power of premonition he has been granted, and thus cannot recognise me; cannot recognise death when it comes for those he loves, or indeed himself.

I see his unwitting demise, his lifeblood pumping wetly to the cobblestones, and although it will not be I who claims him, Venice is, after all, a city of dark and lonely waters.

And so I will be there with him once more, to bear witness when that cold sharp blade lays open his throat.

ANNA ROBINSON

Susan Hampshire in Neither the Sea Nor the Sand, *1972*
written by Gordon Honeycombe, based on his novel
directed by Fred Burnley

A NNA HAD ALWAYS LOVED THE OCEAN. SHE WAS AN INTROSPECTIVE, melancholy child, and would stare at the rolling waves for hours, imagining herself being carried away by them, floating for days and days, feeding on scraps brought to her by friendly gulls. Her younger sister Laura was terrified of the water, but Anna knew the sea meant her no harm; like any loved one, it had black moods and could be momentarily angry or vicious, but she always felt safe and at peace in its embrace.

She never entirely outgrew this dreamy side to her nature. While Laura grew into a practical young woman and soon made a solid marriage with an architect, John Baxter, Anna seemed content to drift; when one day she woke up and found herself married to David, it was as though she had suddenly found herself shipwrecked on the shore of a desert island, marooned with no means of escape. While Laura had two happy children,

Anna remained childless, despite her husband's protestations that motherhood would be good for her.

David had even managed to isolate her from her beloved ocean; they lived in a small Dorset town, hemmed in on all sides by fields and hedgerows, the coastline just out of sight. How Anna longed for a huge wave to sweep in and drown the dull brown landscape that surrounded her, burying it fathoms deep and carrying her far away. But all she could do was retreat into the aquatic calm of her study; she had painted it in marine hues, and would sit there listening to a tape recording of the sea while she worked.

Eventually the gulf between her and David grew too vast. He was a barely glimpsed presence to her, a distant figure waving forlornly from the shore. She had poured out her troubles to Laura, who had told Anna to come and stay with them while she decided what to do next.

Then tragedy struck; the Baxters' daughter Christine drowned in an accident in the pond behind their house. Her sister suffered a breakdown in the aftermath and now John had taken her away to Venice to recover while he worked on restoring a Byzantine church there.

Lost and confused, Anna fled to Jersey. She needed the isolation an island would bring, the whispering counsel of the sea. It was there that she met Hugh Dabernon.

Walking along a lonely causeway one day, she spotted a nearby lighthouse. Approaching it for a closer look, she'd fallen into conversation with the young man responsible for its upkeep. She'd found him darkly attractive, but it was more than that; Hugh had a intensely poetic streak to him which might have seemed affected or pretentious to others, but made Anna feel as though she had suddenly stepped away from the eyepiece of a telescope. Life had previously seemed compressed, monocular; but now the full scale and wonder of the world was revealed to her.

By the end of their first day together, she had already decided she was falling in love with him. But it was ridiculous, surely—she had a whole other life (such as it was), and besides, she could not expect this man she barely knew to simply welcome her into his home, his world. Hugh was still a mystery to her; she sensed a deep longing inside him, but it was something he either could not or would not put into words.

For the rest of her holiday, they were inseparable. Finally, she broke down and asked him if he wanted her to stay. *That must be your decision,* he said quietly.

Hers! Anna, who until this day had drifted through life like a piece of flotsam on the tide. It was no use; she would have to go back to David and try again.

However, when the time came for her to board her ferry and say goodbye to Hugh, a dam burst inside her. Watching him walk away, everything seemed clear for the first time in her life. She ran back to him. He'd said nothing, just gently taken her hand. It was enough.

Hugh had taken her back to his home, a house he shared with his older brother George. The other man was a religious prude, very likely a repressed homosexual, she'd decided. He'd practically wrinkled his nose in disgust at finding a woman in his home. That night she and Hugh had made love for the first time; she'd suspected Hugh enjoyed tormenting his brother with the sounds of their passion.

The next day she'd phoned David and told him she was leaving him. He was outraged, incredulous; for a man she'd only known for a week? As his anger grew increasingly inarticulate, his voice was engulfed by static on the line; it sounded as though he were being swept away by a raging sea.

She and Hugh had run away to Scotland. The bleak surroundings seemed only to stoke the fire between them, bringing them huddling closer together over the flames. She'd rung Laura in Venice to tell her the good news. Her sister too, had seemed transformed, a changed person from the drugged zombie who'd shambled through the wreckage of her daughter's death. *I met an old woman, a psychic,* she told Anna. *She told me that Christine is here with us, that she's happy. John doesn't believe it but there's no way this woman could have known what she knew.*

Anna wasn't sure she believed it either, but she did not begrudge Laura her new-found happiness. It seemed a comforting thought; the notion that the dead remained with us after they'd gone, still loving us from beyond.

All such comfort was stricken from her head the next morning when Hugh collapsed on the beach. He'd been chasing her across the rocks one instant, so joyous and alive and *present*; the next, he was lying limp as kelp on the wet sand, the cold wind already rushing in to fill the rupture left by his absence, the beach around them as blasted and inhospitable as an alien planet.

She'd run for help, but it was too late; the empty vessel of her lover's body lay abandoned on the beach, his spirit carried away by the tides. *You said you'd never leave me!* she screamed.

That evening she'd wandered the deserted beach for hours, a smuggler waiting for a vessel that would never arrive. Crawling into bed, cold and exhausted, she'd imagined Hugh watching over her, much as Laura had claimed Christine was still with her in Venice. For an instant, she almost convinced herself she heard his boots crunching on the gravel outside the cottage, saw his thin shadow slip past the window.

Such was her sudden and overwhelming conviction that he was there that she forced herself to get out of bed and go to the front door. *Hugh is dead*, she insisted to herself. *You saw him die, the doctor pronounced him dead. Don't lose your grip like Laura did.*

She stood by the doorway for a moment, listening to the sound of the wind sighing around the cottage. Then, calmly, unhurriedly, she opened the door, still telling herself there was nothing out there but the night.

Hugh stood in the shadows outside. His sweater was still damp from his fall, the wool encrusted with dried salt and sand. He looked at her, saying nothing.

She did not flinch, nor hesitate.

Come inside, she told him.

As he stepped over the threshold, Anna suddenly remembered—too late—childhood stories about the dangers of inviting the dead into your home. But those were only myths—the reality was that her lover had come back to her: sweet, romantic Hugh. He had not died; it was all a horrible mistake. The doctor that had pronounced him was just an inept old fool. No one could look at Hugh now and imagine he was dead; so what if his flesh were clammy, his tongue mute, his movements stiff and hesitant. He had been through a horrible ordeal, was all. He would recover in time.

The next day she took him back to Jersey, hoping the familiar surroundings would do him good. She was already finding his lack of speech and blank, unflinching stare unnerving. But upon their return, George quickly recognised the truth of the matter. He saw that Hugh was a cold, empty husk; that the imitation of life he offered was as much an illusion as the sound of the ocean roaring from within a sea shell.

George accused Anna of being a witch, of possessing his brother. He insisted on taking Hugh to a priest to have him exorcised. His brother went willingly enough, but on the road to the church he attacked George and forced his van off the road. The vehicle plummeted over the side of a nearby cliff, killing George instantly.

Hugh returned to Anna. Whatever else he was did not matter, he was still her lover. She did not question his murder of George — Hugh, who had been so gentle in life, a killer? *I shall but love thee better after death*, she murmured.

The thought that something darker, something hateful, might have crept into her lover's soul while he'd drifted in that half-light between life and death had not yet occurred to her.

She attempted to return to everyday life; cooking, shopping. The banality of it soothed her after the horrors of recent days. It gave her a focus, enabling her to ignore the fact that Hugh was still little more than a blank-eyed mannequin. She played with him as a small girl might her favourite doll; dressing him, serving him meals he could not eat, imagining his replies to her constant cheery chatter.

It was only when Hugh kissed her that the illusion was finally banished. The feel of his wet, slug-like lips on hers, the taste of his charnel breath, like trapped air rushing out from an exhumed grave. She locked him in a room and fled. How could she have been so stupid? She'd thought they could still share a life together, but Hugh had no life left within him to offer her.

She finally understood the truth. The dead are singleminded; they know only what they lack and pursue it relentlessly.

When she released him from his makeshift prison, she finally saw him as he truly was: a decayed, black-eyed scarecrow, a ghastly, shambling parody of himself. He still wanted her, but now she realised exactly *what* it was he desired; for her to join him in death.

Appalled, she picked up a heavy candlestick and tried to extinguish whatever spark it was that animated him, but it was no use. She had loved him, invited him in, and he would not so easily be returned to the cold outer darkness that had spawned him.

Still, he would not take her unwillingly. Repelled by her assault, Hugh trudged silently from the house, his wordless devotion thwarted. Anna watched him as he shambled slowly along the nearby beach, heading back towards the causeway where they had first met. She knew the sea was calling to him, as it had so often called to her.

She could have simply let him go and gone on with what remained of her life. But, faced with the prospect of an existence without Hugh, something inside her crumbled. She could not envisage being without him. He had tried to come back to her, but it was impossible; he no longer had a place in the living world. Very well, she would have to go to him.

Anna set out in desperate pursuit, the ocean applauding her as she ran. She must not, could not lose him again.

She finally reached the causeway, to find Hugh patiently waiting for her at the water's edge. He gently took her hand, ready to lead her away into his realm. She gazed out at the churning sea, and was suddenly afraid of it, for the first time in her life.

But then she heard Hugh's soft voice in her mind, reassuring her. *It all begins again out there*, he murmured.

Hadn't she always known this moment would come, ever since she was a small girl? Now, she was no longer a child, and there was no reason to remain on dry land any more. She could finally give herself freely to the waves.

The two lovers walked slowly into the sea, and soon vanished from view beneath the incoming tide. As the cold water embraced her, Anna thought, *Let the ocean take our love and whisper stories of it across the world, a thousand messages washed up on a thousand shores.*

LAURA BAXTER

Julie Christie in Don't Look Now, *1973*
written by Allan Scott & Chris Bryant
based on the story by Daphne du Maurier
directed by Nicholas Roeg

LAURA BAXTER STANDS AT THE UPSTAIRS WINDOW AND STARES out at the pond behind the house. Her memories dance across the surface of the water, the driving rain fragmenting them, turning them into a pointillist blur of grief and loss.

The downpour pauses to draw breath for an instant. The swirl of scattered colour on the pond begins to cohere, forming an image of John's face.

And suddenly, she is back in Venice, her husband's lifeless features staring up at her from the canal where his corpse had been left to drift, just another decaying Venetian relic. His jaw hangs slack in silent protest; another gaping mouth has been opened in his soft throat.

Laura opens her own mouth to scream, and now it is months earlier, and she is still screaming, looking on in horror as John pulls the wet dead thing that scant moments before had been their daughter Christine from the depths of the pond. John is screaming too, and their voices rise in a chorus of wordless suffering, an aching lament of their loss and failure.

She closes her eyes, straining to blot out the awful memories, but try as she might, she cannot shut out that ghastly sound, and the shrieking goes on, and on, and on, until she thinks her eardrums might burst.

Then a door opens in her mind, and time has skipped forward again. Now Laura is only hours returned from Venice, where she and John had retreated to try and heal from the loss of Christine. Instead she had lost John too, given him up to the city's dark and lonely waters.

Laura stands in the somber gloom of her empty house, still wearing her coat from the long journey home, and she clasps her hands to her ears, not understanding where the incessant shrieks are coming from. After all, there is no one here left to scream.

Finally, she realises it is simply the insistent cry of the telephone. She considers ignoring the call, shunning the world completely, but what if it's her son's school, what if something has happened to him too, and so she reluctantly answers. The message does not concern her boy, but it is another notification of tragedy nonetheless: her sister Anna has disappeared while on holiday in Jersey; she is thought to have taken her own life by walking into the sea.

Laura hangs up and slumps to the couch. She feels utterly empty, hollowed out; at any moment her body might collapse and crumple like a discarded snakeskin. She has always feared the water; an instinctive, nameless dread she carried within herself like a lurking cancer. And now that tumour has finally blossomed and spread, engulfing not only her but most of her family.

Hot tears form in her eyes, surprising her; she had thought herself incapable of shedding any more. Tasting the salty residue of her own misery on her tongue, she thinks to herself, perhaps it would be for the best if she simply never stopped, just remained here on this couch and slowly drowned in her own sorrow.

And now it is now again, and Laura is standing at the upstairs window, and the only tears in evidence are those falling from the heavens and trickling down the glass. The house around her is cold and dark and she shivers, a sudden chill sinking its tiny teeth into her flesh; what little of it remains, at least. Laura can barely bring herself to eat these days; her skin is stretched taut over the torture rack of her bones. Everything smells of decay to her now; when she tried to cook herself a steak the other night she could barely stand the reek of carrion that flooded her nostrils when she tore open the butcher's paper.

She'd taken the steak and carried it straight to the bin, and even that small task had been unbearable, the clammy dead meat reminding her of the feel of John's flesh as she knelt at the edge of the canal cradling him. She'd collapsed to the kitchen floor and retched uncontrollably; thankfully there was nothing in her stomach but bile. Still, it was sweet as nectar compared to the acrid taste of her own guilt and shame.

She returns to the kitchen now, not in search of food but the simple warmth and comfort of herbal tea. As she fills the kettle, her gaze drifts to the kitchen window. The storm outside has redoubled its assault, its small fists beating furiously on the pane, demanding admittance. Laura squints; she can barely make out the garden beyond through the distorted lens of the rain-streaked glass, but for a moment she thinks she sees several dark figures standing at the edge of the pond, watching her.

(*seeing is believing*)

The kitchen swims in front of her for a moment, and she stumbles backwards towards the kitchen table, her outstretched hand seeking the comforting solidity of its surface.

And then she is falling, falling into the past, collapsing to the marble floor of a Venetian hotel restaurant. She and John had been having lunch, where they'd met the two English sisters, Heather and Wendy. Heather was blind and an alleged psychic; she'd claimed that Christine was still with them, laughing and happy.

Laura had always been practical, level-headed, but when she'd heard Heather's words she'd been hit by a tidal wave of need. She'd desperately yearned to feel that her daughter was at peace, that Christine didn't hate her parents for their negligence and failure to save her.

(*of course it was John that let her play by the pond but*)

Heather's reassurances were an affirmation, a lifeline. Laura had been overcome at first, hence the fainting fit, but afterwards she felt restored; the ground seemed solid beneath her feet for the first time in months.

John was scornful of Heather, had dismissed her as a charlatan, but even he could not deny the immediate change in Laura. John's world was a place of bricks and mortar, of foundations and supporting walls, of geometry and maths and physics; he had no space for the irrational in his worldview. But, for a time at least, he had gratefully accepted his wife's return from the dark realm she had inhabited ever since Christine's death. At last their love seemed replenished; they were *together* again, rather than merely being present in the same space.

(*let him not go let him not go*)

Laura slumps into a wooden chair, the kitchen around her slowly righting itself. She looks at her hand, still flat against the surface of the table, her finger tracing the pattern of the tablecloth as it had once traced the patterns of the hairs on John's naked chest.

They'd made love in Venice for the first time in months, reaffirmed their union between the crisp white sheets of their hotel bed. John had surprised her with the force of his need, his hunger; she'd felt almost as though he was devouring her.

Had part of him sensed that this was to be their last time together? She'd found him again that evening, only to lose him almost immediately thereafter.

(*let him not go there is DANGER*)

There she is, searching for John in the labyrinthine passageways of Venice, desperately calling his name. The ancient city seems to rumble around her, rousing itself, like a vast machine slowly grinding back into life. Perhaps it anticipates the blood sacrifice that is to come. She hears footsteps—running *to* her? Running *away*? She cannot tell. Venice's streets are a maze of whispers and echoes and above all *lies*; forever promising to lead you to safety, only to bring you to another dead end.

She rounds another corner and suddenly it is not a Venice waterway that stretches out in front of her, but the English Channel. She is a child again, warily dodging the eager fingers of the tide that grab at her feet, while her sister Anna frolics happily in the surf. *Come on, silly*, Anna calls encouragingly, but Laura will not. She knows the water is dangerous; worse than that it is *hungry*, its vast depths contain an aching emptiness that can never be filled. Anna scowls back at Laura, her hands stuck impatiently on her hips, her red swimsuit bright against the grey wash of the ocean.

(*red means run*)

Her head aching from the rush of memories, Laura flees the kitchen, her tea forgotten. She stumbles back upstairs to the bathroom, fumbling in the medicine cabinet for her tranquillisers. They'd first been prescribed to her after Christine's death and she used to hate the numb smear they made of her days, but now she welcomes it. There is nothing for her in the present and the past is a festering wound, so narcotic oblivion seems to be all that remains.

She crawls into her son's bed, welcoming the refuge of its small single mattress. Her own bed is a cold, empty desert without John there beside her; she feels as though she may get lost in it, never to return. Within moments she is asleep, even before her medication takes hold.

Instantly, she is back in Venice, riding alone in a gondola, the looming buildings dark around her. She sees three figures watching her from atop a nearby bridge, but cannot discern their faces in the shadows. Laura turns to the gondolier, a small figure dressed in a red coat, and begs them to stop, to let her off. But the gondolier does not look at her, just shakes its head in mute denial. The gondola drifts on, leaving the shadowed city behind, a stygian gulf opening up before it, and then Laura is lost to the darkness.

(*oh Laura*)

She is awoken the next morning by a whispered voice in her ear. It was John, she is sure of it. However, in the depths of her drugged slumber, she could not be certain whether his words were a sigh of longing or an admonition. She forces herself upright and looks around her son's bedroom, as though expecting her husband to be there to greet her.

But she is alone, save for the frozen faces of footballers and rock stars that peer down at her from the walls.

Laura eases her legs out of the bed. As her feet hit the floor, wet leaves crackle under her tread. She looks down, still groggy and confused from the pills. A damp trail of muck and leaves leads in from outside the room, its progress terminating beside the bed.

Suddenly wired with adrenaline, Laura leaps out from beneath the covers. She follows the trail back through the house, down the stairs and along the hallway and into the kitchen. There, on the black and white tiled floor, the muddy marks form themselves into recognisable footprints, tracing a path back to the kitchen door and all the way down to the waiting pond.

She is elated, terrified; the rush of competing sensations is almost too much for her, a tempest erupting inside her skull. There is only one person that might understand.

She fumbles in her handbag to retrieve the number, then hurries to the phone, dials.

A voice answers within seconds: *Hello, dear.*

This is Laura, Laura Baxter from Venice.

I know. I knew even before the phone rang. Heather's voice is calm, matter-of-fact.

Oh, Heather. I'm so sorry to bother you, but you see … well, I had a visitor. I thought I was dreaming it, but I wasn't. John was here, you see. He came to me.

I understand.

And it's not just him. I think Christine is with him, and my sister too. She died as well, you see. She drowned in Jersey while we were away. I lost them all, but now they've come back to me. John, and Anna, and little Christine …

Laura's eyes drift over to the window, searching the empty garden beyond. The only movement she can see outside is the sheets of rain gusting in the wind.

Laura, dear …

What should I do, Heather? What do they want from me?

A small sigh on the other end of the line. *Do you remember I told you that my abilities were as much a curse as a gift?*

Yes. You saw John die, I know you did. And you tried to warn us …

They are a curse inasmuch as while I can sometimes offer comfort, it makes the living greedy, you see. They will not let go, will not let the dead rest. And the dead are attracted to our need, like bees to honey.

Sharp pins begin to prickle at the corners of Laura's eyes. *But I love them, so very much! How can I just let them go?*

64

You must, Laura. For their sake, and yours.

I can't.

The dead are defined by their lack, you see. They will try and warm themselves with the heat of your love for them, but theirs is a cold that can never be warmed. And finally, they will take you with them, down into the darkness.

Laura's vision blurs as the tears come. *Perhaps I should go with them.*

Laura, no!

There is nothing left here for me now.

It is not your time! It is wrong, it is against God. Heather's voice is horrified.

God took my family from me! What do I care what He wants, Heather?

And now, Laura sees something beyond the window.

Three figures, drifting slowly up from the pond. A man and a woman, each holding hands with the little girl stood between them.

As if she can sense their arrival herself, Heather's voice grows desperate, pleading. *Laura, please. Come and stay with us here. We can talk. I can help you.*

I'm sorry, Heather.

Laura hangs up, cutting off the older woman's appeal.

She moves to the window, gazing out at the family she has lost. Behind her, the phone starts to ring, screaming out a warning, but Laura does not heed it. She watches as John slowly beckons to her.

She should go to join them, every bone and sinew in her body crying out for her to throw the door open and run to her loved ones, but something holds her back.

She is still frightened, you see. Still frightened of the water, of its vast crushing emptiness, and of what might lurk in its depths. She knows John and the others have come to her from far below its surface, and that they wish to take her back there with them; down into the freezing dark, the tenebrous deep she has dreaded ever since she was a child.

Perhaps part of her always knew this moment would come, and her childhood fears were simply a inchoate premonition of the terrible choice that awaited her decades later.

Laura Baxter stands by the window, suspended somewhere between hope and madness, and waits for the driving rain to obscure the three figures from view.

PROFESSOR PARKIN

Michael Hordern in Whistle and I'll Come to You, *1968*
written and directed by Jonathan Miller
based on the story by M.R. James

PROFESSOR PARKIN LIVED IN A LAND OF MUMBLES AND VAGUE gestures, forever shrouded in a haze of miscommunication. He viewed the world around him as one might gaze upon a dirty fishtank; the glass smeared and clouded, the denizens within flitting into sight one moment, before dissolving back into the murk the next.

He did not regret this state of affairs in the slightest; the world and the people that populated it (his students included) seemed on the whole to be dreary and tedious in the extreme. He rarely understood what people wanted from him, and in return, they were usually quite unable to decipher the slurry of mumbles and grunts that served as his usual mode of conversation. His antipathy extended to most physical matters, which ranged from necessary but wearying to outright distasteful. He had never attempted to expand or derange his senses; nor had he ever enjoyed the intimate company of a woman (or a man for that matter; Parkins' sexuality was entirely obscure). Instead, he preferred to dwell as much as possible in the intellectual realm, viewing himself as a being of pure thought tethered only to the material plane by the tedious necessity of the flesh and its attendant demands.

If pressed, he would admit to enjoying a brisk walk by the sea (albeit always out of season when the coast was largely deserted). He relished the solitude, the lonely sigh of the waves, the chill virgin wind that tasted as though no other living being had ever breathed it. He had often fantasised of an apocalyptic scenario that left him as the last man on an unspoiled earth, free to wander in peace, blessedly unmolested by the attentions of others.

In the absence of any imminent realisation of this fantasy, Parkins would wait until the swarms of tourists had retreated back into their hives for the year, then, once the weather was sufficiently inclement, book himself a week's holiday along one of England's coastlines. The bleakly beautiful shores of Norfolk were a particular favourite of his, unspoiled as they were by much in the way of human activity.

And so it was that he found himself back in that area of the country in the late autumn of 1968. He'd found himself a comfortable hotel, not extravagant but expensive enough that he could expect an acceptable standard of dining and a reasonable class of guest (if he must be bothered by other people, he would at least prefer a certain level of manners and education).

He'd also heard that there were some remaining Roman archaeological sites in the vicinity. No doubt they would soon be swept away by the implacable forces of coastal erosion, and so he should take the opportunity to study them while he still could.

When he'd enquired to the hotel porter as to whether he could expect to encounter many other people along their particular stretch of coast at that time of year, the old man had looked at him funnily. *Depends on who you want to meet, sir. There's nothing but dead folk up that way.* Apparently there were the remnants of a burial site perched on the very edge of the crumbling cliff face a mile or two away. The old Colonel also staying in the hotel pronounced the place *spooky*, but it all sounded ideal to Parkin. He found the company of the dead entirely preferable to that of the living.

Parkin spent a quite agreeable morning trudging along the beach in search of his destination. The sands were deserted, the wind bracing but not biting. As he dawdled on his way, he silently revelled in the pleasurable melancholy of the English seaside. For an instant, the professor envisaged the beach as it would look drenched in warm golden light, carpeted with lazy sunbathers, and he shuddered inwardly.

Finally, he came upon the burial ground. He glanced up at the adjacent cliff to see a line of gravestones lurching crookedly along its summit, like the dorsal plates of some great dinosaur. A simmering of uncharacteristic excitement in his belly, he scrambled up the crumbling slope to inspect the site. In truth, much of it had already been lost to the elements; still, he spent the next hour or so wandering amongst the stones, inspecting the faint ghosts of their inscriptions and taking a few rubbings where he could.

Parkin guessed he must be significantly more exposed to the coastal climate up here on the clifftop, as a damp chill soon began to cling to his bones, and a constant shiver prickled at his neck. His feeling of contented solitude had also abated; he somehow did not feel entirely alone in the graveyard, despite the fact that there was not another soul as far as his eye could see.

He suddenly remembered the Colonel at breakfast calling it *spooky*, and crossly dismissed the thought, irritated at his own suggestibility. Coming across an interesting-looking gravestone on the verge of falling into the waves, he smothered his feelings of disquiet and busied himself with inspecting it, recognising that he might be the last person who would ever be granted the opportunity.

And then, a prize! Protruding from the eroded grave soil at the edge of the cliff was a thin yellowed object. At first he'd thought it must be a finger bone, pointing accusingly from beyond, but it appeared to be some kind of a whistle, carved from osseous matter and bearing a faint inscription. His discovery was caked in filth, so he pocketed it for later cleaning and study.

Satisfied with his reward and feeling increasingly clammy, Parkin set out for home. Walking back to the hotel, he at least satisfied himself that his feeling of being observed was not just a childish fancy; another walker could be seen in the distance behind him, keeping steady pace with his progress.

Back in his room, Parkin set about carefully cleaning his prize. Upon closer inspection, the inscription proved to be Latin: *Quis est iste qui venit*, which the professor quickly translated as *Who is this who is coming?*

Intrigued, he gave an exploratory blow into the whistle. The sound that resulted was thin and mournful; it put him in mind of a night wind gusting round a cemetery.

As if in reply, the turbulent sea air outside his window began to batter insistently at the glass. Parkin had to fight a sudden urge to fling the window open and welcome the gathering darkness inside.

He slept restlessly that night, a turn of events the professor put down to the cheese soufflé served at dinner. As a result, he was in no mood for the debate at breakfast the next morning. The Colonel—who Parkin was rapidly coming to view as an impressionable old fool—asked him if he believed in ghosts, of all things!

Of course, the man was quite unable to keep up with the philosophical discourse Parkin embarked upon in response. As he set off on another brisk coastal walk after breakfast, the professor mused to himself that normal folk really should leave thinking to the professionals.

The rest of the day passed without incident, but upon retiring for the evening, Parkin endured an even worse night's sleep than the previous one. He was assailed by dreams of being pursued along the beach by a terrible, amorphous apparition; at first glance, the chasing figure seemed to be little more than a collection of rags held aloft by the breeze, but if he gazed upon it too long, the billowing ribbons of cloth seemed to form themselves into unsettling likenesses—a clutching hand, a grimacing face.

In their disturbing tangibility, they were unlike any nightmare Parkin had ever experienced—he could *taste* the salt in the air, *feel* the wet sand sucking at his heavy tread—and indeed, he could not even be sure they *were* dreams. They flooded his mind as soon as he dared close his eyes, and seemed to come at him from *without*—were they received visions of a possible future?—rather than being conjured up from his own unconscious.

Exhausted and out of sorts, he remained within the hotel the next day.

The haunted wail of the wind outside was deterrence enough for Parkin, although the lingering dreamsickness from the previous night played no small part in keeping him away from the beach. The foundations of Parkin's rationality were slowly crumbling away, as though eroded by the same coastal elements he had come here to enjoy.

Certainly his temper was not improved when the maid enquired which of the two beds in his room she should prepare, given that the professor seemed to have occupied both the night before? Suddenly, Parkin began to fear the failing light beyond the hotel windows.

He would never speak of what he witnessed in his bedroom later that night. When the Colonel burst into the professor's room, alerted by his cries of alarm, he insisted he saw nothing save for an impression of furtive movement in a darkened corner. But when he put on the overhead light, the room was entirely empty save for the terrified Parkin.

So shaken was the professor that he insisted on spending the rest of the night in the Colonel's room, huddled in an armchair with a candle burning nearby. To spare his dignity, the hotel owner roused a maid to discreetly change Parkin's soiled sheets and nothing more was said of the matter.

The next day Parkin cut short his holiday and left, although not before he had hurriedly returned to the ancient graveyard and replaced the bone whistle. Standing over the mound, perhaps it was only his imagination, but the soil of it seemed sunken, emptied, as though the earth below had given up its dead. For a moment, he imagined the grave as a comfortable bed, inviting him to crawl inside and sink into its welcoming depths.

His journey back to Cambridge passed without incident; for once in his life, Parkin felt more at ease while other people were present. However, once he was alone and back in his rooms, a dread sensation crept over him. He could not rid himself of the pervasive scent of the sea, even after he changed into clean clothes. And what he had once considered to be the comforting solitude of his rooms now seemed inhospitable, alien. Every half-heard creak and rattle suggested the presence of another, lurking just out of sight, taking stealthy possession of his private space.

We know little of what transpired over the next few days until Parkin traveled to London to consult a medium, Mrs Rosa Fludd. Given this uncharacteristic display of credulity on the professor's part, we can only imagine his scepticism had been rigorously tested to an even greater degree than before. In desperation, he had made some circumspect inquiries and had finally been recommended the old lady as the genuine article.

Perhaps he had imagined some bohemian psychic, living in shabby but stylish comfort, but when he reached the squalid warren of Mrs Fludd's housing estate, he almost turned back. How did the lower classes live like this, Parkin wondered. Only his greater terror of that which pursued him forced his hand.

He was greeted by the woman's niece, a disdainful troglodyte who yelled at him not to track mud on the carpet while she herded him through to Mrs Fludd's room. The old woman herself seemed harmless enough, although she grew immediately uneasy once Parkin entered. *You've brought it with you*, she said. *It wants something. They don't ever let go till they get what they want, you know.*

She sat down with the professor at her table and reached out for his hands, an intimacy Parkin found uncomfortable. She closed her eyes and began to drift into a trance. Before long her breathing grew laboured and heavy, as though she had lost the habit of it.

When her eyes finally opened again, Parkin thought for an instant he could see the sea reflected in them, black and hungry. She stared at him for a moment, her face distorting like an ill-fitting mask. Suddenly she lunged at him, her tongue squirming through her lips as though it were an earthworm. Parkin found himself being wrestled to the floor, Mrs Fludd's face looming up towards his own, her mouth a bottomless well of need, her groin thrusting unspeakably against his. He shrieked in utter horror.

The next thing he knew, the niece was pulling him away from the old woman, screaming at him, *I'll get the fuckin' Old Bill onto you, you sick old pervert!* She was blaming *him*—Parkin, who had never known a moment's desire for a woman, *any* woman, and certainly not this wizened creature lying sobbing on the threadbare carpet in front of him. Struggling to his feet, he pressed a few banknotes into the niece's hand, mumbled an incoherent apology, and fled.

This was the last confirmed sighting of Parkin before his death. When he was found in his bedroom a few days later, his body appeared completely drained of vitality, save for a single aspect (of which more in a moment). His flesh was withered like old fruit, his skin flaking, his eyes clouded and sunken. Given the short period of time elapsed between his visit to London and his body being discovered, the possible reasons for the advanced deterioration of the corpse were a mystery to all.

Qui venit had been crudely scratched into the wooden headboard of Parkin's bed, probably with his own fingernails. Those present at the scene described the frozen expression on the dead man's face as a ghastly mixture of ecstasy and terror, each entirely inseparable from the other. Decorum prevented them from openly discussing the most shocking aspect of his demise, but young men will inevitably gossip about their elders, and so whispered rumours quickly spread throughout the halls of the college.

They concerned the one part of Parkin's anatomy that seemed entirely undiminished by death, and, as the rest of him lay utterly spent, remained proud and tall, the gathered bedsheets bunched around it.

RICHARD

Paddy Considine in Dead Man's Shoes, *2004*
written by Paddy Considine & Shane Meadows,
additional material by Paul Fraser
directed by Shane Meadows

R ICHARD HATED HIS BROTHER.
    Their father had walked out when Anthony was still a toddler. After that, their mother had to work two jobs to make ends meet, so the two boys were often left to fend for themselves. If Richard wanted to go out to play, he had to take his brother along, no arguments. Even though Anthony ruined *everything*. He couldn't ride a bike, couldn't kick a ball, couldn't tell a joke. It wasn't too bad if they played soldiers because they would tie Anthony up and pretend he was a prisoner of war, but even then he would start to cry if separated from Richard for too long. The other kids called Anthony a spastic; Richard knew that he wasn't, not really, and would feel obliged to defend his brother, often getting into fights with the bigger boys. *He's just special, that's all.*
    It was different when they were alone. Then Richard too, would call

him a spaz. When Joey Deacon appeared on *Blue Peter*, Richard would point at the television screen and say *That's you. You're a Joey too.* He would then contort his hands and twist his mouth in grotesque imitation, which always made Anthony laugh. If their mother caught Richard doing it, he'd get walloped around the back of the head, but it never made him stop. They'd lie in their respective beds at night, and Richard would hiss in the darkness: *Spastic. I hope you die in your sleep. I hope you choke on your stupid fat tongue and suffocate.*

But Anthony never did. He kept on growing up, kept on being there, forever at Richard's side; and the older he got, the more of an embarrassment he became.

As Richard entered his teens, he watched as his mates slowly drifted into petty crime and drug abuse. Richard resisted the pressure to do likewise; he was worried what the chemicals might do to his brain, worried he might end up like his brother. *Nothing but a spastic.* And as for crime, forget it. He knew the other kids from the village were all stupid goonies, and if you were stupid, you got caught. If you got caught, you went to prison, and that was even worse than growing up in a shitty village in the shitty Midlands.

Richard wasn't stupid. So he kept his head down, and his nose clean, and the day he turned eighteen he enlisted to join the army. He'd wanted to go sooner, but he needed parental permission, and his mother wouldn't let him. *If you go away, who'll look after Anthony?* So he waited, and hated his brother even more for making him wait. And all the while, there was a beast growing inside him, raging and howling and thirsting for blood and pain.

The day he left, both his mother and Anthony cried, but Richard didn't care. He vowed never to come back to the village, never to see them again. His mother would write to him after he was posted overseas, and enclose notes from Anthony, childish scrawls that hurt Richard's eyes to look at, but Richard never replied. He was glad to get away from them both, and although he'd just missed out on the Gulf War, he soon found himself deployed in a far bloodier conflict, as part of the peacekeeping force sent to the Bosnian War.

For the next decade, he moved from warzone to warzone, from Bosnia to Kosovo to Iraq, losing himself amongst the horrors of battle, gladly forgetting who he was and where he'd come from, welcoming the torpor that gradually enveloped him. He'd finally made some good friends in the army: Jay and Gal, two dead-eyed squaddies whose thirst for violence rivalled his own.

In Basra, driven half-mad by the heat and the monotony, a gang of soldiers stationed at Camp Breadbasket beat and humiliated a group of Iraqi prisoners; Richard and his friends were amongst the group. Freed from the obligations of family, he'd finally been able to take part, to lash out at someone weaker, someone unable to defend themselves. The fucking Iraqis were no better than Anthony, stupid and weak and helpless. All the anger that had built up inside him throughout his childhood came spilling out; the beast he'd nurtured for all those years was at last set free. He felt liberated; *this* was what he'd wanted all along.

Soon afterwards, he received a letter from his mother, the first in months. Anthony had been found dead by his own hand; he'd hanged himself in an abandoned wildlife park outside nearby Riber Castle. His mother knew some of the local lads must have been involved; without Richard there to look after him, they'd been leading Anthony astray, giving him drink and drugs, and anyway, he never would have ventured all the way up to the castle on his own. But the police weren't interested; it was a clearcut suicide, and who was really bothered about the death of the local simpleton anyway?

Richard had desperately wanted to ignore the letter, to tell his mother that he simply couldn't get away for the funeral; didn't she understand that other people's lives depended on him now? But one night soon after he received the message, Anthony came to him. Richard awoke to find his brother sitting on the end of his bed, teeth bared in that permanent idiot grin, so close to a grimace. *I missed you, Richard.* He'd screamed and woken the others in the bunkhouse, but it hadn't been a dream like Jay and Gal said; Anthony was still there, stood quietly in the corner. Couldn't they see him?

He was already under scrutiny after the mistreatment of the prisoners had come to light, the army busily trying to keep a lid on the scandal. The doctors said he was under psychological strain caused by the stress of wartime and the death of his brother. They were idiots, quacks; Richard *knew* Anthony was real because he told him things that only Anthony would know. The names of the lads that had taken him up to the castle, whereabouts they lived, the things they'd done.

He was granted indefinite leave to attend Anthony's funeral and recover. But Richard knew there was no recovering, not from this. He'd tried to flee from his responsibility, but you can't shut out the dead, nor outrun them. Anthony would remain there at his side until he could finally rest; until Richard had made his brother's tormentors pay for his death.

And in doing so, perhaps Richard might somehow atone for his own failure.

He'd hurried away after the funeral, unable to face his mother. He'd fled into the surrounding countryside and lived rough for a time, never speaking to a soul save for Anthony, the ever-present spectre of his guilt. The last thing he saw at night and the first thing he saw when he awoke. But even in death, Anthony was too kind-hearted to judge his brother. He didn't even want Richard to hurt the other lads, not really. He just didn't want to be alone.

Richard fasted, prepared himself. The things he'd seen and done in wartime had forged him, honed his violence, but this was something different, something older: a kind of blood ritual. Richard only dimly understood it, but he could feel something far greater than himself urging him onward. Something ancient, buried deep in the earth and soil, crying out for vengeance. Before, he'd only killed according to the dictates of his commanding officers; now, the very landscape itself guided his hand.

Finally he was ready. He returned to the village, finding it barely changed from the place he'd so gladly left behind all those years before. The people were the same, still drugged and coarse and stupid. Making them pay was almost too easy; even the most violent of them could not stand against a trained, methodical killer. They were helpless as lambs against the ravening animal he carried inside himself, caged behind meat and bone. He donned his army regulation gas mask and became a faceless monster, inhuman and remorseless.

One by one he murdered them all, by knife, by fist, by axe, by gun. By the end, even the devoted Anthony had abandoned him, sickened by his violence.

When Richard came to the last man responsible, a soft and helpless father of two, he already knew that it would not be enough, that it could *never* be enough. He understood that the beast would keep on demanding more and more, and if the army would not take him back, his rage would continue, unchannelled and indiscriminate.

He took the man up to Riber Castle, the site of Anthony's death. There, he carried out an exorcism. He told the truth, for the first and the last time in his life. He told the man how much Anthony disgusted him, that yes, they'd all been right all along, he really *was* a spastic.

And thus freed, he pressed his knife into the man's hands and forced him to thrust the blade into Richard's own belly.

His hands red with Richard's blood, the man fled, weeping. Richard was left to bleed out on the floor of the outbuilding, welcoming the calm he felt settling into his bones, the peace he'd never previously known. By the time the ambulance arrived, he was already dead.

Within a month, he was laid to rest next to his brother, just as he'd instructed. They would never be separated again.

And yet, I am not at all certain his story ended there.

For if you go to the village today and ask about Riber Castle, the local kids all speak fearfully of it as a haunted place. None of them will set foot there after dark. For to do so is to risk the attentions of the revenant they claim haunts the grounds, a terrifying faceless apparition dressed in a gas mask and army fatigues.

And no one who encounters the spectre returns to tell the tale.

Of course, you will find tall stories like this up and down the country. England's counties are a patchwork of ghosts; these myths are part of the air we all breathe.

But still, I wonder whether men like Richard can ever really find peace.

A.J. STOKER

John Bryans in The House That Dripped Blood, *1971*
written by Robert Bloch
directed by Peter Duffell

YOUNG ARCHIE BROWN LEARNED VERY QUICKLY THAT THERE WERE
houses, and then there were Bad Houses. Growing up in the town of
Biddlecombe, on the haunted shores of Cornwall, everyone knew to avoid
Windward House. Ever since Mary Meredith had fallen to her death from
the cliff edge outside the house, the building had acquired a reputation.
Although its owner, old Commander Beech, scoffed at the notion of it
being haunted, he did admit that there had been *disturbances*. And ever
since the last set of tenants had hurriedly moved out, the house had sat
empty, gathering stories to itself like dust.

Archie and his friends would regularly trek out to Windward, hoping
to spot a spectral face at the window, or hear the ghostly sobbing that
some claimed could be heard there after dark. Disappointingly, they never
did.

Nevertheless, Archie could tell it was a Bad House. He had an uncanny feeling about such things. Once, he and a friend plucked up their courage and sneaked inside through an open window. The friend quickly deemed it a letdown; it was simply a big old empty house, no ghosts at all. Why, there weren't even any cobwebs, and everyone knew a haunted house should be festooned with them.

Archie knew better. When he climbed the stairs to the locked room on the first floor, he could *feel* it. The cold heart of the house, beating steadily behind the door, sending out insistent pulses of chill and dread that seeped into the marrow of his bones.

When the brother and sister from London bought Windward House, the residents of Biddlecombe could talk of little else. Despite selling at a knockdown price, Commander Beech was considered to have conducted a canny bit of business. It was generally agreed that in a matter of months, possibly even weeks, the Londoners would abandon the property, and matters would return to their rightful order, with Windward House being left to slowly succumb to the elements.

Much to Archie's interest, things didn't quite turn out that way. The Londoners were apparently made of sterner stuff—much to the disappointment of some of the more insular locals, who were given to muttered disparagements about soft city types. Long-standing family mysteries were solved and unquiet ghosts laid to rest. Archie came to the conclusion that perhaps even Bad Houses simply needed the right owner, and wondered whether there might not be a profitable career in trying to find them.

When he came of age and left Biddlecombe, he changed his surname to Stoker, a theatrical flourish he believed might appeal to the morbidly artistic types he expected to be his natural clientele. After all, while talk of unnatural deaths and hauntings in a property quickly discouraged your average punter, writers and artistes loved it, treated it as a delightful eccentricity that would only serve to inspire them and bolster their public image.

(Of course, many of them would learn to their cost that such things were not to be taken lightly, but so what? If the property subsequently needed to be resold, then Archie would be only too happy to continue the search for a more suitable owner.)

Moving to the Greater London area, he set up shop as a property agent, and began scouring the newspapers for any unfortunate incidents that might suggest a suitable prospect. It took time to establish his *bona fides*— homeowners were understandably reticent about discussing such matters, particularly when it came to putting a house on the market—but discreet word of mouth about the rare expertise he offered soon spread, and given that, if offered the choice, most other agents would happily plump for an easy life and steer clear of any problem properties, Archie's business was soon thriving. England was a haunted country, he mused, and it stood to reason that as time went on, more and more houses would fall prey to such 'disturbances'.

One of the first properties he managed was the old house in Shepperton. The building, while not reputed to be haunted exactly, had a reputation for bad luck dating back to its original construction, when random accidents onsite had claimed the limb of one builder and the life of another. Archie inspected the house with interest, and while he agreed that the property was not literally haunted—no cold spots here—he sensed a certain *wrongness*, almost as though the building itself possessed a malign will of its own.

Proving Archie's instincts correct, the first tenant to rent the house was a writer, a hack horror novelist named Charles Hillyer seeking solitude and inspiration. Archie considered himself an honest sort and duly warned the man and his wife of the house's reputation, but as he expected, it only served as a lurid enticement.

Within a matter of weeks, both Charles and his wife were dead, murdered by the woman's lover Richard—or was it Dominick?—who subsequently disappeared without a trace, leaving only a scrawled note atop Hillyer's unfinished manuscript, saying that it was all he could offer by way of a confession.

Of course, none of this could precisely be attributed to the property itself, but Archie knew a Bad House when he saw one. Other tenants followed—the ageing bachelor, the loveless widower, the ham actor—and he attempted to warn them all. But they seemed irresistibly drawn to the house, willing insects lured to a Venus Flytrap, and one by one, they met their respective ends.

When the police inspector turned up at Archie's door, investigating the actor's disappearance, he tried to explain to the official exactly what the house was, but knew deep down it would be fruitless. Soon afterwards the inspector himself vanished, but Archie gave little further thought to the matter. He had tried to tell the man, and besides, he had a growing number of other properties to concern himself with.

Soon afterwards he made a quick sale on a derelict old country cottage — the smarmy PR type looking to renovate the ruin ruthlessly beat the asking price down to a mere fifty pounds, and insisted he was doing Archie a huge favour as he did so — but Archie had already glimpsed the sticklike figures of the woman and her two children through the empty windows of the cottage, unmoving but watchful, their ragged clothes hanging loosely from their shrunken limbs. He knew that there was no prospect of building over the past here, that no amount of luxury renovation could hope to plaster or paper over the cracks in reality that spiderwebbed the site.

The Christmas after the man moved in, he, his wife, and two other friends were found dead in the upstairs room, apparently having perished of starvation.

The tabloids had a field day with the bizarre story, and when a reporter came knocking on the door of A.J. Stoker and Company, looking for a fresh angle, Archie was only too happy to oblige. The publicity wouldn't hurt, not given the peculiar turf he had staked out, and besides, Archie had begun to feel as though he was an instrument of something greater than himself; that there might be some higher moral order to what he was doing. Perhaps, he mused, it was somehow his ordained purpose to introduce certain people to the perfect property, destined for them and them alone.

When it came to selling the house in Ilchester Place, Archie wouldn't set foot in it himself, not given the almost palpable sense of evil he got from simply standing on the pavement outside. He assigned it to one of his younger, cockier employees, far less sensitive than he; and when the lad sold it to the Lofting woman, Archie was seized by an uncharacteristic regret. She was beautiful, obviously fragile, and he felt sure she would fall easy prey to whatever lurked in the house. Still, she had the means to offer an outright cash sale, and this was the business he was in. When Mrs Lofting was found some months later, her throat slashed, seemingly dead by her own hand, he told himself that this was the path she had been on all along, irrespective of his involvement. When the decomposed corpse of her estranged husband was later discovered in the cellar, and Mrs Lofting was subsequently linked to a series of other mysterious deaths, well, that settled the matter for Archie. Perhaps she'd deserved the house after all. Once again, a disturbed soul had been paired with a disturbed house and paid the price; as he saw it, Archie's only responsibility in these transactions was to facilitate them as smoothly as possible.

As England moved into the 1980s, the property market boomed. Always a natural conservative, Archie watched the reshaping—dare he say it, renovation?—of the country with tacit approval. Like many small businessmen of the time, he prospered. His personal finances, along with his waistline, began to swell rapidly. He started to give thought to easing into a comfortable retirement. But when the Cricklewood house came his way, he knew he could not resist.

"SUBURBAN HOUSE OF HORRORS" exclaimed one tabloid headline. "JILL THE RIPPER" was another. Housewife Julia Cotton had seduced and murdered a number of businessmen at the address and concealed their mutilated bodies in the attic, all under the nose of her oblivious husband Larry. And when he had finally discovered her crimes, she'd swiftly killed him too. Shortly afterwards, she herself was slain— police were investigating the whereabouts of Larry's missing brother Frank in relation to her death.

Archie inspected the property and found it benign enough, save for the lingering smell of decomposing flesh and a vaguely hellish atmosphere, which he supposed was only to be expected. But he could sense no lurking presence within its walls, no vestige of malefic intent. It was simply a good old fashioned murder house, one that he felt sure he could find the right buyer for. Horror novels were booming; no doubt some ghoulish hack with more royalties than taste would be tempted by the prospect of converting the bloodstained attic room into an office.

But as it turned out, perhaps Archie had finally found the property he himself deserved. Mere days after he began advertising the house, an unmarked parcel was delivered to his office. Intrigued, he opened it to find a small but ornate puzzlebox, obviously an antique. No one seemed to know who had delivered the parcel, or where it might've come from.

Intrigued, he began to toy with it between business calls, trying to unlock a way inside. A nameless compulsion seized him. He could not explain it, but felt certain that if he could only discover the key, he would, at long last, find himself right where he belonged.

JO GILKES

Jane Wymark in Baby, *1976*
written by Nigel Kneale
directed by John Nelson-Burton

J O HAD NO GREAT DESIRE TO MOVE BACK TO THE COUNTRYSIDE;
she'd been raised there as a child, as had generations of her family
before her. She found it bleak and unwelcoming, its damp verdancy
oppressive. But her husband Peter had insisted; his veterinary work in the
city was slowly choking him with its monotony. He longed to live amongst
people for whom animals were not simply a pampered indulgence, but a
necessity. Besides, the clean air would be good for Jo and their unborn
child.

Jo sat quietly as he patiently explained matters to her. Peter was a
medical man, she should listen to him about these sorts of things. Why,
didn't she understand that the pollution of the city might well have
contributed to her previous miscarriage?

Jo had long since learned not to challenge her husband about important life decisions. He seemed to go through his days in a state of constant near-fury as it was, forever seething over some perceived slight or piece of random bad luck. He had never struck her, but she was certain the repressed potential for violence was there. And she could not let anything threaten this pregnancy. For years she had felt hollow inside, like an empty jar. Her doctor had prescribed pills but they'd only intensified the numbing emptiness. This new life growing within her finally gave Jo the purpose she craved.

Peter had found a position working with an older vet, Pummery. *He's a drunken old Paddy, but an easy-going sort,* he'd said. As it turned out, they'd be living close to the roots of Jo's family tree. *My ancestor lived in the village here, back in the early eighteenth century,* she told Peter. *Grandma used to tell me stories about him. He was a judge, a respected man. Apparently he killed witches.*

Peter had laughed. He was always amused by backward country folk and their superstitions. He put his hand on her swollen belly and kissed her. *There, don't you see? It was meant to be, all of it.*

They'd found an old cottage with plenty of land around it; it needed work but it was going cheap. Jo didn't want to live on a building site, all that noise and dust, but Peter told her to stop waffling. *The work will be finished in plenty of time for the birth, I've found a couple of good local men,* he explained. *And it'll give you something to do all day while I'm working. Besides, think of the little one having all those fields to run around in!*

She should have known better than to argue. Instead, she just needed to concentrate on preparing for the arrival of their child; once the baby was born she would at last have someone who loved her unconditionally, who viewed her as something more than a needy, hysterical distraction.

Things seemed to be going well until the old workman started putting ideas into Jo's head. He told her the lands around the cottage were reputed to be *tainted*: cows could not carry to term there; birds' eggs would be addled in the nest. His co-worker instructed her to pay the old fool no mind, he just liked to exercise his tongue over a cuppa, and most of what came out of his mouth was superstitious stuff and nonsense.

But Jo couldn't shake the idea from her thoughts; after her miscarriage, she'd often wondered whether there was something intrinsically wrong with her. Perhaps her womb was toxic, poisoned. Now she'd discovered that the land her ancestors were raised on was itself blighted. Had her family borne this infection down through generation after generation?

She tried to confide her fears in Peter but he simply sighed in irritation, pointing out that she'd had numerous checkups and the doctors all said their unborn child was fine. He told her to ignore the local yokels and get on with decorating the nursery, lest she end up with a baby and nowhere to bloody put it.

The next day he found the *thing* bricked up in the wall. They were expanding the kitchen, knocking some brickwork down to create an alcove, when Peter uncovered the old jar. It had been sealed up within the structure of the cottage, deliberately entombed. She immediately thought of the Poe stories she'd read as a child; all those women buried alive, their tortured shrieks permeating the walls that imprisoned them. But of course it was just a jar.

She hadn't wanted Peter to open it inside the house, was worried about the germs it might contain, but predictably, he laughed off her concerns. Inside was the *thing*, shrunken and shrivelled and utterly grotesque. Had this dessicated homunculus ever really lived?

Peter examined it with excitement; what on earth could it be? Was it a lamb, a pig, a monkey? She didn't understand how he could bear to touch it. It didn't matter what you called it, she instinctively *knew* what it was: an abomination.

From that moment on, she never felt alone in the cottage. Peter refused her pleas for him to destroy his prize discovery; his fury when she tried to burn it was such that it was as if he'd discovered her in the act of aborting their own child. She began to hear strange noises, guttural croaks and caws that put her in mind of some great carrion bird. Shadowy figures skulked in the periphery of her vision.

Peter put it down to lack of sleep; as Jo's pregnancy had bloomed, so had her attendant insomnia. She was exhausted and frayed, quick to temper. Pummery and his frightful wife took to turning up on their doorstep with bottles of whisky; Jo would sit there in silence as Peter got drunk with them, thinking *is this our future? Whisky and cow shit?*

One night she finally snapped, screamed at them all. She could see them silently making excuses for her, the patronising pity in their eyes. *She's just a wee bit hysterical. Some women aren't cut out for pregnancy.*

She became obsessed with the history of the cottage and the land it was built on. One afternoon she sat down with the old builder and gave him a tot of Peter's whisky to loosen his tongue. He told her of the old stories, of how the bones of a devil had once been unearthed in the fields outside and the evil that had infected the village as a consequence. A witch cult had arisen, led by a beautiful girl called Angel Blake. They'd worshipped Satan himself in the forest that bordered Peter and Jo's property.

The legend was that Jo's ancestor, the Judge, had slain Angel and broken up the cult—but some claimed she'd survived, had crawled back into the dark woods, sustained by the demonic infection that burned in her veins. There she had lurked in the shadows, her body twisted by agony and hate, her beauty warping into rank monstrosity. She'd cursed the Judge and the village, planted seeds of corruption deep in the earth that would flower when the time was right.

Jo felt as though she had been summoned here, to this blighted place, to face the consequences of her ancestor's actions all those centuries before. Did Angel Blake still haunt those woods? And what of the dead creature they'd discovered nestling within their walls?

The old man had grown vague, evasive. It was clear he did not wish to talk of it. *It'd have purpose*, was all he said. *It'd have been suckled.*

Jo was now sure they had to escape, to try and shake off the curse they had brought down upon themselves. She felt marked, singled out for some dire retribution she did not yet understand. For one brief moment it seemed as though Peter would assent—some momentary humiliation at work had soured him on his bucolic fantasy—but Pummery soon talked him round. She was trapped and vunerable, like a rabbit caught in a snare, helpless to protect her unborn child.

One morning she'd even ventured into the woods alone, as though offering herself up freely, trying to preempt whatever doom might befall her and her family. She'd sensed the witch there, lurking just out of sight, its dead, wet scent mingling with the pervasive stink of decayed leaves and fungi that shrouded the woods. Jo knew it was hungry, could feel its craving, and all of a sudden she'd felt overwhelmed, dwarfed by its voracious, insatiable need. She'd turned and run, although she now knew she could not hope to run far enough to avoid the fate that had been ordained for her.

A fusillade of kicks inside her belly awoke her one night. She could not tell whether her baby was signalling alarm, or excitement. As she lay there listening to the sounds of the dormant house, Peter sleeping beside her, she slowly became aware of a stealthy creaking noise downstairs. She considered waking Peter for a moment, but knew it was useless. This was to be her reckoning, and hers alone.

She slowly made her way downstairs, one hand vainly cradling her swollen stomach for protection. She gagged at the charnel stench that arose to meet her. As she turned into the living room, she saw it sitting in the rocking chair — the creature that had once been Angel Blake. Its dead flesh was garbed in muck and mould and filthy rags, its unseeing white eyes stared back at her.

The witch had been summoned here by the call of its familiar, the unspeakable mockery of life that lay suckling at its mistress's putrid teat; and now it would take its due.

Jo screamed, and instantly she felt the thing's cold fingers clutching inside her, squeezing the nascent life from her womb. She collapsed sobbing to the floor, her hand clasped wetly between her legs, hopelessly trying to staunch that which was flooding out of her.

That was how Peter found her some time later, caked in blood and loss, her sorrow ebbing into the tainted ground, already saturated with centuries of misery. He was too preoccupied with his stricken wife to notice the now-vacant rocking chair still gently creaking back and forth in the background.

Jo was rushed to hospital, barely surviving the miscarriage. Afterwards, she did not speak for days, staring blankly into space. No one knew what she was really seeing; that hideous ruined face, the ghastly parody of motherhood that had taunted her as she lay there, barren once more. Peter had rapidly grown impatient with her, his initial concern clouding into angry incomprehension at her mute withdrawal. She was still young, they could try again. She needed to pull herself together. Didn't she understand how lucky she was that he'd come downstairs in time to save her life?

None of that mattered. As Jo lay there, silently healing from her ordeal, she could feel herself changing. She'd been emptied of life once more, but this time things were different. The witch had left her a small blessing in exchange; she could still bring something new into the world. She could feel the bones of her right hand beginning to warp and stretch; the manicured nails thickening and curling into claws; the coarse dark hair sprouting up her wrist and arm. What was growing in her now was not life, but *power*.

She could not wait to return home to show her husband.

JOHN MORLAR

Richard Burton in The Medusa Touch, *1978*
written by John Briley
based on the novel by Peter Van Greenaway
directed by Jack Gold

EXTRACT FROM LITERARY MAGAZINE BANANAS, PROFILE OF NOVELIST JOHN MORLAR, NOVEMBER 1975:

Morlar's fifth novel, Skeleton Keys, *was recently published to critical hostility and indifferent sales.* The Times Literary Supplement *called it 'a paranoid's fantasia, akin to being screamed at by a crank in Speaker's Corner for 400 pages. One can almost make out Mr Morlar's spittle flecking the paper.'*

Morlar himself professes indifference about the novel's reception. 'It's people who can't write, writing for people who can't read. They won't recognise that this bloody country is just leftover scraps from the Empire, bits of fat and gristle curling up on the plate. But when we all end up scraped into the swill, then they'll see I was right.'

NEWS ITEM FROM THE LONDON EVENING STANDARD, 16TH DECEMBER 1975:

CRITIC DIES IN FREAK ACCIDENT

Peregrine Devlin, a staff editor and critic for the Times Literary Supplement, was killed yesterday in a fire at his block of flats in Chelsea. Officials say that he boarded the lift to return to his home, unaware that a blaze had recently broken out on an upper level. The lift subsequently failed, leaving Mr Devlin trapped between floors, where he died from smoke inhalation.

In a bizarre postscript to the incident, it emerged that the notoriously acerbic Mr Devlin had recently been embroiled in a public argument with the author John Morlar. Upon encountering the critic in a London restaurant, Mr Morlar had become enraged at a recent review of his novel Skeleton Keys, *written by Mr Devlin. Onlookers reported that he angrily told the critic, "I hope you burn in your very own private hell…"*

EXTRACTS FROM THE PRIVATE JOURNAL OF JOHN MORLAR:

MORE BLOOD ON MY HANDS, IF INDEED THE PUTRID GREASE THAT OOZED THROUGH DEVLIN'S VEINS CAN BE CALLED BLOOD. I SHOULD NOT PERMIT MYSELF TO GET INVOLVED IN SUCH PETTY VENDETTAS. I DON'T KNOW WHAT THIS POWER WANTS FROM ME, BUT I IMAGINE IT IS NOT THE MEANINGLESS DEATHS OF VERMINOUS LITERARY CRITICS. THE MOMENTARY SATISFACTION THESE PATHETIC ACTS GIVE ME IS FADING EVER MORE QUICKLY. I SUPPOSE THIS IS WHAT AN ADDICTION MUST BE LIKE.

SO BE IT. I AM ADDICTED TO CATASTROPHE.

———

I AWOKE FROM A DREAM THIS MORNING WHERE I STOOD AMONGST THE RUINS OF LONDON. ST PAUL'S CATHEDRAL, BUCKINGHAM PALACE, PARLIAMENT, ALL LAY IN RUBBLE. THE AIR WAS THICK WITH THE SALTY PERFUME OF BURNT FLESH AND THE THAMES RAN RED WITH BLOOD. THIS SHABBY LITTLE COUNTRY HAD FINALLY BEEN PUT OUT OF ITS MISERY AND WAS LYING DEAD; DUMPED IN A PAUPER'S GRAVE, FLIES SETTLING ON ITS VACANT, STARING EYES. I LOOKED AT THE

MISERY AND DEVASTATION AROUND ME AND I KNEW THAT I WAS THE CAUSE.

I WOKE UP LAUGHING.

———

I TRIED TO TELL DR ZONFELD ABOUT MY VISION. I ASKED HER IF THERE WAS A RECOGNISED OPPOSITE TO A MESSIAH COMPLEX, BECAUSE WHATEVER I MAY SUFFER FROM, IT IS MOST ASSUREDLY NOT THAT. JESUS CHRIST NEVER GOT HIS SAINTLY HANDS DIRTY, I SAID. I, ON THE OTHER HAND, AM HERE TO WADE IN THE MUCK AND THE FILTH. I'M UP TO MY NECK IN SHIT AND BLOOD.

JOHN MORLAR—NOTHING BUT A BLOODY BIN MAN, SENT TO DO GOD'S DIRTY WORK.

I THINK SHE WAS OFFENDED. SHE PRIMLY TOLD ME THAT 'MESSIAH COMPLEX' IS NOT A DEFINED CLINICAL DISORDER, AND THAT THE CORRECT TERMINOLOGY FOR MY CONDITION WOULD BE 'GRANDIOSE DELUSIONS'.

MY DELUSIONS, ALAS, ARE NOT GRANDIOSE ONES. THE FACT THAT I COULD BRING THIS PIGSTY WE SO LAUGHABLY CALL 'GREAT' TO ITS KNEES, SIMPLY BY THE POWER OF MY MIND, IS NOT A DERANGED FANTASY, BUT PLAIN, IRREFUTABLE FACT.

ZONFELD REFUSES TO SEE THIS. PERHAPS A DEMONSTRATION IS IN ORDER.

———

I HAVE RECENTLY BEGUN TO SUSPECT THAT I AM BEING FOLLOWED. SLY SHADOWS LURK AT THE EDGES OF MY VISION, BEHIND ME ON THE STREET, OUTSIDE MY HOME AT NIGHT. I KNOW TOO MUCH, YOU SEE.

I UNDERSTAND THAT WHAT PEOPLE CALL 'CORRIDORS OF POWER' ARE NOTHING BUT SEWAGE PIPES, AND THAT THE ESTABLISHMENT MEMBERS SCURRYING THROUGH THEM ARE NO BETTER THAN RATS, DRIPPING WITH THE COUNTRY'S EFFLUENT. THEY BATHE IN IT, CLOAKING THEMSELVES IN ITS RANCID STINK, CALLING THEMSELVES PATRIOTS FOR DOING SO.

I SEE THEM, PLOTTING TO STEAL THE LAND OUT FROM UNDER OUR FEET. THEY WANT IT ALL: THE DIRTY WATER, THE FAILING POWER, THE POLLUTED AIR WE BREATHE. IT'S ALL PROFIT TO THEM. THEY

WANT TO TURN THE WHOLE BLOODY COUNTRY INTO ONE GREAT LICE-RIDDEN SWEATSHOP, AND TO MAKE US PAY FOR THE PRIVILEGE. THEY SING THEIR OWN TWISTED ANTHEM: 'BRITONS NEVER, NEVER, NEVER SHALL BE SLAVES...UNLESS WE BREAK THE BASTARD UNIONS FIRST.'

I SEE ALL THIS, AND MORE. ALL THE DIRTY LITTLE PLOTS AND SECRETS. WHEN I TELL HER THEY ARE WATCHING ME, ZONFELD JOTS SOMETHING PITHY DOWN IN HER NOTEBOOK, NO DOUBT A REFERENCE TO MY INCIPIENT PARANOIA.

WELL, LET THEM COME. I UNDERSTAND MY PURPOSE NOW. I SHALL GRASP THE PILLARS WITH BOTH HANDS, AND BOW MYSELF WITH ALL MY MIGHT. I WILL BRING THE WHOLE BLOODY TEMPLE CRASHING DOWN.

———

I WAS RIGHT.

A MAN CAME TO SEE ME TODAY, PROFESSING HIMSELF A FAN OF MY WORK. HE BROUGHT A COPY OF MY FIRST NOVEL ALONG FOR ME TO SIGN, CLEARLY UNREAD. HE WAS TALL, DARK, WELL-EDUCATED. HE STANK OF GOOD BREEDING AND THE GARRICK. SAID HIS NAME WAS FREMONT.

WHEN I POINTED OUT THAT THE BOOK HAD OBVIOUSLY NEVER BEEN READ, HE CHUCKLED. 'I SAID I WAS A FAN OF YOUR WORK, MR MORLAR. NOT YOUR WRITING, WHICH QUITE FRANKLY I FIND HYPERBOLIC AND OVERWRITTEN. NOT TO MENTION HYSTERICALLY MISGUIDED.'

I'VE HAD WORSE REVIEWS. I CALMLY POURED US BOTH A DRINK AND TOLD HIM: 'WELL THEN, YOU EITHER WORK FOR THE TIMES LITERARY SUPPLEMENT OR THE GOVERNMENT. BUT GIVEN YOUR NOTICEABLE LACK OF BODY ODOUR AND THE FACT THAT BOTH YOUR EYES FACE IN THE SAME DIRECTION, I'M GUESSING THE LATTER.'

HE TURNED TO ADMIRE THE CARAVAGGIO MEDUSA ON MY WALL. 'IT HAS COME TO OUR ATTENTION THAT YOU HAVE A GREAT TALENT, MR MORLAR. A GIFT FOR DISASTER. WE SHOULD LIKE TO PUT THAT TALENT TO GOOD USE.'

I SAID NOTHING. HE TURNED BACK TO LOOK ME IN THE EYE, HOLDING MY GAZE FOR A GOOD FEW SECONDS. IMPRESSIVE. NOT MANY PEOPLE CAN DO THAT.

I EVENTUALLY REPLIED: 'SEEING AS YOU'RE FAMILIAR WITH MY 'HYSTERICALLY MISGUIDED' OEUVRE, YOU MUST OF COURSE REALISE I'M ABOUT AS LIKELY TO REQUEST TO BE SKINNED ALIVE AND LOWERED INTO A VAT OF SALT AS I AM TO AGREE TO THAT.'

HE DRAINED HIS GLASS. 'EVERYONE HAS A PRICE, MR MORLAR. I AM QUITE WILLING TO DISCUSS YOURS. I UNDERSTAND THAT YOU HAVE NO GREAT LOVE FOR YOUR COUNTRY, BUT REALLY, OLD CHAP, LOOK AT YOUR ALTERNATIVES. WOULD YOU RATHER SUCKLE ON THE COLD, WITHERED TEAT OF MOTHER RUSSIA? OR PERHAPS YOU'D PREFER TO LAP UP UNCLE SAM'S CONGEALED BURGER GREASE?'

I MOVED TO THE FRONT DOOR AND OPENED IT FOR HIM. 'AS FAR AS I'M CONCERNED, JOHN BULL CAN CRAWL INTO THE SAME ROTTEN CESSPIT AS MOTHER RUSSIA AND UNCLE SAM AND YOU CAN ALL GLEEFULLY BUGGER EACH OTHER SENSELESS FROM NOW UNTIL ARMAGEDDON. AND THAT'S MY LAST WORD ON THE MATTER, HYSTERICAL OR NOT.'

HIS SMILE LOOKED LIKE SOMEONE HAD SLASHED IT INTO HIS FACE. STEPPING OUT INTO THE HALLWAY, HE LOOKED BACK AT ME. 'UNDERSTAND THIS, MR MORLAR. WE ARE WATCHING YOU. YOUR LITTLE FEUDS ARE ONE THING. NO ONE WILL MISS YET ANOTHER POMPOUS CRITIC OR ADULTEROUS SOCIALITE. THERE WILL ALWAYS BE A DOZEN MORE TO TAKE THEIR PLACE. BUT IF WE EVER COME TO CONSIDER YOU A THREAT...'

'I COULD KILL YOU RIGHT NOW', I SAID.

HE TIPPED HIS HAT. 'DO CONSIDER MY OFFER.'

LET THEM COME. I CAN FEEL THE POWER BUILDING WITHIN ME NOW. IT WILL NO LONGER BE DENIED.

IT IS TIME TO SHOW THEM ALL.

NEWS ITEM FROM THE DAILY EXPRESS, 28TH SEPTEMBER 1977:

JET CRASH HORROR KILLS HUNDREDS

A Boeing 747 on its final descent into Heathrow Airport crashed into a London high-rise apartment block yesterday, killing everyone onboard. The final passenger tally is not yet known, but is thought to number over 300. No details are yet available as to what may have caused the accident.

The 40-storey apartment building itself was largely destroyed in the crash. Rescue efforts are underway to search the rubble for any survivors, although so far, none have been found. Approximately 500 people are estimated to have lived in the block, an experimental self-contained prototype designed by architect Anthony Royal, who lived in its penthouse. The building recently made headlines when . . .

Extract from the private journal of John Morlar:

ZONFELD CAME TO SEE ME LAST NIGHT. I COULD SENSE HER TEETERING ON THE EDGE OF BELIEF, THAT HORRIFYING ABYSS WHEREIN EVERYTHING SHE KNEW, EVERYTHING SHE BELIEVED, WOULD BE RIPPED AWAY FROM BENEATH HER, LEAVING HER PLUMMETING AND HELPLESS.

I DECIDED TO GIVE HER A GENTLE PUSH.

CROSSING TO THE WINDOW, I NOTICED THE PASSENGER JET FLYING IN THE DISTANCE. I HAD NEVER ATTEMPTED ANYTHING ON THIS SCALE BEFORE, BUT IT PROVED SURPRISINGLY SIMPLE. THERE WAS THE BRIEFEST MOMENT OF PAIN—A HOT NEEDLE PIERCING THE VERY CORE OF MY BRAIN—AND THEN, EUPHORIA. AS WE WATCHED THE BOEING PLUNGE INTO THE HIGH-RISE AND EXPLODE IN A MIASMA OF BURNING JET FUEL, MY BODY FELT TRULY ALIVE, RELEASED FROM THE GRUELLING MUNDANITY OF EVERYDAY EXISTENCE THAT KEEPS ME ANCHORED TO THE EARTH. I FELT AS THOUGH I MIGHT BEGIN TO FLY, ASCEND INTO THE HEAVENS TO GAZE DOWN ON ALL THE HELPLESS INSECTS SWARMING BELOW.

SUCH IS THE NATURE OF MY ADDICTION.

AND ZONFELD? HER ICY PROFESSIONAL POISE WAS SHATTERED, HER DOUBTS RIPPED AWAY, LEAVING ONLY TERROR. SHE FINALLY SAW ME FOR WHAT I WAS. I WAS NO LONGER A PATIENT, A HELPLESSLY-DELUDED WEAKLING IN DIRE NEED OF HER LOFTY MINISTRATIONS, BUT A MONSTER. SHE COULD SMELL THE BLOOD ON ME, ALL THOSE DEATHS I WEAR LIKE A GRUBBY SHROUD.

I GAZED INTO HER EYES AND I KNEW, IN THAT MOMENT, HER

PROFESSIONAL OATHS MEANT NOTHING. SHE WOULD SEE ME DEAD IF SHE
COULD, EXTERMINATED, EVERY ABOMINABLE SHRED OF ME STAMPED OUT
UNTIL IT WAS DUST.

I TOLD HER THAT THE ACHILLES 6 SPACE MISSION WOULD BE NEXT.
I TOLD HER THAT THE AWED ONLOOKERS WOULD CHOKE ON THE ASHES
OF THE ASTRONAUTS AS THEY RAINED FROM THE HEAVENS.

I WONDER, WILL SHE TRY AND STOP ME? CAN SHE SUMMON THE
STRENGTH?

DO I WANT HER TO?

News item from the *London Evening Standard*, November 5th 1977:

WRITER ATTACKED IN MYSTERY ASSAULT

*The novelist John Morlar was assaulted in his London home yesterday by an
unknown assailant. According to reports, he was discovered by a neighbour
in the early hours of the evening, badly beaten and unbreathing, although
he later revived. He is currently on a life support machine, in critical
condition. Police are appealing for anyone with relevant information on the
incident to come forward.*

*Morlar had become notorious in London literary circles for his vicious
attacks on what he saw as establishment hypocrisy, and his ongoing feuds
with a number of critics, most notably...*

Excerpted from transcript of interview between intelligence operative
codename Fremont and John Morlar, 14th April 1978:

FREMONT: GOOD MORNING, MR MORLAR. HOW ARE YOU FEELING TODAY?

MORLAR: (unintelligible)

FREMONT: SOME WATER, PERHAPS.

(slurping noises)

FREMONT: IS THAT BETTER?

MORLAR: WHERE AM I?

FREMONT: IN A PRIVATE CLINIC. YOU'RE GETTING THE VERY BEST
OF CARE. ABSOLUTELY TOP NOTCH. DO YOU REMEMBER ANYTHING?

MORLAR: ZONFELD.

FREMONT: AH YES. WELL, SHE'S DEAD. OVERDOSE. SHE MADE QUITE A MESS OF YOU THOUGH, DIDN'T SHE? ANYTHING ELSE?

MORLAR: (unintelligible)

FREMONT: DO SPEAK UP.

MORLAR: WINDSCALE.

FREMONT: AHA. NOW WE'RE GETTING TO THE POINT. WINDSCALE, YES. QUITE IMPRESSIVE WORK, COMING FROM A HALF-DEAD VEGETABLE ROTTING IN AN HOSPITAL BED. LUCKILY THAT FROGGY DETECTIVE WAS ABLE TO WARN US IN TIME TO PREVENT TOO MUCH DAMAGE. ONLY ABOUT A DOZEN DEAD, I BELIEVE. OF COURSE, WE'LL HAVE TO SEE HOW MANY OF THE WIDER POPULATION WERE CONTAMINATED. TIME WILL TELL. STILL, WELL DONE YOU.

TELL ME, DO YOU REMEMBER THAT LITTLE CHAT WE HAD?

MORLAR: YES.

FREMONT: EXCELLENT. AND DID YOU BY ANY CHANCE RECONSIDER?

(NO REPLY)

FREMONT: I SEE. STUBBORN, AREN'T YOU? WELL, THE THING IS, MR MORLAR—MAY I CALL YOU JOHN? I FEEL LIKE WE'RE GETTING TO KNOW EACH OTHER SO MUCH BETTER NOW.

THE THING IS, JOHN, IS THAT WE WERE PUT IN A POSITION WHERE WE HAD TO RECONSIDER FOR YOU. I MEAN, WE CAN HARDLY HAVE YOU GOING AROUND BLOWING UP OUR NUCLEAR POWER STATIONS, CAN WE? AND YOU CLEARLY WEREN'T IN ANY FIT STATE TO NEGOTIATE. SO WE WERE FORCED TO TAKE MATTERS INTO OUR OWN HANDS, RATHER.

MORLAR: WHAT DID YOU DO?

FREMONT: IT'S COMPLICATED, BUT LET ME SEE IF I CAN PUT IT IN A NUTSHELL. I USED TO WORK WITH A DOCTOR CALLED BROWNING. QUITE A BRILLIANT MAN. ANYWAY, HE DEVELOPED A PROCESS FOR IMPROVING THE HUMAN BODY. FUSING BLOOD AND TISSUE WITH SYNTHETIC BONES AND MUSCLES. SO MUCH MORE DURABLE, YOU SEE? HE CALLED IT 'COMPOSITING'. THE RESULTS WERE REMARKABLE. IT TOOK A LITTLE WHILE TO PERFECT THE METHODOLOGY—SOME OF THE ORIGINAL SUBJECTS HAD CERTAIN...COMPULSIONS, BUT WE'VE IRONED OUT THE TEETHING PROBLEMS NOW.

SO WE'VE GOT THIS PROCESS...AND THEN HERE <u>YOU</u> ARE, A BRILLIANTLY DESTRUCTIVE MIND IN A RUINED, DYING BODY. IT WAS OBVIOUS, REALLY. WE JUST TOOK YOUR BRAIN AND POPPED IT INTO A NEW BODY. I THINK YOU'LL BE AMAZED AT THE IMPROVEMENT.

MORLAR: BULLSHIT!

FREMONT: SHALL I SHOW YOU? HERE'S A MIRROR, LOOK.

MORLAR: (unintelligible)

FREMONT: I KNOW IT MIGHT TAKE SOME GETTING USED TO. BUT YOU HAVE PLENTY OF TIME. YOUR NEW BODY IS YOUNG AND STRONG. AND AS I SAID, EXTREMELY DURABLE.

MORLAR: I'LL KILL YOU ALL. I'LL SEE YOU DROWN IN YOUR OWN FILTH.

FREMONT: OH, JUST ONE MORE THING. WE WERE AWARE OF YOUR REPUTATION FOR...RECALCITRANCE. AND WE THOUGHT PERHAPS YOUR TEMPER MIGHT NOT BE IMPROVED BY YOUR NEW CIRCUMSTANCES. SO WE TOOK A SMALL PRECAUTION.

(NO REPLY)

FREMONT: THERE IS A TINY EXPLOSIVE CHARGE EMBEDDED AT THE BASE OF YOUR SKULL. SO, ANY MISBEHAVIOUR, ANY MORE NASTY ACCIDENTS...AND BOOM. WE'LL SEE IF THAT MIND OF YOURS CAN SURVIVE BEING SPLATTERED ALL OVER THE DRAPES.

I'M SURE IT WON'T COME TO THAT THOUGH, JOHN. I FEEL LIKE WE'RE GOING TO BE THE VERY BEST OF FRIENDS.

MORLAR: I'D SOONER BE FRIENDS WITH THE SYPHILITIC CORPSE OF ADOLF HITLER.

FREMONT: WE'LL PROVIDE YOU WITH A NEW LIFE, A NEW IDENTITY. YOU CAN GO EVEN BACK TO WRITING IF YOU WISH—OBVIOUSLY JOHN MORLAR IS OFFICIALLY DEAD, BUT LET'S FACE IT, WHO THE HELL READ HIM ANYWAY?

MORLAR: (unintelligible)

FREMONT: AND IN RETURN, ALL WE'LL NEED FROM YOU IS THE OCCASIONAL FAVOUR. NOTHING MUCH, REALLY. WE JUST WANT TO POINT THAT GIFT OF YOURS IN SLIGHTLY MORE...BENEFICIAL DIRECTIONS. JUST IMAGINE THE POSSIBILITIES.

MORLAR: GO TO HELL.

FREMONT: HMM. PERHAPS I WILL. BUT I'M NOT IN ANY GREAT RUSH. HOW ABOUT YOU?

(End transcript)

EXTRACT FROM THE PRIVATE JOURNAL OF JOHN MORLAR:

MORE DREAMS OF DISASTER. SPACECRAFT EXPLODING, GREAT TOWERS FALLING. ARE THEY MEMORIES OF THE PAST, OR CATASTROPHES OF THE FUTURE? AM I RESPONSIBLE..?

OH, THE IRONY, THAT I, JOHN MORLAR, SHOULD END UP LIKE THIS: AN ARTIFICIAL MAN, A SIMULACRUM. A PUPPET OF THE BASTARD ESTABLISHMENT, DANCING TO THEIR LOUSY TUNE. NOTHING BUT A WORTHLESS FAKE.

I MUST BIDE MY TIME. THIS CANNOT BE THE END OF IT. PERHAPS MY MIND <u>COULD</u> EXIST OUTSIDE THIS SYNTHETIC PRISON. THERE MUST BE A WAY.

HE CAME TO SEE ME AGAIN THIS MORNING. FREMONT. HE SAID THAT ONCE I AM FEELING STRONGER, THERE IS A SMALL MATTER HE'D LIKE TO DISCUSS. HE SAID WINDSCALE WAS ONLY A DRY RUN AND HE WAS SURE I COULD DO BETTER NEXT TIME. REALLY MAKE MY MARK ON THE WORLD.

HE SPOKE ONE WORD. RUSSIAN, I THINK.

CHERNOBYL.

EDMUND & DOROTHY YATES

Rupert Davies & Sheila Keith in Frightmare, *1974*
written by David McGillivray
directed by Pete Walker

DOROTHY YATES MAY HAVE BEEN A GIFTED DIVINATOR OF THE future, but her own past was an impenetrable haze of myths and lies. Subsequent to her arrest for the murder of Barry Nichols in 1957, still shocking in its specifics even now, she was committed to an insane asylum and diagnosed as a 'pathological cannibal'. With the benefit of decades of hindsight, we can perhaps make allowances for the less-than-rigorous nature of psychological treatment of the era, but nevertheless, her doctors' assessment that Dorothy's condition had arisen out of the childhood trauma of being forced to eat her favourite pet rabbit for supper, is still, frankly, ludicrous. However, the prognosis was then widely accepted and used as the basis of her treatment, leading to her eventual release in the early 1970s and the ensuing catalogue of atrocities thereafter.

The actual truth of the matter—never revealed to the doctors by

Dorothy or her husband Edmund—is this: 'Dorothy' was discovered by Edmund as a fourteen year old girl late one night in 1934, helplessly wandering the platform of Russell Square tube station. She was dressed only in rags, filthy and stinking, her skin simmering with sores and boils.

Edmund's first instinct upon seeing her was to flee in horror, but something in the pathetic creature's forlorn gaze stopped him. She had no name, no language, could not communicate, but it was obvious she had suffered more than any human being should ever have to suffer.

Still only eighteen himself, Edmund was known for his kindly nature and charitable deeds, and so, in an act of pity, he coaxed the poor girl into coming home with him. Fortunately, he lived alone in a private residence left to him by a beloved aunt, so there was no one present to witness him usher this reeking, pitiable wretch across the threshold of the house. He set about cleaning her up and restoring her to some semblance of health, fully intending to place her in an orphanage once she was recovered.

In the process, however, the nature of their relationship gradually shifted. Edmund began to view her as less of a desperate charity case and more of a pet project; naming her Dorothy after his deceased aunt, he dedicated himself to socialising her, teaching her language and manners. It was a long and difficult task, but he relished it nonetheless.

Edmund had always been a shy man and somewhat uneasy in the presence of others; this was the first extended period he had ever spent in any sort of female company, however unconventional. Dorothy, for her part, seemed to adore him. And in the process of nursing her—*civilising* her, he supposed—he grew to love her. Indeed, such were the strength of his new-found feelings that even when Dorothy's true nature was suddenly revealed to him, he could not find it within himself to turn away.

For, as would be discovered many years later, an abandoned tube station and series of tunnels linked to Russell Square played host to a forgotten tribe—feral scavengers descended from a lost group of miners. The miners had been trapped underground while working to construct the train tunnels in the late nineteenth century and callously left for dead. But they had survived—and thrived, after a fashion: piecing together a makeshift home for themselves in the darkness below, breeding copiously...and resorting to cannibalism to survive, preying on whatever unfortunate souls lingered too long on the empty platforms of Russell Square after dark. While they still clung onto rudimentary notions of society and family, the scavengers had lost their language as the years passed and descended to a level only a little above outright savagery.

Dorothy had been born into the prison of that hideous subterranean world, and had never known anything else until Edmund took her in. As an adolescent female, she had not been expected to seek out prey for food, and so did not properly know her way around the maze of tunnels connecting their lair to Russell Square. She had become lost and disorientated, eventually finding her way to the tender care of Edmund.

But while she may have left that squalid underground warren behind her, she could not as easily abandon the monstrous appetites nurtured there.

Edmund returned home one evening to find Dorothy feasting on the corpse of a small boy she had lured into the house. Appalled almost beyond measure, he knew he should call the authorities then and there, but simply could not bring himself to turn on her. Dorothy trusted him, even loved him, in her way, and she had not the wherewithal to comprehend that she had done anything wrong. Even as he struggled to fight back nausea, he understood that none of this was truly her fault. Although he knew nothing of Dorothy's past, he realised that this was simply how she had been taught to survive. It would be his responsibility to show her another way.

And in the meantime, he would simply have to take steps to cover up any unfortunate ... *incidents* such as this.

However, for all that he did manage to teach her, Edmund never succeeded in ridding Dorothy of her taste for human flesh. It was a bloody compulsion, a ravening instinct buried within her like a vein of ore, so deep it was impossible to extract. So although she came to understand over time that her behaviour was wrong, that it might even mean the end of them, she found herself helplessly in thrall to her hunger. And in turn, Edmund was helplessly in thrall to her.

As a result, they had little option but to keep moving around the country and go on concealing the grisly evidence of Dorothy's feeding as best they could. Dorothy eventually proved to have something of an aptitude for Tarot and fortune-telling, and although Edmund generally scorned such phenomena, he could not deny that his now-wife seemed to sometimes possess an almost-uncanny intuition.

Furthermore, her gift enabled them to join a travelling fair, The Pandemonium Carnival, which earned them a reasonable living and helped provide cover for their activities. This state of affairs continued for many years, and while Edmund often mused that it was not the life he would have chosen for himself, he rationalised that it had all arisen out of a single good deed, and in that sense perhaps his path had somehow been chosen for him.

The first rupture in their arrangement came in the early 1950s when Dorothy attacked and killed a young woman, not realising she was a single mother with an infant daughter, Jackie. Previously, Edmund had always been able to help Dorothy select her victims carefully, ensuring that she preyed only on those lonely souls who would not be easily missed. But now there was a orphaned young girl to deal with.

Edmund still possessed enough moral clarity that he could not countenance Dorothy's overeager suggestion that she could simply save the child for later; instead, they left the carnival, adopted Jackie as their own, and moved back to London to start afresh.

Edmund soon came to dote on the girl, but the same could not be said for Dorothy, who viewed Jackie as an incipient rival. She jealously insisted that she and Edmund have a baby of their own; something he had always avoided, for fear of the day when they would inevitably have to explain their mother's aberrant behaviour to the child.

Nevertheless, he acceded to her wishes, as he so often did with Dorothy. She soon fell pregnant; this was to be the second, fateful, rupture in their marriage.

While pregnant, Dorothy's appetites grew increasingly obsessive and out of control. Much as many expectant mothers had uncontrollable food cravings, Dorothy's hunger for human meat became compulsive beyond measure. It was this uncontrollable hunger that resulted in the random murder of Barry Nichols in 1957, another unplanned killing. This time it led to the discovery of the Yates's activities, and their eventual arrest and committal. Jackie and their newborn daughter Debbie were swiftly taken into care, and the system was left to do its work, such as it was.

The Yates's release some fifteen years later was conducted under a heavy blanket of secrecy, for fear of the tabloid storm that might erupt. They were given new identities, and a rented farmhouse was procured in the countryside outside London, to allow Dorothy peace and isolation for her continued recovery. Edmund found work as a chauffeur, and was permitted to make contact with the now-adult Jackie, who had been granted custody of the teenage Debbie. At this stage, all concerned felt it best that Debbie, a defiantly-unruly adolescent, should have no contact with her mother, and so she was kept in the dark about her parents' release.

The subterfuge deepened when Edmund grew to realise that any notion Dorothy had been cured of her compulsion was a complete and utter fallacy. Terrified that his wife would relapse and be taken away from him for good, he and Jackie conspired to supply her with fresh animal brains, under the pretence they were in fact human.

Sadly for them, Dorothy's gifts were everything she claimed they were, and she was not so easily tricked. Unbeknownst to Edmund or Jackie, she quietly began to advertise her services as a psychic, using the trade she attracted to procure a series of fresh victims, concealing their bodies in the abandoned barn behind the farmhouse.

Perhaps Debbie had also inherited something of her mother's intuition; certainly, she quickly realised that Jackie's late night trips out of the house had nothing to do with her claims of a new boyfriend, and soon discovered Dorothy's existence for herself. This revelation, combined with Dorothy's insane appetites, swiftly destroyed the semblance of family normality Edmund and Jackie were trying desperately to maintain.

It became apparent that Dorothy had not simply passed on her intuitive gifts to her daughter; she had also bequeathed Debbie the same inhuman cravings that so compelled her. Dorothy and her long-lost daughter became partners in monstrosity, and as a result, upon his horrified discovery of the barnful of their half-devoured victims, Edmund was forced to choose between his adopted daughter Jackie and the rest of his family. Aghast, he turned away, unable to watch, as Dorothy and Debbie descended murderously upon her.

After the murders of Jackie and the rest, it was clearly no longer safe for them to remain on the farm. Edmund hurriedly began to search for a refuge, and decided he had found one in the form of architect Anthony Royal's new high-rise tower block development. Surely there, within a building designed to offer the soothing blandishments of an utterly generic existence, they would find a semblance of peace and anonymity. Securing a flat on one of the lower levels, Edmund moved his family into the high-rise without delay.

For someone so eager to try and avoid conflict in his own life, Edmund Yates had a weirdly ineffable talent for stumbling into the most bizarre of situations; the sort of freakish horrorshows that would provide lurid fodder for newspapers and books for decades to come. Just as the early 1970s would bring forth the literal unearthing of the details of Dorothy's early life, with the discovery of the last-remaining member of her cannibal tribe; so too would the social experiment of their new home collapse in the latter years of that same decade, rapidly spiralling down into dysfunction to become a concrete snakepit of madness, violence and death.

Many books have been written on the the miniature apocalypse that erupted within Royal's showcase building; learned hypotheses as to the causes of the bewildering entropic slide from order into chaos that claimed the lives of the architect and so many others. Still, given the catastrophic accident that ultimately destroyed the high-rise and scorched the earth of its inhabitants, it is hardly surprising that so few specific details of the lives of its tenants—including those concerning the final months of the Yates family—have ever come to light.

It is safe to say that the initial problems in the high-rise had nothing whatsoever to with Dorothy and her relations; the erratic state of the building's infrastructure and the seething class resentments between the upper and lower floors have already been comprehensively identified as the genesis of what was to come.

However, once the conflicts within the building flared and the precarious social network within swiftly began to buckle under the strain, it is clear that the Yates family took advantage of the confusion. The rumours of cannibalism reported by the few survivors who escaped the tower block can almost certainly be traced back to their door.

As the last remnants of civilisation within the building collapsed, and more and more of the tenants fled or simply disappeared, Dorothy and

Debbie would have found it absurdly easy to indulge their appetites without fear of reprisal or detection. At last, they had found the sanctuary they'd always sought.

Perhaps even Edmund—once food supplies in the high-rise dwindled—cast off the shackles of propriety he had always struggled so assiduously to maintain and joined them in their feasting. And in Debbie, they had a whole new means of attracting prey: a pert, fresh-faced young spider, lurking alluringly at the centre of their web.

Robert Laing, a handsome young doctor living in the building's mid-levels, had already established himself as the sexual locus of the high-rise, desired by women of the upper and lower floors alike. Although he had successfully navigated the transitory chaos of the tower block's descent into anarchy, his cool amorality granting him a certain Darwinian edge, his affectless promiscuity would soon prove to be his undoing. Noticing the flirtatious teenager from the lower levels, Laing instinctively moved to seduce her, beginning a short but torrid affair with Debbie, who managed to surprise even him with the force of her lust.

Indulging her girlish request to come and meet her parents for supper, Laing ventured down some twenty or so floors to visit the Yates's apartment, wherein, after a small pre-dinner sherry, he was quickly introduced to Dorothy's favoured killing implement: an electric drill.

As a doctor well-versed in the dissection of the skull and brain, the irony in the manner of his death would doubtless not have been lost on Laing, had he been in any position to appreciate it. As it was, he was the only inhabitant of the tower block that evening to die of causes unrelated to the conflagration that was about to engulf them all.

For, somewhere on the other side of London, the crazed psychic John Morlar was about to attempt the most destructive display of his malign power to date: sending a Boeing 747 passenger jet plunging into the unsuspecting building looming under its flight path: Anthony Royal's high-rise. His only thought was the extermination of hundreds of innocent people—would he have been at all disappointed to learn that some of the lives he claimed that night were not by any means innocent?

I wonder; as the assembled Yates family closed like a fist around the stricken Laing, sprawled out and bleeding on their dinner table—did they even hear the approach of the aircraft engines over the whine of Dorothy's whirring drill? Was the thick, coppery scent of his blood replaced for the briefest of instants by the stench of burning jet fuel?

Or did they simply die as they had always lived; a pack of starving wolves, seized by a overriding predatory hunger and all but oblivious to the larger world that would seek to destroy them?

GILDEROY

Toby Jones in Berberian Sound Studio, 2012
written & directed by Peter Strickland

L ITTLE IS KNOWN OF GILDEROY—THERE ARE THOSE WHO INSIST
that he never really existed at all—and it is true that perhaps only in the
internet age could such a marginal figure have risen to any sort of
prominence. Only in an environment that thrives on conspiracy gossip,
memes, and creepypastas could an obscure sound engineer who toiled in
the less salubrious areas of the European film industry have been elevated
to the level of cult icon. Decades after he left the business, Gilderoy's
reputation for audio artistry is now only rivalled by the late Alan Splet.

The available facts are these: after having served his apprenticeship at
the BBC Radiophonic Workshop (working alongside Anthony Fielding
and Delia Derbyshire and contributing sound effects to programmes such
as *Doctor Who*), in the early 1970s Gilderoy quit the BBC and struck out
on his own, building an experimental sound studio in his own garden shed.

Some say he chafed under the deadening hand of BBC bureaucracy, which refused to credit him for his increasingly innovative work, but it was also rumoured that he had unrequited romantic feelings for Derbyshire and the two found it increasingly difficult to work alongside each other.

He found employment for low-budget horror outfits such as Amicus and Tigon, but disappointed by the threadbare quality of the productions, preferred to continue to work without credit. Milton Subotsky always spoke highly of Gilderoy's talent, but when United Artists finally agreed to back the producer's dream sword and sorcery project *Thongor in the Valley of Demons*, he and Gilderoy clashed over some of the more experimental sound techniques the engineer planned to employ to evoke Lin Carter's fantasy world. Gilderoy quit in disgust midway through production; the film itself was a box-office disaster, and was quickly buried, thus setting a pattern that would become increasingly prevalent in Gilderoy's subsequent career.

In need of work, he fled to Italy to work on *The Equestrian Vortex*, which would prove to be one of his most notorious credits. Designed to cash in on the international success of Dario Argento's *Suspiria*, the film was an exploitative stew of no-holds-barred sex, violence and occultism. Gilderoy apparently found the working practices of the Italian industry lax and chaotic, and the director Giancarlo Santini an autocratic tyrant (after the furore that greeted the film's release, the elusive Santini never directed again, and it was rumoured the filmmaker was actually one of Aristide Massaccesi's—aka Joe D'Amato—many pseudonyms).

Nevertheless, the bizarre aspects of the film and the freewheeling nature of the production allowed Gilderoy a creative freedom he had never previously enjoyed, and he responded with a disturbingly visceral soundscape; one that augmented the already-shocking visuals Santini had supplied for the film tenfold.

Upon the film's release, it was met with cries of outrage and disgust from the press, and the film's producer Francesco Coraggio was rapidly hauled into court on obscenity charges. All prints and negatives were ordered to be destroyed, and for years the film was considered to be lost. Rumours of circulating bootleg copies have nevertheless persisted throughout the decades since, and lately there has been talk of a full HD restoration in the works — if this comes to pass, it remains to be seen what effect the film's more notorious qualities will have on today's viewers.

One of the few people who saw *The Equestrian Vortex* before it was yanked from release was Dario Argento himself. Struck by Gilderoy's work, he attempted to enlist the engineer to work on his *Suspiria* follow-up, *Inferno*. Exhausted by his experiences in the Italian industry, Gilderoy refused and returned home to England. Argento did not forget him however, and a few years later, when he began production on *Lachrymae*, the final part of his Three Mothers trilogy, he found Gilderoy in a more receptive mood. The engineer returned to Italy, and by all accounts, found himself entirely simpatico with the obsessive, mercurial Argento. Certainly, the manner in which his eerie sound design intertwines with the howlingly abrasive score provided by Goblin (to the extent where one is never quite sure where the music ends and the sound design begins) is one of the highlights of the film.

But yet again, disaster struck. The always-highly strung Argento had a nervous breakdown due to the stresses of production, culminating in his on-set attempt to strangle his then-wife, Daria Nicolodi, after accusing her of being a real-life witch. The director subsequently took a leave of absence from the production in order to recover, and filming was completed by his protege Michele Soavi.

The film never quite recovered from the bad publicity, and its more experimental aspects (Argento grew less and less interested in conventional narrative as the Three Mothers trilogy progressed, and *Lachrymae*, at times, feels like a fever dream captured on celluloid), spelled doom at the box-office. Nevertheless, the perfectionist Gilderoy proclaimed himself happy with his work on the film, and in later years it slowly came to be reassessed. *Lachrymae* is now viewed as the final flowering of Argento's wayward talent, before his precipitous artistic decline set in shortly afterwards.

Perhaps tiring of the continual melodramas of the Italian film industry, Gilderoy rejected the other overtures of work that were coming in and left the country. It was now that the final and perhaps most mysterious phase of his career began.

He next accepted an offer to work on the experimental Polish project 47; little is known of the film, as the shoot had to be abandoned after both leads were mysteriously murdered, an unsolved tragedy which quickly led to stories of the production being cursed.

(This legend was only bolstered when, some years later, the director Kingsley Stewart defied the alleged curse and quixotically mounted a remake of 47 entitled *On High in Blue Tomorrows*. The lead actress Nikki Grace subsequently had a breakdown during production, and claimed, amongst other things, that she was being visited by giant rabbits. However, filming *was* eventually completed, and in fact—perhaps in an attempt to court further publicity—Stewart attempted to trace Gilderoy to work on the film's sound design, albeit without success.)

Gilderoy quickly moved onto *Sword of Death*, an unpromising-sounding European co-production concerning four teenagers disturbing the tomb of Nostradamus; the usual mishmash of black magic and graphic slaughter ensues. However, this project proved to be both (what is assumed to be) Gilderoy's final credit, and also the capstone of his legend.

The production passed without undue incident; a low budget quickie, unhampered by any notions of artistry or pretence at being anything other than what it was—pure exploitation. However, when the film was booked in for a sneak preview at Berlin's Metropole cinema, something went horribly wrong. Official reports attributed it to an outbreak of mass hysteria, doubtless caused by the psychologically damaging effects of watching such horrific and violent material.

However, the few that survived the carnage spoke privately of a plague that swept the cinema, some kind of virulent infection which caused the afflicted to transform into creatures—*demons*, some insisted—that subsequently rampaged through the building, infecting others in their wake and killing dozens more people besides.

Quite what any of this has to do with *Sword of Death* itself, we cannot be certain. The film print itself disappeared after the ill-fated Berlin screening, and no further record of its cast and crew exists. There is no actual evidence Gilderoy himself worked on it, save for claims made in an obscure fanzine interview he allegedly gave some years later. (I say 'allegedly' because some cineastes claim parts of the interview do not tally with the actual facts of Gilderoy's career—what few there are available—and take it as proof the whole thing was a fabrication.)

Whatever the truth of the matter, Gilderoy withdrew from the film industry shortly afterwards. Possibly he was sick of the bad luck that had seemingly dogged his career from the outset, or perhaps he simply acquired a reputation as some kind of Jonah. The arts have always thrived on superstition, and bad word of mouth can be deadly to a career.

So, although he continued to live quietly at home for a period, eventually Gilderoy closed up his studio, sold off his sound equipment and moved away. No one knows where he went, and no trace of him has ever been found.

And yet, his story endures. Recluse, prima donna, genius...the fact that so much of his work is lost, destroyed or perhaps just flat-out mythical has only added to his legend. Of course, a major aspect of that legend is the internet theory that so much ill-fortune *cannot* simply be a coincidence; that Gilderoy is the only thread tying this winding trail of psychosis, disaster and death together, and therefore, perhaps, he is in some way *responsible*.

Those that worked with him describe him as impish-looking; Dario Argento was allegedly fond of referring to the collective responsible for the soundtrack of *Lachrymae* as "the goblin and the Goblins". Is it such a stretch, then, to imagine that there might have been something truly infernal about this unassuming little man; that none of these events were caused by bad luck but by (sound) design? That, as some claim, if you examine Gilderoy's work closely enough, if you begin to separate the dense, intertwined layers of audio that make up his elaborate mixes, you can actually hear the faint sound of his laughter?

DAMIEN THORN

Jonathan Scott-Taylor in Damien: Omen II, *1978*
written by Stanley Mann and Mike Hodges
directed by Don Taylor

Michael Kitchen in Brimstone & Treacle, *1976*
written by Dennis Potter
directed by Barry Davis

*T*HE DAY WILL COME WHEN EVERYONE WILL KNOW WHO YOU ARE. That was what Sergeant Neff had told him. Neff was his new commander at Davidson Military Academy, and while he treated the rest of the cadets like his personal collection of toy soldiers, to be polished, posed, and displayed for his own aggrandisement, with Damien he was different. Quieter, strangely respectful — almost awed.

And he was not the first. Ever since his father's death, when Damien had come to live with his uncle in America, there had been others like Neff. Men and women who seemed drawn to him, compelled to offer guidance and protection. Damien felt as though he were being prepared for something, although he could not comprehend precisely what.

Ever since the tragedies of his early boyhood—the apparent suicide of his mother, his father Robert's resultant religious mania and attempted murder of Damien atop a church altar, only prevented when the man was shot dead by police—he had lived something of a charmed life. His uncle Richard Thorn, a wealthy industrialist, had welcomed Damien into his home and treated him as a son. His cousin Mark, rather than resenting Damien's intrusion, had come to regard him as a brother and best friend. Richard's second wife Ann doted on both the boys, neither her own—but if pressed, Damien might have been forced to admit that she reserved a quiet favour for him.

He was loved, and wanted for nothing. For a time, he viewed the world around him as entirely benevolent.

Paul Buher, the newly-appointed president of Thorn Industries, was another who seemed to take a personal interest in Damien. He was considered by his peers to be cold and calculating, a corporate shark who could smell blood from miles away and would stop at nothing to be first at the feast. But for Damien, he could always spare an encouraging word, or a moment to listen. The boy grew to look forward to Buher's occasional weekend visits to the Thorn family's lakeside retreat. Sometimes he even fancied that the man would find excuses to visit simply so that he could check in on Damien.

One bright spring Saturday, Buher was thrashing Damien at ping-pong—his inherent ruthlessness extended to all leisure activities—when he paused for a moment. *Have you ever thought about what you'll do when you grow up?* he asked.

Work at Thorn, Damien replied. *That's what Uncle Richard wants. With Mark, of course.*

But why stop at that? You're capable of so much more.

Like what? Running for the Senate? President? Damien smiled at the presumption, but Buhler did not share his amusement.

You could, easily. But the President only has the power we grant him, Damien. It's an illusion of authority. Checks and balances.

Damien shrugged, not really understanding. Buher continued. *The thing about power, Damien—true power—it's never given to you. You have to seize it.*

And how do I do that?

You'll understand. When the time comes.

He spoke in riddles, like Neff and all the rest. Still, Damien did feel as though he were on the brink of something ineffable. As he entered puberty, he sensed an irresistible force building within him, tugging at him like a fisherman's line. Of course, his body was changing, but there was something more. A sense of imminent destiny. Did every adolescent boy experience this?

When he asked Mark—a few months older than Damien—if he'd started to feel different of late, his cousin looked confused. *You mean about girls and stuff?*

No, not that. I mean ... inside you. Damien couldn't find the words to express what he really meant.

Like your voice starting to break?

No. Damien grew frustrated. *Something growing.*

Mark giggled. *Better hope it grows a few inches more.*

It was hopeless. Mark didn't understand. Suddenly, Damien felt utterly alone. He longed for a father to guide him. His uncle had been good to him, but he was immersed in his work and rarely around, preferring to let the military academy do the hard work of instilling discipline and common sense into the two boys rather than attempting it himself.

In the end, the answers he sought came from Neff, or rather, from the Bible. Neff instructed him to study the Book of Revelation, suggesting that the knowledge Damien thirsted for lay within. Damien suddenly felt sure the man was a crackpot, another religious fanatic. Since the death of his father, he'd never had any time for organised religion—he even had a phobia of churches, which his therapist put down to lingering trauma—but he dutifully borrowed a Bible and sat down to read.

As Damien scanned the verses within, he began to feel something squirming in the recesses of his mind, like rats scrabbling within the walls of a house. Everyone had heard stories of murderers inspired to kill by the Bible, madmen convinced that God was speaking directly to them through the pages of His Book, forcing them to slaughter in his name. So too did Damien feel as though the words before him were an instruction, a prophecy directed expressly to him. Surely this was lunacy.

He tried to throw the book aside, but could not. Compelled to continue, he read of the rise of the Beast, of Armageddon, and remembered Buhler's talk of seizing power. Horrified at the unbidden thoughts rushing through his mind, he finally managed to slam the Bible closed.

The Mark. If this insane delusion had any truth to it whatsoever, somewhere on his body, he would bear the Mark of the Beast. Surely it was simple enough to disprove.

When he discovered the tiny birthmark hidden on his scalp—666— there was an overwhelming sense of absolute terror as he felt his entire existence plummet away from him. His life was gone, wiped away at a stroke—everything he knew was a lie, perhaps the greatest falsehood ever perpetuated by his true Father, the self-proclaimed master of lies.

But once that terror faded, it was gradually replaced by a cold acceptance. More than that, a sense of purity, and dreadful purpose. He had undergone his unholy baptism, and was now ready to assume his rightful place in the world. No longer was he an orphan, lost and confused—he had found his Father, and his fate.

He was, now and forever, the Antichrist.

With this fateful acceptance, Damien Thorn took his first steps into adulthood. Adolescents are often seized by the urge to tear down everything around them, to remake the world in their own image; but unlike most teenage boys, Damien had the power to achieve it—and the greatest of all teachers in the art of rebellion. But unlike his Father, there would be no one with the divine supremacy to cast him out of the realm he coveted.

So when Mark refused Damien's offer of a place at his side, he killed him. When Richard finally discovered Damien's true nature and plotted to destroy him, he had Ann—revealed as another false disciple lurking in the shadows—kill him too. Then, revelling in his power, he abandoned her to die in an explosion.

There would be no loose ends, no remaining proof of his true identity, no surviving family members blocking his route to ascendance. He would be alone, and desolate, just as his Father was. Such was the nature of power.

After the deaths of Richard and Ann, Paul Buher became Damien's legal guardian. With his entire family dead, Damien became the sole owner of

Thorn Industries, which he turned over to Buher until he was of an age to assume control himself. In the meantime, Buher would mentor him in the ways of the business, and so much more besides.

He would see to it that Thorn Industries helped prepare the world for Damien's rise by increasing their interests in technology and armaments; expanding their influence in international politics; even by the means of buying up large swathes of land in the Third World, putatively to help fertilise and develop it, but in truth to render the people living there as little more than tenants, helpless supplicants, subservient to Damien's will. Buher recognised that a brand new age was dawning, one in which corporations would possess previously undreamt-of power, and he meant to ensure that the lion's share of that power resided in the hands of the Antichrist.

Damien spent the remainder of his teenage years in dutiful preparation and study, not wishing to attract any further publicity. The deaths of his entire immediate family had inevitably drawn press attention, with the tabloids given to gleefully speculating about the 'Thorn Curse'.

Still, he could not resist the occasional small indulgence. When the details of an alleged case of demonic possession in Georgetown emerged in the early 1970s, Damien studied the story with quiet amusement. Two Jesuit priests had died during an exorcism, and Damien saw to it that flowers were sent to each of their funerals. He attached an anonymous handwritten note to each of the wreaths, a quote from Revelation: *During those days people will seek death but will not find it; they will long to die, but death will elude them.*

He went on to study at Yale, and was then awarded a Rhodes scholarship to Oxford University, where he excelled in academia and team sports both, captaining the Oxford Eight to victory and winning the Westchester Cup in polo. Despite the fact that he had only spent the first, dimly-remembered years of his life in England, he felt at home here, and made plans to stay on after his studies at Oxford were complete. He was given to commenting that he liked England because the rigid class system reminded him of the strict hierarchy in his Father's kingdom; he joked that the Seven Princes of Hell would find themselves entirely at home in English high society.

It was during this period that Damien decided he needed to better understand the ordinary people around him. The time was approaching when he would need to gather an army of followers, and how could he do that without learning how they thought? He had led a life of easy privilege, cocooned by wealth and status, and knew nothing of the common man. His Father's first lesson had been that the majority of mankind were weak and stupid, but that was not enough—he had to comprehend their darkest desires, appeal to their most carefully-nurtured hatreds, in order to mould them into the legion he would need to rise up against Heaven.

Choosing the metropolitan anonymity of London for his experiment, he took to wandering the streets and randomly engaging strangers in conversation. Posing as Martin Taylor, a young man recently returned from a stay in America, he would lie about having met them before, then flatter and cajole them into inviting him back to their homes. There, he would insinuate himself into their lives, carefully sowing the corrupt harvest he planned to reap when the End Times dawned.

Tom Bates was an embittered middle-aged man, a lost soul, utterly adrift in both his personal life and the country he saw around him, one he insisted he barely recognised anymore. His daughter Pattie was severely disabled as the result of a car accident; a tragedy that had indirectly been Bates's own fault, although this was a grim secret he kept buried deep inside him. The sick rage he felt at the loss of his daughter—*the vegetable,* as he now called her—he channeled into bigoted screeds about the downfall of England, about the blacks and the subversives and the pornographers that were stripping this once-proud nation of its values. As he regularly informed his long-suffering wife Amy, *The Devil is walking up and down the country.*

The proof of this statement was provided to him one winter's afternoon, when he fell into conversation with Damien on a London street corner. Damien claimed to be a close friend of his stricken daughter and asked to visit her, but such was Bates's inherent distrust of his fellow man that he hurriedly made his excuses and slipped away.

Still, Damien was not so easily discouraged, and had already helped himself to the man's wallet. That same evening, he turned up on the Bates family's doorstep, under the pretence of returning Tom his property. Once inside, he quickly ensured that his visit would be an extended one, tenderly cooing over Pattie, the girl he claimed to have loved. Her mother was immediately taken with their charming young visitor, and Damien found himself invited to stay for the night.

The next morning, he convinced Amy that he could look after Pattie, and that she should take a few hours out of the house and enjoy herself. Then, once her mother was safely gone, he raped the helpless girl, joyously ravaging her twisted wreck of a body.

Ironically, the Bates's took their daughter's subsequent retreat into frozen silence as a small sign of improvement. Despite Tom's bellowed insistences that *There is no God and there are no miracles*, Amy had always clung to the remnants of her tattered faith, to her belief that Pattie would one day come back to them. And now this young man had been delivered to their home, and wasn't their poor daughter better already?

Grudgingly, even Tom began to accept Damien into their household. Anything for a quiet life, anything to shut up the gurgling idiot in the corner, the ruin he had made of his only daughter.

Over drinks that night, Damien coaxed him into a political discussion, keen to extract the poison he could one day put to use for his own ends. Bates admitted he had recently joined the National Front, decrying the city streets full of coloured faces, and bemoaning that the country lacked a sense of direction, or a strict set of values. *All I want is the England I used to know,* he whined.

Damien tried to nudge him further, talking of rounding *them* up and putting them into camps. *Do what Hitler did!* he cried, relishing the discomfort on the older man's face. Tom Bates and his ilk could delude themselves that this was not the logical endgame of their petty bigotries, but Damien knew otherwise. Who understood the nature of evil better than he?

It was all simply a matter of degrees. Once evil became commonplace, men like Bates would never question or defy it; they just needed to be gently led across the arbitrary line they had drawn for themselves, like the cowed and frightened dogs they were.

Damien was pleased with his night's work. So, to celebrate, after the Bates's had retired for the evening, he crept downstairs to visit Pattie again. He had been so careful for so long, so cautious, that this rare opportunity to indulge his diabolic appetites was liberating beyond measure.

But something was different. This time, Pattie stirred at his approach; a faint light guttering in her previously vacant eyes, like a flickering candle in the window of a distant house. When he climbed onto her bed and began to paw at her nightdress, she writhed in distress, seemingly trying to summon the strength in her useless limbs to push him off.

Relishing her struggles, he bent down to kiss her.

In the next instant, Pattie found her voice, that lost instrument which had been denied to her for so long, and screamed. It was as if in that moment, she knew exactly what was in the room with her, realised the true nature of the nightmare that crouched on top of her, and screamed her despair to the heavens, in the hope that they might hear her plea. Unwittingly, the Antichrist had pulled her back from the limbo she had been consigned to.

Alarmed, Damien quickly fled from the house. He must not be discovered here—there was still too much left to accomplish. As he crept away into the darkened streets, he considered the implications of what had just happened. Wryly, he recognised that he had conjured a modest miracle of his very own—the sort of thing that would be tediously hosanna'd from every pulpit had it been the handiwork of the Nazarene. In setting out to do evil, he had somehow stumbled into doing good. It was a small but valuable lesson.

Damien appreciated the irony of this minor defeat. Perhaps Christ and His Father were craftier than he had supposed. No matter. He had gained more than he'd lost this day.

He had been granted a glimpse of the future—of the world dreamt of by Tom Bates and countless other small men like him. Not the utopia of peace and harmony mankind had been promised by the Church—it was all too apparent to Damien that Bates did not *want* to live in brotherhood with his fellow man, not if that man's skin were a different colour—but in a society where everyone knew their place, the rule of law was paramount, and the foundations were built upon the shattered bones of the weak.

The tired Christian delusions of love and equality had no place in that world, in that future. The Nazarene had had his moment, and He had failed.

Now, Damien would have his.

PETER QUINT

Peter Wyngarde in The Innocents, *1963*
written by William Archibald and Truman Capote
additional material & dialogue by John Mortimer
based on The Turn of the Screw *by Henry James*
directed by Jack Clayton

*Y*OU'RE SUCH A HUNGRY BOY, HIS MOTHER USED TO TELL HIM.
Always were, ever since you were a babby.
And it was true, the watery milk of her breast would never sate him, and
when he outgrew that, the meager portions served up at the Quint family
dinner table could surely never hope to dull his appetite. Such was young
Peter's hunger that he would roam their village in search of food, a sly fox
on the hunt for easy pickings. Apples from the vicar's tree, or perhaps a pie
cooling on the Widow Rigby's sill. And if the fox should be caught, his
skinny wrist snared in the sinewy vice of the Widow's grasp, why, he'd
already learned from his father how to beguile a woman.

They were simple enough creatures, Quint reckoned. Women valued power, no doubt because they lacked it themselves. They thirsted for it, desired it...or the men that held it.

For his part, he understood that the secret to power was simply taking what you desired; by attempting to cajole or barter, you only admitted you were not powerful in the first place. Still, he also knew the value of a honeyed word, and the effect of a wicked yet alluring smile. So the Widow would send him on his way with a slice of pie wrapped in a handkerchief and a clout around the back of the head, and thus Quint learned the lesson that love and cruelty were inextricably bound together, as inseparable as the rose and the thorn.

When the time came that his parents could afford to feed him no longer, he was sent to work as a stableboy in the big house. He was good with horses, instinctively understanding when to apply a calming hand and when only a riding crop would do. But being only a lowly member of the household staff, his charms and wiles counted for little otherwise, and as he shovelled up yet another barrowload of manure, he would vow to himself that he was destined for better things. He took to stealing out in the dead of night, creeping up to the mansion house and standing there in the dark; his face pressed against the windows, gazing at the finery inside, the heat of his desire fogging the glass.

It was during this time that he became a man. One of the kitchen maids took a shine to his dark looks and took it upon herself to instruct him in the ways of the flesh. She was older; coarse and stupid but womanly in all the right places, and Quint proved himself an excellent pupil. So much so that his understanding of the uses bodies could be put to quickly outstripped hers, and the maid soon called an end to their nightly assignations, alarmed by the force of his unbridled lusts. She took up with a footman instead, finding his comparative lack of sexual imagination a welcome relief.

For his part, Quint could not let such an insult to his manhood stand. He broke the girl's arm as a punishment; then, deciding he had at last outgrown the house, packed up his few belongings and left.

Years passed, and Quint found employment at a succession of other houses, grand old buildings such as Brandham Hall and Gosford Park, gradually advancing in seniority, leaving the stables behind for the relative luxury of a household position. Yet he was forever unsatisfied with his lot, and once he had amused himself by working his way through the more alluring female members of staff (and on occasion, his employers' families), he would leave to seek work elsewhere, that familiar gnawing sensation in his belly compelling him onwards.

It was only when he arrived at Bly that his nameless craving began to diminish. Employed as the valet to the owner of the house, Quint soon found that his master was mostly absent, thus leaving him as de facto lord of the manor. The mansion and grounds were magnificent, the fat old housekeeper no threat to his authority. He would go out riding on the sprawling estate, fancying the lush acres belonged to him. All he wanted for was attractive female company; there were slim pickings amongst the bones of the skeleton staff his master saw fit to install at Bly.

But that would soon change once the two orphans arrived.

Miles and Flora were angelic children; their beauty somehow enhanced by the hints of sadness early tragedy had sketched on their young faces. Their only remaining family was Quint's master, and while he dutifully took them in (and of course sympathised with their loss); as he informed Quint, a man in his position simply had no room—mentally or emotionally—for children. So he sent them to Bly, and the grand old house became the entirety of their life; their home, their school, their playground.

Of course, a governess needed to be found for them, and although Quint had no say in her employment, he could not have chosen better himself. Separated by class they may have been, but Quint and his master shared a slyer, far more fundamental kinship.

So when Miss Jessel turned up on Bly's doorstep, skittish and alluring, Quint thanked the stars for his employer's discerning eye. He had been expecting some hag to take charge of the children, a dried-up spinster, her tired face and body marking her as unworthy of bearing her own family. Instead, Miss Jessel was a fresh spring bud, glistening with dew, ready to spring open under the delicate touch of Quint's fingers.

It took him no time at all to seduce her; she was willing, pliable, almost as if she had not the slightest notion that she might refuse him. Quint found her to be a blank canvas upon which he could paint his innermost fantasies, the gaudy brushstrokes of his lust and perversion. In turn, he instilled in her the same need that drove him, that rapacious hunger, so close to a sickness. Quint became her obsession; the gaping hole he had torn open in her could never be filled.

As the months passed, he grew to find her total dependence upon him repulsive; he would rage at her, beat and bruise her tender flesh, knock her to the floor. But he could never drive her away. She would crawl back to him, a supplicant bitch, her eyes imploring. *Again. Show me how you love me.* If she ever knew the difference between love and hate, she had forgotten it now.

The children were there, of course. Quint and Miss Jessel saw no need for secrets at Bly, and besides, Miles and Flora's education was their responsibility. Quint had never been properly educated himself, and the way he saw it, there were things you couldn't ever learn from books. So when Miles came to him, full of shy questions, Quint saw it as his masculine duty to instruct the boy.

Girls are different from us, aren't they?

Quint chucked and ruffled the boy's blond hair. *That they are, my lad. But the biggest differences are the ones they keep hidden.*

What are those?

It's difficult to explain. But I could show you, if you like.

Miles was always an inquisitive boy, and eagerly agreed. So while Flora was taking an afternoon nap, Quint sat him down in a corner of the master bedroom, and instructed him to quietly observe, and learn. Then he led Miss Jessel into the room, and, over the course of the next couple of hours, proceeded to show Miles the savage truth about the innermost desires of men, and women. Afterwards, as Miss Jessel lay weeping, he took Miles aside and told him, *Your uncle's money would never buy you that sort of an education.*

It would be comforting to view Quint's sudden death shortly afterwards as evidence of a divine hand, or even as proof that the man himself possessed some hitherto-unrevealed streak of awareness and healthy self-loathing, and had therefore taken it upon himself to end the life that had corrupted so many others by its proximity.

However, the truth of it is, it was a bitterly cold night at Bly; the sky was pitch dark, the ground slick with frost, and Quint was full of drink. It was Miles who found him the next morning, his spilled blood already frozen to the touch (as if it were not cold enough already).

And were Miles's shrieks prompted by the sight of his broken, bloodied mentor, or by the sound of that slyly insinuating voice whispering in his ear? *I taught you about life, now I'll show you what lies beyond.*

For Quint's hunger was such that it could never be quelled by death's hand alone. He remained at Bly, an outsider once more, his face pressed up against the opaque window that barred him from the living world. Still, he would not be alone for long; his control over Miss Jessel was such that she required little prompting to join him in his spectral exile. Already destroyed by his death, it took only the merest whisper from him, carried into her room on a faint breeze: *Throw yourself into the lake. Its cold depths will preserve your beauty, and you will relive our time together as you drown.*

And so the lovers were reunited, although one problem remained. The pleasures of the flesh had been their bond, their shared obsession. But their flesh was mortal, cast off and consigned to rot in their respective graves. Without it, what did they have?

Quint, always so adept at using others to his own ends, had the solution. Miles and Flora would be their vessels. So young, so beautiful, so full of potential. Through them, the lovers would live again.

They began their assault on the twin fortresses of the children's psyches. Possessing the mind and soul of another is no simple task, and requires patience. But the lovers had time, and so they began to appear to Miles and Flora in dreams, gradually asserting their influence while the sleeping siblings were at their most vulnerable. Before long they had gained a foothold, and although their control was not yet absolute, it was enough that when Miles was sent away to boarding school and separated from Flora, Quint quickly saw to it that he was expelled for indecent behaviour. The shaken headmaster informed Miles that he was a contaminating influence, a blight on the purity of the school.

Standing unseen at the boy's shoulder, Quint smiled. He had taught Miles well.

But upon the boy's return to Bly, Quint encountered another hurdle in the form of the parson's daughter, Miss Giddens. The master had finally got around to appointing a replacement for Miss Jessel, and this time had avoided employing someone quite so young and impressionable. Quint instantly recognised the woman for what she was: a pious, middle-aged frump, frustrated by desires she could never allow herself to articulate, let alone act on. He could well imagine her squirming demurely yet delight-edly under the master's appraising eye. The problem was that her repression made her suggestible, open to wild fancies and capable of recognising the dark undercurrents at Bly for what they were. Before too long, she had glimpsed the shades of the two lovers, witnessed them silently stalking the grounds, watching their prey—the children.

A battle of wills ensued. At first the lovers attempted simply to terrify the woman, to frighten her away from Bly, but although Quint could sense her sanity growing brittle, the woman clung to her damnable faith like a dinghy in a tempest. Even when those around her began to doubt her claims, to perceive her as the greater threat to the children, she persisted in her doomed crusade.

So Quint tried another approach. If he could not shatter the governess's equilibrium, he would assault her virtue. After all, he was well practised in such matters.

One night, when the woman came to tuck Miles into bed, Quint swiftly entered him and took control. As Giddens leaned down to kiss the boy goodnight, Quint seized her face and hungrily pulled her mouth to his.

All at once he could tell it was the first time she had been kissed in this manner; he could taste her fear, but also her desire, black and forbidden and long-suppressed, like rot at the root of a tree. He knew that were Miles only a little older, he could take the governess now and make her his.

However, the boy was still immature and weak, and the woman easily pushed him away, shocked; both at Miles's actions and the sudden revelation of her own lusts. Still, Quint was satisfied. He had tasted her weakness and knew now that she could not triumph over him.

In the end, neither side could claim victory. Giddens' obsessive need to save Miles drove her into a mania, and when she terrorised the boy into acknowledging Quint's presence, she succeeded only in cutting his young life short. Quint's claws were sunk too deep, and Miles could not safely break free of his influence; instead, something splintered inside him and he fell down, stone dead.

In the aftermath of Miles' death, the governess was diagnosed as a hysteric and committed. The master allowed Bly to fall into disuse, and when he died without an heir of his own, it was left to Flora. She would never speak of her time there, and refused to ever set foot in the house again. And so the great mansion was left to decay; a body without life, a palatial carcass.

For decades Quint haunted the barren grounds of the estate, once teeming with vibrant life, now faded and stricken with neglect; hungering for resurrection as Quint himself hungered. In time, Miss Jessel's spectre simply faded away, consigned to limbo; her thwarted desire for Quint was not enough to sustain her existence.

But Quint had always been a patient man, and he knew an opportunity would eventually present itself. He waited, as he had always waited.

And then, one day, the world changed. Quint could sense it; the thundering drumbeat of doom in the air, the bitter taste of smoke and dying drifting in from the city. The country was at war again, the greatest war the world had ever known, and the cities and their populations were at risk. Bly was requisitioned for use by the government, and soon became home to a boy's school.

Quint watched greedily as the pupils arrived, coachloads of them, clutching their battered suitcases like shields. Bly had been allowed to deteriorate, but still seemed impossibly grand, impossibly old to these urban refugees, the grime of the city still clinging to their skin. *Do you think it's haunted?* Quint heard some of them mutter.

He would not get carried away by the glorious banquet that was suddenly laid out before him. He must choose wisely. He would wait, and watch, and select just the right victim—lonely and ignored, a stray from the herd. He would not risk any outside interference this time.

The boy was small for his age and somewhat fey, but Quint recognised his nascent beauty and knew he promised to be the perfect instrument. In Quint's hands, he would be shaped and honed to cruel perfection. He was sensitive and intelligent, the sort of boy that attracted troublesome attention from his inferiors, and thus preferred his own company.

Quint bided his time, then appeared to the lad when he was out skimming stones across the lake one afternoon. He was stealthy in his approach, materialising only as a reflection on the water's surface, so as not to unduly alarm his quarry.

As the ripples on the lake subsided to reveal Quint's smiling features, the boy looked around sharply, then froze. Quint murmured, *You don't have to be afraid of me. I'm a friend.*

God knows the boy had few enough of them. He stared at Quint's reflection for a few seconds, then stuttered. *Are you ... d-dead?*

Not as such.

You're alive?

No. But I could be, with your help.

You need my help?

Quint nodded. *Of course, I can help you in return. That's what friends do.*

The boy considered this. *What's your name?*

Peter Quint. And yours?

The boy mouthed Quint's name silently to himself, then carefully sat down on a nearby rock. *I'm Hugo,* he said finally. *Hugo Barrett.*

HUGO BARRETT

Dirk Bogarde in The Servant, *1963*
written by Harold Pinter
based on the novel by Robin Maugham
directed by Joseph Losey

BARRETT LET HIMSELF INTO THE CHELSEA TOWNHOUSE AND gazed around carefully, a predator entering unfamiliar terrain. The building was large by modern standards, although hardly as grand as Bly, but he supposed it was what passed for luxury in this shabby new world. The walls and floors were bare and unadorned; much remained to be done here. It was an unfinished work, much as Barrett himself had once been, all those years ago. But just as Peter Quint had taken the formless clay of that young boy and sculpted him into the lean, cunning wolf he was today, so too would Barrett remake this house in his own image.

He had been born in London to stolidly middle-class parents. His life was laid out for him from birth; he was to one day take over the running of the family business, and any early impulses towards deviating from this path were firmly stamped out by his father. The Hugo Barrett that was sent away to Bly during the war was a meek, unassuming boy; save for the blooming maturity of adolescence, the version that returned was identical in appearance, and yet in all other respects might have been a different person entirely. In actual fact, for all intents and purposes he was, although his parents had no real way of knowing this.

All they understood was that their son had transformed from the compliant drone they had sent away; his eyes, once watery and unquestioning, now burned like hot pokers, searing into whoever they beheld. His manner was mocking, almost devilish. Even his accent had changed; his cut glass enunciations softening and slurring into a Lancastrian tone. *Stop speaking in that ridiculous voice,* his father demanded. *It's how real people talk,* replied Barrett, with a defiant grin. *Those who never got taught how to pretend.*

Hugo's parents could only imagine he had been exposed to some deplorable influences in his time away; a sound enough explanation, although not quite in the manner they supposed. Certainly his father's attempt to correct his son's new-found insolence by way of a firm beating was doomed to failure even before Barrett seized the strap away from him and used it to strike his father across the cheek. *There,* he said. *You won't try that again, now will you?*

From that day on, his mother and father learned to fear him, and Barrett was largely abandoned to his own devices until he left home at sixteen. There was to be no more talk of the family business.

The day before he moved out, Barrett led his mother to her bedroom and raped her, simply to ensure his parents would never try to contact him again.

Thus freed to make his way in the world, Quint's influence led Barrett to seek employment as a household servant. For a period after the war, it seemed as though the aristocracy were losing their grip on the land, but Quint recognised that there would always be something servile about the the English character, and while some social barriers had been brought down, there was still work to be had for those who could fetch and serve with alacrity.

Such lowly employment would once have been unthinkable for young Barrett, but it was a game of wits Quint had long understood, and relished;

the upper classes would never admit you to their world unless it was as an inferior, a hireling. However, once you had a foothold in their territory, they were easy prey; weak and stupid, their flesh soft and milky. They consigned their servants to the shadows, not wishing to be reminded of their craven presence, but from there, it was all too simple to strike.

His search for a suitable position had finally led him to this West London townhouse, wherein he was to meet Tony, the young man destined to become his new master. Barrett scoffed inwardly at his first sight of the man; lounging in a deckchair, already lost in a boozy doze despite the early hour. They were so transparent in their vapidity, these people. They pretended they had nothing to hide, safe in the assumption that no one could possibly question or challenge them.

Barrett stared down at Tony and within seconds, knew everything there was to know about him: his idleness, his lack of curiosity, his dilettantism, his incipient alcoholism. This would be absurdly easy.

With practiced ease, Barrett charmed his way into the position. From there on, it was a process of increments; first making himself indispensable to his master's needs (there were many, all of them utterly trivial), then slyly pitting Tony against his girlfriend Susan (who was always suspicious of Barrett; Quint wondered if part of her could sense his shadow lurking behind the servant's eyes). He quietly made sure Tony always had a drink within easy reach, slowly nudging him down the treacherously gentle slope of dipsomania; then finally, the *coup de grace*, installing the slatternly Vera into the household under the guise of housemaid. *She's my sister, sir. Our mother is ill so she's become my responsibility. You won't regret it sir, she brightens any room she's in.*

In reality, Vera was a Soho whore Barrett had plucked off the streets. And so, his influence spread through the pristine rooms of the house like gangrene.

Not that the outside world saw him for anything other than an enviously attentive servant. One night, they entertained a visiting guest from Chicago: Richard Thorn, head of the business conglomerate Thorn Industries. Tony had some harebrained plan for clearing acres of Brazilian jungle to build cities for Asian peasant populations and wanted to pitch it to Thorn, who were doing their own research into feeding the world's poor.

Richard listened carefully as Tony made his execrable pitch, politely pointing out the several obvious fallacies in the Englishman's carelessly-prepared sums and statistics. The evening would have been a total disaster were it not for Barrett's excellent meal and solicitous yet unobtrusive presence. As Tony felt the foundations of his grand scheme crumbling beneath him, he became drunker and drunker, and Barrett eventually had to help him up to bed even before the coffee had been served.

Upon his return, Thorn was preparing to leave, but as Barrett showed him apologetically to the door, Thorn pressed a vellum business card into his hand and said, *You ever need a job, give me a call.*

Prompted by Barrett, Vera had begun an affair with Tony. Frequent were the nights where she would fuck the servant, then trot obediently downstairs and fuck the master. This small reversal of hierarchy Barrett was able to insist upon. *I'm not having his slops,* he curtly told Vera. *I don't know where he's been.*

Oblivious, Tony became obsessed with the girl, who had ushered him into a world of sordid pleasure he had barely known existed previously. Matters came to a head one evening when Tony and Susan returned home unexpectedly, to find Barrett and Vera making use of the master bedroom as though it were a dark wood. Upon hearing Susan's appalled cry, Barrett strode out onto the upstairs hallway, quite naked. He stared cooly down at the emasculated Tony, taunting him with his evident superiority.

The pair were obliged to leave the house. Vera went back to her Soho bedsit, and Barrett bided his time. He knew that Tony could not manage without him. A short time later, he contrived a seemingly chance meeting with his erstwhile master in the local pub. Barrett affected a suitably chastened air, and meekly offered to buy Tony a drink. To observe them, barely able to meet each other's eye, you might have intuited a surreptitious homosexual pickup. Indeed, Barrett had long suspected the master harboured secret lusts for him.

Whatever the reason, Barrett was welcomed back into the household. His victory complete, he began to assert his authority more openly. While they continued to enact the superficial rituals of master and servant, for all intents and purposes they were now social equals; they took their meals together; divided the coffee and Sunday papers between themselves; even began to host parties together.

For a time, the townhouse became one of the more exclusive social hubs of Sixties London; if you study the *Swinging Faces* series of photographs by Thomas Anthony, several of them were taken on those carefree nights (if you look carefully, you can make out the elusive Barrett in the background of one of them, his features blurred and obscured, like a lingering ghost). Rumour had it that Barrett had paid Jennings to take additional covert photographs for his own personal use; compromising images of some of their more notable guests, to be filed away for future leverage.

And then there were the other, private parties, the ones that didn't make it into the society columns; select groups of girls invited for Tony and Barrett's personal amusement. By this point, Tony's alcoholism was such that he could barely function; after drunkenly pawing at a few of the guests, he would collapse limply to a sofa, content to watch Barrett attending to his own pleasure. One night Barrett went too far; driven by Quint's darker urges, he almost choked one of the girls to death. Some faint spark of decency ignited within Tony, and he roused himself from his stupor to intervene, only for Barrett to forcefully slap him to the floor. *Pay her off and see she gets in a taxi*, he told his master.

Tony was going under fast, and even a last-ditch intervention from the spurned Susan could not save him. She blundered into one of their private *soirées* — was she horrified at what she found, or secretly excited? — and, realising that she was as welcome here as a beggar at a society ball, tried to pull Tony away. But any small comfort she could offer him had long since been superseded by the bottle, and instead she stumbled into Barrett's waiting clutches.

He lunged at Susan, kissing her forcefully; but it was less a kiss than a violation, much as young Miles had similarly violated Miss Giddens all those years before. For a fleeting instant, she wanted him, and then she tasted it on his tongue: the rot, the foul corruption at the core of his being. Susan pushed Barrett away, and slapped him viciously; was this the first time Quint had ever been struck by a mere woman?

A few weeks later, Tony was dead, killed by a cocktail of brandy and sleeping pills. He left the townhouse and a lump sum to Barrett, whose ascent to the moneyed classes was now complete. Or so he thought.

As it turned out, Tony's peers would not accept a former servant into their ranks (not least a man whom they judged responsible for the destruction of one of their own), and the bright young things of Swinging London would only tolerate an ageing bachelor for as long as he had the money and the wherewithal to entertain them.

So, as his inherited funds and influence gradually dwindled, Barrett withdrew, haunting the empty rooms of the townhouse just as Quint had once haunted Bly. He took to wandering the drinking dens and fleshpots of Soho, engaging in all-night gambling sessions with the nefarious likes of Jack Carter and Harold Shand, a far cry from the elite company he had once enjoyed. But here, he was at least accepted, as long as he paid his debts — which were multiplying all the time.

Stumbling through the city streets one night, Barrett found himself propositioned by a young brunette. Perhaps it was the drink, or the dim light of the alleyway, but it seemed to him that she resembled the long-deceased Miss Jessel. A familiar urge rose inside him, and once they were safely back in her bedsit room, Barrett began to hurt the woman. It had been too long since he had satisfied such needs.

When she started to scream, he grew alarmed — he could not hope to rely on the same tight-lipped discretion of a country estate in a Soho brothel — and put his arm around her neck to quieten her. Within moments, she was dead.

Barrett fled the scene. For days, he worried that he would be connected to the crime. He had been impulsive, foolish. He felt adrift, as though he had no place in this new world that was changing so rapidly around him. For years he had fought to be accepted, to claim a place, and now he was in danger of losing everything.

In the end, the murder was attributed to the then-active Necktie Killer, who had already been terrorising Soho for some weeks. Barrett had successfully avoided one pitfall, but he could not escape the next. He was forced to sell the townhouse to pay off his mounting debts; the sort of men he had been gambling with were not to be trifled with. They had real power; all at once he recognised the paltry limits of his own influence, which had never extended much beyond the walls of the various grand houses he had sullied with his presence.

All of a sudden he was reduced to nothing, no place to go, only a few coins remaining in his pocket.

But as he gathered the few belongings he could carry, he discovered something discarded in a desk drawer—Richard Thorn's long-forgotten business card.

Perhaps he could begin again. Barrett dialled the private number listed on the card.

The phone at the other end rang for some time before it was finally answered. A low, purring voice spoke. *This is Damien Thorn.*

Oh, I'm sorry. I was phoning for Richard Thorn, Barrett replied.

Was that a crackle on the line, or a quiet chuckle? *I'm sorry. I'm afraid my uncle died in a fire some years ago. Was there anything I could help you with?*

The old survival instincts had not abandoned him. He fell into an obsequious apology. *Oh, I'm sorry, sir. Sorry for your loss, and for bothering you. You see, it was just that your uncle offered me a job once. As his personal valet. But of course, that isn't your concern, sir.*

There was a pause on the other end. *Well, my uncle was an excellent judge of character*, the voice said, in a slyly mocking tone Barrett recognised all too well. *You'd better come in and see me once I'm back in London.*

When Barrett was ushered into the office of the young head of Thorn Industries a couple of weeks later, he'd thought that the combined decades of his and Quint's experience had prepared him for anything. It had not.

The two men gazed at each other for a moment, each instantly cognisant of the fact that they both shared a secret; a hidden self they kept carefully concealed from the world around them. Leaning back in his chair, Damien smiled and bade Barrett to make himself comfortable, offered him a drink.

Thank you for seeing me, sir, Barrett said, as he took his seat.

Perhaps we should look at it as ... seeing each other, his prospective employer replied.

And with that, Damien showed him his true face.

The servant fell to his knees.

Master, said Barrett.

COUNT DRACULA

Christopher Lee in Taste the Blood of Dracula, *1970*
written by Anthony Hinds, directed by Peter Sasdy
Dracula A.D. 1972, *1972*
written by Don Houghton, directed by Alan Gibson
The Satanic Rites of Dracula, *1973*
written by Don Houghton, directed by Alan Gibson

THE LEGENDS OF COUNT DRACULA IN HIS HOMELAND ARE LONG and terrible, but for the purposes of this history, we must restrict ourselves soley to an account of his activities in England.

We can date his first appearance in this country back to the late 19th century. Weller, an unscrupulous dealer in antiques and esoterica, had discovered the Count's remains while on a buying trip around Europe. As something of a dabbler in the occult, Weller was only too aware of the dreadful folklore surrounding Dracula. Awestruck, he gathered up the Count's cloak, signet ring, and a small amount of his dried blood. He saw no particular monetary value in the items; for him, they were dark fetish objects, rare prizes he could use to impress the rich dilettantes he relied upon to make his living.

Dilettantes like Lord Courtley.

Courtley was a loathsome aristocratic brat, disinherited by his father for his own dabblings in the Black Arts. Handsomely saturnine in his looks but practically penniless, he relied upon the favours of prostitutes to survive. To Weller, he was nothing but a nuisance; an entitled pest who would strut around his shop perpetually trying to wheedle deals, while offending the other customers with his high-handed ways.

In an attempt to lord it over Courtley, one day the dealer had proudly shown him Dracula's remains. The effect was immediate.

Courtley was nothing if not a creature of appetite, and he gazed at the remains with palpable hunger, like a starving orphan stood before a banquet. *I must have them, Weller,* he breathed. *Do you know what you have here? Power beyond your imagining. And you're keeping it locked up in a damn box!*

With a touch of glee, Weller had taken the items and replaced them back in their box for safekeeping. He regretfully informed Courtley that they were not for sale, certainly not at any price the young lord could afford.

The insult was clear, and entirely intentional. Courtley turned and stalked out of the shop without another word.

However, Weller had not reckoned with his frustrated client's resourcefulness. Courtley returned to the shop within the week, with three well-to-do middle-aged men in tow. Their uneasy furtiveness led Weller to suspect they had only very recently made Courtley's acquaintance, probably in one of the numerous London brothels he liked to frequent.

The young lord insisted that his new-found companions were ready to fund the acquisition of Weller's prized relics, money no object. Weller attempted to demur, but Courtley was relentless. He nipped and harried like the jackal he was, until the asking price had been driven so high that Weller could not possibly refuse it.

The dealer took the gentlemen's money, and wished them well. He suspected that no good could possibly come of their transaction, but what customers did with their purchased items was hardly his concern. In truth, Weller was secretly glad to be rid of his prize, despite its impossible rarity. He had always felt somehow unclean after handling the remains, and while it was surely only his imagination, a cold shadow seemed to have fallen over his premises ever since he had returned home with them.

As Weller had surmised, Courtley's decadent posturing and privileged viciousness meant nothing in the face of the true evil his meddling unleashed. He led his new-found disciples to an abandoned, deconsecrated church. Here, Courtley performed a blasphemous rite the young man only dimly understood; in doing so, he succeeded in resurrecting Dracula, but not before his three terrified benefactors had turned on him and beaten him close to death.

As the Count took possession of Courtley's dying body and reshaped its flesh into his own image, he could not rid himself of the young lord's final memories; the heavy boots and clubs crushing the life out of him as he lay writhing on the floor. Taking this assault as an insult to his own person, Dracula vowed to make the men pay for Courtley's death.

Why would a personage such as Dracula, the anointed Prince of Darkness of the Devil himself, stoop to involving himself in the petty squabbles of men? Perhaps he simply loathed the hypocrisy of these three so-called gentlemen; so pious and upstanding to their families and community, while secretly indulging their every fantasy and perversion under the guise of charity. There was no hypocrisy in Dracula; he had chosen evil, devoted himself to it, and was as pure an exemplar of it as had ever existed. In this sense, he was a true fanatic; to worship in Dracula's church, one must be devoutly and steadfastly corrupt. In comparison, the banal everyday cruelties of mankind are nothing but a casually-muttered prayer, a half-hearted genuflection to the dark forces lurking all around us.

Dracula struck at the men through their children. Enlisting the daughter of one of them—Alice—as his catspaw, he methodically corrupted their hitherto Christian families, before using the children to execute them, one by one. It was a simple display of his power. Such was the ease of it that he perhaps grew overconfident; this was a new, supposedly civilised country that understood little of his kind, and there was no learned Van Helsing here to challenge him.

Satisfied that he had avenged their insult, he prepared to turn his attention to the wider world beyond. But he had reckoned without Alice's suitor Paul. The young man tracked his fiancée to the abandoned church, and by conducting a ceremony to reconsecrate it, managed to defeat Dracula. Once again, the Count's body was destroyed.

But not his influence. Paul thought he had freed Alice from Dracula's control, but once stained by his touch, a soul is not so easily wiped clean. The young couple made plans to be married, but on their wedding night, when Paul joined his bride in their marital bed, Alice took a knife she had concealed under the pillow and cut his throat. Collecting the blood that gouted forth, she took the ashes she had secretly removed from the church and resurrected Dracula once more.

Dracula repaid her loyalty by feeding upon Alice, then abandoning her. He would not make the mistake of lingering too long and risking discovery again. He had a new kingdom to build, a fresh country to conquer.

In the following months Dracula consolidated his power, carefully amassing wealth and disciples. He might have succeeded in corrupting England completely, had it not been for his old nemesis Lawrence Van Helsing. Visiting London on a lecture tour, he stumbled upon evidence of his old enemy's activities and managed to track him to his lair. The Count attempted to flee in his carriage, but the indomitable Van Helsing was not so easily escaped. He threw himself onto the vehicle as it sped away through Hyde Park with little regard for his own safety. The two adversaries fought bitterly atop of the speeding carriage, and when it finally crashed, the fatally-injured Van Helsing saw to it that Dracula was staked and killed by one of the shattered wheel spokes scant moments before he himself expired.

But once again, the vampire was saved by one of his followers. A faithful disciple had followed the carriage to the crash site, and duly gathered up the remains of his fallen master. However, perhaps fearful of the attention that Van Helsing's death had stirred up, he did not immediately act to revive the Count. Instead, Dracula's remains were safely preserved, handed down from descendant to descendant, until the right time came for him to be restored to the world.

That day did not arrive until a full century later. In Dracula's absence, two world wars had been fought and won, and England had grown soft and lazy in their stead. An atmosphere of self-conscious modernity had enveloped the country; the young were busily rejecting everything their parents stood for, and understood nothing of the sinister creatures dwelling beyond the bright lights of civilisation that had so terrified their ancestors. It was a society of easy pleasures, of woolly platitudes and primary colours.

Surely now, Dracula would enjoy his final triumph. In this docile, incurious world, the force of his evil would be akin to a wildfire rampaging through a drought-stricken cornfield.

A familiar pattern began to repeat itself: a young decadent named Johnny, descended from Dracula's loyal custodian of a century before, gathered a group of thrill-seeking teenagers to the nearby Saint Bartolph's: another deconsecrated church, another blasphemous rite, another resurrection.

Was this perpetual cycle of death and rebirth beginning to erode the towering black peaks of the Count's resolve? He seemed a diminished figure in this bright new world. Perhaps even this most arrogant and prideful of old monsters was awed and a little afraid of what he glimpsed beyond the boundaries of the ruined church. There were few dark places for him to hide in the garish, neon-soaked city, and the polluted blood of its denizens was tainted with countless intoxicants; all seemingly freely available in this numbed, unclean society, so alien to him.

Consequently, Dracula did not learn from his previous mistake, and chose once more to stay close to the more familiar gothic surroundings of his lair. This was a fatal error.

His disciples were not the only ones who had faithfully carried their cause down through generation after generation; so too, had the hated Van Helsing left his own mark upon the world. Dracula's old adversary had sired a son before his death, and had taught him well about the obscene cult of vampirism. That knowledge had been handed down through the years, passed from heir to heir, its current beneficiary being one Professor Lorimer Van Helsing.

And so, another Van Helsing waited in London, ever-watchful and prepared. One hundred years had now elapsed since Dracula's previous resurrection, and he had begun to think that perhaps the family duty (or curse?) would spare him, as it had his father and grandfather before him. Nevertheless, he did not wear his inherited mantle lightly, and he did not shirk it. In their own way, the Van Helsings were as fanatical as Dracula himself.

So when the police inspector came to him with photographs of a drained, mutilated corpse, he knew his moment had finally come.

Van Helsing's granddaughter Jessica had unwittingly participated in the same ceremony that resuscitated Dracula, and it was through her group that Lorimer was able to track down his acolyte, Johnny. Discovering that Dracula had already infected the boy, Lorimer was forced to destroy him, but by now, his own existence had been revealed to the Count, who had swiftly moved to counterattack his foe. He had Jessica seized and brought to the church, where he intended to make her his consort as a final act of revenge against the Van Helsing family.

Following her trail to St Bartolph's, Lorimer prepared to face his family's adversary. Once again, Dracula would do battle with a Van Helsing, and once again he lost. The Van Helsings understood that Dracula's fatal weakness had always been his poisonous ego, swollen to bursting over centuries of tyranny. He simply could never comprehend how these human insects might ever be a match for him. But the Van Helsings had always combined an innate scholarly intelligence with a certain steely nerve, and so it was that Lorimer lured the Count to a trap within the church graveyard, and once more put an end to him.

Lorimer was well-versed in the history of Dracula's long cycle of death and rebirth, and was not foolish enough to believe that he had laid the vampire to rest for good. However, he knew that the site on which St Bartolph's stood was scheduled for redevelopment, and so he buried Dracula's remains deep in the earth, praying with every scrap of faith he could muster that this would be sufficient to keep the Count from rising again.

What he could not be expected to know was that Dracula had come to the attention of a new benefactor, one whose capacity for evil dwarfed even the Count's own.

The church was demolished shortly thereafter, and the land purchased by a development company, Canis Ltd. Lorimer made a point of regularly passing the site on his daily walks, and when he saw notice of the sale, he took a certain relief in it. He hoped that the ground would soon be built upon, and Dracula's remains lost to the earth forever.

However, Canis were merely a shell company, and the actual buyer was a large multinational, Thorn Industries. The purchase had been instigated by its young owner, Damien Thorn.

The next time Dracula awoke from his black sleep, it was in a freezing Thorn Industries warehouse somewhere on the outskirts of London. The building was deserted, the only witnesses to Dracula's return Damien's manservant Hugo Barrett and Damien himself, still only 20 years old at this point. The body of the young woman Hugo had calmly exsanguinated in order to facilitate the resurrection dangled limply from a rope above the Count.

Dracula rose to meet his new supplicants, only to find them less servile than his eminence deserved. A red fury bloomed within him. *Kneel before your master!* he commanded.

Hugo casually lit a cigarette. The flare of his lighter ignited tiny flames in Damien's eyes, capering like twin devils as he gazed up at the Count. *Times have changed, Count,* he said. *This is not your country, and you are no longer master, but servant. My servant.*

Dracula thought of killing him right at that moment, but something in the young man's stare stopped him. Still, the insult could not go unanswered. *I serve but one master,* he said coldly.

Damien smiled, and got to his feet. *He who you call Master, I call Father. And so, as you serve him, you shall serve me.*

They locked eyes. Dracula attempted to crush the young man within the steely fingers of his hypnotic will, but found Damien utterly impervious. In that moment, the Count knew he spoke the truth. This was the Antichrist written of by John the Evangelist; his Master's heir, herald of the Last Days.

Damien calmly explained to him the preparations that were underway: the slow accumulation of power and influence, the massing of a worldwide network of acolytes, all in readiness for the Armageddon that would arrive in little more than a decade. To this end, he had resurrected Dracula, the most resolute and monstrous of his Father's servants on Earth.

Still, the Count had to understand that there could be no more petty vendettas, no more careless outbreaks of vampirism. In order to be effective in this new modern world, Dracula would have to learn its new codes and rituals. Thorn Industries would help establish him in that most unquestioned and influential of modern social positions, the business magnate. In return, he would operate from the shadows, an instrument of Damien's will, ruthless and cunning.

Biding his time, Dracula agreed. A new identity was created for him: D.D. Denham, reclusive head of the Denham Group of Companies, specialising in property development, oil and chemicals. Damien made sure the Count had the best business minds available to him for counsel as he acclimatised himself to the landscape of contemporary commerce. As it turned out, Dracula was a natural businessman; his implacable will and predatory instincts were perfectly adapted to the ruthless capitalist machine he found himself a part of. A machine whose choking fumes would quickly come to smother most of the world, much as Dracula had once hoped to spread his own diseased gospel across the planet.

Over the next two years, the Denham Group prospered. Dracula installed himself in a secure penthouse atop their headquarters, newly erected upon the site of his most recent defeat, a symbolic act of defiance he found fitting. Compared to his own ancestral home, it was sterile and tasteless, but in this modern world it was what passed for a symbol of his status.

From here he carried out his new master's will: a corporate takeover here, a mysterious death there. And he was safely inured from his enemies; protected as he was by the labyrinthine barriers of corporatism, the Van Helsings of the world simply had no idea Dracula even existed, let alone flourished.

But his new position sat ill with the Count. He was accustomed to being his master's chosen prince on Earth; now he had been supplanted by this upstart boy, who carried with him all the natural arrogance of one born into royalty. Dracula's own pride had been forged over centuries; he had earned his power and standing, and all of the blood spilt in doing so had been freely offered up to the Dark Father who dwelt below. Why then, should he be expected to kneel now, after so long?

I have been so long master that I would be master still, or at least that none other should be master of me. Dracula had spoken those words once, long ago. And now here he was, reduced to the level of a lackey, practically a scrivener. What had Damien earned? He had simply oozed into the world, thrust out by a mangy wild dog—*a dog!*—and laid claim to it as his birthright. In Dracula's kingdom, dogs had no rights; the boy was nothing but a cur, fit only to be kicked and gutted.

Dracula decided upon a plan. He would usher in his own Armageddon, before Damien's had even begun, and in doing so humiliate the Antichrist and elevate his own standing before Satan. As much as his master might dote on his only son, surely he could not ignore the offering of an entire planet, the complete destruction of everything that the despised Christ and his Father loved and cherished so highly.

He began to assemble his own horsemen of the apocalypse: the government minster, the titled heir, the general, the scientist; all fell prey to his will. He instructed the scientist, a genius in his field, to begin work incubating a new strain of bubonic plague, one so deadly and virulent that it would sweep across the face of the Earth before anyone could hope to stop it.

However, unbeknownst to Dracula, he had another opponent in play, one as mercilessly dedicated to advancing his own cause as the Antichrist himself.

The intelligence agent Stratton-Villiers, the man codenamed Fremont, had noted the recent rise to prominence of the Denham Group with interest. Making it his business to have a spy in every boardroom, Fremont had subsequently learned of the existence of the Psychical Examination & Research Group, a thinktank funded by Denham and headquartered at a quiet country retreat, Pelham House. In actuality, the house was the hub of Dracula's secret network, a nest of hired thugs and vampiric followers dedicated to the Count's cause: total apocalypse.

Knowing nothing of Dracula's existence, Fremont instructed his men to place a mole on the inside of Pelham House. The spy was quickly discovered and tortured near to death, but managed to escape and report back to his superiors. Before he died, he provided evidence that the research group was a front for obscene Black Mass rituals, and revealed the participation of Dracula's anointed four horsemen. Given that John Porter, the government politician recruited by Dracula, was the minister responsible for overseeing Fremont's own unit, it left the secret servicemen with an interesting problem to solve.

They enlisted the expertise of Lorimer Van Helsing, who swiftly discovered evidence of Dracula's involvement. But there was more at stake now than the unfortunate few who had already fallen victim to the Count's appetites; to Lorimer's horror, he realised that Dracula's objective was nothing less than the complete annihilation of the human race.

In desperation, he prepared to confront his nemesis at the Denham Group headquarters. But the Count was no longer a newborn in our world; this office building was his fortress now, and he was more than ready for Van Helsing. Lorimer failed in his attempt to kill Dracula, and was taken prisoner.

But yet again, Dracula's ego proved to be his downfall. Such was his loathing of the Van Helsing family, responsible for so many of his defeats, that a quick simple death was not deemed sufficient for Lorimer. Instead, Dracula had him brought to Pelham House, where he would become one of the Count's chosen horsemen, infected and doomed to carry his plague out into the world. As an additional twist of the knife, Dracula would force Lorimer to watch while he finally claimed Jessica Van Helsing as his consort.

A suitably vicious plan perhaps, but it came to naught. A fire started in the building and quickly rampaged out of control, claiming the lives of Dracula's acolytes and incinerating their vials of plague bacilli along with them. His designs for Armageddon in ruins, Dracula fled the burning house, hotly pursued by Lorimer. Succeeding in snaring Dracula within the clutching branches of a hawthorn tree, Van Helsing calmly executed the vampire for the second time.

Perhaps at the end, Dracula might even have considered this defeat something of a blessing. His upstart bid to supplant the Antichrist had been a catastrophic failure, and surely neither Damien nor his Father would have looked kindly upon it.

When Agent Fremont and his men arrived to secure the area, Lorimer led him to the Count's remains, telling him that they must be secured for the safety of all mankind. No longer must Dracula be allowed to continually return from the grave and wreak havoc amongst the living. Fremont assured him that he would take personal responsibility for dealing with the matter.

In this much, he was a man of his word.

Some weeks later, Dracula was reborn once more. This time he found himself imprisoned, caged within a custom-designed plexiglas tomb. The room around him was dark, save for the single light illuminating the well-dressed man who sat opposite him, safely outside his plastic prison.

Agent Fremont.

Dracula bared his teeth in a hiss. *You would imprison me?*

Fremont looked at the vampire with amusement. *Just a precaution, old boy. Needed to level out the playing field a bit. So that we might have a little chinwag.*

Release me! The Count hammered his fist against the plexiglas, to no avail.

Oh, I'd be delighted to. If we can find a bit of common ground, that is.

Dracula quietly seethed. *What do you propose?*

Fremont got to his feet and began to pace around Dracula's prison. *I hear you have a castle, back in the old country. Quite impressive. I've seen photographs.*

It dwarfs the pitiful shacks inhabited by those in your age, both in scale and in magnificence.

Fremont relished his adversary's arrogance. *No doubt. Oh, by the way, do you know who lives there now?*

Dracula glared at him, saying nothing. The thought of someone else living in his castle was too appalling to contemplate.

Fremont continued. *A Romanian Communist general. You're familiar with the Communist regimes of Eastern Europe?*

The vampire spat violently. *Upstart peasants!*

Quite. We're not great admirers of them over here, either. So you see, we do have some common cause.

Dracula considered. *You would barter with me?*

Something like that, possibly. Fremont cleared his throat. *We were thinking that perhaps we could help you get back to your country. And that, once you were there, you might want to reclaim what's yours—to begin with, your castle. And then, your influence…*

The Count's eyes gleamed. *My influence?*

We know you have a gift for…persuasion. For enlisting people to your cause. *Well, we rather thought our cause could become your cause. Imagine you, secretly working to . . . turn the Communists. Controlling them, under our instruction, of course. We could make rather a splendid team, don't you think?*

Why would I help you?

Aside from you being freed to take your ancestral castle back? Well, old boy, if you don't, I can promise you you'll never see daylight again. Oh, sorry — figure of speech. Silly me.

Fremont moved closer to the plexiglas, close enough that Dracula could see the vein pulsing warmly in his neck. *Look above you, Count. There's a sprinkler unit mounted on the ceiling of your cell. If we don't reach agreement, one signal from me and it gets turned on. I hear you're not a fan of running water. Oh, and I had the water tank blessed by a padre for good measure.*

He paused for effect. *After that, your ashes would be sealed up and entombed in the deepest, darkest vault I could find. No one would ever hear of Count Dracula again. You'd become a fairytale, nothing but a bedtime story to frighten children with.*

Dracula considered this. Perhaps non-existence *was* preferable to being a catspaw for these squabbling insects and their petty politics. *None other should be master of me.*

He was on the verge of refusing Fremont when the other man spoke again, as if reading his mind.

Oh, one more thing. A small enticement to sweeten the deal. We could deliver you Lorimer Van Helsing.

The Count could hardly believe it. *You would give him to me?*

Easy enough to organise, once we were satisfied you were carrying out your side of the agreement. He's an anthropology professor, I believe. Perhaps a lecture tour behind the Iron Curtain can be arranged. I'm sure he'd jump at the chance to visit your old stamping grounds. Fremont looked pleased at the clean simplicity of it.

You would sacrifice one of your own?

No doubt you play chess, Count Dracula. And you're an excellent player, I'm sure. So I imagine you understand the principle of sacrificing a piece to gain an advantage.

Dracula smiled, but his smile was no less terrible than that of the man facing him on the other side of the plexiglas.

He's an old man. We'll deal with the granddaughter. No one else will miss him.

The bargain was struck.

JIM & EMILY UNDERWOOD

Donald & Angela Pleasence in From Beyond the Grave, *1974*
written by Robin Clarke & Raymond Christodoulou
based on stories by R. Chetwynd-Hayes, directed by Kevin Connor

Angela Pleasence in The Godsend, *1980*
written by Olaf Pooley, based on the novel by Bernard Taylor
directed by Gabrielle Beaumont

EMILY UNDERWOOD HAD ALWAYS BEEN WHAT HER FATHER JIM called a Deep One. Born during the war, while Jim was away fighting in the North African Campaign, she owed her life to Julian Karswell; Jim and his wife Miriam had counted themselves amongst the notorious occultist's most devoted followers.

Not long before Emily was due to be born, Miriam had begun experiencing severe pains. She'd been rushed to hospital, only to be informed that her unborn daughter no longer had a heartbeat. The doctors told her that there was unfortunately nothing to be done, but Miriam knew better. She understood the limits of science and medicine, and the boundless power of that which lay beyond them.

She immediately contacted Karswell and begged him for his aid. The occultist possessed an odd fondness for children and agreed to visit her in hospital. Upon arrival, he'd gravely told Miriam that he could indeed revive her baby... but only at the cost of her own life. *Nothing for nothing.*

Miriam readily agreed, on the condition that Karswell saw to it that her daughter's welfare would be taken care of; until such time as Jim returned from the war, or until she came of age if he should not. To the doctors' amazement, the child subsequently revived in Miriam's womb, and was induced shortly afterwards, in case of further complications.

The resulting birth was a traumatic one, although Emily herself emerged into the world silently, offering no cries or tears for the ailing mother she was soon to lose. Miriam lived just long enough to see her daughter's face for the first time, before receding into whatever oblivion Karswell had arranged for her.

Karswell was as good as his word and took Emily in. She came to live with him and his mother at Lufford Hall, and the occultist dutifully raised her as his own until Jim Underwood returned home in 1945. Emily soon grew into a bright, eerily precocious child. She learned to read at a remarkably young age, and quickly rejected the children's books that were gifted to her, preferring instead to sit on Karswell's lap and look through her guardian's collection of valuable grimoires. They would sit there for hours, Emily marvelling at the eldritch horrors illustrated within, her small lips silently mouthing the dreadful incantations Karswell would teach to her. By the time Jim arrived to claim Emily, her vocabulary quite outstripped his; from that day on, he would often marvel at his daughter's facility with 'jawcracking words'.

Taking Emily back to the modest Windsor flat he and Miriam had called home — much of their mutual income had been donated to Karswell's cause — Jim felt suddenly ashamed. His daughter had known only the luxury of Lufford Hall for the first few years of her life, and was now to be reduced to this humble hand-to-mouth existence.

However, if Emily felt any emotion about the sudden downgrading of her circumstances, she did not show it. She looked blankly around the dingy collection of rooms, and simply nodded. She did not resent her social demotion; she told her father she knew full well how fortunate she had been, and that all she wanted was for her future children to receive the same opportunities she had been given early on in life.

They quickly settled into their new life together. Jim's war pension was barely adequate to support the two of them, so he took to peddling matches on the streets. He bore this indignity with equanimity; he and Emily still had each other, and he counted himself lucky for that. Karswell had revealed to him the circumstances of his daughter's birth and Miriam's subsequent death, and Jim had vowed to honour his wife's sacrifice by supporting Emily by any means possible. He promised himself that she would have whatever she desired, as much as it was within his ability to provide it. But whenever he asked Emily what she wanted, she would gaze back at him with those passive, unblinking eyes, like a rattlesnake basking in the sun, and reply, *But what do you want, Daddy?* The occultist had also warned him that Emily was a *unique* child, and it was true that Jim often overheard their neighbours remarking that the girl 'wasn't all there'. He supposed that, despite Karswell's ministrations, part of Emily had indeed died inside her mother, but he nevertheless resolved to love whatever was left.

As the years passed and Emily grew older, Jim began to fret about her lack of friends. Everyday social interactions were entirely beyond her, and her school years had been marked by several instances of bullying, although given the misfortune that inevitably fell upon any child who mistreated her, such incidents never persisted for long. Because, while Karswell's untimely death in the late 1950s had robbed her of her first mentor, he had bequeathed her a portion of his book collection, which she pored over avidly every evening. Jim could see how natural a talent she had for the esoteric, and felt a burgeoning fatherly pride over her increasingly impressive abilities.

So if any child happened to cross her and paid the price, well, that was just the way of things. *Always remember*, he would tell her, *do what thou wilt is the whole of the law.*

Still, he fretted. They would sit at the dinner table together, and Jim would say, *I worry about you, Emily. I worry what you'll do after I'm gone.* And she would smile—her distant, emotionless smile that looked like it belonged to someone else entirely—and say, *Oh, I'm sure I'll meet a nice gentleman someday. And then I'll have babies of my own. Lots of babies.* Then she would drift back into her private reverie, softly singing meaningless songs to herself.

So when Jim met Christopher Lowe outside Windsor station one morning, he quickly decided he could finally give Emily something she wanted. Not because of any upstanding qualities the little man possessed; in fact, quite the opposite. Jim very quickly saw through him, and recognised Lowe for what he was—a repressed little worm, and one who lied about his war service record to boot.

Nevertheless, Jim was not naïve enough to imagine the course of true love would run smooth for Emily, and so he preferred her first lover to be someone more deserving of the unhappy consequences that would likely result. He invited the man home to meet his daughter.

Lowe proved himself a willing participant in the romantic charade; quickly convinced he had a sympathetic audience, he took to voiding his bitterness over the dinner table, while the doting Emily served him a succession of delicious home-cooked meals. His face growing flushed with rage, Lowe would screech impotently about his fat shrew of a wife, his ungrateful son, the soul-destroying nature of his work.

Jim made appropriately sympathetic noises, of course; and for her part, Emily proved herself a strangely magnetic presence, drawing more and more of the man's poison to the surface. Lowe certainly seemed entranced by her; Jim supposed it was yet another of her strange talents.

Matters soon progressed to the point where Jim contrived an excuse to leave them alone for the evening; he returned to find his normally-placid daughter in fits of uncontrollable giggles. *The worm,* she snorted. *The worm has another little worm dangling between his legs. It was so small he could barely get it in.*

Jim cackled delightedly—he enjoyed the rare treat of being able to share laughter with his daughter—and began to make plans for their future. Before she retired for the night, Emily kissed his cheek and whispered to him, *Thank you, Daddy. I got what I wanted.*

Emily swiftly ensured that her new lover's wife would no longer be a problem, and she and her father moved into the Lowe household before the woman's body was even cold. Lowe offered no resistance to their arrival; his life had been nothing but a series of acquiescences, great and small, and he was incapable of deviating from that path now. So when Jim broke the news to him that Edith was pregnant and quietly suggested that the only decent thing for him to do under the circumstances was to marry her, Lowe simply gave a tremulous shrug, like an invertebrate trying to escape back into its hole.

Perhaps he even felt a momentary flicker of relief when his new life was cut short immediately after the ceremony. His new family gathered to celebrate the nuptials, and when Emily asked if he wanted her to cut the cake—was he *sure* it was what he wanted?—he might have suspected what would result, and welcomed it.

Emily's blade pierced the figure of the groom perched atop the cake— so proud, so upstanding, so unlike Lowe himself—and as the icing crumpled under the knife, so too did Lowe. He was dead by the time his body hit the table.

Still, Emily had what she wanted—a baby and a comfortable new home in which to raise it. Nine months went by, and the result of her and Lowe's union was born. Perhaps the boy took too much after his late father—he was a weak, underweight little thing—and scant days after she brought him home, Emily found his lifeless body lying silently in the crib.

Jim wept for his grandson, but Emily showed no discernible emotion. If anything, her hands seemed more at ease cradling the poor dead thing than they ever had done in the short time the child was alive. *Maybe it's me, Dad. Maybe I can't give them what they need.*

Jim assured her that she could try again in time, and when he subsequently crossed paths with the disgraced ex-policeman Johnson in one of Windsor's less salubrious drinking establishments, he felt sure the man could give Emily what she wanted.

True, he was a drunk—Jim discovered he'd left the force after an accused child killer had died in his custody, and although Johnson had been cleared of the man's murder, he'd been pressured into taking early retirement, his life collapsing into a wreck of booze and self-loathing as a result—but he was still a hefty, virile man, and ex-army to boot, which always counted for something in Jim's book.

He lured Johnson home with promises of whisky, and although he seemed more interested in the contents of Jim's drinks cabinet than in his daughter, forever lurking like a quiet ghost in the background, the man met with tacit approval from Emily. Johnson became a regular visitor to the Underwood household, picking disinterestedly at the lavish meals Emily served up for him, but always happy to work his way through Jim's whisky bottle (Jim kept his glass well-filled) and regale them with boozily-vitriolic monologues about his time as a police detective.

And if Jim and Emily did not consider graphic accounts of abuse, rape and murder fit topics for the dinner table, they kept their objections to themselves.

When Jim finally left them alone together for an evening, Emily quickly saw another side of her intended. After helping himself to a few drinks, he suddenly grew violent, enraged at Emily's solemn passivity. He seized her and wrestled her to the floor, his meaty paw around her throat, his breath ragged and excited in his chest. He had kept it bottled tightly inside all these years, the sour ferment building in his belly, but finally *this*, this was what he had always wanted.

Emily saw no reason to deny him. She looked calmly up at him, her eyes fearless. *You can do what you want to me. Whatever you want.*

By the time Jim returned home, Emily had cleaned herself up. There was no sign of Johnson. *He won't be coming back, Dad.*

They found the man's body floating in the Thames a few days later. Few mourned him, but Jim thought it was only right that they attend his funeral. As they stood amongst the scattering of Johnson's ex-colleagues at the graveside, Emily could already feel the dead man's bitter seed budding inside her. This time she would take no chances.

She found a couple that would suit her needs, a safe distance away in the countryside, and watched them from afar. The Marlowes were bland and affluently happy, and had four children already—to Emily, the kids seemed to be more of a lifestyle accessory than anything else, something that just happened to have been delivered along with the imported furniture. She felt certain the couple would barely notice another.

So, when she was almost due, she contrived to meet the family while they were out for a Sunday walk. The woman seemed desperate for someone to talk to, and invited her to their home for tea. Emily had never been good with people, and the woman's husband in particular quickly grew to find her awkward presence disquieting, but it was no matter. By the time he tried to usher her from the house, Emily could feel the baby announcing itself, eager to arrive.

The man rushed to fetch a doctor, but by the time they returned, the woman had already helped Emily to deliver her daughter. Emily watched her cooing delightedly over the little girl; it was as if she was already bored of her own offspring. Satisfied she had made the right choice, Emily allowed the couple to bed her into their spare room for the night. Then, once the family had retired, she quickly rose and dressed herself.

She gazed down at her newborn; the baby woke and stared silently back up at her mother, as if reading her thoughts. *This is all yours now, little cuckoo. Take what you want from them.*

With that, Emily stole away into the darkness, leaving her child behind. There would be other fathers, other children, other homes. All she took for herself in return was the Marlowe family's future.

AMY SUMNER

Susan George in Straw Dogs, *1971*
written by David Zelag Goodman
based on the novel by Gordon M. Williams
directed by Sam Peckinpah

*H*OME, AMY THOUGHT. *I'M FINALLY HOME.*
She'd been born in Cornwall in 1950, the daughter of Rick and Stella Fitzgerald, née Meredith. The family had lived in Windward House, a large clifftop residence that Rick and his sister Pamela had purchased at a knockdown price from Stella's grandfather some years before. The house possessed a tragically storied history, and had stood empty for over a decade. (It also enjoyed an ill reputation amongst local people, who deemed it haunted.)

Scoffing at such superstition, the Fitzgeralds had snapped up the property, only to discover the truth of the rumours. More happily, Rick Fitzgerald and Stella had fallen in love, and together, they'd finally succeeded (it was thought) in laying the ghosts of the past to rest. The couple were soon married, and thus Stella was finally returned to the ancestral family home she had always loved. Amy was born soon afterwards.

And they all lived happily ever after, as Rick would frequently tell guests over cocktails.

But the happy ending of one story is often only the beginning of another, sadder, one. Some claimed what happened next was simply the result of post-partum depression; others insisted that the pervading air of gloom had never truly been banished from Windward House.

Whatever the truth of it, Stella threw herself off the clifftop some months after Amy's birth, much as Mary Meredith, the woman originally thought to be Stella's mother, had done a quarter of a century before.

Rick, blaming himself, had fallen into a deep depression. He became distant, leaving Amy's upbringing entirely to Pamela. Drinking heavily, he soon became convinced that the house was now haunted by Stella, much as it had once been haunted by Mary.

Unable to abide living there any longer, he signed the house over to Pamela and took Amy away to a small village near Land's End, where he rented an isolated farmhouse—Trencher's Farm—for them both. There, he would sequester himself away in his study for days on end, composing a never-to-be-finished requiem for Stella.

The young Amy grew up never knowing her mother, and idolising her distant father, a withdrawn figure who would occasionally emerge for meals, but mostly entrusted Amy's care to his housekeeper or, when she came to visit, her aunt Pamela. Often lonely, she grew into a petulant, demanding girl, craving the love and attention she had never been granted. She would sneak into her father's study while he was asleep and sabotage his work, randomly adding minims and semibreves to the staves of his composition. But if Rick even noticed, he never said anything.

Once she entered her teens, Amy took to hanging around with local boys like Charlie Venner or Norman Scutt, whom Pamela decried as *coarse*, and *a bad influence*. She'd pleaded with Rick to pay more attention to the company his daughter was keeping, but when he banned his daughter from seeing them, she simply waited until Rick was once again locked away in his study, then sneaked out. Amy was fast developing into an attractive young woman, and enjoyed the attention she got from Venner and the others.

Rumours of Amy's activities eventually got back to Pamela, and she'd insisted that Amy be sent away to boarding school. Rick had acquiesced, only breaking the news to his tearful daughter a few short days before she was due to leave. Heartbroken and furious, she'd never said another word to him; Rick would die from liver cirrhosis during her first term away.

Years passed, and having no real home to return to upon completing school, Amy used money from her inheritance to travel to America and enrol in a university there. It was so different to what she'd known in England, where the tumult of the late sixties had barely touched her. Here, there was a dangerous air of uncertainty, a livewire sense that anything was possible, or indeed permissible. Two very different wars were waging, abroad and at home. The atmosphere crackled with civil unrest, student revolt; rock 'n roll and sex and violence were the currency of the times.

It was here that she met David Sumner.

David was a young science professor, preppy and bookish. Amy wasn't taking any science classes, but she'd noticed him around campus, head frequently buried in an incomprehensible book. He'd seemed utterly removed from the uproar around him, almost desperate not to acknowledge it. It was obvious that he found the certainty of algebraic equations far more comforting than the anarchy threatening to engulf them all. But he had an impish quality she found appealing, and a lithe sensitivity she'd never known in a man before, certainly not in the boys back home.

One day she introduced herself in the canteen. She'd been teaching herself chess, and had bought a small travel kit. She wandered over to him and placed the board down on the table. *Do you play?* she said.

He looked up at her and blinked. *I don't play games*, he babbled, trying not to notice her apparel. She'd dressed for the occasion and chosen her shortest miniskirt, somehow neglecting to wear a bra to boot.

Amy smiled. *Oh, you'll play them with me.*

They were married six months later.

Amy had looked forward to completing her degree and settling into life as a campus wife. She enjoyed the atmosphere of intellectual freedom they dwelt in, the cocktail parties and drunken debates. It would only be a matter of time before David was awarded tenure, and for the first time she could remember, Amy found herself enjoying a sense of possibility. Even if her existence with David was sometimes stifling, there were campus rumours of late night activities that might spice things up if need be; tantalising whispers of key parties and intoxicated bacchanals.

But as it turned out, David had very different ideas. Distressed by the hum of impending violence in the air, like a storm about to break, he told Amy he wanted to take a sabbatical, get away from America for a while. *If we stay here I won't have any choice but to get involved, and I don't want to be involved,* he told her.

Amy resisted at first, but after the shootings at Kent State, David doubled down on his insistence, displaying a steely nerve she hadn't previously suspected he possessed. They fought for weeks, until Amy finally gave in. *I'll give you a year,* she said. *Just until everything blows over here.*

David had fallen in love with Amy's stories of Cornwall, and pushed for them to relocate there, anticipating a sojourn filled with bucolic peace and quiet. Amy reluctantly agreed; her aunt Pamela had already informed her that Trencher's Farm had remained unoccupied since her father's death, with many of his old belongings still in it. Perhaps if she went back and faced down those old ghosts, she could put it all behind her for good. They took out a year's lease on the farmhouse and headed to England.

To her dawning horror, Amy found that nothing there had changed. Unlike her adopted country, England seemed to pride itself on standing still; the idea of civil unrest—so impolite!—remained a complete anathema to much of the population. Even worse, Venner and his cronies still lived in the nearby village, a lurking pack of feral dogs. Emboldened by maturity and their daily intake of ale, they loitered in the lanes as Amy ran her errands, openly ogling her legs, her ass, her breasts.

Things were no better at the farm. Claiming Rick's old study for himself, David had settled down to work, shutting himself away for hours on end and ignoring Amy. He was just like her father: the eternally absent male. Suddenly she felt thirteen years old again.

Amy found herself assuming the same role of petulant ingenue she had played all those years before. The old lines and stage directions sprang easily to her mind. She would saunter into the study and alter the equations on David's blackboard, taking a sulky delight in disrupting him, prodding at him until he snapped. *I love you, Amy—but I want you to leave me alone,* he told her. Once again, she was being sent away.

She'd begged him to spend some time with her. Noticing a poster for a travelling fair playing nearby, she'd coaxed David along. *We'll eat candyfloss and you can win me a goldfish,* she told him. David allowed himself to be convinced.

As they walked under the garishly-painted archway welcoming them to the *Pandemonium Carnival,* she'd felt excited; she was out on a date with her husband. This was what adult married life was meant to be; she was certain Rick would have been proud of the young woman she'd become.

But as they settled into their seats in the big tent, she could sense David growing tense beside her. This was about as far away from liberal academic America as you could get; the notions of entertainment out here in rural England were more vulgar, far less *enlightened.* Like so many of his political persuasion, David loved the idea of being one of the common people, only to find the unvarnished truth of their lives repellent.

Amy didn't care; she entered fully into the spirit of the show, oooh'ing and aaah'ing as the freakshow was paraded before them. David said nothing, remaining stony still in his seat.

He was not moved to speak until the ringmaster finally capered into the arena, a croaking goblin wearing minstrel makeup.

Amy felt David's fingers clutching her knee, hard enough to hurt. *We're leaving,* he hissed.

What are you talking about? she said.

David took his glasses off, as though he couldn't bear to see anymore. *Amy, look at him! He's wearing blackface! I've never seen anything so appalling in my life.*

David, it's just a bit of fun . . .

Yeah, and I suppose they'll start burning crosses as an encore next. Come on!

He'd stood up and dragged her out by her wrist. They'd fought ferociously in the car home, Amy mocking David's wishy-washy liberalism. *You really don't get it, do you?* he'd retaliated. *People are out fighting against that crap in the streets!*

Then why aren't you out there with them? she'd screamed in reply. They'd driven the rest of the way home in silence.

Matters had only got worse after that. David had retreated back into the silence of his study, barricading himself behind tripwires of mathematical formulae. In response, Amy had quietly encouraged the attentions of Venner and the others, taunting them with the ripe unavailability of her body. Part of her understood that Charlie was little more than an oaf, hardly better than the giggling idiots he called his friends, but another part of her, that long-lost teenaged girl who'd been so abruptly banished from her home, pined for the bygone simplicity of a time where his coarse masculinity and firm body would have been enough to satisfy her.

She'd revelled in the Pavlovian power she had over the local men, but Amy's immaturity was such that she'd never truly learned the limits of that power in the adult world. Lured by her scent, emboldened by David's impotence, the men began to steal into the house, first stealing her underwear, then strangling the Sumners' pet cat and hanging it in their bedroom cupboard.

Suddenly afraid of what she'd unleashed, she'd begged David to confront them, but as usual he'd prevaricated, complicated the issue with windy obfuscation. How Amy despised his weakness! Venner might have been an animal, but at least he was a *man*.

Just how much of an animal would soon become clear. The men had invited David out hunting, and like the trusting fool he was, he'd accepted, eager to be accepted into a world he'd never understood. He'd left the henhouse completely unguarded, and Venner, the cunning fox, crept in. He'd come calling for Amy, and she, thinking they both understood the game they were playing, let him inside.

She quickly learned that the rules of the brutal world Venner inhabited were a far cry from those of the university campus she'd so recently left behind. He'd forced himself upon Amy, despite her screams. She'd struggled and fought, but in the end it was easier to submit.

Struggling not to be subsumed by the despair that welled within her, she took refuge in a private fantasy, telling herself she was a girl again, and that this was the first time she'd been denied all those years ago. Despite the pain and humiliation, she almost managed to convince herself that she welcomed Venner's assault.

Tears in her eyes, she summoned the will to embrace her attacker. This way, she could pick herself up and go on with her life, and David need never know. She could envisage his easy intellectual disgust if he ever found out; Amy knew he would instinctively believe she had invited this degradation upon herself. His weakness would never survive this; she had to find an inner strength her husband did not possess.

And then, just as she'd thought her torment was over, Norman Scutt had crept into the room. Venner had stepped aside and allowed his friend a turn at Amy. Suddenly she realised that Charlie was just as pathetic as her husband, that all men were little better than craven pack animals, jostling and snapping for position.

Once again, she screamed and struggled, but was too exhausted to prevent Scutt viciously raping her. This time there was nowhere for her mind to hide, no possible way to convince herself that this was anything other than the purest horror.

When David returned home that evening, she could barely bring herself to look at him. The self-loathing she nurtured was only matched by that which she felt for him. He finally admitted Venner and the others had humiliated him like a schoolboy, left him wandering alone on the moors. *They really stuck it to me out there*, he told her.

She said nothing. How like a man, to equate a petty social embarrassment to the sort of violation she had been forced to suffer!

She began to make private plans to leave David, but then events in the village took an even more violent turn. Henry Niles, the local simpleton, was suspected of abducting a teenage girl, Janice Hedden. Fleeing from a pursuing mob, he had stumbled into the road and had been hit by David and Amy, returning home in their car. David had insisted on taking Niles home to call a doctor, not realising Janice's vengeful father and the others were out searching for him.

A heavy fog had billowed in from the sea, surrounding Trencher's Farm. It was a night for monsters, and it did not take them long to arrive. The mob tracked Niles to the farm and angrily laid siege to the building. Amy begged David to turn the man over to them, but he refused. To her dismay, she realised that something primal had been awakened within him, that he meant to meet the villagers' violence with retribution of his own.

The battle quickly escalated, and once the first blood was split, David knew that no amount of reasoning would offer a solution now. He could give them Niles, and they would still kill him. They would kill him for defying them, for being married to a woman they desired, for being American. To save himself, he would have to become like them.

So when Amy refused to help him, his mask was finally ripped aside. *Do as you're told or I'll break your neck,* he told her. At that moment, Amy feared her husband more than Charlie Venner or even Scutt.

Soon, five villagers, including Venner and Scutt, lay dead or injured. A victorious David surveyed the carnage, a cold smile on his face. *Jesus, I got 'em all,* he whispered proudly. Amy fought the urge to vomit. Worse even than the carnage she had just witnessed was the revelation of David's hypocrisy; in the end, he was everything he had claimed not to be, merely another brute. The final irony was that he had *not* got them all; one of the mob had survived the battle, and took David by surprise. Amy looked on as the man beat David to the ground; the victorious machismo of just a few moments before was forgotten, and he was reduced to a spineless, pleading worm once again.

Amy considered letting the man murder him, but knew her own life would be forfeit if she did. Horrified, she picked up a shotgun and killed the attacker. Now she too, was complicit, dragged into the maelstrom of her husband's violence.

David left her alone in the wreckage of their home as he drove Niles away to safety. Amy stared dully at the shattered house, at the bloodied bodies, at the ruins of everything she had known. Once she had been tearfully sent away from this house, but now, she could simply not bear to remain here any longer. Quickly, she threw a few belongings into a bag, then wrapped herself in a heavy coat and left, pausing only to scrawl David a farewell note. *I don't like this game any more,* was all she wrote.

Outside, the fog lay like a sodden shroud, wet and choking. She stumbled out onto the main road, heading away from the village, barely able to see her own feet beneath her. Within minutes, she was cold and exhausted. She did not know how long she would be able to walk for; all she understood was that she could not go back. Perhaps she might just lie down and hope to die of exposure out here, or else find her way to the sea and throw herself in, as her mother had done before her. Surely it could only be a release.

Her suicidal reverie was interrupted by an approaching sound; what sounded like horse's hooves clattering on the tarmac. Was it a trick of the fog, an aural distortion? But no—moments later, a horsedrawn carriage emerged out of the murk and pulled up beside her. She could just about read the painted sign on the side of the vehicle, announcing 'Papa Lazarou's Pandemonium Carnival!'

She strained to see the driver. *Please, can you help me?* she whispered up to the indistinct shape sitting atop the carriage.

In reply, a darkly-painted face loomed down at her, emerging from the mist as if it were a brass rubbing taking form before her eyes. A strong hand seized hers, pulling her up onto the seat. Before Amy knew what was happening, the driver had whipped the horses back into motion, and they were speeding away into the night.

The driver still held her hand tightly in his own. She looked up into the grinning face of the carnival ringmaster, Papa Lazarou. Exclaiming with glee, he reached down and deftly plucked Amy's wedding band from her finger. Before she could say anything, he gave a sandpaper cackle:

You're my wife now, Amy!

David Sumner never saw his wife again.

DEACON

Gordon Kennedy in The Borderlands, *2013*
written by Elliot Goldner and James Moran and Sean Hogan
directed by Elliot Goldner

DEACON HAD ALWAYS BEEN WILFUL, PRONE TO DISOBEDIENCE. AS a small boy, his despairing mother first tried cowing him with threats to report his behaviour to the family priest, and when that fell on deaf ears, terrifying him into submission with stories of legendary bogeymen that lurked in dark places, hungering after unruly, godless children.

For, despite his staunchly Catholic upbringing, the young Deacon always had his doubts about God. He simply could not reconcile the evil he already recognised in the world with the existence of a supposedly all-powerful and loving deity. On the other hand, he knew, without any vestige of doubt, that there *were* monsters; both human and inhuman.

So when his mother told him of the insatiable Rawhead, a towering carnivorous beast that roamed the countryside devouring everyone in its path, and Bloody Bones, a mysterious subterranean creature that dwelt in caves and tunnels ready to prey on the unwary, he was quite certain she was telling the truth.

From that day forth, he refused to play in the fields and meadows lying outside the bounds of the small village his family called home, and enclosed spaces were anathema to him. These measures provided him with some small sense of safety, although he could do nothing about the black winter nights when the wind seethed outside his window—how could he be sure that it was not the wail of a wendigo or banshee?—and neither could he ward off the monsters awaiting him in the depths of his dreams, where there could be no escaping them.

As he grew older, his parents became dismayed by his budding agnosticism and arranged to have him sent away to Saint Anthony's, a Catholic boarding school. The establishment was somewhat down-at-heel, but the fees were affordable, and the priests teaching there were renowned as strict disciplinarians.

Deacon quickly fell under the sway of Father Goddard, a harsh, unyielding man who nevertheless recognised the boy's keen intelligence and spirit, and undertook to realign them in the service of the Almighty. He would hold regular evening chats with Deacon, whereupon they would discuss his burgeoning doubts and fears about the world, and Goddard would firmly and systematically rebut them. He had no patience with fence-sitters, and could summon a Biblical quote for every occasion, reciting the relevant scripture in his richly-commanding baritone.

Despite the fact that he was rapidly leaving childhood behind, Deacon still found his sleeping hours tormented by nightmares of the nameless things that lurked beyond the world of man, and would confess these terrors to the priest. *But Father, there are monsters in the Bible,* he would insist. *Leviathan, Behemoth, the Nephilim. So how can you say they don't exist?*

In response, Goddard would sigh impatiently. *I gave you more credit than that, Deacon. You're a smart boy. These are metaphors, like many things in the Bible. They aren't* real.

Such was the force of Father Goddard's will that Deacon eventually began to submit to the Catholic faith. There was some murmured talk at the time that perhaps the priest's interest in Deacon went beyond the purely spiritual, but nothing ever came of such disreputable gossip, and by the time scandal erupted at the school some years later, after Goddard was found to have murdered another boy he was mentoring, Deacon had left St Anthony's far behind him.

If he enjoyed any private insight into why Goddard had committed such an act, he never spoke of it. Still, perhaps there was something to be said for his childish fears of monsters after all.

Although Deacon never actually entered the priesthood—he still retained enough of his instinctive rebelliousness that such an avenue was advised to be unsuitable—fate finally brought him to the Vatican, where he joined an research team tasked with investigating any alleged miracles reported to the Church. Such cases were common enough that the Vatican thought it prudent to examine and document them carefully, lest rampant fraud and rumour damage the Church's standing and reputation. Deacon's tendency towards religious scepticism was therefore considered a distinct advantage, given that the overwhelming majority of these cases were proven to be false in some respect.

Deacon showed himself to be an able recruit, and was soon entrusted with his own team. Was there a part of him that relished undermining the faith that had been foisted upon him? Colleagues from the time have since suggested that he sometimes seemed like a man quietly at war with himself, and he is known to have begun drinking regularly during this period. His increased alcohol intake was noted by his superiors but not officially commented upon—it had not yet advanced to the point where it was in danger of interfering with his workload, and certainly the Catholic faith has never looked askance at its followers enjoying a drink or two.

All of this was to change after the events in Belém.

Belém is a busy city in Northern Brazil, and seemed an unlikely spot for a miracle. However, word had reached the Vatican that a Catholic shrine there had gained a reputation as a site of healing; devotees were already proclaiming it to be the new Lourdes. Such was the fevered excitement around these rumours that the Church despatched one of their senior cardinal priests, Renaldi, to look into the matter. Deacon was not initially part of the group, but when communications from Renaldi grew erratic, he was quickly sent to Belém in pursuit of the team.

Deacon later took to offering a more partial account of events, but the official record shows that he arrived in the city to discover the priests alive, albeit in a confused and suggestible state; some were already claiming they had experienced ecstatic visions at the shrine. Cardinal Renaldi announced himself satisfied that something miraculous had indeed occurred there; regardless, Deacon insisted on further investigation, as unshakeable in his scepticism as ever.

There is some dispute over what happened next; what we do know is that Deacon was supposed to accompany the team back to the shrine, but was apparently too inebriated to make the trip. Renaldi and the rest of the group travelled there without him and were never seen alive again.

When their bodies were found in the jungle some days later, the coroners discovered they had been dosed with large quantities of dimethyltryptamine (DMT), a naturally-occurring psychedelic. One of the priests had apparently gouged his own eyes out; the accepted theory was that it must have been in response to the intensity of the hallucinations he was experiencing.

In his report, Deacon concluded that the shrine had been a fraud all along, and that the dead men had either been mistakenly given too large a dose of DMT in an effort to convince them of the veracity of their visions, or else they had simply been murdered to prevent the perpetrators of the fraud from being exposed.

The truth will probably never be known. For his part, Deacon was not publicly censured for his negligence—his superiors realised that if he had accompanied the group as planned, he would doubtless be dead too—but his reputation within the Vatican suffered significantly as a result. Many priests privately held him responsible for the men's deaths, and it was quietly decided that the next time Deacon was assigned an investigation, he would be very carefully monitored.

Deacon himself was not oblivious to the whispering campaign being waged against him. He sank into a deep depression, his drinking only worsening as a result.

So when the purported miracle at the English country church came to light, it was judged an ideal opportunity to permit Deacon back into the field. The parish was small, the church remote and ill-attended, and there would be no obvious risk to life or limb involved. Discretion was therefore thought to be assured.

An unexplained incident had been captured on amateur video taken at a christening; however, the footage was crude and most likely faked. It was considered to be a relatively open-and-shut case, one which could be wrapped up with a modicum of fuss and thus allow Deacon to ease back into his responsibilities.

That said, no chances were to be taken; the Vatican insisted the investigation be thoroughly documented on video and employed a technician, Gray Parker, to oversee the process. In addition, Father Mark Amidon — one of Deacon's more vocal detractors within the Vatican — was tasked with acting as overseer.

Upon studying the footage of the christening, Deacon had little doubt he was embarking on a wild goose chase. However, he understood that this was something of a probationary mission, and accepted the assignment without complaint. He joined Gray at their small rental cottage, realising with some consternation that the technician had rigged the entire building with CCTV cameras in advance of his arrival. Amidon had been delayed en route, so the pair went ahead and commenced the investigation, introducing themselves to the parish priest Father Crellick, and installing more closed circuit cameras around the church.

Deacon decided very early on that Crellick was a fraud, judging the man to be a liar and a poor one at that. The church had only recently been reopened, having been closed since the 18th century, and the congregation was sparse and unenthusiastic; a cynic might suggest that a confirmed miracle could be just the thing to boost attendance.

Nevertheless, due process was observed, and Deacon undertook a careful examination of the church records, studying the journal of Pritchard Mandeville, the last minister to serve at the site before its closure. He discovered that Mandeville had also founded a nearby orphanage, similarly long since closed.

Finding themselves unwelcome in the area — the villagers were surly at best, and outright hostile at worst — the team resolved to wrap up the investigation as quickly as possible. Their video cameras did indeed capture further incidents in the church — objects moving, ghostly cries — but nothing that could not be explained away by simple fakery.

However, when they attempted to confront Father Crellick and provoke a confession, the man broke down and threw himself off the church tower. Once again, an investigation involving Deacon had resulted in a tragic death.

Wracked with guilt, Deacon resolved to return to the church, rationalising that this would be the final evidence they needed; if no further incidents were recorded, it would be proof Crellick alone was responsible.

But when his nighttime journey to the building was interrupted by strange events—disembodied cries in the darkness, momentary glimpses of a spectral figure that appeared to be Crellick—Deacon found both his nerve and his scepticism buckling. Inside the church, he discovered a hidden doorway, opening onto a set of stone stairs leading deep underneath the church. When he attempted to investigate further, he was driven back by the ghastly sound of Crellick screaming in torment.

Amidon was furious with him for attempting to prolong what he now viewed as a closed case. He suspected Deacon of faking the latest incidents himself, and vowed to have him dragged before a disciplinary committee.

In desperation, Deacon contacted his old mentor from the Vatican, the elderly priest Calvino. The old man travelled to meet them at once, informing them that the church grounds had originally been a site of pagan worship, and in his view needed to be reconsecrated to drive out whatever forces were still lurking there. In the face of Father Amidon's continued protests, they decided to journey back to the church.

All at once, Deacon felt like a small boy again. He had finally discovered *something*—a supernatural force that could not be explained away by fakery or church dogma. This was older than the Church—could it be more powerful? He could not admit such shameful thoughts to the others, but remembered his mother's cautionary tales of Rawhead and Bloody Bones and felt the same nascent dread enveloping him.

Deciding to make a joke of it, he asked the group if anyone else had ever heard these same stories.

Amidon's wry response caught him off-guard: *I remember a story back from when I was a kid in Dublin. God, I haven't thought about this for years. Rawhead! There was all this talk about how he'd been set free from his prison in the earth. Somewhere over in County Wicklow, it was. Some farmers had released him and he'd gone on a rampage. Killed kids and all sorts. Finally they managed to drive him back underground. All nonsense of course, but people really believed it had happened. A big ten-foot monster! That's Ireland for you. Rawhead the King, they called him.*

The priest chuckled in amused remembrance, but Deacon could not find it within himself to join in the laughter. Suddenly, he knew. His mother had been right. There *were* monsters after all, and they still hungered for him.

They proceeded into the darkened church, and commenced the ceremony. Deacon immediately sensed that something was wrong. He could feel the power building around them; a dark, ancient energy thrumming in the stone walls. His faith meant nothing here, his God was entirely absent. Jesus Christ was the real folk story, not the ancient pagan legends. Calvino's holy incantations might as well have been a harmless nursery rhyme; as soon as he began to chant the finishing ritual, the building started to erupt around them. Lights exploded and objects flew through the air; they could hear Crellick's unearthly screams echoing around the walls.

An irresistible wave of force knocked Deacon to the ground. He looked up, and in the instant before the church went completely dark, he thought he saw Father Calvino's eyes burst in their sockets.

When Deacon came to, Calvino had vanished. A trail of his blood led through the church and down the hidden stairway. Amidon was catatonic, bleeding from both ears. Gray was unharmed but terrified, and attempted to flee the building. However, another wave of force slammed the door closed before he could escape, and he had little option but to join Deacon in his bid to locate the stricken Calvino.

The two men descended the stairs, heading deep underground. Below, they found a maze of tunnels, extending out across the countryside, far beyond the bounds of the church. Hearing distant sobs and cries of distress, they ventured further into the catacombs.

But instead of Calvino, what they discovered was evidence of a ritual slaughter: the remains of children—*their bloody bones*, Deacon suddenly thought—sacrificed centuries before by the false priest Mandeville, to whichever dark master he served there.

Suddenly, they caught a glimpse of Amidon further ahead—had he followed them down here? An alarmed whisper in the back of Deacon's mind warned him he was being manipulated, *lured*—but he ignored it. He must make amends this time, save lives where he had failed to before. They pressed on, the walls of the tunnels growing tighter around them. Deacon choked back panic, offering prayers under his breath. The words brought him little comfort here—once uttered, they seemed to shrivel and die in the chill subterranean air—but they were all he had.

Finally, they crept into a small crawlspace, convinced that Amidon was to be found on the other side. But upon investigation, the passageway proved to be a dead end. Frustrated, they turned around to retrace their path. Deacon told himself his anxious mind was playing tricks, but increasingly, the ground beneath their hands and knees felt unpleasantly soft and clammy, and the air reeked of spoiled meat.

To their horror, they discovered that their exit had simply vanished, as though they had been swallowed up by the earth itself.

As a viscous fluid began to ooze from the walls surrounding them, instantly beginning to dissolve their clothes and blister their skin, Deacon quickly realised that was almost exactly what had happened. However, they had not been swallowed by the earth, but by something abominable lurking within it. They had found Mandeville's master, the ancient god hidden below.

Behind him, Gray began to scream, his mind disintegrating as rapidly as his body. *You said it wasn't real!* he sobbed accusingly.

Deacon might have laid the same accusation at Father Goddard's door. He tried to drown out the man's shrieks by loudly reciting the Lord's Prayer, but it was no use. It was meaningless doggerel to him now; he was in the presence of true evil, and could not help but fear it. He felt the skin on his face bubbling; horrified, he looked down at his hands to see the flesh sloughing off the bones.

And now, finally, he joined Gray in screaming, reduced to a child once more. He cried for Father Goddard, shrieked for his mother. Why had he not listened to her?

He *was* a bad boy, he had been all along, and now Bloody Bones had got him.

RAYMOND TUNSTALL (MR PIPES)

Keith Ferrari in Ghostwatch, *1992*
written by Stephen Volk
directed by Lesley Manning

I T IS NOT COMMONLY RECOGNISED THAT THE ROOT CAUSES OF THE
Fox Hill Drive incident in 1992—the most severe paranormal
manifestation ever recorded in this country—can be traced back to Julian
Karswell, but like so much of England's dark, unwritten history, it is the
ghost of his name that haunts the margins. Only in this case, it was his
negligence, rather than any deliberately wicked intent, that was to lead to
so many subsequent tragedies.

Raymond Tunstall was, like so many of Karswell's followers, a small,
colourless man; a fringe dweller in the choked conformity of 50's Tory
Britain. Above all, what Karswell promised his disciples was freedom;
freedom from society, from laws, from conventional morality. This
attracted a wide spectrum of people, ranging from libertines to anarchists
to petty criminals. All were keen to avail themselves of the licentiousness

that Karswell offered; all looked forward to the prophesised day when the world would be gifted to them, when their appetites and desires would be given delicious, unchecked rein.

None more so than Raymond Tunstall himself.

As he saw it, Tunstall had lived his entire adult life trapped in the agonising hairshirt of middle-class Christian morality. His skin writhed with the torment of what he had to endure, day in, day out. He had not asked for this existence: it had been imposed upon him by those who considered themselves better and more righteous than he.

And yet, it was *they* who had scarred the world with their insane wars; *they* who had brought society to the precipice of destruction, blithely promising heaven while every day forcing the world closer to a nuclear hell. All Tunstall wanted was to nurture everything that was good and innocent. God knows there was little enough beauty in the world. Whatever there was should be loved and cherished. And what was more beautiful than children?

It was not that Tunstall was the only child molester to be found amongst Karswell's ranks. On the whole, they were grudgingly tolerated rather than accepted by the other cultists, but Karswell himself found his paedophile disciples to be some of his most avid devotees, and had no wish to lecture others on their sexuality, however forbidden. This was in spite of the fact that the doctor was known to be (platonically) fond of children himself, and often allowed the local youngsters to play in the grounds of his estate.

When quizzed on this apparent contradiction, Karswell was given to smugly quoting Scott Fitzgerald's dictum that the test of a first-rate intelligence was the ability to hold two opposed ideas at the same time and still have the ability to function. Alas, his own first-rate intelligence did not extend to keeping the village children away from certain members of his congregation.

When Tunstall was discovered with the young girl, such was Karswell's anger that it was said a violent thunderstorm boiled in the skies over Lufford Hall for the whole of that night. But his rage was not simply down to the child's violation; he was also obsessive to the point of paranoia about protecting his cult's privacy. Wanton illegality led to gloating newspaper headlines, which in turn brought unwanted attention and further intrusions. It was therefore expected that Tunstall would quickly suffer the same fate as the other unfortunates that had previously crossed the occultist.

However, Karswell decided that, in this instance, it might benefit him to be seen to act in accordance with the law. Consequently, Tunstall was banished from the cult, turned over to the police, and was told that any attempt to fight the charges would result in the most dire reprisals. He stood trial, was promptly found guilty of child molestation and committed to a psychiatric hospital, where he would remain until after Karswell's untimely death.

Upon his eventual release, Tunstall found lodgings with an aunt and uncle, Mr and Mrs Sellers, who had promised Tunstall's dying mother that they would care for her troubled son. The house on Fox Hill Drive was a new build, and the Sellers had no inkling that the land had originally been acquired cheaply by the developer due to its unsavoury reputation. Still, the couple had never experienced anything untoward themselves, and so there was no earthly reason for them to anticipate what would happen next.

Unfortunately, thanks to the years he had spent under the tutelage of Julian Karswell, Raymond Tunstall was of an altogether more suggestible temperament.

Shortly after moving into the property, Tunstall began to be plagued by nightmares, visions of an evil old woman. He insisted to his social worker that the woman was taking possession of his body and controlling his actions. He began to wear a long black dress, and would often be seen walking the streets of the Fox Hill estate muttering to himself. Local children were warned to stay well away from him, but before too long, a young girl went missing from a nearby playground.

Angry residents laid siege to the Fox Hill Drive address; several incidents of vandalism were reported. Horrified by the turn of events, Mr and Mrs Sellers fled the property and took a long holiday abroad, essentially washing their hands of their nephew. It was during their absence that Tunstall took his own life, hanging himself in a small cupboard under the stairs. His body was not discovered for close to two weeks. The missing girl was never found.

It took years for anyone to draw a link between Tunstall's visions and the legend of Mother Seddons, a baby farmer who had lived in the Fox Hill area around the turn of the century. For twenty-five years, Seddons had taken in unwanted children for money—and, it later transpired, murdered untold numbers of them (some estimates suggested the tally could be as high as four hundred). Her story had certainly contributed to the housing estate's ill-starred reputation, but despite her notoriety as a local bogeyman, there was no evidence that Tunstall himself knew of the case.

After Tunstall's suicide, scattered rumours would continue to dog the area for the next couple of decades, but it was not until Pamela Early and her two daughters moved into the Sellers house that Fox Hill Drive entered its final, most infamous chapter.

Shortly after their arrival, the Early children began to complain of nocturnal visitations by an apparition fitting Raymond Tunstall's description. An unsettling pattern was beginning to emerge. Indeed, parapsychologists have remarked on the similarity between the causeology of this case and the famous 'Stone Tape' haunting at the Taskerlands mansion in the 1970s. Both incidents share a gradual accretion of activity; manifestation layered upon manifestation, like strata of sedimentary rock. As Mother Seddons haunted Tunstall, so in turn did he haunt the Early family. Whatever walked in Fox Hill Drive did *not* walk alone. (There is no record of whether Seddons ever claimed to have been similarly afflicted.)

The visitations quickly progressed into full-blown poltergeist activity. Objects would be thrown around the room, and one of the children began to exhibit signs of physical abuse and trauma. Paranormal experts were called in to investigate, but were powerless to prevent the escalation of events.

Under the circumstances, it was impossible for the Early family to stem the flow of local gossip, and before too long, local newspapers were running salacious items about the haunting of Fox Hill Drive. These reports soon found their way into the national press, ultimately leading to the incident coming to the attention of the BBC.

One might question why Pamela Early would want to see her family's trauma turned into the stuff of primetime television viewing; certainly there were those who doubted her motives at the time. Equally, one wonders what led the BBC to think that the events at Fox Hill Drive would make for the stuff of good Halloween light entertainment, spooky but none-too serious. Did no one question whether a team of comedians and children's television presenters were appropriate choices to investigate a case involving a long history of trauma, abuse and (as it turned out) much, much worse?

The result was the infamous *Ghostwatch* debacle, broadcast on BBC1 on Halloween night in 1992. The details of the ninety-minute broadcast have already been exhaustively scrutinised by sceptics and adherents alike and need not concern us here; suffice to say that it rapidly metastasized from a seemingly-benign televisual ghost train ride to something vastly more sinister, which was to cost the lives of more than one of the participants.

No, what is far more relevant to this history is the suppressed account of what happened *afterwards*.

By the time *Ghostwatch* had ceased transmission, it was apparent something had gone horribly wrong. The broadcast had somehow acted as a collective séance, enabling Tunstall's spirit (or 'Mr Pipes', as he had been christened by the Early children) to channel himself into the nation's airwaves. As he began to manifest before millions of viewers, the programme was hastily abandoned (due to the usual 'technical difficulties'), and the BBC rushed to mollify a frightened and enraged audience, with little success.

For weeks to come, *Ghostwatch* was the stuff of tabloid headlines and furious debate. Probing questions were asked in Parliament, and for a time it seemed as though the BBC's charter might be in jeopardy. Still, the reports and headlines only ever concerned themselves with the programme itself; no one ever publicly addressed the continuing fallout from the broadcast. Some tried, but a blanket D-notice had already been put into effect, blocking all further media coverage.

A D-notice ordered by the familiar figure of one Agent Fremont.

Fremont's specialist unit—officially, they had no title, but some referred to them as The Gravediggers (although never to Fremont's face)—had been called in to investigate the lingering aftereffects of the *Ghostwatch* incident. Simply put, the haunting had not ended with the transmission. Instead, the locus of the event had shifted from a corporeal location to an entirely non-physical space: Tunstall's spirit was now literally a ghost in the machine, freed from its ties to Fox Hill Drive and at liberty to transmit itself via Britain's television networks.

In the weeks after the initial broadcast, sightings of the spectre rapidly proliferated. He was glimpsed in an increasing number of television programmes, always involving children. YouTube compilations of clips from the period purport to show Mr Pipes (his nickname rapidly adopted by the nation's frightened youth) in a wide range of 1990s programmes, including *Blue Peter*, *Live and Kicking*, *Knightmare* and *Grange Hill*. The ghost was never seen on set, only ever on the nation's television screens during transmission.

Most alarming was the fact that the children involved in the broadcasts subsequently began to complain of paranormal incursions in their own homes: whispering voices, spectral manifestations, even physical attacks. Initially, the incidents were written off as a form of mass hysteria, a result of too many impressionable children having seen the original *Ghostwatch* broadcast, but after the first child went missing, the matter was immediately referred to Fremont.

A spook to catch a spook.

But despite his unit's expertise, the intelligence agent soon found himself stymied. The problem was the non-specific nature of the haunting: how to exorcise a ghost that seemingly no longer possessed any ties to the physical world?

Citing the 'Stone Tape' precedent, Fremont ordered the Fox Hill Lane property demolished (despite the fervent protests of Pamela Early, whose daughter Suzie had vanished inside the house and was still missing), hoping this would diminish Tunstall's influence. It had no appreciable effect. Teams of psychics were consulted, but found it impossible to communicate with the ghost.

There was simply no way to predict when and where Pipes would manifest next. And while they struggled to find a solution, two more children disappeared.

Finally, the case of Anna Madden was brought to Fremont's attention. While still a young girl, she had exhibited remarkable psychic abilities; not the more common gifts of telepathy or telekinesis, but the power to actually influence reality within her dreams, and to compel others to share that dreamt reality.

When Fremont contacted Anna's parents, they were initially reluctant to help, wanting only a normal life for their daughter. Nonetheless, Agent Fremont was nothing if not brutally persuasive, and before long Anna found herself staked out in the wilds of children's television, a frightened fawn to bait a hungry predator. She was included in the studio audience for several children's shows, in the hope that her presence would lure Tunstall's attention.

Anna had a simple method for controlling her dreams: she would exactingly draw an image of a place (a building, a field, a beach), and when sleep came, she would immediately find herself there. Fremont therefore devised an exquisitely cold-blooded plan: she was given photographs and video footage of the house at Fox Hill Drive and asked to sketch it.

The stratagem initially seemed to bear fruit. Anna reported visiting the house in her dreams. She described it as an eerie, foreboding place: the air constantly filled with the cries of cats, the sky outside entirely absent, a furious blizzard of electronic noise in its place. She claimed to have met a young girl called Suzie there, frightened and alone, who warned her to leave before Mr Pipes arrived home.

Encouraged, they kept sending her back into the dream world, until finally, Tunstall showed himself. Anna awoke screaming from her sleep; such was her hysteria that it took a tranquiliser to calm her down. She said that a man had appeared to her in the dream, although he wore a long black dress, and (confusingly) sometimes seemed to be a woman. His face had been horribly mutilated. He had forced her into a dark cupboard under the stairs, where she could feel his cold fingers all over her, like graveyard worms squirming on her flesh.

Her parents were understandably horrified. They insisted that Anna be returned to their custody before she was placed in any further danger.

Fremont thanked them for their assistance, and assured them he would release their daughter in accordance with their wishes—but first he must have a doctor examine Anna. He could not in all conscience release her until everyone was satisfied that she had been given a clean bill of health.

The parents had little choice but to agree. They were taken to an anteroom and given hot coffee while they waited. The beverage was drugged, quickly rendering them both unconscious. Meanwhile, under the guise of examining Anna, Fremont's doctor insisted on administering a mild sedative, claiming it would enable her to get back to sleep without suffering any further dreams.

In reality, it was a large dose of pentobarbital, which plunged Anna into an induced coma. One from which she would never awaken.

By keeping Anna in a coma, Fremont reasoned that Tunstall could be trapped in her mind indefinitely. Better one haunted girl than an entire haunted country, he decided. Anna Madden would be an unwitting hero, never conscious of her sacrifice, but that did not lessen its magnitude. After all, most people are not born heroes; rather, they have heroism thrust upon them. Anna was no exception.

There were no loose ends—Fremont had always prided himself on his fastidiousness. Anna's unconscious parents were taken from the building and later died in a staged traffic accident. Collateral losses were always regrettable, but these things had to be weighed against the good of the nation.

Anna herself was taken to a secure medical facility, where she is cared for to this day. Should she ever be awakened from her chemical sleep, the likelihood is that she would be hopelessly insane.

The spectre of Mr Pipes never manifested on television again. The site of the demolished house on Fox Hill Drive was kept vacant, although nearby neighbours would complain of the sound of cats wailing for years to come.

HELEN STEPHENS

Anna Massey in Peeping Tom, *1960*
written by Leo Marks
directed by Michael Powell

IT HAD BEEN WELL OVER A YEAR SINCE MARK LEWIS'S DEATH, AND Helen was still afraid.

Afraid of the world outside the house she shared with her mother; afraid of people; but mostly just afraid of men.

She'd been so trusting, so willing to believe the best in others. A lifetime spent caring for her blind mother—a sour, prickly woman who used alcohol to dull her pain the same way most people used aspirin—had tutored her in the art of maintaining a cheery smile, of freely offering love to those who could not or would not accept it. As Helen had seen it, the universe erred on the side of benevolence more often than not, and as a grateful recipient of that benevolence (life with her mother could be trying, but she wanted for little otherwise), she had a duty to extend it to others.

Then, she had met Mark.

She supposed that she had loved him, a little. Certainly she had taken her first tentative steps along that road. When first they'd met, he'd simply been the strange young man who lived upstairs, the landlord they never saw. (Mother was always fond of making drunkenly morbid pronouncements about what he might be getting up to in his upstairs lair.)

Nevertheless, there had been an immediate connection, albeit a tentative one. It had not taken her long to intuit that Mark's hesitant manner was not simply shyness, but a mark of the psychological damage that had been wrought upon him. Still he'd seemed so kind, so fundamentally decent. She'd convinced herself that all he really needed was to be loved and cared for, to be taught how to trust again.

They'd made plans to collaborate on a book project, and she'd begun to daydream of the possible future they might share together. Perhaps even a future (she only ever dared envision this in the small dark hours of the morning, when truth and insomnia make uneasy bedfellows) away from her mother.

Then had come the revelation that Mark was a psychopath, a murderer of women; helplessly in thrall to a knot of twisted urges that no amount of love could hope to unravel. Rather than hurt Helen, Mark had ended his own life, and Helen's blissful daydreams faded into stark nothingness, like an undeveloped film negative ripped into the light.

And how her mother had relished it! Of course, she'd always been wary of the possibility of her daughter abandoning her, and had continually warned her against the strange young man who lived upstairs—all for Helen's own good, of course.

So when Mark finally stood exposed as a monster, the latest tabloid bogeyman (they'd initially christened him 'The Clapperboard Killer', until 'Peeping Tom' finally stuck), her mother's poisonous self-satisfaction had been almost toxic, choking the oxygen out of the cramped rooms they shared together. Helen could not be trusted to make her own decisions, she announced. She was naïve and easily led, and should be thankful she had a loving mother to protect her.

So when they learnt that Mark had bequeathed the house and all his possessions to Helen, it was Mother who made the decision to stay on. Helen had wanted to sell the property, get far away, but her mother wouldn't hear of it.

We finally have a bit of security, she said. *If you try and sell it, you'll only get a rotten price, after all that's happened. Why don't you think of my happiness, for a change? It's not like anyone actually died* in *the house.*

The matter was settled. The other tenants had moved out, and Helen and her mother were left alone. Slowly, Helen began to wither, like a flower left in the dark. Her mother pretended not to notice (her blindness was always a useful tool, when it suited her), and blithely encouraged Helen to carry on with her writing. *You need to grow up and get over it. I always told you men can't be trusted. And a bit of work will do you good.*

The book Helen had been planning was a novel for children, concerning a magic camera that photographed people; not as they were, but as the innocent infants they had once been. How pitifully sentimental that seemed now! She imagined Mark as a child, already corrupted by his father's sadism. There was no innocence, no magic in the world. Without telling her mother, she burnt the manuscript in the fire.

Inevitably, the vice of tension in their flat had slowly tightened over time, despite Helen's unending efforts to please. One night a particularly viperous screaming match had erupted between mother and daughter; Helen had fled the room in tears, wanting only to put as much distance between herself and her mother as possible. But her only two options seemed to be to leave the house (almost unthinkable) or to flee upstairs, to Mark's old apartment. This too, had once seemed an impossibility; the thought of setting foot upstairs usually made her want to vomit.

Now, in the face of her mother's vicious intransigence, whatever ghosts might lurk upstairs seemed almost benign in comparison; a faded snapshot of what once was bad, instead of a flesh and blood golem of everything that was awful now.

She slowly mounted the stairs and crept inside the flat. The front room was in chaos, books and clothes tossed everywhere; the police had been belligerently thorough when they searched the premises. She tiptoed carefully through the clutter. What she needed to face lay in the darkness of the rooms beyond: the monster at the heart of the labyrinth.

Helen emerged into Mark's photography studio and gasped. The still-pungent smell of developing fluid shocked her back into the past; for a moment she was sure Mark was present with her in the room again. She was seized by the impulse to turn and run, but fought to suppress it. Mark had shown her what her own fear looked like, grotesque and distorted, and she must face it down, conquer it. In that sense at least, he had done her a small kindness.

She stumbled hesitantly forward into the shadows. Around her were cluttered shelves of Mark's film and photography equipment—the police had confiscated everything they considered evidence, but the remainder had been left to Helen. She ran her hands along the dusty metal shelves, asserting ownership of the space. Mark had always claimed to be working on a documentary, and she supposed that, in a perverse way, the footage he had shot of his killings was precisely that. But now, it was long past time she told her own story.

At the end of the room stood a ghostly monolith: Mark's projection screen. Placed before it was Mark's canvas chair, his name stencilled across the back in imitation of a director. She eased herself down into the seat and sat quietly in the darkness, until the funereal silence around her began to grow oppressive. Instinctively, she reached out towards the nearby film projector and switched it on.

There was no film loaded on the machine's spools, but Helen found the bright light of its bulb and the *clack clack clack* of its mechanism reassuring. She closed her eyes and began to drift away.

Once again, it was as though Mark was back in the room with her, standing in anticipation behind the chair as she watched his handiwork, willing for her to truly *see*.

Helen . . .

A faint voice, all but drowned out by the projector noise. Her eyes snapped open. For an instant, she glimpsed a man's shadow cast on the white screen, looming darkly over her own. Stifling a cry, she spun around.

She was alone in the room. When she looked back at the screen, there was nothing there but absence. Her hand trembling, she shut the projector off and hurried from the apartment.

By the time she returned downstairs, her mother had already downed a couple more tumblers of scotch and smugly took the audible quaver in Helen's voice as ample confirmation that she had won their skirmish.

Helen did not sleep that night. As she tossed and turned in her bed, she kept expecting to hear Mark's stealthy footsteps creeping up and down the floorboards over her head. *I don't trust a man who walks quietly*, her mother had always said. Was it possible that his spirit was still lurking in the house? Did he mean her harm?

But no—the voice, faint as it was, had sounded plaintive, almost desperate. Lying there in the dark, she remembered Mark in his final moments. He could have been a character from her own story, magically revealed as a small boy once more, intent on sparing her the pain he had suffered and in turn perpetuated on others. He did not want to hurt her, she was sure of it.

The conversation was stilted at breakfast the next morning, and mother and daughter contented themselves with listening to the wireless while they ate. For a few short moments, Helen gazed out at the quiet suburban street beyond their front window and almost convinced herself that it represented the natural way of things, neatly-ordered and peaceful and kind. People *were* decent, weren't they? The inhabitants of their street wanted only to be good friends and neighbours. She had nothing to be afraid of.

The news headlines offered up a polite retort, delivered in the impeccably emotionless tone of a BBC newsreader. A young nurse had gone missing from a village in East Sussex; police had linked the incident to the previous disappearance of a female art student, Miranda Grey. Despite an extensive manhunt, the student had never been found, and consequently, fears for the safety of the young nurse were growing.

Those poor girls. Helen's mother busied herself with spreading butter on a piece of toast, as though it were her own satisfaction, thick and delicious. *Could you pass the marmalade, dear?*

I'm sorry, I just finished the last of it, Helen lied. She removed the half-full marmalade jar from the table and placed it safely in her lap. *I'll buy some more later.*

After breakfast, Helen had retreated back to her own room, claiming a headache. She drew her curtains and lay down in the semi-darkness, unable to banish Mark from her thoughts. *Show me*, she'd told him on that last night. *Show me, or I'll remain frightened for the rest of my life.*

Unwillingly, he had done as she'd asked. Helen had been granted a fleeting glimpse beyond the veil, a furtive peek at mortality. She had looked death in the eyes, felt its sting on her bare throat, yet still she was afraid.

Mark Lewis was dead, but there were others like him, faceless little men who abducted women; stole them as offerings for their own desires and gratifications. They saw themselves as gods, these squalid, paltry men, and were not the women they claimed simply the sacrifices a god was due?

Helen refused to be afraid of them any longer.

She sat with her mother playing cards that night, and made sure her mother's whisky glass was kept full. Later, she crept from her room and made her way back upstairs, careful not to make any sound that might cause her sleeping mother to stir.

Seating herself in front of the screen once more, Helen turned on the projector and waited for Mark to come to her.

Over the following months, Helen immersed herself in film and photography. She enrolled in courses at the Blake School of Art, and worked diligently to master the equipment Mark had left her. Before long, her teachers were commending Helen on her keen eye, and the unflinching clarity of her images.

Of course, it was not they who were her *real* instructors.

Her mother did not approve of course, insisting that *all this filming isn't healthy*. Still, she could not deny the improvement in Helen: she was out in the world again, mixing with people, her fears seemingly conquered. As much as she preferred to keep her daughter close, Helen's mother knew when she was beaten. So after a time, she conceded this particular battle, and choked back her objections with another glass of scotch.

If she could have seen Helen slipping up to Mark's old rooms after midnight, she might have felt differently. Mark came to Helen every night now, a shy spirit, and softly whispered to her what she must do.

He instructed her on how to build her own magic camera; not like the one she had written about—that was childish, the stuff of fairytales—but a device like the one Mark had used. Something to show men their true faces, to make them afraid.

Careful to conceal her interest from her mother, Helen continued to monitor the details of the missing women. The nurse had still not been found, and now a third girl had been abducted. Helen could delay no longer.

So late one night, she held a private view for Mark. She laid out her photographs, projected her films, demonstrated the deadly camera rig she had customised. He said nothing the whole time, an unobtrusive shadow lurking silently over her shoulder, like a film extra nudging into shot.

When she was finished, she closed her eyes in anticipation. *What do you think, Mark?*

A quiet voice sighed. *Beautiful, Helen. You are ready.*

The projector flickered into life again.

Helen watched as Mark showed her a succession of images. She saw a young man, living alone in a large country house. Good-looking enough, but she could tell immediately his features were merely a facade, a handsome mask of learned expressions and emotions. Helen looked on as he stalked a succession of young women—the student, the nurse—their faces familiar from blurred newspaper photographs. He observed them from the driver's seat of an anonymous white van, biding his time, choosing his moment.

And, finally, he would strike, drugging them and bundling them into the back of his vehicle. Then he would take them to his lair, collecting them like specimens, imprisoning them in a cellar until they learned to love him. Of course, they never could.

In contrast, Helen's own tragedy was that she *had* loved Mark, but then Mark had never expected anything from her, never demanded her adoration. She could never bring herself to hate him. But this man—this creature, with his ego and boundless, poisonous need—how Helen loathed him.

A final image flickered onscreen before the projector went dark: a sign for Forest Row, a small village in East Sussex. Helen gathered her things, carefully loaded her magic camera into its carrying case, and returned downstairs. She packed a few items for a short trip, then slept until morning.

As dawn broke outside, its light slowly revealing the world as though it were a developing photograph, Helen quietly dressed, then stole into the next room.

She sat down on the edge of the mattress, gazing down at her mother's sleeping face. For a instant, she had to resist the urge to take a picture.

Mother. Mother, I have to go away for a little while.

Her mother stirred and muttered something, her voice thick with sleep and alcohol.

I just wanted to say goodbye.

The sleeping woman gave a small snore in reply.

Helen considered this, then reached over for the nearby spare pillow. Carefully, she held it down over her mother's face. The ensuing struggle was short, and never really in doubt.

For once in their relationship, Helen had succeeded in having the last word.

She caught an early train into Forest Row. By the time she arrived, the warm sun had already soaked the village green in a wash of comforting, buttery light. Helen looked around at her surroundings. This was the sort of idyllic image that England so often sold to itself, a picture postcard perfection the country preferred to believe represented its true face.

Helen knew it was a lie. There were monsters here.

She left the village and walked along the outskirts until she came to a large house, the same one she'd seen in Mark's film. Pausing in the shade of a large tree, she looked down and noticed something at her feet—a freshly-dug earthen mound. Another mound, not as fresh, lay a couple of feet away.

Helen moved away from the tree. Taking out her stills camera, she began to shoot pictures of the house and the surrounding fields. She noticed a face appearing at one of the house's upper windows, but ignored it and continued to work.

Within moments, the door to the house opened, revealing its owner. He looked subtly different now—fear did that to a face—but Helen recognised him nonetheless. The young man waved indignantly at her. *Excuse me!* he shouted. *This is private property! You can't do that here!*

Helen lowered her camera. She approached the man, fixing a smile on her face. *Oh, I am sorry. It's for a special project, you see.*

It doesn't matter what it's for. You just can't.

196

The man appeared flustered, increasingly so as Helen drew closer. *It's just that this house is so perfect...*

She faked a stumble, almost tripping into his arms. *Oh! I do apologise. It's just so very warm, and I haven't had anything to drink.* She blinked at him, enjoying his discomfort. *Do you suppose I might come in for a glass of water?*

He looked quietly horrified. *Inside?*

Yes, if it's not too much trouble. Unless...unless you're hiding a dead body or something in there!

She laughed, and once he understood that she was joking, he laughed too. The tension between them eased slightly. *No. Nothing like that.*

Then may I?

He glanced around for a moment, making sure they were not being observed. Then he nodded. *Follow me.*

Thank you so much. And in return, I'll show you my magic camera. Perhaps I can even film you.

He looked quizzical. *Film me? What for?*

Helen smiled cryptically.

Oh, but you see — I'm making a documentary.

LORD SUMMERISLE

Christopher Lee in The Wicker Man, *1973*
written by Anthony Schaffer
directed by Robin Hardy

Struan Rodger in Kill List, *2011*
written by Ben Wheatley & Amy Jump
directed by Ben Wheatley

L ORD SUMMERISLE WAS FOND OF PRONOUNCING THAT, *HERE, THE old gods are not dead.*

But what if that were no longer true?

The first Lord Summerisle's genius for agronomy had transformed a bleak outcrop of volcanic rock into a verdant paradise, fertile and ripe. The fruits of its soil had brought years of prosperity to the islanders, but now the crops were dying on their vines, and the island of Summerisle was dying with them.

Panic had set in amongst the community. Their livelihood was rotting away before their eyes, threatening them with ruin. How would they survive? They were an insular people with their own laws and rituals, and it was unthinkable for them to leave the island, or to open it up to tourism. In desperation, they looked to their leader, the current Lord Summerisle.

The lord's love for his island home could not be doubted—like his father, and his father before him, he had been taught to cherish nature, to respect its elemental power and offer appeasement when necessary—but love does not equal understanding, and when the harvest began to fail, he did not possess his grandfather's agricultural genius to fall back on.

Instead, as mankind will, he turned to religion—to the darkest and most abhorrent of the old ways. A blood sacrifice was required. The gods of the sun and the orchards must be pacified.

The rituals decreed that for a sacrificial offering to have its optimal power, the victim must give themselves freely, and should embody a symbolic trinity: king, virgin, and fool. Complicated, but not beyond a man of Summerisle's talents. The search commenced.

He was no agronomist, but Summerisle's inherited title had taught him something about power, and influence. His ability to cajole and manipulate was without peer. A suitable candidate was found, and a plan hatched—Sergeant Howie, a pious dullard of a policeman from the mainland, would be lured to the island under the pretence of a missing persons investigation.

Some people doubted it would work—there was so much that could go wrong—but Lord Summerisle's conviction was unshakeable. He would attend to every facet of the plan himself. It would not fail. Had history not shown that Christians were the meekest of souls, forever eager to rush to their own slaughter? Did they not model themselves in the image of a man they called the Lamb of God, who had willingly offered himself up for sacrifice?

His fervent appeal convinced the islanders—all save for one: Lord Summerisle's own son. He had grown distant from his father's teachings over the years, and now that their land was dying, he was all the more convinced that they had been wrong to isolate themselves. Gods did not wish to be worshipped by an insular, dwindling few, he argued. Their power came from mass belief.

The islanders should be taking their worship to the mainland, proselytising, restoring the old ways to prominence. *This* was how they would survive, not by the feeble symbolism of a single blood sacrifice. All over the world, Christianity had failed—now they must seize their moment.

Father and son fought for days—Lord Summerisle admired his son's zeal, but insisted his ideas could not work. If they tried to spread their faith more widely, it would only result in mockery and disdain. Modern society venerated only greed and commerce. Look at what it did to the natural world, with its pesticides and effluents and fertilisers and genetic tampering—all so that a pitiful, poisoned imitation of nature could be delivered to the masses, cheaper and faster and more bountifully then ever.

On Summerisle their devotion to nature was pure, unsullied—and *purity* was what the old gods desired from them.

Summerisle's son quit the island in disgust. *This will be your last year on Summerisle,* he told his father. *The crops will fail again, and so you too will have failed. What then?*

The lord would not hear of it. He set about enacting his plan.

Everything went perfectly, for a time. Howie was as big a fool as had been suggested (the lord was not a murderer by temperament, and did not relish the idea of taking human life, but he had to admit that he would consider it a more pleasant world without the policeman in it), and was shepherded through the twisting maze of Summerisle's scheme with nary a misstep. Finally, he was ready for his appointment with the wicker man.

As Howie burned alive, screaming hopelessly for Christ into a sky that held only a god far older and less merciful than He, Summerisle and the rest of the islanders danced until their feet bled. They believed in their hearts that the gods had now been appeased. Surely the perfect culmination of their plan was evidence of divine providence? *I know it will work!* Summerisle cried joyfully to his people.

It did not.

Come the next harvest, the crops withered and died as before. Bereft, Summerisle retreated inside his estate, unable to comprehend his failure. He had done everything the old gods demanded, so why had they abandoned him?

He donated large sums from his personal fortune to the local community, hoping to stave off disaster. But the islanders had never before known want or hardship, and what they viewed as relative pennies did little to dispel their anger.

Whispers began to spin across the island like the strands of a cobweb, gradually tightening to snare their victim. There was muttered talk that the islanders had been misled, lied to, that perhaps their leader was as big a fool as the man they had sacrificed. Perhaps his son had been right all along and there was no longer a place for them on Summerisle.

Hearing of his father's failure, the son returned to the island. Sensing his opportunity, he began to seed his own harvest; one of rebellion and betrayal. He told the islanders that his father's time was past, that the old gods now demanded new forms of worship. He insisted that Summerisle's soil turning barren was an omen, a sign that they should gather together and seek new lands, new earth in which to sow their devotion.

Some could not countenance ever leaving the island and abandoning all they had known, but Summerisle's son found more than enough converts amongst the ranks of the disenchanted. He promised them all a new dawn was coming.

Just one task remained. He told them they must close the chapter on the old ways, and make amends for all the years they had taken their gods' benevolence for granted.

One final blood sacrifice would be necessary—that of Lord Summerisle himself.

When they came for Summerisle, he did not resist. He understood the scale of his failure, and had expected that he would suffer the consequences. He had tried to be a good leader to his people, but there was no room for sentimentality in the natural world he so cherished.

Still, when the mob came for him, his only son at their head, Lord Summerisle found himself frightened for the first time he could remember. It was not his impending death that scared him, but the fact that he gazed into his own son's eyes and found nothing there but fanaticism, for a bloody cause Summerisle did not understand. *The past is gone*, his son told him. *The future is not yet here. There is only ever this moment.*

Summerisle knew that the gods he worshipped were dispassionate, some would even say uncaring; after all, what was mankind in the face of the monumental power of the elements? Nevertheless, his gods were not malign—and all he saw in his son's eyes was malignity, an unslaked thirst for blood and pain. Where he beheld awe in the universe, the younger man saw only vast, infinite nihilism. This was existence as his son understood it, a cosmos of meaningless violence and conflict and suffering. *This* was the new land he meant to lead his people to.

As they took Summerisle to the clifftop, he mourned the passing of the community he had devoted his life to nurturing. Whatever would come after him, he was quietly grateful he would not live to see it. He only hoped the island would eventually return to nature, and that he might be permitted to roam its hills and grasslands as a hare, or a bird.

He lay down on the floor of his wicker cage and stared up at the glory of the setting sun, and when the hungry flames greedily claimed him, he did not cry out or scream as Sergeant Howie had done.

The new Lord Summerisle stood and watched the fire until his father's body was ash and bone. The next morning he left the island once more, taking with him a hand-picked inner circle. He promised those still remaining that they would be sent for in time.

With his inherited title, Lord Summerisle found it a simple matter to insinuate himself into the upper echelons of British society. Over the next few decades, his deft fingers found purchase in government, the Law, the Church, and big business, to say nothing of more illicit concerns. The new lord possessed none of his father's scruples about how he made his money, and there were far more profitable crops to be harvested than mere apples.

The influence he amassed over those years also allowed him to slyly goad the reemergence of those traits the modern world had blithely labelled reactionary, but which he saw as vital tenets of his ancient faith: isolationism, racialism, nativism. In this respect, the soil of his new home proved fertile indeed.

But despite his growing power, the lord found himself concerned. He sensed other influences massing in the country, as shadowy and insidious as his own. He had no fear of the Church, impotent and lumbering as it was, but there were other, darker, religious forces to be wary of. His father had been fond of saying that Jehovah had been given his chance and blown it; but what of Lucifer? Did He and his acolytes finally mean to seize *their* chance?

Summerisle would not see his faithful forced to kneel before despots of any stripe. He decided a champion was needed: a warrior knight to lead their cult into the coming battle. So, much as his own father had once done with Sergeant Howie, he began a careful process of selection, scouring the country to identify suitable candidates for what he termed 'reconstruction'.

His followers submitted lists of possibilities: scores of vicious, psychotic men who believed in nothing and yet found the meaning they craved from following orders, as long as those orders were to fight and maim and kill. Summerisle noted with a certain wry amusement that at least his timing was good: the then-extant Iraq war serving as something of a useful audition process.

Finally, a shortlist was drawn up. Each candidate would be thoroughly tested to judge their suitability. Summerisle favoured two men in particular; coincidentally, both had served in the same regiment in Iraq. Their names were Richard and Jay.

However, before they could begin Richard's reconstruction, the soldier suffered a mental breakdown as a result of the death of his mentally-handicapped brother. While the murderous rampage he subsequently embarked upon was impressive enough, Summerisle regretfully ruled him out on the basis of his lack of emotional detachment: his champion would need to cast off the civilised bonds of family duty, not be driven by them.

After that disappointment, he decided to personally conduct Jay's test himself. The man now earned an intermittent living as a mercenary, along with his partner Gal. It was therefore a simple enough matter to entrap him with the promise of well-paid wetwork.

Upon meeting him for the first time, Summerisle quickly assessed his candidate to be little more than a brutal thug—a borderline sociopath, crippled with PTSD, unencumbered by ideology or morals. He might be perfect—if he could successfully navigate his reconstruction, wash away the stains of his trauma, and emerge, baptised in blood and newly-purified.

Gal was useful inasmuch as he provided a steadying influence on his psychotically-wayward partner, but otherwise the lord had little interest in him. He gave the two men a list of targets, paid them handsomely, then forced Jay into taking a blood oath. The mercenary had taken his first unwitting steps towards a new existence.

Summerisle had cast off many of his father's old beliefs, but he still understood the importance and power of symbolic acts. The names he gave the mercenaries—the 'kill list', they called it—represented the three pillars of civilised society that Jay must reject to progress on his journey: organised religion, education, and government. In actuality, the three men were all members of Summerisle's cult, who had willingly offered themselves up for sacrifice—such things were still seen as an honour amongst the faithful.

The two mercenaries killed the priest and the librarian easily enough, although Jay's savagery was already threatening to careen wildly out of control. This left only the MP remaining, but Gal subsequently proved to be a wilier puppet than Summerisle had imagined. Upon discovering a hidden cache of the cult's documents while looting the librarian's house, the mercenary had realised that he and Jay were simply pawns in a much larger game they did not understand. They had abandoned the job, retreated back to their homes.

Summerisle deemed it necessary to send a small message in response: Jay's family cat had been slaughtered and strung up on their doorstep. He had no patience with recalcitrance. The two men realised they no longer knew who to trust—everyone seemed to be watching them, plotting from afar. Jay was growing feverish, paranoid; his body turning upon itself. Summerisle's blood magic was beginning to reshape him, reconstructing his flesh and bone for the tasks ahead.

The mercenaries demanded a second meeting with their employer, intending to resign from the contract. Summerisle listened quietly to their protests, then calmly informed them that both they and their families would die unless they completed the list.

Jay and Gal were experienced enough in their field to know a deadly serious man when they saw one. They reluctantly submitted.

They travelled to the MP's country estate and waited for darkness, expecting another straightforward hit. However, the lord had decided the time was right to give the two men a small demonstration of what they were really facing. When night fell, the disbelieving mercenaries were treated to the spectacle of a group of Summerisle's cultists gathering for a firelight ritual, their bodies naked, their faces shielded by grotesque wicker masks.

Panicking, the two men opened fire. They succeeded in killing their target and several others besides, but found themselves cornered after they attempted to escape the grounds. Gal was mortally wounded, and in agony, begged Jay to end his life. His eyes devoid of emotion, Jay shot him in the head—killing his only friend, and one of the last remaining ties to the old life he was being groomed to abandon.

The rite was almost complete. Jay took his family and fled to their country cottage, but their movements were being carefully monitored, as they had been all along. The family's respite was short-lived. Jay and his wife vainly attempted to defend their home and child, but were soon overcome.

Jay had one final test to pass.

He awoke with flames cavorting in his eyes, to find himself surrounded by a gathered ring of cultists, a knife clutched in his hand.

Before him stood a cloaked hunchback, also brandishing a weapon. Jay was heavily drugged, confused, but his years of training soon asserted themselves—his core instincts to fight and to kill. At heart, it was all he really knew.

The two combatants joined in battle, but it was barely a contest—within minutes, Jay's opponent lay twitching on the ground, its life dripping from his blade. Victorious, Jay stripped away its cloak—to reveal his dying wife, the lifeless body of their son strapped to her back. He had slain them both.

As she lay there on the earth, shuddering as her punctured heart gave up the last of its blood, she looked up at Jay and laughed madly. In her final moments, she recognised that the man who had once been her husband no longer existed—before her stood only a monster, a chimera of Lord Summerisle's making.

His family's blood on his hands, Jay had successfully completed his initiation. Friends, loved ones, civilised society—he had cast them all aside.

As he stood there at the centre of the circle, a mute statue forged of male rage and violence, the cultists moved to anoint him their champion. He did not resist as they placed the crude wicker crown atop his head. Perhaps a part of him had always secretly longed for this.

His coronation complete, the assembled worshippers applauded wildly. Lord Summerisle stepped forward from amongst their ranks, leading the applause. Gazing into the firelight, he remembered his father's face for a moment.

Where you found only a fool, I have found a king, he thought.

OLIVIA RUDGE

Samantha Gates in Full Circle, *1977,*
written by Harry Bromley Davenport and Dave Humphries
based on the novel by Peter Straub
directed by Richard Loncraine

THE INSCRIPTION ON OLIVIA RUDGE'S GRAVESTONE CLAIMED
that she died aged only nine years old; what it did not say was that she
had never really been born at all, not in any conventional sense at least.

Her mother Heather had been a wealthy socialite, famed for her
decadent parties. Exclusivity was of the utmost importance to Heather;
only those she deemed 'interesting' were invited, and if you failed to
maintain Heather's interest, that invite would quickly be rescinded.
Regular attendees included the actors Edward Lionheart and Charlotte
Inwood, notorious underworld figures such as the Kray twins and London
wrestling magnate Kristo, and the charismatic occultist Dr Julian Karswell.
A tell-all book detailing what went on behind the closed doors of 25
Ilchester Place on those nights remains as yet unwritten, but one whispered
clubland rumour of the time had it that a select group of party guests

witnessed Karswell conjure up the Prince of Darkness himself, right there in Heather's drawing room.

Heather quickly fell under Karswell's sway; she was bored, rich, and 'fast' (as the lexicon of the era had it), and the latter two qualities certainly appealed, for as long as it suited him. She joined the growing ranks of his cult, and her money helped fund his subsequent purchase of Lufford Hall. As was his habit, Karswell eventually moved on to younger, prettier devotees, and thus, freshly-spurned and entering her forties, Heather was suddenly seized by the incipient loneliness of middle-age. She decided that she wanted a child, but an earlier botched abortion had left her unable to conceive one.

She begged Karswell to help her, and eager to be free of her attentions, he agreed. Having acquired the papers and effects of the deceased black magician Oliver Haddo, Karswell drew upon his forerunner's magical research into the creation of life, and—as he proudly boasted—bettered it. The result was an apparently normal baby girl.

Karswell named her Olivia, in tribute to Haddo, and proudly presented her to Heather. For a time, all was well; Heather had no particular interest in what she saw as the more monotonous aspects of motherhood, but there were maids and nannies for that, and as Olivia proceeded to grow into a precociously beautiful young girl, Heather was able to bathe in the flattering glow of her reflected light.

It was not until Olivia entered her third year that the first signs of trouble began to manifest. Heather had a fondness for cats, and several pampered thoroughbreds had the run of Ilchester Place, second only to Olivia in the hierarchy of Heather's somewhat wayward affections. One frosty January morning, the maid ascended the stairs to Olivia's bedroom, carrying her a breakfast tray of juice and porridge. But upon entering the room, what the maid found was not a sleepy little girl snuggled warmly in her bed, but a bloody operating theatre. Heather's prize Siamese lay crudely dissected on top of the mattress, its limbs removed, its belly hacked open and innards laid out on the topsheet for inspection.

Olivia stood calmly to one side, her hands slathered with gore, the clotted crimson shockingly vivid against her porcelain skin.

The maid fled screaming, but Heather's reaction to the incident was more forthright. Upon seeing the slaughter for herself, she slapped Olivia across the face, then proceeded to take a belt and whip her bare buttocks raw. At no point did her daughter utter a single whimper of fear or pain, let alone shed a tear.

Instead, that night, as Heather fled to the boozy respite of a friend's dinner party, Olivia coaxed another of the animals up to her mother's bedroom and proceeded to enact the same bloody ritual; the only difference this time was a surer knifehand, a greater surgical refinement to the cutting strokes. Olivia was a fast pupil.

One by one the household staff handed in their notice; Heather was left alone with the blank-faced little girl she increasingly regarded as an abomination, a creation of pure evil.

She tried appealing to Karswell for help with the monster he had ushered into the world, but as his mother spirited Olivia away for a bowl of homemade ice cream, he merely looked at Heather and shook his head. *You get nothing for nothing,* he said, and she thought she glimpsed real sadness in his eyes as he uttered the words. Of course, he had always taken a certain fatherly pride in Olivia.

So from then on, the two of them remained shut away in the sepulchral environs of 25 Ilchester Place, all parties ceased, curtains pulled firmly closed against the outside world. Heather took refuge in prescription pills and alcohol, content to abandon Olivia to her own pernicious devices; Olivia's only interest in her mother by this point was as an acquiescent source of nourishment and shelter, and for her part, Heather was quite certain that this was by far the most preferable of all possible arrangements.

When Olivia finally reached school age, Heather for once embraced her parental duties with fervour and enrolled her daughter in the best local school she could find. Let the authorities deal with the girl; surely, in time, they would realise what sort of creature they had on their hands and act accordingly.

But Olivia was preternaturally cunning, and her icy charisma was such that she quickly gathered around herself a group of acolytes, boys and girls swept along by the implacable force of her will. She taught them to lie, to bully, to hurt. She instructed them in the finer points of mutilation, practiced upon whichever form of small animal was closest to hand.

However whenever trouble of some sort or another was discovered by a teacher, it was always one of the group that was found responsible, never Olivia herself.

Growing bored of petty cruelties, she fastened her attentions upon a small child she saw playing in the local park: Geoffrey Braden, a chubby boy of about four years old. She won his affection by surreptitiously feeding him sweets; then, once she had gained the boy's trust, she summoned her acolytes to the playground and held another lesson. Leading Geoffrey to the sandpit, she sexually mutilated him as the group looked on, then thrust his screaming face deep into the sand and suffocated him.

Although witnesses had seen her leading Geoffrey away, Olivia of course evaded blame and a local vagrant was tried and hanged for the murder. Heather, however, knew the truth. After all, she had had to wash the boy's blood from Olivia's skirt, her trembling hands rubbing furiously at the stained fabric. Growing weaker by the day with addiction and self-loathing, she finally mustered the strength to act.

While Olivia slept one night, Heather crept into her room and stabbed her daughter in her bed. Such was the ferocity of the assault that the knife blade snapped off in Olivia's ribcage. Overwhelmed by the vicious delight she took in the act, Heather finally discovered she had something in common with her daughter after all.

When Heather was tried for the crime, she insisted that there had been no murder, because Olivia was not really dead: *evil never dies.* It was a mantra she would repeat for the rest of her days; to the judge and jury during the trial, and afterwards, when she had been judged insane and committed for life, to the doctors and nurses of the psychiatric institute.

But no one listened, at least not until the fateful day decades later when Julia Lofting came to visit.

And Olivia? Just as she had never truly been born, exactly as her mother insisted, she never truly died. She simply waited.

Forever nine years old, she still had her house, and her old toys—the wind-up clown was a particular favourite—and if every now and then a local pet was found mutilated, well, she had to pass the time somehow.

Pass the time as she patiently waited for a new playmate to come and visit.

CHARLES CROSSLEY

Alan Bates in The Shout, *1978*
written by Jerzy Skolimowski & Michael Austin
adapted from the story by Rupert Graves
directed by Jerzy Skolimowski

ANY ACCOUNT OF THE MYSTERIOUS LIFE OF CHARLES CROSSLEY can only ever be a piecemeal approximation of the truth, given his stated tendency to embroider the facts—as he would always say, daring you to disbelieve him, *I like to keep it alive.* (The fact that he spent the last few years of his life in a mental institution might also cast some doubt over his veracity as a narrator.)

Upon his death, he had the appearance of being a man in his mid-forties, but he sometimes insisted he was much older. Given that his sohourn in Australia is shrouded in mystery, the exact timespan of the years he spent living there is impossible to verify. He had been known to claim that he was in the vicinity of Hanging Rock on that infamous Valentine's Day in 1900, when several schoolgirls mysteriously disappeared. (Typically for Crossley, he would also insist that he knew exactly what had happened to the missing girls, but always refused to expand on his story.)

This could simply be dismissed as the fantastical ramblings of an unhinged mind; still, it should be noted that some eyewitness accounts did report seeing an unidentified man answering to Crossley's approximate description in the area on that very date.

There does at least seem to be some evidence to support his account that he spent eighteen years living amongst the Aboriginal people in the Australian Outback, not least the murder warrant issued against him for the murder of the children he fathered during his time there. John Grant also mentions encountering a man resembling Crossley in his memoir of his time spent teaching in the Outback, *Wake in Fear*. He writes:

'I would sometimes encounter another Englishman in The Yabba: I knew him only as Charles, a ravaged scarecrow perpetually dressed in a long coat, despite the appalling heat. I never witnessed him remove the coat, nor shed as much as a single bead of perspiration. His eyes were like shattered ice, blue with unknowable loss. The locals would give him a wide berth, fearful of attracting even the briefest glance from those cold eyes—and these were men who, in their way, were as foul and dangerous as any of the myriad reptiles or insects of the Outback. When Charles and I would socialise together, no one would dare approach our table—and I never saw him pay for a single drink.'

The mysteries of his early life aside, it is at least a matter of record that Crossley returned to England in the mid-1970s. A virtual nomad, he wandered the country without motive or purpose, until chance (no doubt Crossley would have argued that destiny or fate were in fact responsible) finally brought him to the doorstep of Anthony and Rachel Fielding.

The Fieldings were an avowedly bohemian couple who had fled London for the bleak seclusion of coastal Devon, ostensibly so that Anthony could have peace and quiet to work (an experimental composer, his compositions owed much to theories of *musique concrète*). In truth, he seemed as much devoted to conducting illicit affairs with local women as to his art, leaving his wife Rachel a hurt and frustrated exile in their isolated cottage retreat.

It was at this point that—as if summoned out of the arid desert of a fever dream—the dark figure of Charles Crossley entered their lives.

Crossley liked to jest that he came to the Fielding's for lunch and stayed for breakfast, enjoying Rachel for dessert in-between. It does appear as though a brief affair did take place between the two of them, although whether one believes that was down to Rachel's obvious dissatisfaction with the state of her marriage, or (as Crossley claimed) the magical influence he exerted over her, ultimately depends on the credulity of the individual listener.

Still, the liason did not seem to impinge on Anthony Fielding's own fascination with Crossley and his lurid tales of magic and infanticide. Not content with merely cuckolding his host, Crossley proceeded to sneer at Anthony's compositions, telling him that in comparison to the ancient energies Crossley could summon from within his own body, his music was nothing, empty and facile. Crossley told him that he possessed the secret of death magic, a 'terror shout' that would instantly kill anyone exposed to it. It had taken him nearly two decades to master.

Anthony begged him for a demonstration of the shout. In a letter he later wrote to his friend and occasional collaborator, the enigmatic sound technician Gilderoy, Fielding described how Crossley led him out into the eerie isolation of the surrounding sand dunes early the next morning:

'I had of course walked the dunes by myself many times, but this was different. It was as though Crossley had led me into another world, like we had stepped across a liminal threshold to somewhere other. Perhaps it was just a suggestion prompted by his bizarre stories of the Outback, but I suddenly felt sure this was what the Aboriginals mean when they talk about The Dreaming.

After we had walked for what seemed like hours, Crossley stopped and began to prepare himself. Such was the silent power of his concentration, the desolation I glimpsed in his eyes, that I was suddenly very glad I had brought the wax along to plug my ears. You might think me a gullible fool, Gilderoy, but I found my hands trembling with a terrified urgency to protect my ears before he even took a single breath.

Then, he Shouted.

That simple word does not begin to do it justice. No word in our language could. He shrieked, he howled, he roared. He did all of these, and none of them. It was something else entirely. Despite the fact that my ears were protected, I could feel the physical force of his Shout reverberating within me, shaking the ground upon which I stood. My flesh felt insubstantial against it, like a faint pencil sketch that could easily be erased from existence. To see him, it was as though he was wrenching some ancient, elemental power up from deep beneath the earth. If you think of Francis Bacon's 'Head IV', then perhaps your mind's eye can approximate the sight.

But in truth, nothing I can write will properly communicate it to you, Gilderoy. I felt as though a fourth-dimensional bomb had been detonated. It was utterly terrifying and transcendent all at once. I only wish you could have been there to witness it too.'

(Fantastical perhaps, but we should note that the lifeless bodies of a shepherd and his flock of sheep were found in the sand dunes neighbouring the Fielding's cottage later that same day. There was absolutely no evidence of foul play, and no cause of death could be found. Ultimately, the coroner was forced to return an open verdict.)

Meanwhile, the authorities had managed to trace Crossley to the vicinity, and in due course, police arrived to arrest him on the outstanding charges over the murder of his children. A struggle ensued, and those present reported hearing a brief but unbearable sound, as though 'a hole was being torn in the sky'.

One policeman died in the course of the arrest; another was admitted to hospital suffering symptoms akin to shellshock. Again, doctors were at a loss to diagnose the causes.

Crossley refused all offers of legal representation and acted as his own lawyer during his trial. Whether or not one believes he was a fool to do so depends on your interpretation of the outcome. Without counsel to guide his testimony, Crossley was free to expound at length about his magical abilities, with predictable results. The judge promptly ruled that he should be committed to an institution — which may of course have been what Crossley intended all along.

Then came another twist in Crossley's tale — Rachel was pregnant with his child. When she wrote to him in the institution to say that she was keeping the baby, he gave her his blessing, but insisted that she should keep the child away from him, for its own safety. *I think I shall die in this place*, he wrote, *and I have precious little to offer, but I shall see to it that whatever worldly possessions I have are passed onto my son (it will be a boy), after I am gone.*

Taking him at his word, Rachel never visited Crossley during or after her pregnancy (despite the fact that he was often heard to claim, in his mania, that random members of staff or visitors to the institute were, in fact, the very same Fieldings from his story). When she finally gave birth to the child — it was indeed a boy — she christened him Joseph.

Crossley was fascinated by the existence of the son he would never know, and spoke frequently of him to his doctors. He was seized by a desperate compulsion to leave something behind for Joseph, and, in what was perhaps the strangest encounter of Crossley's entire bizarre existence, his opportunity would shortly arrive.

Intrigued by Anthony Fielding's letters, his friend Gilderoy contacted Crossley, asking to work with him in an attempt to capture his 'terror shout' on tape. Crossley agreed, on condition that, in return, Gilderoy supervise the recording of an audio memoir that Crossley would recite for his son.

Work commenced quickly. Gilderoy rented lodgings near the institution, and the two men would meet daily: taping Crossley's memoirs in the mornings, and in the afternoons, beginning the painstaking task of devising a recording method able to capture the unearthly resonance and destructive force of the shout.

The project, conducted in the utmost secrecy, took months: Crossley's recordings were a simple enough matter, although elongated by the narrator's constant digressions and obsessive need to retell the same story in different ways.

As for their other collaboration, even Gilderoy's genius laboured mightily to safely and accurately record a sound that was entirely supernatural in origin. Believing the sessions might be good therapy for their patient, doctors had allowed the technician to requisition and soundproof a small room in the institution, and it was there that the two men struggled with their Sisyphean task. Staff members spoke of a rubbish skip outside the hospital being piled high with ruined audio equipment, blackened and charred by massive electrical surges.

Eventually, the work was either completed or abandoned. Crossley did apparently manage to complete his recordings to an extent he deemed satisfactory (although given his proclivity for infinite variation, it would always have to be regarded at something of a work-in-progress). Several hours' worth of audio tape were indeed delivered to his son Joseph upon Crossley's death, although no one else has ever heard their contents (esoteric scholars worldwide have long clamoured for copies or transcriptions to be made available, without success).

Regarding Gilderoy's role in the affair, as is so often the case, it is impossible to separate the verifiable facts from the miasma of penny dreadful horror stories that has formed around them.

The most popular legend is this: Gilderoy *did* finally succeed in his aim of recording Crossley's shout. So secretive was the technician that when Crossley enquired as to what exactly he meant to do with the tape, Gilderoy simply replied, *I'm sure I'll find a use for it somewhere.*

But what use could one possibly find for a sound so awful, it would instantly kill any listener?

The—no doubt fabricated—story has it that Gilderoy had also somehow managed to obtain a dupe bootleg copy of one of Mark Lewis's snuff films: the infamous 16mm recordings he made of his 'Peeping Tom' murders. The films were recorded silent, so Gilderoy worked on creating his own soundtrack from scratch, with a grotesque climactic flourish: as the sequence reached its harrowing apogee, instead of the victim's dying scream, Gilderoy dubbed on Crossley's shout.

He called the film, simply, *fine* (assumed to be a sly reference to the time he spent working in Italian exploitation movies). Reports that Gilderoy held a single screening of *fine* for a small private audience—all of whom died or were driven insane by the experience—are completely unsubstantiated.

And Crossley? His death, like so much of his life, was an enigma. The official record shows cause of death as cardiac arrest, but some witnesses still insist that they watched him summon a bolt from the heavens with the unearthly power of his voice, the lightning blast instantly striking him dead.

We shall probably never know the truth, which is doubtless how Crossley would have wanted it.

JOSEPH SOLOMON

Steve Oram in A Dark Song *(2016)*
written & directed by Liam Gavin

F OR MOST OF HIS EARLY LIFE, JOSEPH FIELDING'S REAL FATHER
was nothing more than a hollow voice on a tape, a forbidden name
that drew coughs and averted glances around the family dinner table. An
absence.

Until that day when Joseph lay strung out and dying in a filthy Soho
alleyway, and Charles Crossley walked out of the desert to save him.

Joseph was born to Rachel Fielding in the late 1970s, the product of her
brief affair with Crossley. She had been adamant about keeping the child,
despite her extant marriage to Anthony Fielding. Anthony, who had
watched helplessly as Crossley seduced Rachel in their own marital home,
agreed to stand by her.

But after Joseph was born, Anthony found he could barely stomach
looking at the boy, and increasingly retreated into his work, leaving Rachel
to bring up her son alone. (Still, as his wife could testify, Anthony's love was
at best a diluted, tasteless brew, and even if the boy had been his, it is

doubtful he would have been any more than a distracted, occasional presence in Joseph's life.)

Joseph grew into a sullen, angry child, resentful of his mother and yet utterly dependent on her. He was a poor student at school, unruly and quick to fight with the other boys. As he entered adolescence, his attentions turned to the girls of his peer group, his budding pubescent longings quickly souring into something hostile and perverse. When he was caught exposing himself to two female classmates, he was summarily expelled.

Rachel decided to homeschool Joseph, and it was then she finally gave her son the collection of tapes that Charles Crossley had left behind for him. Although Rachel could not bring herself to listen to the material beforehand, she hoped that a father's influence—even that of Crossley, who had murdered all of his previous children—could only do the wayward boy some good.

Joseph quickly became obsessed by the hours of recordings, locking himself away in his bedroom and replaying them constantly. On the rare occasions that Rachel was permitted to enter the room, she would find pages and pages of densely-scribbled notes, entire passages transcribed verbatim from the tapes. Moreover, there would be scores of elaborately-drawn diagrams and symbols stuck around the bedroom walls.

It was all gibberish to Rachel, but if pressed to describe them, she would have defined the images as *occult*.

Her mistake was in mentioning the drawings to Anthony. Rachel's husband had a passing familiarity with esotericism, and upon seeing the symbols for himself, he angrily tore them from the walls and confronted the boy.

I won't have this crap in the house, he yelled in Joseph's face. When the boy responded with a tirade of obscenities, Anthony struck him across the face.

Rather than escalate the fight, Joseph merely withdrew from the room, locking himself away in his bedroom. Despite his mother's tearful entreaties, he refused to come out. She had no way of knowing then that she would never see her son again.

That night, Anthony developed a severe fever, which quickly worsened to the extent where he was struck blind. He was immediately rushed to hospital, although the doctors there could diagnose no physical cause for his distress. Amongst all the confusion, Joseph quietly packed a few belongings and left home for good, pausing only to burn Crossley's tapes. He left no word of explanation for his mother.

Anthony remained afflicted by the blindness for a week, until it lifted as suddenly as it had descended. No explanation for the attack was ever found.

Joseph travelled to London, and eventually found a room in a squat. He remained there for some months, acquainting himself with the big city and developing a healthy appetite for intoxicants of all varieties. Possibly it was only his resourcefulness in sourcing illicit substances that maintained his precarious foothold in the squat, because otherwise his manner was as abrasive as ever, hardly endearing him to the other members of the household.

He also used this time to further his occult studies. He refused to let a lack of funds stand in his way, and became quite adept at stealing whatever volumes he desired from esoteric booksellers or the homes of private collectors.

However, there remained one skill he could not master: the art of attracting the opposite sex. Still a virgin, he looked on in frustration as numerous young women drifted in and out of the house. For Joseph, they were a teasing mirage, a lustful dream he could not make flesh. When he tried to talk to them, they were inevitably bored or repulsed. How could he be so skilled at the higher arts of magic and esotericism, and yet so clumsy at this, the most prosaic of human activities?

In desperation, he turned to his father's example. Crossley had always eschewed the tedium of seduction; rather, he had simply used his magic to take what he desired. A young anarchist couple occupied the room adjacent to Joseph's, and the girl's habit of wandering around semi-clothed had prompted many furious fits of masturbation on his part. Enough was enough. No longer would he watch from afar, ignored.

While the couple were out one morning, he stole a glove from amongst the girl's belongings. That night he conducted a blood magic ritual to bend her will to his, then strode into the couple's bedroom and ordered her to follow him back to his own room.

The girl's only response was to burst out laughing. Her partner's was more forthright—he promptly got out of bed and gave the would-be seducer a painful beating, cracking two of his ribs. Joseph was forced to flee the squat immediately, under threat of the violence being repeated tenfold if his 'ugly fucking mug' wasn't gone by morning.

It was winter, and he had nowhere else to go. Despite his desperate circumstances, returning to his parents' home—beaten and battered, a complete failure—was unthinkable. So instead, he drifted further into alcohol and drug abuse, flooding his veins with honeyed, narcotic bliss in an attempt to stave off the predatory January cold.

It worked, for a time—inasmuch as when he reached the point of near-death some weeks later, he could not feel the streaks of urine freezing on his thighs: the blood vessels under his skin withering like blighted crops; nor his heart gradually stumbling to a halt. Joseph knew only that he was lying in an endless desert, and although he could hear the wind keening desolately around him, he was not cold.

Even while semi-conscious, he dimly understood that the end of his life was near. So when he heard footsteps slowly approaching across the sand, and opened his eyes to see a dark silhouette crouched over him like a carrion bird, Joseph thought for a moment that Death had arrived to claim him.

But then the figure's stark features came into focus, and Joseph somehow knew that he was looking at the face of his father, despite never having glimpsed so much as a photograph of Charles Crossley.

Crossley reached down and grabbed his son by the arm. *Come on*, he said.

Jospeh found he could not resist his father's command. He struggled weakly to his feet. *Am I dying?* he asked. *Are you here to take me with you?*

Crossley stared back at him. There were no answers to be found in his bottomless gaze. *You can follow me, or not*, he said. Then he turned and began to trudge away over the desert wastes, a cloud of dust rising to obscure his retreating figure.

What choice did Joseph have? He staggered off behind his father, following the erratic trail of Crossley's footprints across the dunes, like a line of musical notation he could not decipher.

They walked for hours, Joseph falling to his knees more than once. Crossley never faltered, never once looked back to monitor his son's progress, and more than anything, it was the wordless challenge of his callous disregard that kept Joseph struggling onwards.

Eventually, the desert winds began to subside, and the billowing sands surrounding them parted to reveal a building—a gloomy-looking townhouse, shuttered and long-abandoned. The house was located in a fashionable residential square, the rest of the houses expensively-comfortable and well-maintained. It put Joseph in mind of a decayed tooth in an otherwise perfect smile.

25 Ilchester Place, W14. It squatted at the end of its row of buildings like a poisonous mushroom, cold and damp, ready to infect the rest of the square with its toxic spores. Joseph could sense the appalling wrongness of it from where he stood. The house felt *shunned*, as though the other residents had agreed to collectively pretend number 25 simply did not exist.

Crossley's voice was a conspiratorial whisper. *You can stay here,* he said. *For as long as you need. People don't come here. You can get well. But...*

He trailed off, his eyes opaque.

What? Joseph asked. *There's something wrong here, isn't there?*

His father looked him up and down. The fouled and filthy rags of his clothes. His emaciated frame. He was a child who could not be entrusted with his own care. *Are you protected?*

What do you mean?

Crossley seized him by the shoulders. *Are you* protected, *I said! Do you know how to protect yourself?*

Finally, Joseph understood. *Yes!* He rolled up his sleeves to show Crossley.

On his arms were inked several crude tattoos, mystical symbols of protection. However, their linework was blemished in several places by infected trackmarks—because for all their magical power, they could not protect Joseph against himself.

Joseph tugged his sleeves back into place, ashamed of his own weakness. But his father seemed satisfied. He motioned around the side of the house. *You can get inside that way. Be careful. Don't speak to anyone you meet.*

Crossley began to walk away, the desert winds rising to engulf him once more.

Joseph suddenly felt bereft—there was so much he wanted to say. He called out plaintively after the retreating figure: *I listened to your tapes! They taught me everything!*

Crossley paused for a moment. *You listened, but did you hear?*

Before Joseph could reply, his father was gone. The street around him was now silent and empty, filled with the unruffled early morning quiet of a wealthy London neighbourhood. The sort of neighbourhood it would not benefit Joseph to be seen in.

Creeping around the side of the building, Joseph easily broke inside, and entered the darkened house. He could tell it had been closed up for years—the air was musty, thick with neglect and decay. But for him, it represented a haven.

Searching the kitchen, he found some old tins of food. He located a can opener and sat down to a cold feast, gobbling beans and vegetable soup straight from the tins. It was amongst the finest meals he had ever known.

As he finished eating, greedily licking tomato sauce from his fingers, he suddenly became aware he was not alone. He looked around to see a young girl staring at him. She couldn't have been more than ten years old, blonde and angelic-faced and yet somehow abhorrent.

Joseph had experienced several visions in his life, numerous paranoid psychedelic hallucinations and crazed mystical ecstasies, but yet, none of that had prepared him for this, for the simple sight of a little girl watching him coyly from the shadows.

Somehow, he knew that this was the worst of all.

Hello, she said. *I'm Olivia. What's your name?*

I can't talk to you, Olivia, Joseph said, averting his gaze.

Why not? You're in my house. This is my house, you know.

He got up from the table. *Well, it's a big house. I'm sure there's room for the both of us.*

Not unless I say so. And I don't say so. The girlish sing-song arrogance of her voice masked something indescribably vicious lurking underneath.

Olivia took a threatening step forward, then froze like a statue, halted in her tracks.

Joseph smiled. *You can't touch me, Olivia. So looks like we're just gonna have to get used to each other.*

Her face rippled for a moment, as though it was the surface of a pool and something unspeakable was about to erupt from its depths. She hissed and spat like a striking cobra.

Joseph affected an air of casual nonchalance. Ignoring Olivia, he wandered from the room and made his way upstairs to the master bedroom. He even managed to control his trembling until he was safely out of Olivia's sight.

Wrapping himself in a moth-eaten bedspread, he lay down and went to sleep, although not before he had securely locked the bedroom door. He doubted it would keep Olivia out if it came to it, but the token gesture made him feel better.

Joseph spent the next few weeks nursing himself back to a semblance of health. There was no power in the house, but he kept himself warm by burning pieces of furniture in the fireplace. He fed on the remaining cans of food for as long as he could, and in time, he regained enough strength to go out and forage for more supplies.

Olivia generally left him alone. He could feel her presence sometimes, unseen but full of hate, and would catch occasional glances of her sallow face in reflected surfaces. Still, it seemed as though she was resigned to the fact that she could not hurt him; and given that hurting was all she understood, she had settled instead for giving him a wide berth.

Similarly, on his occasional forays outside the house, Joseph noticed the neighbourhood inhabitants doing their level best to completely ignore the fact of 25 Ilchester Place's existence. They would avert their eyes so as not to catch a glimpse of its exterior, and cross the road rather than walk directly past it.

Nevertheless, Joseph's own person had attracted unhappy looks from the upper middle-class neighbours, and he did not wish to draw unwelcome attention. So, once his mind and body were sufficiently healed, he conjured a simple glamour to protect both he and the house from prying eyes. In the immediate vicinity of the building, it would be as though neither of them really existed. He would be practically invisible. How he longed for that, to go completely unseen by the world.

As his strength gradually returned, he found other aspects of his physical being reasserting themselves. He had still never experienced a woman's touch, and the fact that he had almost died after being rejected by one served only to fuel his resentment. But what could he do? He had no immediate prospect of attracting a woman; neither could he pay for one.

Then it came to him. A dark unbidden fantasy came bubbling up out of the murk of his subconscious. Instinctively, he was appalled, but neither could he banish the thought from his mind. He felt something primal stirring within him.

Searching the house, he found some chalk. Setting to work on the hardwood floor of the living room, he carefully drew out a binding circle. Then, taking a small bowl from the kitchen, he sliced open his palm and filled the receptacle with blood. Placing the bowl within the circle, he knelt down beside it, his body trembling with forbidden excitement.

She *was* a very pretty girl.

Reciting the necessary incantations, he summoned Olivia to the circle. Within moments, she materialised, visibly seething at his presumption.

I'll kill you, she hissed.

I don't think so, Joseph replied. *Listen to me. I want you to pick up the bowl and drink it.*

I won't!

I command it, Olivia.

Her body straining to resist him, Olivia bent down and picked up the bowl, raising it to her mouth to drank down his blood.

When she let the bowl fall from her lips, they were red with a life she herself did not possess. When she bared her teeth, they were stained with rubies.

You fucking cunt, she said.

I want you to . . . The words died in his throat. *I want you to...take off your dress, Olivia.*

She was his to command. Sullenly, she obeyed.

He gazed upon her porcelain skin, unspoiled as fresh milk. She was not yet a woman . . . but it was enough, for now.

He unbuttoned his trousers. *Now, I want you to touch me, Olivia.*

She sneered. *The last boy I touched, I cut it off with a scalpel. I'm going to do the same to you.*

Shut up and touch me!

Her hands were small and exquisitely gentle.

For a time, it were as though the house on Ilchester Place existed entirely apart from the world. While he managed to stay off harder drugs, Joseph would drink and smoke weed constantly, and enjoy Olivia's attentions whenever the mood took him. He was unaccustomed to such contentment, and had little desire to emerge from the blissful cocoon he had spun around himself.

Still, he would often think of his father, and wonder for what purpose Crossley had emerged from the underworld to save him. In their brief time together, he'd seemed disgusted at the wretched path his only son had taken. Joseph longed to somehow prove himself. Crossley struck Joseph as a man who'd striven to impose his will on the world, but his son wanted no such thing—in truth, he would prefer to withdraw from it entirely.

How then, to win his father's approval?

Perhaps, he thought, the answer was mastery. He and his father would never view the world in the same way, but if he could match him as a magician, perhaps then Crossley would see him as something more than a pathetic weakling.

Joseph returned to his studies, and managed to build himself a crude website, advertising his services as a mystic. (He decided to change his name from Fielding, preferring something that implied wisdom and power. He soon settled on Solomon—obvious, but that was what selling yourself was all about.) He was a proficient enough magician that word of mouth soon brought him a steady flow of work—love and revenge were perennially popular areas amongst his clientele.

But he could never forget it was merely petty street magic he was peddling, a far cry from the kind of mystical supremacy he aspired to. His idol was Julian Karswell—how Joseph wished he could have studied under him! *There* was a man who understood power. Karswell had even claimed to have successfully completed the Abramelin Ritual. A spell to summon one's own guardian angel, it was amongst the most difficult and elaborate rites a magician could attempt.

In truth, Joseph lacked his father's natural talent for magic. He had the knowledge, but not the skill. This was not helped by his propensity for self-destruction. He would attempt magic while drunk or stoned, and forget lines of incantations or other important aspects of the rituals.

As his reach proved to continually exceed his grasp, his bitterness and self-loathing grew.

He took to beating Olivia. He could not really hurt her, of course, but it satisfied him to have an outlet for his rage. And what did it matter? She would already gladly kill him if ever given the chance.

As it was, she seized any available opportunity for a display of retribution. One night, Joseph brought a prostitute home. He was already drunk and forgot that the woman was not protected against the evil in the house as he was. The next morning he found her in the bathroom, the mirror on the medicine cabinet smashed, shards of glass embedded in her throat like a lethal necklace. As the woman's blood puddled stickily around his feet, Joseph heard Olivia giggling from afar.

By now, Ilchester Place had become a prison, of sorts. He was entombed here by his own failure, locked up with a nameless, loathsome thing wearing the face of a little girl. He should flee, get far away, but was afraid to. The memory of that freezing cold Soho alley still haunted him.

Then Joseph received the email. A woman named Sophia Howard had heard about the Abramelin Ritual, and its power to grant any wish. There was a man she desired. Could Joseph help her? She would pay him well.

He was simultaneously ecstatic, and terrified. Here was a chance to finally prove himself. And the money she was offering—he could get away from this corrupted house, from Olivia. If the ritual succeeded, he could even achieve his own, long dreamt-of fantasies.

He could finally—*truly*—be made invisible from the world.

But what if he failed? The consequences could be fatal, or worse.

He emailed her back, setting out the terms. A month later, she told him to meet her in Wales. She had rented an isolated house there, perfect for their work.

He packed a bag, Olivia watching him as he gathered his things. He did not look at her, or tell her where he was going.

As he finally made to leave, she muttered, *You're going to die there.*

Upon reaching Wales, he nearly turned around and came straight back home. Sophia Howard was a stupid posh bitch, and had lied to him, as women do. It turned out that her son had been abducted and murdered, probably due to her own carelessness. Her *real* wish was to see him again. She was unstable, had spent time in a psychiatric hospital. There was so much that could go wrong.

And yet. She offered him all the money she had: tens of thousands of pounds, more than Joseph had ever seen. She agreed to submit herself utterly to his control, to cook and clean and slave for him. She did not even blanch (more than a little, anyway) when he mentioned ritual sex. And she was not by any means unattractive.

He agreed to begin work.

The Abramelin Ritual would take months to perform, possibly years. If he succeeded, this would be Joseph's crowning accomplishment. (He lied and told Sophia that he had conducted the ritual several times before.)

He wondered if his father was watching.

Sophia took to her assigned role without complaint—Joseph admired her obsessive dedication, but still, that did not stop him from abusing the privilege he had been accorded. He would watch intently as she cleaned the house—quietly enjoying ogling her arse and her cleavage as she crouched on the floor scrubbing—then delight in pointing out spots she had missed. If a meal she had prepared was not to his satisfaction, he would insist she go back and begin again.

Sophia hated him for it, but Joseph was already quite accustomed to the scorn of women.

As the ritual continued—day after day, week after week—Sophia complained that nothing was happening, but Joseph could sense reality beginning to shift around them. Doors opened of their own accord, and they would hear disembodied footsteps echoing around the empty building. Sophia would also insist that she could hear a dog barking at night, when no such animal lived anywhere near the house.

Joseph did not tell her of his own experiences. He would wake at night to find Olivia sitting on the end of the bed, quietly watching him. She never spoke, only smiled. He did not know whether it was truly Olivia but it frightened him nonetheless—he was not at all certain his magical protections would work here, in the liminal realm they now inhabited.

Perhaps it was the sight of Olivia, perhaps it was the weeks of abstention, but Joseph's baser appetites finally got the better of him. One night he made Sophia strip naked and expose herself to him while he masturbated. When she realised it was not actually part of the ritual, she exploded in rage. *I'm just a man*, Joseph pleaded.

She was sick of the whole thing, wanted to call it off. Now Joseph was truly afraid. If they did not properly finish their work together, they could be stranded in this house for eternity.

He finally convinced her to go on, but then Joseph made a fateful discovery: Sophia had been lying to him once again. What she *truly* desired was not merely to see her son again, but to enact vengeance on his murderers.

The ritual was ruined. Everything had been wasted. They would have to begin again. Not only that, but Sophia would have to be purified, baptised anew. Retrieving a stashed bottle of whisky from hiding, he got drunk for the first time in months, steeling himself for what lay ahead. Then, he filled the bathtub in preparation.

Sophia climbed into the water, suspecting nothing. Joseph began to recite the words of the purification rite, then pushed Sophia's head under the surface, holding her there until she drowned.

Once he was sure she was dead, and the conditions of the purification ritual had been satisfied, he hurriedly revived her. Sophia was unharmed by the ordeal, but furious at yet another deception. When he took her to the kitchen to recover, she flew at him. In the ensuing struggle, Joseph was accidentally stabbed with a carving knife.

He slumped to the floor, the blade protruding from his belly. Knowing he could not possibly leave the house and go to hospital, the pair did the best they could with the wound, cleansing it with whisky and applying a makeshift dressing. The occultist resignedly told Sophia it was the price he had to pay for hurting her.

He could not sleep that night; the throbbing in his ruptured stomach seemed to take hold of his entire body. Still, he continued on as best he could the following day—what other option was there?

But as time passed, it became clear that something was seriously wrong.

Joseph was often weak and distracted, losing his focus and forgetting parts of the ritual. Sophia began to worry his wound was infected, but he insisted that they press on regardless. *This is the price of our rage,* he said.

Joseph had never cared about another human being in his life, but now he began to worry about Sophia, this shattered, angry woman who had no more of a place left in the world than he did. He feared what would happen to her if he did not survive to see the end of the ritual.

His nights became a feverish blur, his bed a roiling sea of tears and sweat. He would hear Olivia's voice whispering in his ear. *It won't be long now,* she said. *And then you'll be mine. To play with forever.*

Soon, he no longer had the strength to get up. Sophia tended to him as best she could, but they both knew it was hopeless. He implored her not to leave him alone. *She comes when you're not here,* he whispered. Sophia had no idea who he was talking about, but it did not matter—she knew from her own experience that they were no longer alone in the house.

Finally, Joseph began to slip away. Sophia squeezed his hand and spoke comfortingly to him, but he did not hear her. His eyes gazed into the distance—what was he seeing? *Is God here now?* he whimpered.

In Joseph's mind, he was once more lying in an endless desert waste. But now it was night in the desert, and cold—so very cold. He could taste grains of sand, dry and bitter on his tongue.

Again, he heard approaching footfalls, heavy in the sand. Joseph closed his eyes. He could not face his father, not now. Crossley had given him a chance at life—something he had cruelly denied to his other children—and Joseph had wasted it, frittered it away on anger and abuse and cheap conjuring tricks. *I'm sorry,* he sobbed. *I'm sorry I failed.*

There was no reply. Finally, Joseph succumbed to the silence and opened his eyes.

His father's dark ragged figure loomed over him, immense. Crossley stared down at him, a sharpened white bone pointed accusingly in his hand.

Then, a black chasm opened in his face, like the ground being rent asunder by an earthquake. He began to shout.

The sound swallowed everything.

JACK GOODMAN

Griffin Dunne in An American Werewolf in London *(1981)*
written & directed by John Landis

T HIS HAD ALREADY BEEN THE WORST VACATION OF JACK GOODMAN'S young life, and now he was dead.

Not merely dead, but *undead*; an animated corpse, rotting right where he stood. Which at this moment was outside a shabby porno cinema in London's Piccadilly Circus, wincing as the incessant rain (seriously, did it ever stop raining in this goddamn country?) drummed its fingers on the exposed bone of his skull, a rattling sensation which made him feel like a walking Quonset hut.

He'd thought it couldn't get any worse, not after the bad teeth, the disgusting food, the cold and the wet (in summer!), the long trudges across blighted country landscapes that blurred into endless washes of brown, like a stepped-in dog turd smeared across a sidewalk ('picturesque', David had called it).

Turns out it can *always* be worse. Turns out the horrors of English food—the colourless, exsanguinated meat, the congealed slop of vegetable matter, the greasy instant coffee—were nothing compared to having your flesh torn apart by viciously hooked claws, your bones gnawed by razored yellow teeth, the foul carrion reek of a monster's breath as it slobbered greedily over your exposed entrails, steaming in the cold air—

And after all that, you couldn't even look forward to Paradise. No, you were still stuck in *England.*

Merrie Olde England, with its warm beer and cold pubs, three channels of television (no cable!), and naked girls in the daily newspaper (OK, that part wasn't so bad). Stuck here *forever*—or at least until your best friend decided to off himself, or had the job done for him.

Because get this—Jack had been killed by a *werewolf.* An honest-to-god, real-life Lon Chaney Jr. imitator. Not only did they have history in this godforsaken island (and boy, did they love to rub all that history in your face), they also had *monsters*—a fact that the Brits were conspicuously less eager to toot their horns about.

He and his good buddy David Kessler had been out traipsing the Yorkshire moors after dark (because what the hell else did you do for entertainment in Yorkshire, right?), only to be attacked by said werewolf. Good buddy David had hightailed it out of there leaving Jack to get ripped apart, and had escaped with just a few duelling scars to show for his bravery.

The upshot of all this was that David too, was now a werewolf, and undead Jack was doomed to remain in Limbo (or in England, which kinda amounted to the same thing), until the monster's bloodline was ended.

In short: one way or another, David Kessler needed to bite the dust, pronto.

Jack had left David behind in the cinema. He'd wanted to catch the end of the movie (*See You Next Wednesday,* an entertainingly-terrible British skinflick), but the full moon had risen, and David had started to change, and Jack still got a little nauseous watching him feed. It was all a bit too close to home.

So he'd drifted back outside, back into the wet and the cold, at a loss what to do next. That was one of the main problems of being undead: too much time to kill. He'd done the London tourist thing already, traipsed wetly around Big Ben and St Paul's and the Tower of London, but he'd soon discovered one of the drawbacks of historical buildings was that they all had their own ghosts, ghosts who'd been trapped in this goddamn country for *centuries*, and they were all eager for someone to talk to. And if there was anything more boring than talking to a dead guy, it was talking to a *medieval* dead guy. All those *thees* and *thous* made Jack's head hurt.

Slowly, he began to wander back towards the neon lights of Soho. One of the few advantages of being dead and mostly invisible was that you could look at naked girls without paying. Although even that was losing its appeal now that he didn't have any blood left to pump to you-know-where.

Trudging through the rain-slick streets, he mourned the loss of his potency, of the mediocre Debbie Klein (and her decidedly non-mediocre body) and all the other girls he would never know, never get to schtup.

Lost in thought, he turned into Windmill Street and nearly collided with another dead guy. Fairly long-dead, by the looks of him; Jack guessed this as much from the hideous paisley waistcoat he was wearing as the few scraps of parchment skin that still clung to his skeleton.

The dead guy doffed his straw hat. *Hello there, fellow traveller!*

He sounded like a complete — what was the word the Brits used? Not twat, but *twit*. Yes. This guy was definitely a twit.

Jack nodded, returning the greeting. *Er, hi.*

Ah, you're a Yank! First time in London?

And the last.

Hahaha! Good to see your sense of humour hasn't rotted with the rest of you. The dead guy extended a bony hand. *Saw you wandering around earlier, meant to say hello. Name's Paul Foote.*

Jack shook the proffered bones and introduced himself in turn.

Pleased to meet you, Jack! Jack supposed Foote looked pleased enough, although dead guys often did. That was the trouble with corpses, you could never tell what they were thinking. *Listen — are you otherwise engaged at the moment?*

Otherwise...? Er, no, not really. I was just gonna check out some of the local nightlife...

Foote continued to grin. *Good man! Lucky I bumped into you like this. You see, there's a place where a few of us get together for the occasional soirée.*

Quite informal. It isn't much, but it's somewhere the dead can go to get out of the rain. How about it?

Jack shrugged. He figured he had nothing to lose—being dead did that for you. *Sure, why not?*

Groovy! Follow me! Foote put a guiding hand on the small of Jack's back, exactly where his right kidney had once been.

The next moment, they materialised in front of a derelict building, the windows dark and boarded-up. Before them, a stairway carpeted in a mulch of newspapers and other discarded trash led down to a basement door.

Foote beckoned him on. *Down here, old chap. It's not quite the Ritz, but we've tried to make the best of it.*

Jack gingerly followed him down the steps and through a doorway. Inside, they emerged into a long-disused nightclub space. Anyone living would have quickly been driven out by the suffocating pall of mould and dust that lingered in the air, but the dead had no such problem.

Much of the furniture lay broken and splintered in the corners of the room, but the patrons had gathered whatever was still useable and arranged it close to the stage area. Someone had managed to obtain some candles for the tables, and their flickering light illuminated the cadaverous hollows of the gathered crowd's faces (what was left of them, at least) as they sat and watched the evening's entertainment, a solo pianist. A cobwebbed disco ball hung overhead, a tarnished reminder of the full moon that had brought them all to this place.

Foote led Jack towards a table adjacent to the stage, already occupied by another dead guy in a white safari jacket. Jack glanced up at the pianist, dressed in a wide-lapelled shirt and a brown cardigan. (Man, someone needed to give these dead guys some fashion tips.) The performer picked his way through *Moon River* and seemed to be making a creditable job of it, despite the old out-of-tune piano and an occasional missing key.

Arriving at the table, Foote introduced Jack to their companion. *Bennington, this is Jack.*

Bennington did his best skeletal impersonation of a sneer. *Ah. A new boy.*

Jack immediately decided that if you looked up 'plummy' in the dictionary, you'd find a picture of Bennington in his better days underneath.

Foote took a seat, and motioned for Jack to do the same. *There's been some . . . activity recently. I've seen quite a few fresh kills moping about the streets.*

So I've heard, Bennington sniffed. *Bloody Americans, always sticking their noses into other people's business.*

The pianist finished the song, and was met with a chorus of boos. Bennington immediately lost interest in Jack. He'd gathered a small pile of dessicated peanut shells on the table in front of him, and began to lob them at the performer's skull.

Jack whistled, or tried to. It was difficult without your lips. *Tough crowd.*

There's a reason for that. Foote turned to him conspiratorially. *He's not actually one of us.*

Jack gazed up at the pianist, who seemed grimly resigned to his lot. *He looks pretty dead to me.*

Oh, he is. But you see, he wasn't a victim. Foote explained: *He was a werewolf. His name's Jan Jarmokowski. He's the reason I'm here, and Bennington, and a few of the others. In life, he was a famous concert pianist. So it was decided an eternity playing easy listening standards to an unappreciative undead audience might be an appropriate punishment.*

Jarmokowski gritted his teeth and went into *Release Me,* to more scattered boos.

Jack didn't quite understand. *But if he's dead—why are all of you still here?*

Foote sighed. *The bloodline, old boy. The bloodline wasn't severed. He bit a man, you see. A man named Tom Newcliffe. Thing is, everyone thought old Tom had gone off to top himself, but he lost his nerve at the last second. Fired that bullet into the wall and ran off into the woods. So here we are.*

Bennington sneered again. *You can never trust a darkie.*

Jack coughed into his tattered sleeve. That was the other thing about the Brits, they were so goddamn racist. Christ knows the US had its problems, but here they still had primetime sitcoms laughing at funny foreigners. All in good fun, what what?

Foote diplomatically changed the subject back. *Funnily enough, it was actually Tom who bit the fellow who killed you. Small world, eh?*

Certainly too small for Jack's liking. If it had only been a little larger, he might never have left the US in the first place.

Onstage, the tune came to a sudden halt as Jarmokowski's right index finger bone parted company with the rest of his hand and clattered to the floor. The pianist stopped in mid-tinkle and bent down to retrieve it. Holding it aloft, he got to his feet and gave an apologetic half-bow to the audience.

I'm sorry for this interruption to the performance, ladies and gentlemen. I just need to take a short...werewolf break.

Groans from the crowd. Bennington pelted the pianist's retreating back with more peanut shells.

Jack left his chair and followed Jarmokowski over towards the bar area, where he was attempting to reattach his runaway digit. Jack raised his hand in silent greeting, then immediately lowered it, wondering whether it might be interpreted as mockery. *Hi,* he said.

The pianist gave him a suspicious glare. *Why are you talking to me? No one talks to me.*

Jack shrugged. *I was just wondering—what's it like? Being a wolf, I mean. They call it a curse and all that, but none of you guys seem in a particular hurry to kill yourselves or anything. So it can't be that bad, right?*

Jarmokowski carefully screwed his finger back into place. *You really want to know? It's better than anything. The power you have in your body, it's like you're plugged directly into the mains. Your veins sing with it. It's better than coke, better than anything. You can drink or fuck all night, do whatever you want. I'd play here for another thousand years in exchange for just one more day as a wolf.*

So I probably shouldn't hold my breath waiting for my buddy to kill himself, right? Jack sighed.

Sorry, friend. Didn't they read you fairy tales as a kid? You can't ever trust a wolf. If he told you that, he was probably just trying to make you feel better.

Jack slumped against the bar, beaten. *Shit.*

The pianist turned towards the stage. *I have to get back to work now. They get rowdy if they think I'm skiving off. But look—if you need cheering up, I do take requests.*

Jack watched him wander back to his piano. He wondered if he could sneak out of here without Foote or anyone noticing him leaving.

He was about to start skulking towards the exit when a wave of dizziness hit him. Bright lights flared before his eyes; his feet seemed untethered to the earth. All of a sudden he only felt half-present in the room, as though he were drugged, succumbing to anesthesia.

In between the flashes of light, he began to glimpse images, vivid and immediate: a cornered werewolf, crouching angrily in a dark alleyway; the frightened face of the hot English nurse David had been banging; a sudden flourish of gunfire.

And finally, David's naked body, human once more; riddled with bullets, what remained of his life pooling around him on the cold concrete.

Jack realised what this meant. He slammed his fist excitedly on the bar. *I'm outta here! I'm outta here!* He stumbled back towards Foote, ecstatic. *David's dead! They got him! I'm going home!*

Foote pushed the chair Jack had previously vacated towards him. *Steady on, old boy,* he said warningly. *Take a load off.*

You're not listening! I'm out! Fuck this country! And fuck all you stiffs! I'm done! Jack could feel his body flickering, like a faulty lightbulb.

Bennington snorted. No one spoke.

And then, suddenly, Jack was back—back in the derelict bar, back with the dead guys, back in England. The weightless sensation had left him.

He looked around in disbelief. *What the . . . ?*

Foote patted the chair. *I did tell you to sit down. Bad news is much better dealt with sitting on your arse.*

Jack slumped into the seat, dazed. *But David's dead. I saw him die!*

Of course, of course. But the bloodline, *dear boy.*

What?

Foote sighed. *That nurse he was shagging.*

Jack still didn't get it.

She's carrying David's little cub.

Bennington snickered nastily. *And won't she get a hell of surprise the first time she offers it her tit on a full moon!*

Onstage, Jarmokowski grinned down at Jack and went into the opening bars of *One for My Baby.*

Jack grabbed a handful of Bennington's peanut shells and flung them at the pianist.

IAN & JOANNE

Edward Woodward & Samantha Weysom in The Appointment, *1981
written & directed by Lindsey C. Vickers*

CROMBIE WOODS HAD FIRST ACQUIRED A REPUTATION AS A haunted place back in the 1950s. What had previously been considered nothing more than a pleasant recreational spot and useful shortcut suddenly became dogged by ill talk of strange lights glimpsed in the dark woods at night; of whispered voices coaxing the unwary into the forest, and sightings of mysterious black hounds, traditional harbingers of doom and misfortune.

For years the small patch of woodland was shunned by local people, but as the decades passed and previously dire warnings lost their potency, becoming nothing but spooky stories to be shared delightedly amongst the area's children, Crombie Woods again became a favoured walking location.

Until 1978, when the disappearance of schoolgirl Sandy Freemont reminded the inhabitants of the nearby town that however fanciful they may appear, fairy tales and ghost stories often carry important lessons; stern imprecations that we ignore at our own peril.

Sandy had taken a shortcut through the woods on her way home from school orchestra practice. A precociously gifted violinist, she had been talked of as a shining musical prospect and future star of classical music. Happily, she was also a modest girl and well-liked amongst her peers — or so it was believed.

For, as Sandy learnt to her cost, the bright heat of talent can also foster the rot of envy, like meat spoiling in the warm sun.

Her body was found in Crombie Woods two days after her disappearance. She had been mutilated almost beyond recognition, clawed and torn into a shredded pulp. Because the wounds could not possibly have been inflicted by human hands, it was assumed that the corpse had been posthumously savaged by the feral dogs that were still sometimes glimpsed lurking in the woods.

As far as the coroner could ascertain, there was no evidence of sexual assault, but nevertheless, the apparently motiveless nature of the crime gave rise to the theory that the murder must have been committed by a lone maniac. Still, no suspect was ever arrested for the crime, and after pressure from local parents, the footpath was securely fenced off. Once again, Crombie Woods had become a horror story to frighten the young.

Understandably, no one ever noted the distinct similarities between the details of Sandy's murder and those of a series of other strange demises recorded decades earlier, in the 1940s and 50s: a chain of deaths culminating in that of the notorious occultist, Dr Julian Karswell, at Bricket Wood railway station. His body, too, had been horrifically mutilated, and although the police at the scene were quick to ascribe the blame to a passing train, others present insisted upon a more supernatural explanation for the claw-like wounds that ravaged the deceased man's flesh.

The truth is that Karswell had summoned and bound a major demon, using it to viciously strike at his enemies. But upon his death at the demon's own hands, it had found itself released from all magical restraints and free to roam the material plane at will.

Seeking the refuge of dark and lonely places, the fiend had ensconced itself within the shadows of Crombie Wood. Over time, the demon's vile influence infected the roots and tendrils of the woodland, and its malefic familiars — three black hellhounds — began to venture out beyond the forest and stalk the sleeping town's dreams. It was then that Crombie Wood acquired its reputation as a place to be feared.

Karswell's opponents had prided themselves on ridding the world of a great evil that night at Bricket Wood, but in truth, they had only displaced the larger threat.

Some years later, Joanne, a classmate of Sandy Freemont, was making her way home through Crombie Wood, oblivious to the fact that she was not alone. Watching her from the darkness, the demon sensed that the girl carried an absence within her. She was an empty vessel, waiting to be filled.

For Joanne was an unremarkable girl; pretty enough, and doted upon by her parents, but mediocre in all other respects, affectless and boredly content to drift through life. *She lives in a dangerous world of make-believe*, her mother Dianne always insisted. If pressed, Joanne would have claimed to be happy enough with her lot, but in truth, even at such a young age, she recognised her own lack, and envied the ambition and talent she saw in some of her peers.

In girls such as Sandy Freemont.

As Joanne walked daydreaming along the forest path, a low voice called to her from amongst the trees. Other girls might have taken fright and run, but something within Joanne had been waiting for this summons. She knew she was no fairy tale heroine; what she desired from life was different, and much darker.

And so, instead of seeking a trail of breadcrumbs out of the dark woods, she chose to plunge deeper into its shadows.

There, in the verdant darkness, the demon appeared to her, wearing the face of her father Ian. A part of Joanne understood that it was not actually her father standing before her, but the mere association was enough; the churn of emotions prompted by his face, the maelstrom of love and respect and fear (and other feelings she dare not admit), was sufficient to tear open her heart and soul and allow the creature inside.

And as it entered her, she welcomed it.

What do you most desire? it asked.

Joanne did not hesitate. *There's another girl at school,* she said. *Her name's Sandy. I want what she has. All of it.*

If I grant you this, so too must you offer something of yourself. The demon's voice was soft with anticipation.

I don't care. Take whatever you want. Just give me Sandy.

After Sandy's body was discovered the following week, one of the many gaping holes she left in the world was the loss to the school orchestra of its star violinist. A hole the school's music teacher never expected to be able to fill.

Imagine his surprise then, when Joanne promptly presented herself to him for an audition. *I can play violin quite well,* she said bashfully. *But you always had Sandy—poor, poor Sandy—so I never thought to audition before. But now... I thought maybe I should do it for her.*

Not expecting much, the teacher politely agreed to listen to her play—and had been astonished. Joanne's musical gift was everything Sandy's had been—it was almost like listening to the murdered girl play. (In all honesty, although he never would have admitted it, Joanne even possessed a slight edge over her predecessor—an air of devilish abandon that served to liberate her playing.) And all this from a girl he had previously considered a sulky non-entity, a bored faraway presence in his music lessons! By the time she finished her recital, he had tears in his eyes.

She lowered her instrument and looked at him dully, her voice as weirdly emotionless as ever. *Was it OK?*

It was, and more. Joanne became the musical star of the school, swiftly going on to win acclaim and awards across the country. Sandy Freemont's accomplishments were swiftly all but forgotten. (There were those that thought it a shame, even disrespectful, that Sandy's star should be eclipsed so quickly, and so completely at that, but they kept their feelings to themselves.)

Joanne herself took to her new status calmly, as though it were nothing less than she had been due all along. The demon asked comparatively little from her in return: occasional small offerings or services of the flesh, nothing she minded giving. And if every now and then, some other unfortunate should go missing in the vicinity of the wood, well, they were always carefully chosen and never of sufficient status or importance to attract too much fuss.

Certainly none that could be attributed to an adolescent girl, especially one destined for such great things.

As for Joanne's parents, if they ever questioned the change in their hitherto-mediocre daughter, they did not do so too deeply. They had always cherished Joanne to an extent disproportionate with her accomplishments, so now they merely told themselves that their years of encouragement had finally paid off. Joanne was simply a late bloomer, held back by her natural diffidence.

Ian in particular became more attentive than ever. There were those in their extended family who privately believed he and his daughter's mutual adoration had always been somewhat inappropriate, even unseemly on occasion.

Perhaps he cannot really be held responsible; the demon delighted in coaxing the murkiest of emotions from within its human victims. Perhaps Ian simply rationalised the incremental shifts in his daughter's behaviour towards him—the lingering hand on the knee, the bedtime kiss slightly too close to the edge of the mouth—as quirks of blossoming girlish adolescence. Perhaps those instances late at night, where he lingered outside Joanne's bedroom door, hand poised to grasp the doorknob—yet never quite daring to turn it—were evidence of the demon's wiles and growing influence upon him, rather than expressions of his own deepest desires.

Whatever the reality, the culmination of the forbidden dance Ian found himself drawn into would prove disastrous.

Three years after Sandy Freemont's murder, Joanne was preparing for an end of term school concert recital, one in which she would perform a complex solo violin piece by Paganini. As was the family custom, she was fully expecting to bask in the glow of her parents' admiration, and in anticipation of this, a pair of front row seats had been reserved for them.

However, at the last minute, Ian was summoned away on an urgent work trip and found himself unable to attend. Despite his profuse apologies, his daughter immediately grew petulant, churlish. *Aren't I special to you anymore?* she pouted.

Wearying of her sulkiness (and perhaps reluctant to be reminded of quite how special she was to him) Ian ordered Joanne to bed.

This was to be his final act of authority as a parent.

That night his sleep was restless. He dreamt of his wife, flirtatious and alluring in a red cocktail dress, only for her face to reshape itself into that of Joanne. His sleeping mind recoiling from the implication, the dream then shifted into an anxious premonition of his work trip. He drove through a blasted granite landscape, quite alone in his vehicle, yet haunted by the persistent sense that he was being accompanied on his journey.

The dream rapidly became nightmarish; out of nowhere, three black dogs leapt at his car, sending him skidding off the narrow mountain road and into the waiting chasm beyond. As his stomach plunged away from him, he awoke with a childlike whimper.

Any momentary disappointment that it was Dianne beside him to offer comfort and not Joanne was immediately banished from his mind. If only Ian had known that his wife was also suffering portentous nightmares of his death, it might have given him pause; perhaps even such a stolid, unimaginative man as himself could have recognised the warning and been saved.

He set out early the next morning, determined to avoid seeing his daughter.

No matter, she had an appointment of her own.

Stopping by Crombie Wood on her way to school, Joanne made an offering to the darkness—a small collection of correspondence from her father, and some smiling photographs of them both. Did the saccharine nature of Ian's postcard endearments—*Miss You! Daddy xxxxxxx*—make the gift all the sweeter?

Ian made good time on his journey north, although his mind was still haunted by the terrors of the previous night. The piercing sound of nearby roadworks seemed to suggest the frantic squealing of car tyres; the three black dogs painted on the side of a passing lorry were surely just a coincidence, although an uncomfortable one. Stopping at a phone box, he called home, eager to hear the comforting sound of a familiar voice. His brief talk with Dianne offered some reassurance, although the call was cut short before she could recount the details of her own dream.

That reassurance was soon banished. As Ian continued on his journey, and his car entered an all-too familiar granite landscape, precipitous and forbidding, his hands tightened anxiously on the wheel. For an instant, he was sure he was back in bed dreaming, so recognisable were his surroundings. He dropped his speed, inching through the mountain pass as though he were a superstitious child, desperate to avoid stepping on the cracks between paving stones.

When he finally emerged on the other side of the pass into the neighbouring countryside, he felt like sobbing with relief. It had just been a stupid dream after all — mere jitters, no doubt brought on by his spat with Joanne. What else could it have been? The similarity of the details were unsettling, but there was, after all, a reassuringly banal explanation — he must have driven these roads before and half-forgotten them.

As it turned out, it was not the journey he had forgotten, but something far more personal. During his anxious call to Dianne, his fretful hands had slipped off his wristwatch — and he had stupidly left it there, in the phone box.

He was almost tempted not to go back for it, but it had been a birthday gift from Joanne — the back engraved MY DEAR DADDY ALWAYS LOVE JOANNE. Imagine her fury if he lost it on the same trip that had prevented him from attending her concert! Sighing, he turned the car around.

Ian could not know that his daughter's anger had already been sufficiently roused, and that it in turn had summoned forth a far more frightful fury, one that would shortly consume him utterly. Fatally, his recollections of the previous night's dream had not been coherent enough to offer a true warning.

As he made his way back through the mountains, he did not understand that he had indeed been granted a premonition: not of the initial passage along the route, but *of his doomed return back*.

When the emergency services arrived at the scene a short time later, they found only the scorched trails of Ian's tyres on the deserted road, like the desperate clawmarks of some great wounded beast, arterial petrol sprayed all over the tarmac. His vehicle lay shattered in the gully below, a twisted metal casket for the ruined remains of its driver.

And if the attending ambulancemen felt an unseen presence in that empty pass; if they fancied they heard the distant sound of laughter carried aloft on those chill mountain winds, then they kept it to themselves.

That night at the concert, there was widespread admiration for Joanne's decision not to cancel her appearance, despite the tragedy of her father's death. She insisted that he would have wanted her to go on with the performance, and tearfully dedicated it to his memory.

As she finished her solo, she accepted the resultant standing ovation with a lowered head and duly respectful modesty. Alas, her mother was understandably not present to witness it.

In the wake of Ian's death, Dianne withdrew to the family home. There were rumours of heavy drinking and of late night screaming fits. The townspeople pitied Joanne, who soldiered on with admirable dedication, never letting her family's misfortune get her down or interfere with her dedication to her musical talent.

On the rare instances Dianne was glimpsed in town, she appeared dishevelled and wild-eyed. On one occasion she insisted to the local greengrocer that she was a virtual prisoner in her own home, a victim of diabolic forces. She whispered fearfully to him that she was slowly being driven mad by the three black dogs that visited her at night and passed their dark dreams onto her.

Shortly after Joanne's eighteenth birthday, Dianne committed suicide. Given her inability to recover from the trauma of her husband's death, no one who knew the family was particularly surprised. The house and all of Dianne's belongings were bequeathed to Joanne, as was only fitting. And if anything, losing both parents at such a young age seemed only to spur Joanne on to greater heights. She quickly established herself as a violinist of international renown, and as she entered her twenties, she toured the world many times over, playing to adoring audiences and packed houses. She later confided in interviews that when she took her bows each night, she often imagined her parents sitting there in the front row, beaming proudly up at her.

A wealthy and successful virtuoso, Joanne now owns a number of residences in various cities across the world. But she still maintains the house her mother left to her, and has been observed by local people to visit several times a year.

And there are those amongst them who swear that, on moonless nights, the exquisite sound of a violin can sometimes be heard from deep within Crombie Wood.

PHILIP

Sean Harris in Possum, 2018
written & directed by Matthew Holness

ONE OF PHILIP'S EARLIEST MEMORIES WAS OF BEING TAKEN TO the Norwich Hippodrome by his uncle Maurice. The variety show that night had featured the ventriloquist Maxwell Frere, and Maurice, a keen amateur puppeteer, was eager to catch the man's act.

Philip was a quiet child, and sat placidly through the earlier routines on the bill without the slightest flicker of emotion registering on his young features. At the interval, his uncle turned to him and scowled. *Liven up,* he said. *The look on your face, you might as well be watching paint dry.* Philip blinked back at him, a startled rabbit. Thawing somewhat, Maurice reached over and squeezed his nephew's thigh, a trifle too hard. *Never mind, boy. We all enjoy ourselves in our own fashion, don't we?*

Everything changed when Maxwell Frere came onstage, however. At the first glimpse of his dummy Hugo, Philip sat bolt upright in his seat, quivering. Once the act got underway, Hugo snapping and cackling sardonically at his hapless handler, Philip began to weep. When his sobs became audible over the noise of the audience, the dummy swivelled its head to seek out the culprit. Its glaring eyes pinned the sobbing boy to his seat like a butterfly.

Philip screamed.

Not missing a beat, Hugo immediately shrieked back: *Now I know why some animals eat their own children!*

Philip had wet himself, and Maurice was forced to take him home. On the bus back, his uncle made the boy strip off his sodden trousers and underpants in full view of the other passengers, before finally wrapping him in a raincoat. When Philip was sat back in his seat, he'd leaned in and whispered in his ear. *You were right to be afraid. Sometimes they have a life of their own. That poor sod won't be able to control him for much longer.*

Philip had dreamt of Hugo for the rest of that week, nightmares of the dummy scuttling after him like an insect, its dead eyes staring, its grinning mouth stretching impossibly wide to devour him. But eventually, his fear gave way to a horrified admiration. Philip decided he wanted to *be* Hugo. The dummy was witty, always had a comeback, and could rely on his handler to guide his every action.

In stark contrast, Philip's body felt alien to him, a clumsy vehicle he had little idea how to control. When he tried to speak, his tongue lay like a slumped corpse against the gravestones of his teeth. He wished someone could puppet *him*, put all those clever words in his mouth.

It wasn't long afterwards that Maurice came to stay with them. When Philip asked his mother why Maurice couldn't live in his own house anymore, she shushed him and said, *We're all the family he's got, and we have to look after him.* Philip didn't think she looked at all happy about it, though.

Maurice moved his things into the spare room, perching his collection of carved puppets on top of the wardrobe. Sometimes he let Philip play with them, and he began to teach the boy the rudiments of puppetry. Philip thought his parents seemed uneasy whenever he spent time alone with his uncle—his mother would always find studiedly casual reasons to look in on them—but eventually they began to relax, happy that their odd little boy had found a hobby.

One day Philip turned round to his uncle and asked, *Do the puppets like it when we touch them? Because they can't stop us, can they?*

Maurice smiled and replied, *Of course they do, lad. We're always very gentle with them, and we help them do things they can't do themselves. Besides, sometimes it's nice to be touched.* Philip absorbed this, cradling one of the puppets in his hands. Then his uncle gave him a gobstopper from his jar of sweets, and whispered, *Would you like me to show you sometime?*

Philip had no idea quite what he meant, but assumed this was to be another lesson in puppeteering, and nodded eagerly.

So that night, and for many nights afterwards, Maurice stole into his bedroom and taught Philip exactly what it meant to be a puppet; to have another's hands on you, inside you, controlling you.

Many years later, Philip took that lesson, those poisoned memories of Maurice's long hairy fingers crawling over his body, and turned them into Possum. He was a puppeteer himself now, and had a collection of funny animal puppets he'd created from scratch. While he was still uncomfortable in his own skin, he'd discovered that it was far easier for him to talk in the voice of others: the high-pitched squawk of Percy Parrot, or the yammer of Max the Stuttering Monkey. Children loved his naughty puppet menagerie and their antics.

Possum was different.

Philip had carved a replica of his own face, and given it elongated arachnoid legs. He'd had no plan or design when he sat down to create Possum; it was as though it had crawled fully formed into the world. *Little Possum, black as sin.* None of his other puppets had minds of their own, but Possum wasn't like the others. Without intending to, he'd put something inside the puppet, some unspeakable urge he'd nurtured within the darkest cave of his soul, and it gave Possum life.

Before long Possum had destroyed all of Philip's other puppets: Max, Percy, and the rest. It was jealous, possessive, would never let him out of its sight for long. You could never catch it moving; it would wait for its moment, then, as soon as you averted your gaze, spring like a hunting spider.

Philip began to dread what the puppet might do. He thought of

Hugo on that long ago childhood night, the way the dummy had seemed to move and speak with its own baleful intent. He wished he could speak with Maxwell Freer and ask his advice, but the man was long dead; he'd been committed to an insane asylum and ended up swallowing his own tongue.

Panicking, he decided to kill Possum. Philip returned to his childhood home; a wordless compulsion told him it had to end there. His parents had died in a mysterious fire years before, but Maurice was still there, wallowing in the foetid pit he'd made of the house. They circled each other warily, a pair of mangy strays. His uncle found Possum one day, and reacted with a puzzled mixture of admiration and disgust. He appreciated the bizarre craft in the puppet, but also recognised it for what it was; he knew a predator when he saw one.

Philip tried abandoning Possum; drowning it; burning it. Nothing worked. It always survived, found its way home. Time was running out. A local boy had gone missing—had Possum taken him? The police were looking for a man of Philip's description in connection with the disappearance.

Philip felt choked by an inchoate guilt; he was sure he'd done *something*, committed some indescribable act, but he could not say exactly what. Maurice lingered ever-present in the background; a mocking audience of one, silently heckling him.

It was only when Philip discovered the kidnapped boy concealed in his parents' old bedroom that he realised what had to be done. It was not Possum that needed to be destroyed. Maurice had snatched the child, imprisoned him for his own perverse pleasure. When Philip came upon the boy, his uncle attacked him, confident that he still had Philip in his thrall. But his nephew found the strength he'd lacked all those years before, and managed to overpower and kill Maurice. Philip released the boy then fled from the house, leaving Maurice and Possum, the twin monsters from his past, safely behind him.

But upon returning to his home town, he was spotted at the train station and swiftly taken into police custody. He was immediately charged with his uncle's murder in spite of his protestations of self-defence. The kidnapped boy subsequently identified Philip as the man he'd seen staring at him on a train the day he was abducted, and so the police decided that he was also to be prosecuted as an accessory in his uncle's crime.

Philip sat alone in his cell. It was stark and cold and stank of urine, but he finally felt safe: Possum could not reach him here. Despite the injustice that was being done to him, in a strange way, Philip at last felt in control of his life.

When the burly detective came to visit him—Johnson, his name was—Philip expected the man to beat him, but instead he just sat on the end of the bed and studied him. Philip thought he saw a veiled look of unwilling recognition in Johnson's black eyes.

Finally, the detective spoke. *It won't go well for you, you know. On the inside. You should think about that.*

They'd taken Philip's belt and shoelaces away when they brought him to the cell, but Johnson now produced the belt, and pressed it into his hands. Then he got up and left without another word.

Philip thought about it, and supposed the man intended for him to kill himself, but he had no intention of doing any such thing; *he* was the one who had been wronged, couldn't they see that?

It was only after the lights went out that night and he heard the stealthy sound of long legs scuttling around his bed that Philip began to reconsider.

They found him hanging limply from the window bars the next morning, the belt taut around his neck, his unsupported trousers puddled around his ankles. As the policemen took him down and waited for the ambulance to arrive, they voiced their quiet satisfaction that another nonce had got what was coming to him, thus sparing the taxpayers' hard-earned money.

They did not realise—how could they?—that Philip could still hear every word.

For while he was indeed dead, his stiffening flesh quite beyond his ability to animate it, Philip found himself unable to leave his body. He was helpless, trapped within a cage of slowly-decomposing meat and bone.

He could do nothing to resist as he was dumped onto a stretcher, then unceremoniously carted off to the morgue. There, he was consigned to darkness once more, before finally being taken out for his post-mortem.

Philip could feel the cold slab numbing his back and buttocks, his chest being rudely opened up by the wicked scalpel and shears.

As the coroner proceeded to hollow him out, he thought to himself, *It's finally happening. I'm finally becoming a puppet. Limp and empty, theirs to control.* He imagined himself sat on Maurice's knee, a packed house laughing along with their routine, the funny putdowns he'd get to make at his uncle's expense.

But he was a puppet without strings or gears, a broken marionette. As they sewed his eyelids shut and abandoned him to the shadows forever, he suddenly longed for that childhood sensation of careful fingers exploring his skin; at least then he would not be alone.

There was nothing worse than being a rejected toy who had once known life and laughter, only to be coldly discarded and put away in a box. As Philip lay there, sealed tight in his casket, slowly being lowered into the earth, he finally realised the cruelty of what he'd done to Possum; he'd granted it a semblance of life, but, appalled at the hidden part of him it represented, refused to dignify it with his touch. No wonder Possum had tormented him for so long; it was as much victim as predator.

It was only later, when he heard the sly movement in the earth outside the coffin, the chitinous limbs prying at the polished pine lid, that he had cause to regret these thoughts. It had sensed his weakness, his need; it always could.

And now it had come for him. Philip was incapable of movement, could not cry out nor raise a hand to defend himself.

No matter, it had fingers enough for both of them.

The wood of the coffin lid splintered.

Possum was here.

PROFESSOR BERNARD QUATERMASS

Brian Donlevy in The Quatermass Xperiment *(1955) & * Quatermass 2 *(1957)*
written by Richard Landau & Val Guest and Nigel Kneale & Val Guest
based on the television serials by Nigel Kneale
directed by Val Guest

Andrew Keir in Quatermass and the Pit *(1967)*
written by Nigel Kneale, based on his television serial
directed by Roy Ward Baker

THE OLD MAN SAT OUTSIDE THE GRAVEYARD AND WAITED. AND as the minutes slowly ticked past, he remembered.

Once upon a time, his name had been Quatermass. Not an easy name to forget, although he supposed he was mostly forgotten now. He'd done his best to ensure that, of course.

Years ago, he'd been the head of the British Rocket Group, hailed as a genius, a national hero. He'd launched Britain's first manned space flight and planned to build bases on the moon. It had all been a beautiful fantasy of course; another fairytale chapter of the utopian post-war dream Quatermass and other idealists like him had attempted to will into reality.

But the dreams had soon curdled into nightmares: Victor Carroon, the only survivor of the ill-fated space flight, returned from his voyage infected, no longer human. The plans for the moonbases had been taken and subsequently used to provide safe refuge on Earth for more creatures like Carroon, as part of a shadow conspiracy to surrender the planet to alien beings.

On both occasions, Quatermass had acted decisively and stopped the invaders, but found he could not prevent his country from being shaken out of its collective fantasy; slowly emerging, still exhausted, into a shabby reality of prejudice and inequality, poverty and ignorance, the promised utopia all but forgotten.

Quatermass's own awakening had come in the subway tunnels of Hobbs End, where extension works on the London Underground had uncovered a Martian spacecraft, millions of years old; and around it, the fossilised remains of mutated pre-humans. He quickly realised that the Martians had fled their dying planet and experimented on humanity's ancestors to embed their own genetic code within them; essentially colonising Earth by proxy. Mankind itself had sprung from this poisoned gene pool; we *were* the Martians, forever doomed by our own twisted biology to hate and kill one another.

The psychic influence of the previously-dormant spacecraft had caused violent mass riots to break out on the streets around Hobbs End; even Quatermass himself had succumbed to its influence. Only the heroic sacrifice of another scientist, Dr Matthew Roney, had saved London.

Shattered by his experience, Quatermass was given leave from the Rocket Group. His body quickly healed, but his idealism could not; as he now saw it, he had been living a lie all this time. What if his desire to travel to the stars, his great humanist dream, was nothing more than an expression of the insidious Martian instinct to colonise and conquer? He had already seen the first signs of his work being co-opted and corrupted by the British Military; what might be the consequences if he continued down this path?

Now that his eyes had been opened, everywhere he looked, he saw those same vile alien urges asserting themselves within humanity; spiralling racism and hatred and violence. He would not be a part of it.

Quatermass quit the Rocket Group with immediate effect. He remained in London for a time, drifting into an uneasy romance with Barbara Judd, a fellow survivor of the riots. When she fell pregnant, Quatermass, seeing no future for the child, pressed her to take advantage of the recently-passed Abortion Act, but she refused. Instead, they agreed to marry.

The marriage did not last much beyond the birth of their daughter Paula. Quatermass was depressed and drinking heavily; Barbara, who had proven extremely susceptible to the psychic effects of the Martian spacecraft, was still exhibiting symptoms of trauma. One afternoon, Quatermass returned home to find her standing blank-eyed over the baby's cradle, a red-hot iron poised in her hand.

Her husband's well-timed interruption broke the trance; Barbara had burst into tears and fled the house, not to return for several days. They subsequently agreed to separate, with Quatermass taking sole custody of Paula.

He decided there was nothing to keep them in London any longer, and purchased a remote cottage in the Scottish Highlands. There, he would live with Paula for many years, homeschooling her throughout her early life, and supporting them with his savings and occasional consultancy work for aerospace companies.

Despite his earlier misgivings about bringing a child into the world, he loved his daughter deeply; what little remained of his youthful hope and idealism, he freely imparted to her. For her part, Paula proved to have inherited her father's intellect and keen scientific mind. Eventually, she would leave to attend sixth form college, then Oxford. Quatermass remained alone in the cottage, now a virtual recluse.

One day in 1990, he received a phone call from his daughter: there was a man she wanted him to meet. A suitor, a boyfriend? No, nothing like that. This was purely a professional matter. He did not like receiving visitors at home, but agreed to meet the man for Paula's sake.

She arrived at the cottage the following week, an older gentleman at her side. He was tall, imposing; his thin smile never reaching his eyes. Paula introduced him as Mr Fremont.

Quatermass poured them all a scotch. He seemed to be making an effort to be affable for Paula's sake, but as they raised their glasses, he looked at Fremont, then sprang: *Fremont. That isn't your real name, is it? I remember you from the Rocket Group days. You were one of those spooks, forever skulking around trying to catch us selling secrets to the Russians. A double-barrelled surname, wasn't it?*

The other man's smile widened, signaling a rare display of genuine amusement. *You have me, Professor. I didn't think you'd remember after all this time. Yes—my real name is Stratton-Villiers.*

Paula looked at them both in wonder, but before she could interject, Quatermass brusquely continued: *And you're trying to recruit Paula, is that it? Unfortunately, she doesn't need my permission, but if I were her, I'd tell you to crawl back into whatever dark hole you oozed out of.*

His daughter's face reddened; Stratton-Villiers kept on smiling, unabashed. *Obviously, the family name has an illustrious history,* he replied. *And when Paula proved to be such a remarkable student, it seemed only natural to approach her. To offer her the opportunity to follow in her father's footsteps.*

Quatermass scoffed, before Paula finally spoke up. *I wanted you to know, Dad. And Mr, uh, Fremont said he was okay with you knowing. That you'd proven your loyalty many times over.*

Stratton-Villiers leaned forward confidentially. *I run my own covert unit now, Professor. Completely autonomous.*

I know who you are, said Quatermass wearily. *They call you the Grave-diggers, isn't that right?*

The other man's smile was finally wiped away. His tone became curt. *Officially, we don't have a name. We are tasked with investigating…unusual phenomena. Including the sort of phenomena you yourself have a great deal of familiarity with.*

Quatermass rose to his feet. *Whoever you are, whatever you are, I'm out. This is not a package deal. Paula is a grown woman and can ignore my advice if she likes, but this is not bloody buy one Quatermass, get one free.*

Stratton-Villiers drained his glass, then stood up. *This was purely a courtesy visit, Professor. Certainly we would consider you a valuable resource if you permitted Paula to consult you, but we shall of course respect your wishes should you refuse. I'll leave you and Paula to say your goodbyes. Thank you for the excellent whisky.*

He slipped from the room like an assassin, leaving Quatermass and his daughter alone. Paula looked at him, pleading. *I would never bother you if you wanted to be left in peace, Dad. I just wanted your blessing.*

Quatermass sunk back into his chair, suddenly exhausted. *It's bastards like him that poisoned everything I tried to do. Can't you see it, Paula? There's something about him, I can't quite put my finger on it. But he reminds me of those damn zombies back in Winnerden Flats, a pair of eyes in another man's body.*

That was a long time ago, Dad.

The old man looked up at his daughter, his eyes heavy with regret. *Do you know why they nicknamed his lot the Gravediggers? Some people say it's because they spend all their time rooting around amongst the dead. But others insist it's because your boss has a nasty tendency to leave a trail of bodies in his wake.*

Paula wasn't listening. If it had ever even been a battle, he had lost it.

Please. I want to do this.

Quatermass shrugged. *I can't stop you. You're a Quatermass, aren't you? You'll do whatever the bloody hell you want.*

That was the end of the discussion.

Paula embraced him warmly before she left, but they both knew something had been irreparably fractured in the relationship. From that day onwards, she would dutifully call him on his birthday, at Christmas, even manage the occasional visit (more and more occasional as the years went by), but Quatermass understood that Paula had chosen country over family; a country he himself had once served but no longer recognised, a country he'd rejected decades before.

He maintained his exile for close to another twenty years. His body slowly weakened and failed, confining him to a wheelchair. But his mind was still bristling and alert. Living in the desolate isolation of the Highlands, alone save for the regular visits of a carer, he could almost fool himself into thinking that the world had ended; that what was laughingly known as the human race, travesty of evolution that it was, had finally followed its programmed instincts and wiped itself out in a monumental racial purge.

He almost wished it were so.

It was Christmastime, late in the first decade of the new millennium, when his life changed again. The holiday meant nothing to him, save for the rare chance it promised to speak to his daughter. So when Christmas Day passed with no call from Paula, Quatermass was seized by an unfamiliar anxiety. He was accustomed to his solitude, welcomed it, but without that small communication, he suddenly felt adrift—no longer alone, but lonely.

Days went by without any word. When Quatermass tried calling his daughter, there was no answer, even from her mobile. He was frantic, convinced that something had happened to her. Surely someone would contact him if so? Was his hard-won anonymity so absolute that no one even knew he existed anymore? He could not eat nor sleep.

It was not until the New Year that he finally received word from her. When the phone rang, he thought his heart might stop. *Better that,* he considered. *Better to die now, than hear something has happened to Paula.*

But when his trembling hand finally managed to pick up the receiver, it was Paula's voice on the other end of the line.

Dad? It's me. Listen, Dad, it's important.

Where the bloody hell have you been? I thought you were dead! His relief flared into anger before he could do anything to prevent it.

Paula seemed not to notice his display of temper. *I'm very sorry. But this is important, Dad. We need you to come. I need you to come.*

Come? Come where? I'm stuck in a bloody wheelchair in the middle of nowhere!

A helicopter will pick you up in the next hour. Please, Dad, I'm begging you.

I told you before, I told all of you—

I know what you said, Dad, but only you can help us with this. It's the children . . . the children, they—

Paula's voice cracked and died in her throat. She took a moment to compose herself before continuing. *I'm sorry. I can't talk about it on an open line. Please, just come.*

Perhaps it was the allusion to children, coming so soon after he feared he might have lost his only daughter, but something softened within the old man. *Very well,* he said. *I'll be ready.*

As Paula had promised, a helicopter landed outside the cottage less than an hour later. A man wearing a hazmat suit emerged to collect Quatermass. He insisted that the professor would also need to don a protective outfit before embarking on their journey, and after much grumbling, the old man acceded.

When the helicopter was back in the air, the agent briefed Quatermass on the situation. There had been some kind of a viral outbreak in rural Warwickshire, an infection that had spread amongst the local children, causing them to become homicidally violent. The virus appeared to be airborne, its provenance unknown. The affected area had been locked down and quarantined, but large groups of the children remained free.

Upon arriving at their destination, the professor was taken to a sterile unit, inside which Paula and Stratton-Villiers were waiting for him. Quatermass was taken aback to see that Paula's boss barely looked a day older than when the Professor had last seen him, some two decades previously.

When the old man remarked on this, Stratton-Villiers gave a wry chuckle. *Excellent genes and a brisk round of golf every Sunday morning,* he explained. Quatermass doubted that this alone explained the man's longevity, but chose not to press the matter further. He suspected that the truth of it would not be at all comforting.

The professor turned to his daughter. Something unspoken hung in the air between them. He wanted to embrace her, to tell her how much he'd missed her, but this was hardly the time. Instead, he asked for a full update on the outbreak.

We found a woman and her teenage daughter driving away from one of the infected sites, Paula explained. *The woman was the only adult survivor, and had apparently had to kill her other two children to escape. She herself appears to be unaffected, although her daughter is exhibiting the first symptoms of infection. It appears the virus is most efficacious on the very young, with a rapid incubation period of little more than hours. With adolescent children, it seems to be more like days. We don't yet know whether it will affect adults, given enough time.*

You have a sample of the virus? Quatermass asked.

Paula nodded. *It's nothing we've ever seen before.*

Extra-terrestrial, Quatermass muttered.

We don't know that, Stratton-Villiers said primly. *It could be a new biological weapon, anything.*

Quatermass barked at him, his eyes never leaving Paula's. *Read the bloody files! I've seen something like this before, in Winnerden Flats. The means of delivery was more primitive then, but the outcome was the same. Tell me, are the infected children exhibiting signs of a group consciousness?*

Paula nodded again. *They won't communicate with us, but we've been monitoring their activities. They seem to act in unison, co-operating without verbal communication. Given their young ages, some of them are still largely pre-verbal, but seem to have no difficulty acting in tandem with the rest of the group.*

The professor thought for a moment. *In Winnerden Flats, the loci of the hivemind were beings hidden within large pressure domes on a nearby base. They couldn't survive in our atmosphere. I don't suppose there's anything like that here?*

No. The area is predominantly rural, residential.

Quatermass sighed. *Well, I'm not sure you have much choice. At this stage, the outbreak is still relatively small-scale and contained. They're only children. If the army move in –*

My thoughts exactly, Stratton-Villiers said.

Paula looked horrified. *Yes, they are only children! We can't just slaughter them like animals! We have to try and communicate with them. Capture them, put them into isolation. We might be able to find a cure—*

Too dangerous. Stratton-Villiers was firm. *If the virus spreads…*

Quatermass tried to be more gentle. *Paula. You already said they won't communicate with you. I know it's a hard choice to make, but what are the alternatives?*

You always found them in the past, Dad. Paula's voice was low and steady. If there was an accusation in her statement, it was a subtle one. *There might be another way. Let me show you something.*

She looked up at Stratton-Villiers, who reluctantly nodded. Together, they took Quatermass into a small anteroom, containing an elaborate computer console and chair. A headset, connected to the console by wires, hung on top of the chair's headrest.

A two-way mirror in the opposite wall looked into an adjoining room: a secure cell containing a hollow-eyed teenage girl. Secured to a chair by restraints, she stared emptily back into the mirror, as though she were seeing beyond it, watching and studying their every move.

Quatermass glanced into the unknowable gulf of her stare for a moment and shuddered.

Ignoring the girl in the cell, Stratton-Villiers stood before the device like a proud father. *This instrument is derived from an invention by a man named Marcus Monserrat, he said. Paula has shown herself highly adept at using it in tests—she seems to possess some low-level psychic ability, which only serves to increase its effectiveness.*

Quatermass winced softly, remembering Barbara, Hobbs End. *What exactly does it do?* he muttered.

It allows the user to communicate telepathically with a subject . . . and perhaps influence them.

No! Quatermass slammed his fist down on the console. *It's too dangerous! Attempting telepathic communication with a powerful alien mass consciousness—it could overwhelm Paula, psychically drown her!*

Stratton-Villiers shrugged. *I myself advised against it . . . but your daughter is quite headstrong, Professor.*

You're her boss, damn it! Order her not to!

Paula gently took her father's hand. *I have to try, Dad. That's part of the reason I wanted you here. So I had someone to ground me.*

There was no reasoning with her. He had taught her too well.

Heartbroken, Quatermass watched as Paula wired herself up to the device. As she switched it on and its electric hum rose to fill the room, the girl in the next room twitched and began to look around. Paula gazed through the glass at her, reaching out for Quatermass's hand once more. She squeezed it tightly.

What happened next took no more than a minute or two, but Quatermass felt as though time had slowed to a crawl. Everything seemed to drift before him in a torpid, dreamlike manner. He might have been at the bottom of a deep ocean, his head pounding with the vast pressure.

Paula's eyes met those of the girl's. The two women stared at each other for several long, frozen seconds, locked in silent—communication? Combat?

A sheen of perspiration broke out on Paula's brow; Quatermass could feel the sweat prickling in the palm of her hand. He tightened his grip, quietly reminding her he was at her side.

She let out a guttural moan, her eyes beginning to roll back in their sockets.

Quatermass looked up at Stratton-Villiers in alarm. *She can't take it! Turn it off, man!*

The other man's eyes were fixed on the subject in the next room. *Wait,* he said. *Something is happening.*

Suddenly, Paula spasmed back in her chair, convulsions juddering her body. Spittle flew from her mouth, splattering the console. Quatermass reached for her, but, hampered by his wheelchair, could not prevent her from tipping out of her seat and falling to the floor. There, her body continued to writhe, twisting like a snake trapped under a hunter's boot.

Quatermass screamed across at Stratton-Villiers. *Help her!*

But the other man simply looked on in quiet fascination, seemingly more interested in the subject next door than in Paula's distress.

Finally, Quatermass had no other choice. He lurched forwards in his chair, toppling from his seat to land painfully on the ground beside his stricken daughter. Gasping with the impact, he forced himself to roll sideways so that he could reach her. With one movement, he seized the headset and tore it from her skull.

His desperate effort was in vain. Paula gave one last agonised shudder, then grew still.

Tears in his eyes, Quatermass turned her unseeing face towards his. Gently, his fingers reached over and parted her lips. *She swallowed her own tongue,* he whispered.

But look, Stratton-Villiers replied urgently. *Look at the girl.*

He helped the unresisting professor back into his wheelchair, and motioned towards the two-way mirror.

There, in the next room, the captive teenager sat limply in her chair, equally lifeless. Her head lay slumped against her chest, a line of drool dripping from her open mouth to puddle in her lap.

Paula's death created a feedback loop, Stratton-Villiers murmured. *It was like a bomb going off in their heads.*

Quatermass's eyes darkened. *You knew. You sent her on a suicide mission.*

Stratton-Villiers bent down to take Paula's body in his arms. Carefully, he returned her to her chair. *Of course not,* he said. *We simply hoped she could communicate with them. You heard me warn her, professor.*

You could have stopped her! Enraged, Quatermass span the wheels of his chair and launched himself at the other man.

Deftly, Stratton-Villiers sidestepped his assault. He darted behind Quatermass's chair, his hands coming to rest on the Professor's shoulders, pinning him in position. Their implacable grip felt like ten screws slowly being tightened into his flesh.

Slowly, Stratton-Villiers leaned over to murmur in the Professor's ear. *Careful, professor. Don't give me cause to forget everything you've done for this country.*

Quatermass slumped in his seat, helpless. He began to sob quietly.

The old man was immediately put on a helicopter back to the Highlands. He was assured that Paula would receive a hero's funeral; arrangements would of course be made for him to attend.

But when the notification came, Quatermass ignored it. He had already said goodbye to his daughter, there on the floor of that sterile little room. He could not bear to endure the hypocrisy of the funeral ceremony, or to look that man, that malevolent puppet, in the eyes again.

Instead, he took to his bed, eating the bare minimum forced upon him by his carer, sleeping as many hours as his body would allow. His last tenuous link with the world had been severed; now, all that was left for him was to die.

It was during these terrible weeks that the dreams began.

At least, he supposed they were dreams, although they felt more like *transmissions*; vividly tangible images being projected into his sleeping mind. They were always the same.

He saw a distant red light, like a cyclopean eye, bright in the surrounding darkness. A featureless humanoid figure emerged from the void. Slowly, it began to shape itself into a young woman. Her blank eyes stared into his, her lips moving, forming unfamiliar words.

Quatermass.

He would always wake up gasping when she spoke his name.

In a bid to blot the dreams out, he started taking sleeping pills, but they proved ineffective. So instead, he resolved to stay awake. This stopped the intrusions for a short time, but soon they began to flood even his waking thoughts. In the fleeting instants when he blinked, he would glimpse the woman's face floating before him, a ghost of a ghost. A door had been opened, and he could not close it.

All Quatermass had left in the world was his mind, and now he was quickly losing that. *What do you want?!?* he screamed to his empty bedroom, before falling into exhausted unconsciousness.

By way of an answer, he dreamt of the woman again; this time standing outside the gates of a graveyard on a hill, its slopes clustered with looming monuments and weathered, mossy graves. He immediately recognised it as the Glasgow Necropolis.

The woman beckoned to him, calling his name, her soft voice tugging him out of the dream.

Using what little strength he had left, Quatermass abandoned his sickbed and arranged for the hire of a car to take him to Glasgow. The journey would be long and expensive, but he did not anticipate coming back.

When they arrived outside the Necropolis, his driver was alarmed at the prospect of leaving the old man alone in a remote spot on such a bitterly cold day, but Quatermass waved him off with a large tip. He wanted no one's pity, or concern.

So now he sat, his wasted frame hunched against the wind, remembering. In truth, the memories were more painful than the cold, and he wasn't sure which would finish him first if he remained here for much longer.

Still, at least Quatermass himself would then only be a distant memory, soon to fade away entirely; as to whether he would be a good memory or a bad one, it was not for him to judge—the world could do that.

Here, now, in this moment, he supposed his life's failures were at least as great as his triumphs.

Right then, a white transit van drove into view. There was nothing visibly remarkable about it, but something put him in mind of a predatory shark, circling its prey. It slowly pulled up beside the professor. The young woman from his dream climbed out and approached him. She looked down at Quatermass as though she were peering at him through a microscope.

Professor Quatermass? Can I give you a ride? Her voice was flat, almost accentless. It sounded artificial, as though learned from a computer.

He nodded in silent agreement. She helped him into the passenger seat of the van, folding up his wheelchair and stowing it in the back. They drove away, drifting back out into the main streets of the city, like a virus entering a bloodstream.

Quatermass looked over at his companion. She was an attractive girl, but dressed in cheap department store clothes, apparently flung together with little regard for taste or fashion. When she glanced back at him, he recognised something in her eyes—or rather, the *lack* of something.

It was the same lack he had seen in the eyes of Victor Carroon; in those of the infected at Winnerden Flats; and in Barbara's eyes outside Hobbs End, or during that terrible moment when she had stood poised over their baby daughter with a red-hot iron in her hand.

He asked, gently: *Why have you come here?*

She spoke matter-of-factly. *For food. Our world is dying.*

Are there more of you?

She nodded.

Are we your food?

She nodded again.

That surely isn't why you brought me here. He found he did not care either way, however.

No. Your body is old and sick. No nutrition.

A part of him admired her candour. *Why, then?*

Your knowledge. It would be useful to us.

I see. Well, it hasn't been much use to me.

The young woman looked quizzical, his wry cynicism lost on her. *I have a place. Will you come with me?*

My dear, I have absolutely nowhere else to go.

A short time later, they pulled up outside a semi-derelict house in the Glasgow suburbs. The young woman carefully placed Quatermass back in his chair and wheeled him inside.

The interior smelled of mould and rat droppings. The professor shielded his nostrils, suddenly missing his cottage, the few meaningful remnants of the life he had left behind. Would this dank hovel be the last place he ever saw?

You live here?

This is just a shell. Upstairs.

Lifting him from the chair as though he were a straw doll, she gently carried him upstairs and into one of the bedrooms. As Quatermass's eyes adjusted to the gloom inside, he looked around and gasped.

The room appeared to be infinite, the same black, endless void he had glimpsed in his dream. Even with the woman clutching him tightly in her arms, he felt unmoored, as though any second he might drift off into nothingness.

He gripped her arm, suddenly frightened.

Please...

You do not need to be afraid.

I don't know what you want of me.

Have you ever wanted to see other worlds, Professor?

It was my earliest dream.

You can see my world, if you wish.

How?

You will leave this body behind. You will no longer know age, or infirmity, or want. Only your mind will travel. There, we can learn from you, and you from us.

Quatermass considered demanding to know exactly what their intentions towards Earth were, then realised he did not care.

He had fought for the world for most of his life, and where had it got him? He was old, alone, poised here on the brink of an unknowable abyss; forever cursed with the wisdom that the planet he had struggled to defend was populated by a cosmic joke; a freak of Martian genetics that would probably destroy itself long before this creature's species ever could.

I have one request. A sudden resolve crept into his voice.

What?

There is a man. His name is Stratton-Villiers. He works for my government. He was responsible for the death of my daughter.

I see.

He is a powerful man, well-protected. But I want him...removed from the world. You understand? If you can do this one thing for me, then all my knowledge, everything I have to offer, is yours.

She considered. *I will communicate this to the others.*

Quatermass looked deep into her eyes, and although he found no discernible emotion there, neither could he see the merest flicker of untruth.

The young woman carried him deeper into the darkness of the room, and away into the stars.

JULIA COTTON

Clare Higgins in Hellraiser, *1987*
written & directed by Clive Barker,
based on his novella

H OW COULD HELL BE ANY WORSE?
This was the question Julia Cotton asked herself as she stood in the kitchen of her new Cricklewood home, preparing a surprise birthday dinner for her stepdaughter Kirsty.

Julia hated cooking, but not as much as she hated Kirsty. Pretty Kirsty, Daddy's little bimbo, content to skate through life on the strength of her good looks and her father Larry's handouts. One day Kirsty too would be hitting the black rocks of middle age and married to a dullard like her daddy, and then she'd see what life was really about, oh yes—

Everything alright, babe?

The aforementioned Larry, also husband of Julia, poked his head into the kitchen. How she loathed it when he called her *babe*.

Julia dug around in the back of her mouth and finally found a smile for him. *Everything's fine! Won't be long.*

Larry looked sheepish. *It's just that we thought we could smell burning...*

Julia wheeled around. Fingers of black smoke were beginning to prise their way from the oven. *Oh, shit!*

I'll, ah, leave you to it then. Larry's head disappeared around the door. If only he could disappear from her life that easily.

The dinner was a disaster, of course. Larry and Kirsty gamely attempted to chew their way through the charred portions of overdone meat, but everyone was privately thankful Larry hadn't skimped on buying the wine. Well, they could both choke, for all she cared.

Julia took a sip of wine and closed her eyes, silently imagining it.

Larry mistook her silent reverie for regret. He reached out and squeezed her wrist. *It tasted better than it looked, honestly. And we really appreciate you making the effort, babe.*

Kirsty assented. *It was a lovely gesture, Julia.*

Neither of them could lie worth a damn. Not like Larry's brother Frank. Now *there* was a man who could spin a yarn to rival the Devil himself, who could sell you a bridge for every day of the week, convince you that he loved you, truly and forever, right before he abandoned you, left you to rot in this stinking suburban hellhole —

I'll get these dishes washed, then. Larry got up and began to clear the table.

Oh no, I'll do it. You and Kirsty go and relax, enjoy the rest of her birthday together.

Well, if you're sure...? He looked across at his daughter for guidance, the blind leading the blind.

I insist. It would mean another fifteen minutes away from Larry's company, at least.

Feigning sadness over the ruined meal, she'd managed to drag it out for a lot longer than that, and was still in the kitchen when Kirsty announced that she was leaving. The two women had reined in their mutual antipathy for long enough to manage a couple of parting air kisses, and now Larry was seeing Kirsty out.

Julia busied herself putting away the washing up. Picking up a kitchen knife, she imagined herself plunging it into Larry's chest. She could do it, she was quite certain of that. If killing a man was what it took to get her out of this house, she could kill and keep on killing, until the corpses were piled high and the walls painted with their blood, running thick and red, down into the carpet and floorboards, soaking into the earth below —

Babe? He was back. *Leave that and let's go up to bed.*

I won't be a minute. You go up without me.

He stepped into the kitchen, seductively insistent. *You were great tonight, in spite of everything. Let me make it up to you.*

Oh God, not *that*. *Larry, I have a headache . . .*

He seized her wrist, his eyes hungry. *Be a wife to me. Babe.*

Before she could question it — feeble, milquetoast Larry, forcing himself upon her? — they were in the bedroom, and Larry was pushing her down on the mattress, tearing roughly at her dress. This was the worst of all. *Larry, no —*

His hand closed over her mouth, cutting off her protests like a cat stifling a baby. This wasn't right, this couldn't be —

As he forced himself inside her, Julia closed her eyes. Alone in her own mind, she could almost believe that Frank had finally come back to her. After all, it was Frank who took whatever he wanted, not Larry. Larry pleaded and whined, but never *took*. So this couldn't be Larry thrusting roughly on top of her, grunting like a rutting pig.

But Frank was dead, wasn't he?

She opened her eyes, Larry's sweating face looming up before her. He grinned like a skull.

And suddenly, she remembered. Frank *was* dead . . . and so was Larry. Frank had murdered him — only minutes before he had killed Julia herself.

She remembered it all.

The house in Cricklewood. Frank's return from the grave, little more than a ravaged skeleton. Julia's determination to provide him with the victims he'd needed to restore himself, a succession of lunchtime assignations that promised sex but only ended in blood.

And finally, the creatures that had emerged from Below to claim them all.

Larry's face began to putrefy before her eyes; the skin stretching and snapping like warm toffee; the eyeballs retreating back into their sockets; the stink of his moist flesh assaulting her recoiling nostrils. But still he fucked her, sweet revenge for all those times in life when he'd desired her and she'd refused him.

Julia screamed.

The scene dissolved in front of her, coming apart like a scrim of wet tissue paper. Within moments, the only intimation of it was the pervading stench of Larry's decomposing carcass.

Julia found herself alone on the floor of a cold stone room. Alone, and naked.

No—not just naked. *Skinned,* the raw meat of her body glistening in the semi-darkness. Her flesh wept at the loss of her skin, her identity. She was no longer Larry's wife, Kirsty's stepmother, Frank's mistress. She was no longer Julia. Now she was no one, just another damned soul.

Because she had been right, in a way—this *was* Hell, and it could not possibly be any worse. For Julia's punishment was this: to live out the endless torment of the same miserable day of her married life for all eternity.

She wept at the realisation, the salt of her tears stinging her exposed flesh. Another few grams of pain to offer up to Hell's scales. But she knew it would not be enough; that those scales could never, ever be balanced.

So Julia continued to weep, as she waited for her torment to begin anew. And there she would have remained, were it not for Sophia Howard.

Seeking vengeance for the murder of her son, the young woman had enlisted the services of the occultist Joseph Solomon. But the notoriously treacherous rite they'd attempted had resulted in Solomon's death, and confined Sophia to a limbo between worlds.

Helpless without her guide, she had been beset by demons and abducted, dragged into the upper reaches of Hell. There, Julia watched from the shadows as they tortured her, the first small enjoyment she had ever known in that foul place.

But as the woman begged forgiveness, something happened. A sudden light had ruptured the darkness, so warm and bright that it brought a momentary joy to even that most dreadful of realms. The demons had scattered back into the safety of the surrounding gloom, leaving Sophia free to follow the illumination back to its source, up and away from the aching depths she had been consigned to.

Julia too, saw her opportunity. Unlike the demons, she did not fear the light.

She followed.

She emerged into a large empty house. Fearful of discovery, of being dragged screaming back to her eternal suffering, Julia concealed herself in a cupboard and waited. She had known a brief, sweet taste of freedom once before, when she had been summoned back to the material plane by that poor fool Channard—but after Hell had claimed the doctor for itself, she too had been cast back into its freezing depths, nothing but discarded bait. She would not suffer that fate a second time.

Exhausted, she slept—the first sleep she had known in decades. But it provided little respite—she dreamt of Hell; of fresh punishment, cruelly meted out for her escape attempt. She awoke with a stifled cry.

It was night, the house seemingly deserted. Creeping out from her hiding place, she began to gather her thoughts. She must get away from here, but where could she go? She was damned, and alone. Who would possibly give her sanctuary?

Then, she remembered. There had been whispers in Hell of another. A favoured son who had failed, and been cast out from the darkness. Perhaps he . . .

She prepared for her journey. Finding little of use in the house, she wrapped her flayed flesh in a blanket, tying plastic bags around her raw and tender soles. She felt humiliated, a pauper in exile. For a fleeting moment, her terror of what lay outside the walls of the house was such that she even considered trying to find her way back to Hell.

No. She would not be cowed, or beaten. She had shed blood before in the pursuit of her desires, and if necessary, she would do it again. Under cover of darkness, she set out on her trek.

Across fields and forests she travelled, concealing herself as best she could during the bright daylight hours. She fed on vermin and other small animals; their thin blood was barely enough to sustain her, but she could feast properly later, once she had found her Master. She called to him in her sleep, her dreaming mind reaching out, and as she grew closer, she was sure she felt a response—very faint, the ghost of a reply—but it was enough of a beacon to guide her.

And finally, as she had departed from one country home, so she arrived at another; once again, isolated and seemingly empty, the lawns overgrown, the windows closed against the world. The only sign of life were the security cameras that tracked her progress across the grounds. A fox cried somewhere in the surrounding woods, a forlorn lament for all that had been lost here.

Julia stumbled up the stone steps and sounded the door knocker. So weak were her limbs that she could barely lift the heavy iron cudgel. For long moments she waited, until she could wait in dignity no more and collapsed to the doorstep.

Finally, she heard shuffling footsteps on the other side of the door. It opened to reveal an old man, anachronistically dressed in a servant's formal attire.

Hugo Barrett's body was bowed with the years, but his devotion remained undimmed.

He gazed down at the bloody apparition on his doorstep, his trained demeanour unruffled, a sardonic gleam still present in his rheumy eyes.

How may I help you? he said.

Julia could only manage a whisper. *I've come to see him. To offer myself to his service.*

Hugo's expression was unchanging. *I'm afraid the Master is not receiving guests.*

Please. I've come a very long way.

I'm very sorry.

You don't understand. I escaped from Hell. There's nowhere else I can go.

He studied her thoughtfully. *Wait here.*

With that, he closed the door once more and slowly shuffled away. Listening to his receding footsteps, Julia felt sure she would die before he returned. Overhead, it began to rain, the heavens rumbling their deep laughter.

By the time Hugo returned, Julia was soaked through and shivering. He held the door open and permitted her entrance, but offered no other aid. These were her Stations of the Cross, and she would have to traverse them alone. He gestured towards the grand staircase. *Up there.*

Julia crawled slug-like up the stairs, leaving a trail of slime and blood behind her. Upon finally reaching the top, she made her way towards the master bedroom.

Inside, the room was pitch dark, its silence absolute. The stink of human waste hung faintly in the air, and something else too — a thick musky odour, almost animal-like.

Julia's eyes were well-accustomed to the darkness. She surveyed the interior.

A shrunken huddled shape lay in the antique four-poster bed that dominated the room. It was unmoving, save for the faint breath of life that still trembled through its frame.

Humiliated, laid low by his failure, the Antichrist Damien Thorn had found a private damnation of his own making, a far humbler domain than the Hell he had planned to usher in on Earth.

Julia crawled to his side. She reached under the bedclothes and took his hand, thin as a bundle of twigs, the untrimmed nails curled like talons. *Master. I am here*, she whispered.

The fingers closed feebly around her own. The shape in the bed did not speak.

Julia's voice grew urgent. *I crawled up out of Hell to reach you. As you were cast out, so too was I. But you are the rightful Prince of Hell, and will rise again. Let me serve you.*

The hand squeezed again, more forcefully this time.

Let me be your consort.

There was no response for a moment, and then Damien's hand gently took her own and guided it down between his legs, where what she found there rose to greet her.

Julia smiled. The needs of men, no matter how weak or how powerful, never changed.

So be it. Her devotion would restore Damien Thorn, just as it had once restored Frank Cotton.

And then Hell itself would learn to fear her.

FREMONT / STRATTON-VILLIERS

Christopher Lee in Scream and Scream Again, *1970*
written by Christopher Wicking, based on the book by Peter Saxon
directed by Gordon Hessler

Christopher Lee in Death Line, *1972*
written by Ceri Jones, directed by Gary Sherman

*Y*OU KNOW, *I'VE OFTEN THOUGHT ABOUT WRITING YOUR BIOGRAPHY.*
The two men sat on the terrace of the small oceanside cottage, sipping from crystal tumblers of brandy and looking out at the granite churn of the Atlantic. Emptiness surrounded them on all sides: jagged gouges of cliff to their left and right, the cold limbo of the sea stretching out in front of them. To look at them, they could have been the last men on Earth.

If one of them had willed it, it might have even been so.

John Morlar glanced over at his companion, a tall black-suited man with an unfashionable but impeccably-trimmed moustache. Morlar was used to getting a reaction from people—he had a peculiar gift for provoking them—but the other man seemed unmoved. As much as Morlar hated him, it was why he looked forward to the man's irregular visits—the constant struggle to needle and unsettle his guest energised him somehow.

Finally, an almost imperceptible wrinkling of the skin around the corner of his companion's eyes signalled some small amusement.

That would be . . . enlightening, said Stratton-Villiers. *What would you call it?*

I was considering 'The Devil You Don't', said Morlar.

Very good. Do you think you have enough material for a book?

Some of it I've obviously had the dubious pleasure of observing first-hand. And you've told me a great many stories over the years. Of course, finding people to corroborate them might be tricky.

Stratton-Villiers nodded. *A certain amount of . . . attrition is only to be expected when you've lived a life as long as mine. Go on. Where would you start?*

I always skip the childhood chapters in biographies. We were all children once. So what? Is there anything in particular I should know about yours?

Stratton-Villiers nursed his brandy, thinking. The game had seized his attention, at least for the moment. *We do have one thing in common, you and I. If you're the sort of biographer who likes to find common ground with his subjects, that is.*

Morlar scoffed. *In your case, I can't say it's a prerequisite. What is it?*

Oh, I killed my parents too. Or had them killed, anyway. He might have been remarking on a slight change in the weather, for all that his tone of voice altered.

I think I've found my opening chapter. What happened?

Stratton-Villiers gestured dismissively. *The same old boring story. Father used to interfere with me when I was a small boy. He would come to my room after dark, stinking of whisky, hands like a pickpocket on a crowded train. Mother knew, of course, but said nothing. I tolerated it for as long as I had to. But as soon as I was able, I took some money and hired an ex-army man to murder them both in their beds. Made it look like a robbery. It was a good clean job, actually.*

What happened to the army man?

A slight pause. *I think he died a few years later.*

Morlar smiled wryly. *The beginning of a familiar pattern.*

Stratton-Villiers sipped ruminatively at his brandy, saying nothing.

You followed a well-trodden path after that. Eton, Oxford. You were recruited at Oxford, yes?

Yes, by George Dobbs. An uncommon note of respect crept into Stratton-Villiers's voice at the mention of Dobbs's name. *I was hoping for a foreign posting when I left Oxford, but they wanted me to monitor Bernard Quatermass's new Rocket Group instead. It was full of ex-Nazis, of course, and Quatermass himself was no one's idea of a safe pair of hands. We were worried about the Russians, but it turned out that what we really needed to be afraid of . . .*

He looked up to the heavens, filled with thick dark clouds that might be concealing multitudes.

There was the Caroon episode, then Winnerden Flats. That hurt us, discovering we'd already been infiltrated to that degree. It prompted me to argue for the creation of an autonomous intelligence unit, specialising in more . . . outré incidents.

Extraterrestrial incursions?

Initially, but our brief was soon widened to include anything remotely off the beaten track of human understanding. Which in those days was fairly limited, point A directly to point B. We soon learned.

This was when you first adopted your codename. 'Fremont'. From the Germanic, isn't it? 'Free' and 'protection'.

A careful smile. You must forgive me the small flourish. I am permitted so few of them.

So Agent Fremont was given his name and his secret unit. Were there more incursions?

Several, yes. Fara, Midwich . . . the Ganymede incident. Close calls, some of them, but there was a silver lining. Eventually, we were able to scavenge the alien technology that enabled Dr Browning to begin his composite program.

Morlar's fingers tightened around his glass. *That was hardly an unqualified success.*

There were some teething problems, as you would expect with any significant technological development. Certain operatives became over-

zealous and exceeded their boundaries. It's all a matter of careful refinement, John. We got to where we needed to be, wouldn't you say?

And Dr Browning? Where did he get to?

A tragic accident. These things happen, unfortunately.

Morlar remained silent.

Stratton-Villiers continued. He was beginning to enjoy himself. *Shortly after that, there was that unpleasant business under Russell Square Underground station. Very grisly set of circumstances. Difficult for everyone. The police inspector who discovered the site later killed himself, I believe.* He thought for a moment. *Ah — then came the Dracula affair. That would make an excellent chapter in your book. Fascinating man, the Count. I very much enjoyed talking to him. And I was really quite proud of our work there, if I may be allowed a brief moment of self-satisfaction.*

You ran Dracula as an operative behind the Iron Curtain, I believe?

Yes.

Quite daring of you. Was the operation a success?

I would say history speaks for itself, don't you think?

Morlar drained his glass. *One area I've been researching recently is the proliferation of Satanic cults in the 1970s.*

Why is that? An edge crept into his companion's voice.

Just a pet project to pass the time. Morlar paused, but Stratton-Villiers did not interject again. *After Julian Karswell died, they seemed to be popping up everywhere. There was Father Rayner and the Children of the Lord, the Yorke family... even Dracula himself was involved, with the cult at Pelham House...*

The other man sneered. *Crackpots and charlatans. We knew about Karswell, of course, but we never much bothered with any of the others. A bunch of grubby little toffs getting their rocks off.*

Right Honourable members of the government, some of them. I'm sure that had absolutely no bearing on your thinking.

Stratton-Villiers looked bored at the insinuation. *I've never thought that a man's religion is anyone else's damn business.*

The thing is, I'm beginning to suspect there was far more to it. My research has only scratched the surface. It feels almost like the beginning of something...

The other man clapped his hands impatiently. *Rubbish! It was nothing but a perverse fad. We had far more important matters to concern ourselves with. You, for instance.*

The gulls screamed mockingly overhead. Morlar suddenly felt heckled, like a bad comedian.

Let's skip that chapter for now. I prefer not to dwell on what might have been.

Regrets, John?

Morlar stared out at the sea. *Perhaps I might yet live long enough to set a few of them right.*

Stratton-Villiers gave a dry chuckle. The sound put Morlar in mind of a snake's warning rattle. *Dreams are necessary to life, are they not?* He finished his brandy and rose to his feet. *Well, I think we should leave it there for now. We can discuss the rest of your imaginary biography next time.*

I've given a lot of thought to the ending.

Sadly, that won't be for you to decide, John.

Stratton-Villiers's shadow sidled up to envelop Morlar. *And of course, if you ever got any ideas about actually writing such a book...* He left the threat dangling in the air, like a hangman's noose swaying in the breeze.

Morlar did not reply. He stood up and moved over to the railing bordering the terrace.

Behind him, Stratton-Villiers picked up his bowler hat, then paused. *I wouldn't want you to think there were any hard feelings, John. I always looked forward to your books in the old days. It was a shame you decided to stop publishing.*

The world changed. I found other means to communicate.

Yes. How is that little website of yours doing?

We're getting close to ten million monthly visits. A readership I could never have dreamt of as a novelist. A note of messianic pride crept into Morlar's voice.

Stratton-Villiers cleared his throat. *Isn't it ironic that as a crank writer, you made a great many important people very nervous while only selling a few thousand books? But now, your readership is in the millions and yet no one gives a damn?*

You're very sure of yourself.

Come on, John. No one actually believes a word you say. You're just another conspiracy peddler. The idiot Americans may bellow about how their President was really born in Africa, but you go one better. You loudly proclaim that several titled members of the British establishment aren't even properly human! His booming laughter was carried aloft by the gusting ocean wind.

Why do you think I named the site 'Cassandra.com'?

You always did have a streak of morbid self-pity.

Stratton-Villiers joined Morlar at the railing. *Perhaps you bastards should give a damn,* Morlar spat. *Look what's happening in this country. Look what's happening everywhere.*

Closing his eyes for a moment, Morlar imagined the railing giving way under Stratton-Villiers's grip, sending him spiralling down onto the eager teeth of the rocks below…

No. He had to keep himself in check. His time would come.

Stratton-Villiers looked at him with interest. *Ah yes. The people are taking back control, are they not?* His voice curdled with sour contempt. *Tell me, how does someone take back what they never possessed in the first place?*

Morlar grew impassioned. *Something is happening, It's all connected. Someone is causing this. Not me, not the site. There's something bigger. I can feel it.*

You should really stop believing your own publicity.

You don't even see it. None of you do. One day soon the whole bloody edifice is going to come crashing down on your pampered heads.

Already tried that once, didn't you?

Morlar ignored him. Stratton-Villiers rubbed his hands together briskly. *Well, good day, John. I must be running along now.*

As he turned to leave, Morlar spoke. *One last thing.*

Do make it quick. Brevity was never your strong suit.

If anything happens to you, what about me? Does anyone else even know I exist?

Now, John. That would rather spoil the surprise, don't you think? Still, don't alarm yourself, old boy. What on earth could possibly happen to me?

Stratton-Villiers left the unanswered question hanging behind him as the metronome click of his footsteps retreated around the side of the house. Morlar turned back towards the ocean, his knuckles white on the metal railing.

Out at sea, the waves began to swell like tumours, black and malignant, dashing themselves furiously against the cliff face below.

John Morlar stood and thought about the end of the world.

Outside the front of the cottage, Stratton-Villiers climbed into his waiting Rolls. He nodded wordlessly to his chauffeur and picked up the half-read copy of the Times from the seat next to him. The car nosed out onto the main road and began the journey back towards London.

Overhead, rain began to bullet from the sky, turning the windows of the Rolls into screens of blurred white noise. The chauffeur turned the wipers on and peered out at the silvered surface of the road ahead.

Could be a long journey home, sir.

Stratton-Villiers grunted, his eyes never leaving the newspaper.

Neither of them noticed the two motorcycles following them at a safe distance behind, their twin headlights flaring in the rain like the eyes of a pursuing demon.

DAMIEN THORN

Sam Neill in Omen III: The Final Conflict *(1981)*
written by Andrew Birkin
directed by Graham Baker

I T ALWAYS CAME AS A SURPRISE TO THE MEMBERS OF HIS INNER
circle that Damien Thorn was something of a Biblical scholar. (Perhaps
they thought his fingers should be singed by the slightest contact with the
Bible's pages, like a cartoon caricature of a devil.) He habitually kept a copy
close to hand, and could quote whole passages verbatim, at great length.

Certainly none of his business associates were familiar with the
teachings of the Good Book—what was the point? Their own bibles were
more likely to be *The Art of War*, or *The Wealth of Nations*. Damien would
often amuse himself by fabricating quotes from fictitious Biblical chapters
(the Book of Hebron?) to see if anyone would catch him. They never did.

To be fair to them, he had inherited his Father's gift for lying.

Sly games aside, Damien's studies had a serious purpose. He knew that
the final battle between Heaven and Hell was imminent, that the
prophecies (as cryptic and unreliable as they were) all pointed towards the

Second Coming of the Nazarene, who would return to Earth to defeat the Antichrist and thwart his plans for Armageddon.

Well, Damien would not be caught unprepared.

He read often of the life of Christ, of his lowly beginnings and life as a penniless carpenter, his torture and death at the hands of the Romans, crucified alongside common thieves and criminals. The contrast between them could not be any greater.

Damien had lived a soft, coddled existence—born into money and privilege, he had never known a moment's want. While he outwardly sneered at the suffering Christ's Father had inflicted upon his only son—all that pain, just so he could cloak himself in pious hardscrabble nobility!—Damien often wondered whether his own upbringing had made him vulnerable in comparison. He could be unspeakably vicious, merciless beyond measure—but would it be enough against a foe whose resolve had been tempered in the burning torment of a slow, agonising death?

Damien understood that Heaven's forces were secretly massing against him. He had carefully monitored the excavations at the site of the destroyed Thorn Museum in Chicago, knowing that buried somewhere in the rubble were the Seven Daggers of Megiddo, the only earthly weapons with the power to destroy him. His acolytes there were under strict orders to unearth the knives and dispose of them, but had failed; Christ's minions discovered the daggers first and spirited them safely away. Damien saw to it that his men were tortured and killed for their failure.

Still, he was confident in his own supremacy. Whereas the Nazarene had only mustered a paltry twelve, he had a worldwide army of disciples, handpicked over the previous decades. He had wealth, political influence, a huge corporation with an outreach that extended to every continent.

So when Christ's assassins began to strike at him, he almost laughed to the skies. The monks selected for the task were lonely, driven men, gaunt with asceticism and poverty. But they had devoted themselves to God, not killing—and their inept attempts to slay Damien were ample proof of the fact.

Furthermore, they did not seem to fully understand the ancient lore behind the Megiddo Daggers. While it was true the weapons could harm him, it required all seven to fully extinguish Damien's existence—and even then the designated strictures of the proper rite must be adhered to precisely. The archaeologist Bugenhagen had known the proper ritual—and had died for that knowledge, almost three decades ago.

But the priests attacked singly, with a lone dagger each. Christ was sending his holy fools on a hopeless errand. They could not hope to kill the Antichrist in this manner.

Damien began to feel more secure than ever. Hell's defences had protected him well for all these years, and were still formidable. Imagine—Christ had already tried to fight one empire with a lowly group of commoners and peons, and had failed utterly. Yet here he was, attempting the same doomed tactic again! Damien's own corporate empire dwarfed the power of the ancient Romans, and he would see to it that the Nazarene failed again, forever this time.

He was aided in his plans by the white hot heat of modern technology. Science had facilitated his own rise to power and yet was shunned by so many of Christ's flock. They denounced the advances made in the fields of physics, chemistry and biology, all because they decided the Bible demanded it. *These* were God's chosen people.

In which case, Damien decided, He deserved to lose.

It was astronomy that looked to have given the Antichrist a vital advantage in this instance—during the early hours of 24th March, 1981, astronomers had excitedly mapped an alignment of stars in the Cassiopeia constellation, and were declaring it to be the second Star of Bethlehem.

If this were the case, then the Christ child had to have been born on the morning of that day.

Damien mobilised his acolytes across the globe, ordering them to murder any male child fitting that description. He was close now, so very close. Six assassins had already failed to kill him, their lives and daggers lost in the attempt. Soon, the Antichrist would be unstoppable, and the Nazarene would join his disciples in death and defeat, finally paving the way for Armageddon.

While he waited impatiently for his ultimate victory, he entered into a casual relationship with a journalist, Kate Reynolds. She did not interest him particularly—he had known dozens like her, ambitious women who would cravenly sell their sex for the briefest taste of the power that men like

Damien enjoyed. But she had a son, Peter, who looked up to Damien, and it entertained the Antichrist to corrupt the boy, to take his previously good heart and blacken it. Damien was not above such small amusements. Besides, as a mongrel, an profane hybrid of jackal and man, he was sterile, and would never have an heir of his own. He began to groom Peter in the ways of power.

It was here that Damien finally miscalculated. Kate realised she was losing her son to something obscene, something she had seen revealed in Damien on the single night they spent together. The horror of it drove her into the care of Father DeCarlo, the one surviving member of the original team despatched to kill Damien. Together, they made a last-ditch plan to destroy the Antichrist.

Damien had grown increasingly desperate after his disciples' failure to kill the reborn Christ. He knew the boy was not dead yet—His death throes would create an unmistakeable rupture at the heart of existence. But despite the hundreds of children murdered across the world, there had been no such disturbance. Somehow, He had slipped through Damien's fingers.

Then, Kate came to him. She proposed a bargain—she would play Judas, betray the Christ child in return for her son. Damien suspected an ambush, of course—he knew a lie when he heard one—but his arrogance and desperation demanded he accept. He could not refuse a chance, however slight, at achieving his final victory.

He travelled to the meeting place, a ruined church, alone. As expected, DeCarlo attempted to attack from the shadows, but Damien, quick as a serpent, used Peter as a human shield. A single Megiddo Dagger was more than sufficient to snuff out one mortal boy's life.

Battering the helpless priest to the ground, Damien began to scream the Nazarene's name. A senseless rage gripped his body. The child was not here, he could feel it. He had been denied again.

In his blind fury, he did not anticipate Kate Reynolds's ambush. In revenge for her son's life, she had taken the priest's dagger and waited for her moment. When she struck, Damien did not react quickly enough to ward off a second assault. The dagger sunk into his back, slicing into his spine.

It was not sufficient to kill him. But the mystical power of the blade was enough to wound Damien grievously. He collapsed to the ground in agony, his body spasming like a hooked fish. He had never known such pain. In his torment, he gazed up to the skies and imagined he saw Christ descending from the heavens to claim the Earth for his own.

Nazarene, you have won nothing, Damien spat.

But it was simply a hallucination, a mirage of anguish and defeat. Damien was crying out his pitiful defiance to an empty sky.

Christ was nowhere to be found; He never had been.

It had all been another lie. They labelled Satan the Deceiver, but could He claim a fraction of the falsehoods perpetrated by the Bible? The actual fact of the matter was simple: the world refused to believe his Father's truth. Humanity would rather wait in vain forever, necks craning up to the heavens like a flock of idiot birds, anticipating deliverance the same way chickens anticipate a handful of grain.

Christ was not returning. He recognised mankind for what they were two thousand years ago, and had abandoned them to the Antichrist. Foolishly, Damien had planned to offer humanity a new kind of deliverance, and had been taught a similar lesson to the Nazarene. He had arrived at his own Calvary, where he too lay pierced and bleeding, just as Christ had that day on the mount.

Summoning the last of his strength, Damien crawled away into the shadows, where he had always felt most at home. Some hours later, his faithful servant Barrett came to search for him. Finding his stricken master, Hugo gently carried Damien to the car.

Lying there in the back seat of the vehicle, Damien ached at his loss, felt a searing absence at the heart of his being. The cause of it was not the humiliation he had suffered, nor the agony of his wound—it was the certain knowledge that his Father, enraged by his failure, had turned His back on him.

Damien could feel his dark power ebbing away by the second. He was little more than human now—worse than that, a lowly cur, fit only to be kicked by his master. *Why hast thou forsaken me,* he murmured in his delirium.

Barrett drove him back to his country retreat, where he would remain for decades to come, vanquished and broken. Crippled by Kate's blow, Damien became bedridden. He handed control of Thorn back to Paul Buher and withdrew from the world, communicating only through his manservant. Refusing everything but the most paltry, basic nourishment, his body rapidly atrophied. As his neglected tendons shrank, his useless legs curled up underneath him—in this, he finally came to resemble the canine mother that had birthed him. His flesh was emblazoned with sores, badges of his despair. Opiate painkillers became his new religion, offering an ecstasy that far surpassed the merely spiritual.

The Nazarene had been released from his suffering after only a mere handful of days, whereas Damien's went on and on—relentless, unending. Months stretched into years. The millennium came and went; those who had prophesied that the end of everything would arrive with it were sadly denied. Little did they know that the creature who had worked so assiduously to bring about that end had all but met his own destruction.

The world went on without Damien, no better or worse than before.

Everything changed the day Julia Cotton found her way to the house. She arrived on her hands and knees, no less of a pathetic wretch than the man she sought. Nevertheless, she was the first person to be admitted into Damien's presence since his fall.

Julia was shocked at what had become of the new master she had come so far to meet; in truth, a little disgusted. Still, she masked her disappointment carefully. She told herself there was a reason she had been compelled to come here. After all this time, she had a calling: she would be Hell's consort.

I will protect thee, she murmured to him, as though he were a small helpless boy again.

Eventually, she managed to coax the enfeebled Damien into a wheelchair, and would take him out into the grounds for walks. He was unused to the fresh air and sunlight, and needed to be swaddled in blankets, his eyes protected behind dark sunglasses.

At first, he said little, but Julia persisted in her attempts at conversation. She meant to usher him back into a world that by all rights should fear him completely. She would bring about his own unhallowed resurrection—so what if it had taken decades instead of days?

It's no use, he said finally, his voice little more than a whisper. *I lost everything. My Father abandoned me.*

Julia's voice was urgent. *You're still a powerful man, Damien. Use that power. Show Him.*

How?

You have money, political influence. Thorn Industries is more successful than ever. While you wasted away, it flourished. The world has offered its throat up to the teeth of corporations like yours. You see, you did win, in a way — just not in the manner you'd expected.

And finally, he did see.

He remembered his youth, his visit to the Bates family all those years ago. He thought back to his discussions with Mr Bates, the hushed talk of *blacks* and *ghettos* and *subversion*. About the need for *proper values* in a land that had all but abandoned them.

That hatred was still out there; Damien could feel it flowing underneath the land like a subterranean river. It only needed to be tapped, brought to the surface.

Perhaps there were *other* ways to usher in Armageddon. He could still win back his Father's respect.

Damien looked up at Julia, suddenly alert. She could instantly sense the change in him.

Yes, he said.

Their work began immediately. As Julia had argued, Thorn was a greater force than ever in the world, its tendrils reaching into everything. Political donations, lobbyists, a fortune spent in advertising — it was a simple matter to chart the course of the most powerful nations on the planet, without their populations ever having the slightest idea whose hand was on the tiller.

Then there was the dark money: the illegal contributions and illicit spending, all in the service of spreading a worldwide plague of disinformation and bigotry. As Damien grew to understand exactly what modern technology could accomplish, he could barely contain his glee.

The Nazarene and his Father only had their Bible; a pathetically outdated relic, increasingly unread. Whereas he — he had the internet: a seething viper's nest of hatred and lies. *It might have been made for me,* he told Julia.

Using his influence, Damien eagerly fanned the flames of populism, and watched as the planet began to ignite, entire countries throwing themselves gleefully upon the fires. He was finally building his Father's kingdom on Earth.

And as the inferno raged, growing ever more out of control, he could feel the power slowly returning to his body. His veins sang with it, like the strings of an unholy violin. The absence he had felt at the core of his being for so long began to dissipate. He could scarcely believe it—this was everything he had longed for.

Lying in bed with Julia one night, Damien felt a watchful presence. He whispered into the darkness. *Father, is that you?*

There was no reply—not yet—but he could feel his Father's eyes upon him, at long last. His years in the wilderness were over.

It would only be a matter of time. More and more of his puppet rulers were in place; civil discontent was rampant; entire countries were divided against themselves. Riots, bloodshed, outright war, were bound to follow.

And when the carnage was done and the carcass of the world was offered up to his Father, the Great Beast would be there at his side to sup on the bones.

Perhaps it was simply the stain of his previous failure, but Damien still, at times, felt a prickling sense of insistent, creeping unease. He tried to mask this discomfort as much as possible—it would not do to admit weakness—but it persisted nonetheless.

One morning Julia found him staring distractedly out of the window and asked him what the matter was.

I don't know, Damien said. *I sense something. Another power in the world.*

She kissed his brow. *You're being paranoid, my love. There is no other power than yours, nothing greater than you.*

He snarled and pulled away. *I'm telling you, I can feel it!*

Not the Nazarene? She looked momentarily worried.

No. It doesn't have His stench about it. I don't know what it is.

What can we do?

Damien's gaze did not move from the window. *Just wait. Wait for it to reveal itself.*

So he did, and it did.

One rainswept morning a lone figure came into view across the surrounding fields. Damien watched in fascination as the man drew closer. There was nothing outwardly remarkable about him—he was middle-aged, dressed in a faded suit and raincoat, carrying a slight paunch from lack of exercise—but Damien could sense the strength he carried with him, like an invisible army marching at his back.

The visitor slowly walked up the driveway towards the house. But rather than laying siege to the building, he politely announced himself by ringing the bell.

Damien wheeled himself through to the upstairs landing. Julia emerged from another doorway to see what the commotion was. They both watched in silence as Barrett slowly shuffled to answer the door.

Opening it, the old manservant peered in bafflement at the visitor standing outside. *Can I help you, sir?*

The man wiped the rain from his eyes. *I'm here to see Damien Thorn.* He spoke in a soft purr, but there was something commanding about his tone.

Barrett blinked. *I'm sorry, sir. Mr Thorn is not receiving visitors.*

The man looked at Barrett for a moment, then smiled. The next moment, the manservant clutched weakly at his neck, then crumpled to the floor.

Calmly, the man stepped across Barrett's prone body, then looked up to where Damien and Julia stood watching. His smile widened.

Julia was prepared. She reached into her purse, producing a small pistol. *I'll handle this, my love,* she said calmly.

She strode down the staircase towards the man, weapon raised before her. *Get out,* she ordered. *Get out or I'll kill you. Don't think I won't.*

Damien knew his consort was entirely capable of cold-blooded murder, but suddenly doubted that facility would be enough. She locked eyes with the man, and her finger tightened on the trigger.

You should probably point that somewhere else, the man said quietly.

Slowly, Julia turned the gun around and placed it against the side of her skull. She did this simply, calmly, as though it were the most natural thing in the world.

Before Damien could even react, she pulled the trigger.

The man waited for Julia's fallen body to stop twitching, then continued on his way, careful to avoid the blood pooling on the marble step. Upon reaching the top, he extended a hand in greeting. *Damien Thorn? I'm John Morlar*, he said.

Damien stared dumbly at the proffered hand for a moment. *I had hoped we could be gentlemen about this*, Morlar said. *It's taken me a very long time to find you.*

Finally, Damien accepted the handshake. As his hand gripped Morlar's, he looked at the other man in fascination. *It's you*, he whispered.

Morlar laughed mirthlessly. *Don't mistake me for some kind of saviour*, he said. *It wasn't so long ago that I wanted to end the world myself. I nearly did it, too.*

So why are you here? People were normally so transparent to Damien, but not Morlar. Up close, he carried hatred with him like a thick cloud, obscuring everything.

Because you represent everything I loathe about this planet, Mr Thorn, Morlar replied. *The greed, the callousness, the hypocrisy. And so I finally realised I might have a purpose in life after all.*

Damien sensed a speech coming. He already got the distinct impression Morlar enjoyed speeches.

Morlar continued. *God may have turned His back on us, but I'll be damned if I'll stand idly by while you and your foul brethren burrow through the trash heap of the planet, like the plague rats that you are. I'd rather burn it all down myself.*

Now it was Damien's turn to laugh. *Damned? You might be, at that.*

I'll take my chances, said Morlar. *Your gift against mine. The winner decides the fate of the world.*

Does it even matter who wins? asked Damien. *Won't the end result be the same?*

Morlar shrugged. *Perhaps, perhaps not. Call it the difference between mercy killing and murder.*

Outside, thunderheads were gathering. Damien uttered a silent prayer. Would his power—weakened as it still was—be enough against this crazed nihilist, this zealot of mass destruction? He begged his Father to lend him strength.

Their eyes met. A sudden lightning flash dissolved the room around them in a white migraine blur. The air split open, and the floor seemed to fall away underneath them, leaving the opponents alone, suspended in space.

Now, nothing beyond this moment mattered. The world trembled, in anticipation of the coming storm.

The two men waited for what would happen next.

Soon, only one would remain.

The Films

A Dark Song (2010)
Absolution (1978)
An American Werewolf in
    London (1981)
Baby (1976) (TV)
Berberian Sound Studio (2012)
Blood on Satan's Claw (1971)
Blow Up (1966)
Brimstone and Treacle (1976) (TV)
Damien: Omen II (1978)
Dead Man's Shoes (2004)
Dead of Night (1945)
Death Line (1972)
Demons (1985)
Don't Look Now (1973)
Dracula A.D. 1972 (1972)
Frenzy (1972)
Frightmare (1974)
From Beyond the Grave (1974)
Full Circle (1978)
Ghostwatch (1992) (TV)
Gosford Park (2001)
Hellbound: Hellraiser II (1988)
Hellraiser (1987)

High Rise (2015)
Inland Empire (2006)
Kill List (2010)
Lonely Water (1973)
Magic (1978)
Neither the Sea Nor the Sand (1972)
Night and the City (1950)
Night of the Big Heat (1967)
Night of the Demon (1957)
Omen III: The Final Conflict (1981)
Paperhouse (1988)
Peeping Tom (1960)
Picnic at Hanging Rock (1975)
Possum (2018)
Quatermass 2 (1957)
Quatermass and the Pit (1967)
Rawhead Rex (1986)
Repulsion (1965)
Satan's Slave (1976)
Scream and Scream Again (1970)
Stage Fright (1950)
Straw Dogs (1971)
Taste the Blood of Dracula (1970)
The Appointment (1981)

The Beast Must Die (1974)
The Borderlands (2013)
The Children (2008)
The Collector (1965)
The Corpse (1971)
The Deadly Affair (1966)
The Devil Rides Out (1968)
The Exorcism (1972) (TV)
The Exorcist (1973)
The Go-Between (1971)
The Godsend (1980)
The House That Dripped Blood (1971)
The Innocents (1963)
The League of Gentlemen (1999) (TV)
The Long Good Friday (1980)
The Medusa Touch (1978)
The Night Caller (1965)
The Offence (1973)

The Omen (1976)
The Quatermass Xperiment (1955)
The Satanic Rites of Dracula (1973)
The Servant (1968)
The Shout (1978)
The Stone Tape (1972) (TV)
The Uninvited (1944)
The Wicker Man (1973)
Theatre of Blood (1973)
Tinker Tailor Soldier Spy (1979) (TV)
To the Devil a Daughter (1976)
Under the Skin (2013)
Unman, Wittering and Zigo (1971)
Village of the Damned (1960)
Wake in Fright (1968) (TV)
Whistle and I'll Come to You (1968) (TV)

ACKNOWLEDGEMENTS

THE UTMOST THANKS MUST GO TO LYNDA RUCKER AND GARY McMahon, for their encouragement and support, to say nothing of beta reading services rendered.

Thanks also to Neil Snowdon, who coaxed the book into being.

I'm grateful to Kim Newman for his insight and enthusiasm (and it would be remiss of me not to give a shout out to the rest of the DVD Night Old Gits: Stephen Jones, Barry Forshaw, Paul McCauley, David Barraclough and Christopher Fowler).

And to the numerous friends and family members who managed not to burst into incredulous laughter when I told them what I was working on, thank you too.